Mario Vargas Llosa was born in 1936 in Peru. He has established an international reputation as one of Latin America's most important novelists.

# MARIO VARGAS LLOSA
# Making Waves

EDITED AND TRANSLATED BY
JOHN KING

**ff**

*faber and faber*
· London · Boston ·

First published in Great Britain in 1996
by Faber and Faber Limited
3 Queen Square London WC1N 3AU
This UK paperback edition first published in 1997

Photoset by RefineCatch Limited, Bungay, Suffolk
Printed and bound in Great Britain by MacKays of Chatham Plc, Chatham, Kent

A CIP record for this book
is available from the British Library

ISBN 0–571–17952–5

2 4 6 8 10 9 7 5 3 1

# Contents

CONTENTS

# Acknowledgements

The articles contained in this collection were originally published in the following publications:

'The Country of a Thousand Faces': 'El país de las mil caras', *Contra viento y marea*, III (1964–88), Seix Barral, Barcelona, 1990, 227–46. An earlier version of this article was published in English as 'A Passion for Peru', in the *New York Times Magazine*, 20 November 1983

'When Madrid was a Village': 'Madrid cuando era aldea', *Contra viento y marea*, III (1964–88), Seix Barral, Barcelona, 1990, 9–13

'Chronicle of the Cuban Revolution': 'Crónica de la revolución', *Contra viento y marea*, I (1962–72), Seix Barral, Barcelona, 1986, 30–35

'In a Normandy Village, Remembering Paúl Escobar': 'En un pueblo normando, recordando a Paúl Escobar', *Contra viento y marea*, I (1962–72), Seix Barral, Barcelona, 1986, 101–104

'Toby, Rest in Peace': 'Toby, descansa en paz', *Contra viento y marea*, III (1964–88), Seix Barral, Barcelona, 1990, 23–7

'P'tit Pierre': 'P'tit Pierre', *Contra viento y marea*, III (1964–88), Seix Barral, Barcelona, 1990, 80–84

'Hemingway: The Shared Feast': '*Paris era una fiesta*: la fiesta compartida', *La verdad de las mentiras: ensayos sobre literatura*, Seix Barral, Barcelona, 1990, 249–58

'A Visit to Buñuel': was originally published under the title 'Cine = Buñuel guiña otra vez un ojo', in *Primera Plana*, 198, 11–17 October 1966, 78–80

'*Luis* Buñuel: A Festival of Excellent Bad Films' was originally published under the title 'Un festival de films execrables', in *Primera Plana*, 169, 22–28 March 1966, 52

'Simone de Beauvoir: *Les Belles Images*': '*Las bellas imágenes* de Simone de Beauvoir', *Contra viento y marea*, I (1962–72), Seix Barral, Barcelona, 1986, 150–55

'Sebastián Salazar Bondy and the Vocation of the Writer in Peru': edited version of 'Sebastián Salazar Bondy y la vocación del escritor en el Perú', *Contra viento y marea*, I (1962–72), Seix Barral, Barcelona, 1986, 111–38

'Literature is Fire': 'La literatura es fuego', *Contra viento y marea*, I (1962–72), Seix Barral, Barcelona, 1986, 176–81

'Literature and Exile': 'Literatura y exilio', *Contra viento y marea*, I (1962–72), Seix Barral, Barcelona, 1986, 200–204

'Socialism and the Tanks': 'El socialismo y los tanques', *Contra viento y marea*, I (1962–72), Seix Barral, Barcelona, 1986, 219–22

'A Visit to Karl Marx': 'Una visita a Karl Marx', *Contra viento y marea*, I (1962–72), Seix Barral, Barcelona, 1986, 144–49

'Joyce's *Dubliners*': '*Dublineses*: el Dublín de Joyce', *La verdad de las mentiras: ensayos sobre literatura*, Seix Barral, Barcelona, 1990, 31–40

## ACKNOWLEDGEMENTS

'The Other Oscar': 'El otro *Oscar*', *Contra viento y marea*, III (1964–88), Seix Barral, Barcelona, 1990, 61–4

'Doris Lessing: *The Golden Notebook*': '*El cuaderno dorado:* el cuaderno dorado de las ilusiones perdidas', *La verdad de las mentiras: ensayos sobre literatura*, Seix Barral, Barcelona, 1990, 213–21

'Letter to Haydée Santamaría': 'Carta a Haydée Santamaría', *Contra viento y marea*, I (1962–72), Seix Barral, Barcelona, 1986, 248–9

'Albert Camus and the Morality of Limits': edited version of 'Albert Camus y la moral de los límites', *Contra viento y marea*, I (1962–72), Seix Barral, Barcelona, 1986, 321–42

'Bataille or the Redemption of Evil': edited version of 'Bataille o el rescate del mal', *Contra viento y marea*, II (1972–83), 9–29

'Sartre, Fierabrás and Utopia': 'Sartre, Fierabrás y la utopía', *Contra viento y marea*, II (1972–83), Seix Barral, Barcelona, 1986, 176–80

'The Mandarin': edited version of 'El mandarín', *Contra viento y marea*, II (1972–83), Seix Barral, Barcelona, 1986, 229–43

'Isaiah Berlin: A Hero of Our Time': edited version of 'Isaiah Berlin, un héroe de nuestro tiempo', *Contra viento y marea*, II (1972–83), Seix Barral, Barcelona, 1986, 260–78

'Faulkner in Laberinto': 'Faulkner en Laberinto', *Contra viento y marea*, II, (1972–83), 299–302

'William Faulkner: The Sanctuary of Evil': edited version of '*Santuario:* el santuario del mal', *La verdad de las mentiras: ensayos sobre literatura*, Seix Barral, Barcelona, 1990, 77–85

'John Dos Passos: *Manhattan Transfer*': '*Manhattan Transfer:* capital del enjambre y la destrucción', *La verdad de las mentiras: ensayos sobre literatura*, Seix Barral, Barcelona, 1990, 41–9

'The World Cup, Spain 1982': articles taken from *El País*, June 1982

'The Story of a Massacre': 'Historia de una matanza', *Contra viento y marea*, III (1964–88), Seix Barral, Barcelona, 1990, 156–92. An earlier version of this article was published in English as 'Inquest in the Andes', in the *New York Times Magazine*, 31 July 1983

'Freedom for the Free?': 'Libertad para los libres?' *Contra viento y marea*, II (1972–83), Seix Barral, Barcelona, 1986, 350–55

'Nicaragua at the Crossroads': edited version of 'Nicaragua en la encrucijada', *Contra viento y marea*, III (1964–88), Seix Barral, Barcelona, 1990, 247–304. An earlier version of this article was published in English as 'In Nicaragua', in the *New York Times Magazine*, 28 April 1985

'My Son the Rastafarian': 'Mi hijo el etíope', *Contra viento y marea*, III (1964–88), Seix Barral, Barcelona, 1990, 305–31. An earlier version of this article was published in English in the *New York Times Magazine*, 16 February 1986

'The Trumpet of Deyá': 'La trompeta de Deyá', *Vuelta*, 195, February 1993, 10–14

'Botero: A Sumptuous Abundance': edited version of the Spanish text 'La abundancia suntuosa'. Published in French as *Botero*, Editions de la Différence, Paris, 1984

'Szyszlo in the Labyrinth': 'Szyszlo en el laberinto', prologue to *Szyszlo*, Ediciones Alfred Weld, Bogotá/New York, 1991, 11–13

# ACKNOWLEDGEMENTS

'Degenerate Art': 'Arte degenerado', *Desafíos a la libertad,* El País/Aguilar, Madrid, 1994, 97–101

'A Fleeting Impression of Václav Havel': 'Impresion fugaz de Václav Havel', *Desafíos a la libertad,* El País/Aguilar, Madrid, 1994, 43–7

'Swiss Passion': 'Pasión helvética', *Desafíos a la libertad,* El País/Aguilar, Madrid, 1994, 55–60

'Letter to Salman Rushdie': 'Carta a Salman Rushdie', published in German in *Die Tageszeitung,* Berlin, 14 February 1992

'The "People" and the "Decent People": On Contemporary Peru': ' "El pueblo" y la "gente decente" ', *Desafíos a la libertad,* El País/Aguilar, Madrid, 1994, 115–19

'The Death of Che': 'La muerte del Che', *Desafíos a la libertad,* El País/Aguilar, Madrid, 1994, 157–61

'Nations, Fictions': 'Naciones, ficciones', *Desafíos a la libertad,* El País/Aguilar, Madrid, 1994, 169–74

'Saul Bellow and Chinese Whispers': 'Saul Bellow y los cuentos chinos', *Desafíos a la libertad,* El País/Aguilar, Madrid, 1994, 79–84

'Visual Contact': 'Contacto visual', *Desafíos a la libertad,* El País/Aguilar, Madrid, 1994, 199–203

'The Penis or Life: The Bobbitt Affair': 'El pene o la vida', *Desafíos a la libertad,* El País/Aguilar, Madrid, 1994, 301–5

'The Truth of Lies': 'La verdad de las mentiras', *La verdad de las mentiras: ensayos sobre literatura,* Seix Barral, Barcelona, 1990, 5–20

# Foreword

> *Ithaka gave you the splendid journey.*
> *Without her you would not have set*
> *out.*
> *She hasn't anything else to give you.*
>
> C. P. Cavafy, 'Ithaka'[1]

Mario Vargas Llosa has been making waves for some thirty-five years. In this period he has become established as one of the world's most prolific and consistently interesting writers, with a dozen major works of fiction and several plays. He has also recently published what is doubtless only a first volume of memoirs, *A Fish in the Water*, which combines memories of the first twenty-one years of his life with a detailed account of his involvement in politics between 1987 and 1990, culminating in a bid for the Peruvian presidency. These works are all available in English language editions. Yet this is only a part of Vargas Llosa's *oeuvre*: then there are another ten volumes in Spanish, and hundreds of uncollected newspaper articles, of literary criticism, chronicles, art and film criticism and political commentary. Of this, only the study of Flaubert, *The Perpetual Orgy*, is widely available in English, together with a book of essays on his own fictional work, entitled *A Writer's Reality*. This volume, therefore, seeks partially to redress the imbalance by providing a collection of Vargas Llosa's writings from the early sixties until 1993. The selection is my own and I have tried to provide as broad a range as possible of Vargas Llosa's recurring obsessions, the development of his literary and political views and his very diverse interests.

The book takes the form of an intellectual odyssey, a journey through different geographical locations and ever changing cultural and political landscapes. It picks up one of the narrative strands of *A Fish in the Water*, with the aspirant writer and scholar heading off to Madrid on a doctoral bursary in the late fifties, and it ends with a series of articles published in the Spanish newspaper, *El País*, where Vargas Llosa now writes a regular column. The order of the articles is

1 E. Keeley and P. Sherrard, eds., *Six Poets of Modern Greece*, Thames & Hudson, London 1960, 41.

in the main chronological, although some are grouped together thematically rather than chronologically, to illustrate an abiding interest in a particular topic, writer or location.

After an opening chapter that serves as an introduction to the first two decades of his life in Peru (autobiographical memories also explored in *A Fish in the Water*, that have been reworked and reinvented in several of his major novels), the selection begins with a memoir of Vargas Llosa's student days in Madrid. For him, Madrid was a sleepy village in the late fifties, light years (albeit only three decades) away from the cosmopolitan, post-modern city of today. Nothing could be further from the setting of an Almodóvar film than Vargas Llosa's daily routine of gentle conservatism, boring classes at the university and visits to the movies to see prints cut to shreds by Franco's censors, often with hilarious consequences. There were also illicit readings in the National Library, where he developed a lifetime's attachment to romances of chivalry, in particular *Tirant lo Blanc* by the fifteenth-century Valencian knight, Joanot Martorell. *Tirant*, he would later argue, was the first in a lineage of fictions by writers – including Balzac, Dickens, Flaubert, Tolstoy and Faulkner – who were 'God supplanters' or 'Deicides' and who tried to 'create in their novels an all-encompassing reality'.[2] Vargas Llosa's own fictions would seek this same 'all-encompassing' critical realism.

From the dusty library benches, *Tirant* could also offer an imaginary model of a committed adventurer, defending Christendom against the Saracens, obeying the chivalric code and seeking the favours of a princess whose complexion was so white that, when she drank red wine, one could watch the wine flowing down her throat. 'How base and loathsome I would hold myself', remarks Tirant, 'if I shunned knighthood's duties! Each man should know his worth and I declare that though chivalry were infinitely more hazardous, nothing could deter me from joining that noble order.'[3] Like the knight errant Tirant, Vargas Llosa would remain an adventurer both in his own robust fictions and in his life. His adventure in the late fifties needed to be pursued in locations other than Madrid. Spain remains in his writings a place of warmth, generosity and hospitality – indeed, he took up dual Spanish and Peruvian nationality in the early nineties when the

2 Joanot Martorell and Marti Joan de Galba, *Tirant lo Blanc*, Picador, London, 1984, p. xx.
3 ibid. p. 50.

president of Peru, Alberto Fujimori, was making life difficult for his erstwhile rival for presidency, and he has recently been elected to the Spanish Academy – but this hospitality alone was not enough for a young man for whom the long dreamed of journey to Europe could only mean one destination: Paris.

France could provide a stimulating intellectual and literary climate for the writer who completed his first two major novels, *Time of the Hero* and *The Green House*, while scraping a living by working nights at Radio-Télévision Française. Paris was the home of the intellectual mandarins, in particular Sartre, who, with essays such as 'What is Literature?', had informed Vargas Llosa's thinking about cultural politics since the early fifties. The new novelists and the new critics in vogue, such as Robbe-Grillet, Butor and Barthes, would not be a source of inspiration for him: he would resist throughout his life any easy assimilation of what he would see as the latest 'fashions' of critical theory. But earlier writers, in particular Flaubert, could offer literary lessons and shared pleasures: the 'perpetual orgy', in Flaubert's terms, of reading and writing. Being 'down and out' in Paris was also the destiny of many American expatriate writers in the twentieth century, from the Peruvian poet César Vallejo to Ernest Hemingway. Yet this hard apprenticeship was at the same time 'a movable feast' of readings and experiences, shared with friends and mentors such as the Paris-based Argentine writer Julio Cortázar who, in 1963, published *Hopscotch*, a dazzling fictional account of Latin America's complex relationship with Europe. Vargas Llosa would explore the nature of his self-imposed literary 'exile' in 'Literature and Exile', included in this volume, countering a belief current in Latin America and elsewhere that a writer living outside the country of his birth is somehow betraying that country. While this inveterate transformer of autobiography into fiction has yet to base a novel on his life in Europe, his Parisian experiences and readings are extensively represented here. There are several vignettes, which can be read either as social chronicles or as short stories, concerning friends and everyday life. Even though the critical canon has Vargas Llosa discovering a sense of humour in his writing in the early seventies, with the publication of *Captain Pantoja and the Special Service*, these essays clearly show an amused intelligence at work throughout his career, enjoying the epitaphs at the Paris dog cemetery or the anarchist views of film-maker Luis Buñuel. One of the reasons he gives, in the essay 'The Mandarin', for his growing disillusionment with Sartre in the sixties was Sartre's tendency 'to turn his disciple against humour, to make him think that laughter was forbidden in any literature that sought to be profound'. (p. 133)

His essays on Sartre and Camus in particular — his first volume of collected literary and political criticism was entitled significantly, *Entre Sartre y Camus* (Between Sartre and Camus, 1981) — reveal what he has called 'the itinerary of a Latin American who undertook his intellectual apprenticeship dazzled by the intelligence and dialectical swings of Sartre and ended up embracing the libertarian reformism of Camus'.[41] They show his way of coming to terms with 'the myths, utopias, enthusiasms, quarrels, hopes, fanaticism and brutalities lived by a Latin American in the sixties and seventies'.[51] For although the writer was in voluntary exile in Paris and later London, his main focus was Peru and the social upheavals occurring throughout Latin America. The Cuban revolution of 1959 had a profound political and symbolic influence in the continent. As his early writings reveal, Vargas Llosa first saw it as a nationalist, anti-imperialist revolution which seemed exemplary and which demonstrated a need for commitment and for political clarity. He would visit Cuba on five occasions in the sixties since, in the early years of the Revolution, the Cubans invited many members of the artistic community to the island, awarded literary prizes and organized seminars and conferences. The group of the Latin American 'boom' novelists who achieved national and international acclaim in these years — led by Julio Cortázar, Carlos Fuentes, Gabriel García Márquez and Vargas Llosa himself — were initially closely identified with this process, none more enthusiastically than Vargas Llosa. Several extracts in this volume — 'Chronicle of the Cuban Revolution', 'Socialism and the Tanks', 'Letter to Haydée Santamaría', 'The Death of Che' — mark his growing distance from the Cuban process. It was a position that he made explicit in 1971 when, together with many other intellectuals throughout the world, including Sartre, he signed two open letters protesting against the crude handling by the Cubans of a dissident poet, Heberto Padilla. But for much of the sixties, Cuba was an example that he felt should be emulated throughout the continent. He was a friend of the Peruvian poet turned

4 Mario Vargas Llosa, *Contra viento y marea*, I, Seix Barral, Barcelona, 1986, p. 11.
5 ibid, p. 9.

guerrilla, Javier Heraud, who was killed in 1963, and he wrote in support of guerilla activity in Peru, although he did not see this as an option open to himself as a writer (see the affectionate homage to his friend Paúl Escobar). He called Frantz Fanon a 'great Third World idealogue' and the campaign diaries of Che Guevara 'one of the fascinating books of our time'.[61] The strength of his feeling in the sixties is in direct proportion to his later vigorous condemnation of what he would see as his mistaken and utopian views.

The political commitment that the volume traces is from the pro-Cuban Left of the sixties to a radical liberalism in the nineties, and politics remains one of Vargas Llosa's constant concerns. It does not, however, supersede his dedication to literature. Apart from the direct political involvement between 1987 and 1990 (which in the event was very soon transformed into a massive political memoir), writing and reading dominate his life. He makes clear the exclusive nature of the literary vocation in his Sartrean study of his friend and mentor, the writer Sebastián Salazar Bondy, and he is speaking of himself when he refers to the discipline shown by Hemingway: 'Because literature is a passion and passion is exclusive . . . Hemingway is in a café and by his side there is a young woman. He thinks: "You belong to me and Paris belongs to me but I belong to this notebook and pencil." That is exactly what slavery means. The condition of a writer is strange and paradoxical. His privilege is freedom, the right to see, hear and investigate everything . . . What is the purpose of this privilege? To feed the beast within, which enslaves him, which feeds off all his acts, tortures him mercilessly and is only appeased, momentarily, in the act of creation.' (pp. 39–40) If the literary vocation is enslaving, he has no doubts about the primary importance of literature as an expression of freedom and discontent, as his memorable essay 'Literature is Fire' states: 'It is important to remind our societies what to expect. Warn them that literature is fire, that it means nonconformity and rebellion, that the *raison d'être* of a writer is protest, disagreement and criticism.' (p. 72) The same sentiments are echoed over twenty years later in the article that closes the volume 'The Truth of Lies': 'By itself, literature is a terrible indictment against existence under whatever regime or ideology: a blazing testimony of its insufficiencies, its inability to satisfy us.' (p. 330)

6  ibid, p. 45, p. 214.

In the development of this vocation, Vargas Llosa acknowledges his attachment at different times to certain writers. To the names Sartre and Camus must be added Georges Bataille, a reference point that criticism on him has tended to ignore. The essay included shows Vargas Llosa's affinity to many aspects of Bataille's literary criticism: literature's relationship to what Bataille calls Evil (obsessions, frustrations, pain and vice); its communication of essentially negative – *maudit* – experiences; the literary vocation as a quest for sovereignty; the fundamental importance of eroticism and the interest in the legendary Gilles de Rais as an example of unrestrained sovereignty. Even when Vargas Llosa explicitly links himself to the *belle lettriste*, harmonious liberal vision of Isaiah Berlin, he feels that this 'healthy' or 'serene' analysis of man and his actions must be complemented by Bataille's exploration of the world of unreason, of the unconscious, 'the world of those obscure instincts that, in unexpected ways, suddenly emerge to compete with ideas and often replace them as a form of action and can even destroy what these ideas have built up.' (p. 147) The realm of Dionysus can hold sway in the most unexpected places at the most unlikely times, as his latest novel, *Death in the Andes*, reveals. While Vargas Llosa would surely agree with Freud's observation that only in the realm of fiction can we find the 'plurality of lives' that we need for existence, the question that he poses is how to keep the boundaries clear between fiction and reality.

This interest in exploring literary and societal taboos attracts Vargas Llosa to Faulkner's fictional world. Together with Joyce, Faulkner has been the main precursor for modern Latin American novelists and Vargas Llosa has explicitly stated that, 'He wrote in English, but he was one of our own.' Faulkner was 'one of our own' because he wrote of a world of 'turbulent complexity', 'backwardness and marginality' which 'also contains beauty and virtues that so-called civilization kills.' (p. 151) When Vargas Llosa is in a remote Amazon settlement, researching his epic novel *The War of the End of the World*, he finds himself witnessing experiences similar to those shared by the inhabitants of Yoknapatawpha County: violence, heat, greed, untameable nature, unrestrained instincts. Faulkner's South is also recognizably Latin America. It was Faulkner's particular genius, for Vargas Llosa, to be able to tell these ferocious stories in formally innovative ways: Faulkner was the first writer he read with pen and paper in hand in order to decipher the structural complexities of the narrative. Unlike many early Latin American writers who told brutal stories with equally brutal techniques of clumsy social realism, Faulkner could demonstrate the art of form to Vargas Llosa's generation.

Many articles express the desire to learn the lessons of international modernism as part of a concern for the development of literature within Latin America. From within the continent, the formal perfection of the stories of Jorge Luis Borges was a constant inspiration, but Vargas Llosa would also engage polemically with the 'indigenist' writers of his own country. (Indeed his next work, in press as I write, is a book-length study of literary *indigenismo*.) He was conscious of being part of a process of narrative innovation, as his essay on Julio Cortázar reveals: the excitement at reading *Hopscotch* in 1963 is contagious. He also prepared in the late sixties a doctoral thesis, published as a book, on the work of Gabriel García Márquez, then a great friend. He has since distanced himself from that writer, their parting of the ways marked by a famous right hook that Hemingway would have been proud of. His engagement with critics from Latin America has also been similarly forthright and bruising. There were famous polemics in the sixties and seventies with the critics Oscar Collazos and Angel Rama over the nature of literature, revolution and the status of literary criticism and this desire to engage remains a constant in his writing. One polemic, with Günter Grass ('Freedom for the Free?') is included here.

The study of García Márquez was completed in Britain, while Vargas Llosa was teaching at the University of London. London became in the late sixties, and remains to this day, his favourite city in which to write. Having survived the shock of a cup of murky, cold tea on the boat train from Dover to London, he took up residence in West London and has returned there, on and off, for thirty years. This, despite the terrifying attentions of Oscar the mouse in his first Earls Court house and the British attachment to lukewarm beer and draughty pubs. This relationship with Britain and Ireland is illustrated in a number of articles. There is an evocation of Joyce's Dublin through an analysis of *Dubliners* and a meditation on Karl Marx in London, who lodged in the most extreme poverty at Dean Street in the 1850s – then a slum, now, in 1966, the centre of 'swinging' London – while writing his greatest works. Vargas Llosa, like Karl Marx, would form a disciplined attachment to the Reading Room of the British Museum. He also reads Doris Lessing and accompanies Salman Rushdie to a football game. In his political analyses of the eighties and nineties, Margaret Thatcher is seen as a liberal reformer. And, in one of his most famous comic essays, the British public school system is put under the microscope for not noticing that, under its charge, his youngest son had become a Rastafarian.

The seventies and eighties would see a return to Peru and frequent stays in Britain, Spain and, in later years, the United States, as Vargas Llosa's growing international stature would give rise to frequent invitations to lecture and teach at campuses all over the country. He returned to a Peru under military rule, but to a regime that proclaimed itself to be socially just and interested in state-directed national development. Initially under General Velasco and later in much more muted form under General Francisco Morales Bermúdez, there was a policy of selective nationalization of foreign enterprises, widespread agrarian reform and state intervention into many aspects of the economy. While many, including Vargas Llosa, pointed to the mismanagement of these regimes – Vargas Llosa was particularly critical of Velasco for placing daily papers and television channels under state control and condemned intellectuals who supported his measures – the military governments had the effect of radicalizing the country. By 1978 Vargas Llosa was talking of antidemocratic socialism and warning of the gains of the far left under Hugo Blanco in the polls. The presidential elections in May 1980 brought back the conservative Fernando Belaúnde Terry after twelve years of military rule. This year also marked the military emergence of Sendero Luminoso, the Shining Path guerrilla movement, which had been founded by a philosophy lecturer, Abimael Guzmán. Within a few years this ultra-violent group – whose literature spoke of the necessary 'quota' of blood sacrifice for each militant – had built up bases in the south central Andes and the shanty towns of Ayacucho, Huancayo and Lima, heralding a decade of what became known as 'Manchay tiempo' – the Time of Fear.

Sendero received countrywide attention with the press and television coverage of the massacre, early in 1983, of eight journalists and their guide by villagers in Uchuraccay, north-west of the capital of Ayacucho, an area in which Sendero conducted operations. The government set up a commission to investigate the killings, with Vargas Llosa as a member. Its report was hotly contested in the country. Vargas Llosa's account of this incident, 'Massacre in the Andes', should be read in conjunction with *Death in the Andes*. Both serve as documents of this time of disorder when 'emergency zones' (where Sendero and the armed forces were locked in violent combat) covered some twenty-seven provinces of Peru. Vargas Llosa's criticism of Günter Grass for depicting Latin America as a place of necessary revolutionary activity should be read in this context. The violent struggles in Peru also colour his views on Central America when he argues, in 1985, for a curb in revolutionary activity and the implementation of democratic reforms in Nicaragua.

The period was also marked by shifts in government economic policy in Peru to combat a grave economic, as well as political, crisis. Belaúnde had tried, unsuccessfully, to impose an International Monetary Fund stabilization plan in return for a loan. In 1985, the populist president Alan García chose a different course, increasing but later freezing prices and imposing a fixed exchange rate and import controls. He also opposed the banking community and the IMF by declaring his own level of debt repayment, a move that led to a virtual boycott of Peru by international financiers. When García announced in July 1987 that he would nationalize all banks and financial institutions in Peru, Vargas Llosa wrote an article in opposition: 'Towards a Totalitarian Peru' beginning a process, outlined in great detail in *A Fish in the Water*, that would lead to his presidential candidacy.

Having opposed Vargas Llosa's liberal reform programme in the election campaign of 1990, the new president Alberto Fujimori performed a U-turn and introduced a programme that became known as 'Fuji-shock'. Prices rocketed – the price of petrol went up 3000 per cent overnight – wages were frozen, public spending was cut back drastically and privatization became the norm. In 1992, with military support, Fujimori flouted democracy by suspending the constitution and abolishing Congress. Vargas Llosa's opposition to Fujimori has been public and trenchant, as can be seen in 'The "People" and the "Decent People"'.

Vargas Llosa is currently based in Europe, but he makes frequent visits to the United States. North American literature has always been important to his literary development, as the essays on Faulkner, Dos Passos and Hemingway reveal. He has also contributed articles to a number of North American newspapers and journals. As his international reputation became established, the visit to the North American campus became a regular event. In many of these university environments he depicts himself, in humorous vein, as somewhat of a fish out of water, or at least as someone swimming against the current critical tides. While his appointment as a visiting professor at Cambridge in England involved him, by his own account, in teaching just one student, in North America a rather larger, more demanding and expectant audience awaited. He could not always satisfy these expectations. In Princeton, he remarks, 'People hope that, in these times of scarcity, at least the Third Worldists might still be revolutionaries. Whoever is not a revolutionary disappoints them. Like me, for example.'[7] This critique of foreign intellectuals who like to place their revolutionary utopias in Latin America is constant in Vargas Llosa's fictions and critical essays, as can be seen both in the polemic with Grass and in 'Swiss Passion'. Other essays comment, through an analysis of recent work by Saul Bellow, David Mamet − 'Visual Contact' − and also of the Bobbitt affair, on the current US interests in contemporary literary theory and the politics of gender, race and minorities.

These recent articles on the United States were first published in a regular column that he now writes for *El País*, entitled *Piedra de toque* (Touchstone), which is syndicated throughout Latin America. They have been collected in the volume, *Desafíos a la libertad* (Challenges to Freedom, 1994). Other essays from this book covering the late eighties and early nineties are included here, and they focus on what Vargas Llosa calls in his introduction to *Desafíos* the 'challenges to the culture of freedom that have emerged with post-communism and a criticism of nationalism and its thousand insidious faces ... religious traditionalism and the new attempts to re-establish the authoritarian tradition in Latin America.' In its place, he argues for internationalism and 'the liberal option as a simultaneous and indivisible alliance of political democracy and economic freedom'.[8] It is from this standpoint that he can talk of the influence on his thought of Popper, Hayek and Isaiah Berlin and of his filial attachment to and unreserved admiration for Popper, Faulkner, Borges and Margaret Thatcher. In this last list there is an interesting tension between a will to define stark clarities and an awareness, from a pluralist sensibility, that such clarities are necessarily elusive and contingent.

While few writers or politicians would mention Borges and Margaret Thatcher in the same breath, even fewer would also be able to analyse

7 Mario Vargas Llosa, *Desfíos a la libertad*, Ediciones El País/Aguilar, Madrid, 1994, p. 227.
8 ibid, p. 9.

Maradona's footballing skills or the work of the Colombian Botero. Like Camus before him, Vargas Llosa is a football fan and in 1982 he was given an ideal assignment: to cover the World Cup in Spain. Several of these columns are included here. His appreciation of Maradona's early footballing skills can be contrasted to his more recent scorn at Maradona's enthusiastic support for Fidel Castro and the Cuban regime. Vargas Llosa has also written extensively on art, as illustrated by the long essay on Botero, Latin America's best known living artist, a short appreciation of the Peruvian Szyszlo and a discussion on art within totalitarian Germany in the thirties, 'Degenerate Art'. In this article he makes reference to George Grosz and would later develop his fascination with Grosz into a lavishly illustrated book.[91]

Art critic, football commentator, film buff, polemicist, political essayist, literary critic, *chroniqueur*, autobiographer, short story writer: *Making Waves* illustrates these many facets of the work and personality of Mario Vargas Llosa.

John King
Warwick, 29 February 1996

9  Mario Vargas Llosa, *George Grosz*, Flohic Éditions, Paris, 1992.

# The Country of a Thousand Faces

The city where I was born, Arequipa, is located in an Andean valley in the south of Peru. It is well known for its clerical and rebellious spirit, its lawyers and volcanoes, its clear sky, the flavour of the prawns and its regionalism. Also for *la nevada* (the snowfall), a kind of fleeting neurosis that affects its inhabitants. One fine day, the mildest of Arequipans refuses to acknowledge a greeting, spends hours brooding, behaves in the most extravagant nonsensical way and tries to throttle his best friend over a simple disagreement. No one gets worried or annoyed because everyone knows that this man is suffering from 'the snowfall', and that tomorrow he will be back to his normal, gentle self. Although my family took me away from Arequipa when I was one and I have never lived there since, I feel very much an Arequipan, and I also think that the jokes that are made all over Peru at our expense – we are known as arrogant, unpleasant and even mad – are the result of jealousy. Don't we speak the purest Spanish in the country? Don't we have that architectural wonder, Santa Catalina, a cloistered convent where some five hundred women lived during the Colonial period? Haven't we been the setting for the most grandiloquent earthquakes and the greatest number of revolutions in Peruvian history?

From ages one to ten, I lived in Cochabamba, Bolivia. With regard to that city, where I was innocent and happy, I remember not so much the things that I did and the people that I knew, but rather the books that I read: *Sandokan,* Nostradamus, *The Three Musketeers,* Cagliostro, *Tom Sawyer, Sinbad.* Stories of pirates, explorers and bandits, romantic love and the poems that my mother hid in her bedside table (which I read without understanding anything, just for the pleasure of what was forbidden) occupied the best part of my time. And because it was intolerable that these magic books should come to an end, I sometimes invented new chapters for them, or else changed the ending. Those additions and corrections to other people's stories were the first pieces that I wrote, the first signs of my vocation as a story-teller.

As always happens with expatriate families, the fact of living abroad accentuated our patriotism. Until I was ten, I was convinced that the greatest fortune that could befall one was to be a Peruvian. My idea of Peru at that time had more to do with the country of the Incas and the Conquistadors than with the real Peru, a country that I only came to know in 1946, when my family moved from Cochabamba to Piura, where my grandfather had been appointed as Prefect. We travelled overland, with a stop in Arequipa. I remember my emotion when I reached the city of my birth and also the fuss that my uncle Eduardo made of me. He was a bachelor, a judge, and a very pious man. He lived with his servant Inocencia in the style of a Spanish provincial nobleman, tidy, methodical, growing old in the midst of very old furniture, very old portraits and very old objects. I remember my excitement when I saw the sea for the first time, in Camaná. I screamed and made a nuisance of myself until my grandparents agreed to stop the car so that I could take a dip on that wild and rugged beach. My baptism in the sea was not very successful because I was bitten by a crab. But, even so, my love at first sight with the Peruvian coast has continued. There are those who have nothing good to say about the two thousand miles of desert, scarcely interrupted by small valleys which have formed along the banks of the rivers that flow down from the Andes, to meet the waters of the Pacific. The most extreme defenders of our Indian tradition, who revile everything Hispanic, accuse the coast of being 'foreign loving' and frivolous and insist that it was a great misfortune that the centre of Peruvian political and economic life should have shifted from the sierra to the coast, from Cuzco to Lima, because it began an asphyxiating centralism which has turned Peru into a sort of spider: a country with an enormous head – the capital – and withered limbs. One historian called Lima and the coast the 'Anti-Peru'. As an Arequipan, a man from the sierra, I should side in this argument with the Andes against the maritime deserts. But if I were forced to choose between this landscape, or the Andes or the Amazonian jungle – the three regions that divide Peru longitudinally – I would probably opt for these sands and waves.

The coast was the periphery of the Inca Empire, a civilization that radiated out of Cuzco. It was not the only pre-Hispanic Peruvian culture, but it was certainly the most powerful. It extended throughout Peru, Bolivia, Ecuador and part of Chile, Colombia and Argentina. In their short existence of little more than a century, the Incas conquered dozens of peoples, built roads, irrigation systems, fortresses and citadels and established an administrative system that allowed them to produce enough to feed all Peruvians, something that no other regime has managed since. Despite this, I have never much liked the Incas. Although I am dazzled by the monuments that they left, like Machu Picchu or Sacsahuamán, I have always felt that Peruvian sadness – a notable feature of our character – was perhaps born with the Inca state: a regimented and bureaucratic society of antmen, out of which an omnipotent steamroller squeezed all traces of individual personality.

In order to maintain power over the peoples that they conquered, the Incas behaved with refined cunning, appropriating, for example, their gods and incorporating the vassal leaders into their own aristocracy. Then there were the *mitimaes,* the transplantation of peoples, who were thrown out of their native lands and made to resettle a great distance away. The oldest Quechuan poems that have come down to us are elegies by bewildered men in foreign lands who sing of their lost fatherland. Five centuries before the *Great Soviet Encyclopedia* and George Orwell's *1984,* the Incas manipulated the past in accordance with the political needs of the present. Each Cuzco emperor ascended the throne with a retinue of *amautas* or wise men, whose task it was to alter history so that it could be seen to have reached its apogee with the ruling Inca, who would be accredited from that moment with all the conquests and great deeds of his predecessors. The result is that it is impossible to reconstruct this history, which has been distorted in such a Borgesian fashion. The Incas had the *quipus,* an elaborate mnemonic system for recording quantities, but they had no writing and I have always been convinced by the argument that they did not want to have writing, since it would be a danger to their type of society. The art of the Incas is austere and cold, without the fantasy and skill that one can observe in other pre-Inca cultures such as the Nazca and the Paracas, which produced incredibly delicate cloaks of feathers and cloth woven with enigmatic figures that have retained their colour and charm to this day.

After the Inca period, the Peruvians had to endure another steamroller: Spanish domination. The Conquistadors brought to Peru the language and the religion that the majority of Peruvians speak and profess. But any indiscriminate glorification of the Colony is as fallacious as the idealization of the Incas. For although the Colony made Peru the head of a Vice-royalty that also encompassed territories which are today different republics, and made Lima a capital with a

3

magnificent court and an important academic and ceremonial life, it also brought with it religious obscurantism, the Inquisition, censorship that managed to ban a literary genre – the novel – and the persecution of the unbeliever and the heretic, which, in many cases, meant the persecution of those who dared to think. The Colony led to the exploitation of Indians and blacks and the establishment of economic castes which have survived to this day, thus making Peru a country of immense inequalities. Independence was a political phenomenon which barely changed a society divided into a minority, who enjoy the privileges of modern life, and the masses who live in ignorance and poverty. The pomp of the Incas, the colonial period and the republic has not made me forget that all the regimes under which we have lived have been unable to reduce to tolerable proportions the differences that separate Peruvians, and that this stigma cannot be compensated for with architectural monuments, warlike deeds or courtly brilliance.

None of this, of course, was in my head when I returned from Bolivia. My family had biblical customs. Everyone – uncles, aunts, cousins – moved in the wake of my grandparents, who were the centre of the family. That is how we arrived in Piura. This city, surrounded by sands, was my first experience of Peru. In the Salesian school, my classmates made fun of me because I spoke like a *serrano,* sounding my *r*s and *s*s, and because I believed that babies were brought by storks from Paris. They explained to me that things happened in a less airborne manner.

My memory is full of images of the two years that I spent there. Piurans are extrovert, superficial, full of jokes and warmth. In Piura at that time, there was good *chicha* (corn alcohol) to drink, the regional dance, the *tondero,* was danced with grace and the relationship between *cholos* (mixed race) and whites was less fraught than in other places; the informality and the boisterous nature of the Piurans closed the gap between classes. Lovers serenaded under girls' balconies and suitors who met with parental opposition abducted their girlfriends: they would carry them off to a *hacienda* for a few days and would then – happy ending, reconciled families – celebrate the religious ceremony, with all splendour, in the cathedral. The abductions were announced and celebrated like the coming of the river which, for some months in the year, brought life to the cotton estates.

This great town, Piura, was full of incidents that fired the imagination. There was La Mangachería, an area made up of mud and reed huts, where the best *chicha* bars could be found, and La Gallinacera, located between the river and the abattoir. Both districts hated each other and there were sometimes pitched battles between *mangaches* and *gallinazos*. There was also the Green House, the town brothel, in the middle of the desert, which at night was full of lights, noises and unsettling silhouettes. This spot, that the Salesian Fathers thundered against, frightened and fascinated me and I spent hours talking about it, spying on it and fantasizing about what might be happening inside. This precarious wooden structure, where an orchestra from the Mangachería came to play and where men from Piura came to eat, listen to music and talk business as much as to make love – couples did that in the open air, under the stars, in the warm sand – is one of my most evocative childhood memories. From this memory *The Green House* was born, a novel that deals with the disturbances that the opening of a brothel causes in the life and imagination of Piurans, and also with the exploits of a group of adventurers in the Amazon. Here I tried to bring together two regions of Peru – the desert and the jungle – which were as distant as they were different from each other. Memories of Piura were also the inspiration for several stories in my first book, *The Cubs*. When this collection of stories came out, some critics saw it as an X-ray analysis of Latin American *machismo*. I do not know if that is true, but I do know that Peruvians of my age grew up in the midst of this tender violence – or violent tenderness – that I tried to recreate in my first stories.

I went to Lima when I was entering adolescence and it is a city that I hated from the first moment because I was quite unhappy there. My parents had separated but were reconciled after ten years. Living with my father meant leaving my grandparents and uncles and aunts and submitting to the discipline of a very severe man who was a stranger to me. My first memories of Lima are associated with this difficult experience. We lived in Magdalena, a typical middle class district. But when I got good marks at school I went to spend the weekends – this was my reward – with an uncle and aunt in Miraflores, a much more prosperous district by the sea. There I got to know a group of boys and girls of my own age, with whom I shared the rites of adolescence. This was what was called 'having a neighbourhood', a parallel family whose hearth was the street corner and with whom you played football, smoked surreptitiously, learned to dance mambo and courted the girls. Compared to later generations, we were archangels. Young people in Lima today make love at the same time as they receive First Holy Communion and smoke their first joint of marijuana when their voices are still breaking. Our wild adventures amounted to no more than slipping into forbidden films – the ones that Church censorship classified as 'inappropriate for young ladies' – or drinking a *capitán,* a poisonous mixture of vermouth and pisco, in the corner bar before going to the Saturday parties where alcoholic drinks were never served. I remember a very serious discussion that the 'men' of the neighbourhood – we must have been fourteen or fifteen at the time – had about the legitimate way to kiss your girlfriend. What Giacomo Casanova chauvinistically calls the 'Italian style', or the British call the 'French kiss', was unanimously rejected as a mortal sin.

Lima was then, in the late 1940s, still a small, safe, peaceful and deceitful city. We lived in watertight compartments: the rich and well-off in Orrantia and San Isidro; the wealthier middle classes in Miraflores and the poorer middle classes in Magdalena, San Miguel, Barranco; the poor in la Victoria, Lince, Bajo El Puente, El Porvenir. Middle class children almost never saw the poor: we did not even know that they existed. They were out there, in the neighbourhoods, dangerous and remote places where, so we were told, crimes were committed. If he never left Lima, a boy from my background could spend his life under the illusion that he lived in a Spanish-speaking country made up of whites and *mestizos,* in complete ignorance of the millions of Indians – a third of the population – who spoke Quechua and lived completely different lives.

I was fortunate enough to break through this barrier to some degree. Now it seems like luck. But then, in 1950, it was a real drama. My father, who had discovered that I wrote poems, feared for my future – a poet is condemned to die of hunger – and for my 'manhood' (the belief that poets are always homosexuals is still to an extent widespread among certain groups), and in order to protect me against these dangers, he thought that the ideal antidote was the Leoncio Prado Military School. I spent two years in that institution. Leoncio Prado was a microcosm of Peruvian society. There were boys from the upper classes, whose fathers sent them there as if it were a reform school, middle class boys who wanted to have a career in the military and also boys from the lower classes, because the school gave grants to children of the poorest families. It was one of the few institutions in Peru in which rich, poor and middle income groups, whites, *cholos,* Indians, blacks and Chinese, people from Lima and the provinces, all lived together. I found the imprisonment and the military discipline, as well as the brutal and bullying atmosphere, quite unbearable. But I think that in these two years I came to know real Peruvian society, those contrasts, tensions, prejudices, abuses and resentments that a boy from Miraflores could not even suspect existed. I am grateful to the Leoncio Prado for something else: it gave me the experiences that provided the raw materials for my first novel. *Time of the Hero* recreates, with many inventions, of course, the life of this Peruvian microcosm. The book had a striking reception: one thousand copies were ceremoniously burned in the school square and several generals attacked it severely. One of them said that the book had been written by a 'degenerate mind' and another, more imaginatively, said that it was a novel financed by Ecuador to undermine the Peruvian military. The book was successful, but I never quite knew if this was due to its own merits or to the scandal that it provoked.

In the past twenty years, millions of emigrants from the sierra have come to live in Lima, in slums – euphemistically called 'young communities' – which surround the old neighbourhoods. Unlike us, middle class boys from Lima today discover the reality of the country just by opening the windows of their houses. Now, the poor are everywhere, as pedlars, tramps, beggars and muggers. With its 5.5 or 6 million inhabitants and its enormous problems – rubbish, inadequate transport, insufficient housing and crime – Lima has lost a great deal of its charm: its colonial districts and jalousied balconies, its tranquillity and its noisy, wet carnivals. But it is now truly the capital of Peru because all the peoples and all the problems of the country are represented there.

They say that hatred is mixed in with love and this must be true because I spend my life speaking badly about Lima and yet there are many things in the city that move me. For example, the mist – the gauze that covers her from March to November, which so impressed Melville when he came through here (he called Lima, in *Moby Dick*, 'the strangest, saddest city thou canst see' because it 'has taken the white veil' and 'there is a higher horror in this whiteness of her woe'). I like the *garúa*, the invisible drizzle which feels like spiders' feet on one's skin and makes everything wet, turning the city dwellers somewhat batrachian in winter. I like the beaches with their cold water and big waves, ideal for surfing. And I like the old stadium where I go to football games to support Universitario de Deportes. But I realize that these are very personal weaknesses and that the most beautiful aspects of my country are not in the city but in the interior, in the deserts, the Andes or in the jungle.

A Peruvian surrealist, César Moro, aggressively entitled one of his poems 'Lima the Horrible' and years later another writer, Sebastián Salazar Bondy, took this expression as the title for an essay written to demolish the myth of Lima, the idealization of the city in stories and legends and in the words of *criollo* songs. He contrasts the supposedly Moorish and Andalucian city – its filigree lattice windows hiding mysterious and diabolical veiled ladies who tempted gentlemen with powdered wigs – with the real, difficult, dirty and festering Lima. All purveyors of Peruvian literature could be divided into two tendencies: those who sanctify Lima and those who criticize her. The real city is probably not as beautiful as some say or as dreadful as others proclaim.

Although, as a whole, it is a city without personality, it has beautiful spots: certain squares, convents and churches and a jewel of a bullring, the Acho. Lima has had a passion for bullfighting from colonial times and the Lima fan is as knowledgeable as any in Mexico or Madrid. I am one of the enthusiasts who try never to miss a bullfight during the October Fair. My uncle Juan, one of the infinite relatives on my mother's side, instilled me with this passion. His father had been a friend of Juan Belmonte, a great bullfighter who had given him one of the matador suits that he wore to fight. The suit was kept in my uncle's house like a relic and was shown to the children of the family on important occasions.

Military dictatorships are as common to Lima as the bullfights. Peruvians of my generation have lived under them for more years than under democracy. The first dictatorship that I experienced personally was that of General Manuel Odría, from 1948 to 1956, years in which my generation passed from childhood to adulthood. General Odría overthrew a lawyer from Arequipa, José Luis Bustamante, a cousin of my grandfather. I knew him because, when we lived in Cochabamba, he came to stay at my grandparents' house and I remember how well-spoken he was – we listened to him open-mouthed – and the money that he slipped into my hand before leaving. Bustamante was the candidate of a Democratic Front in the elections of 1945, an alliance in which the APRA party, under Raúl Haya de la Torre, held a majority. The Apristas – a centre left party – had been severely repressed by dictatorships. Bustamante, an independent, was the APRA candidate because it could not put up a candidate of its own. No sooner was he elected, by a great majority, than APRA began to act as if Bustamante was its puppet. At the same time, the reactionary, troglodyte right unleashed a hostile campaign against the man that they considered to be an instrument of their *bête noire*, APRA. Bustamante kept his independence, resisted pressures from left and right and governed with respect for freedom of expression, unions and political parties. His government only lasted for three years, punctuated by street violence, political crimes and uprisings, until Odría's coup. I still maintain the admiration that I felt as a child for that gentleman with the bow-tie, who walked like Chaplin, because he was a rarity among the rulers of my country: he left office poorer than he had entered, he was tolerant of opponents and severe with his supporters, so that no one could accuse him of taking sides, and he respected the law to such an extent that he committed political suicide.

With General Odría, barbarism returned to Peru. Although Odría killed, imprisoned and deported a great many Peruvians, his eight-year rule was less bloody than other South American dictatorships of the period. But, as compensation, it was more corrupt, not only because public officials lined their own pockets but, more seriously, because lies, perks, blackmail, denunciations and abuses took on the form of public institutions and contaminated the whole life of the country.

During this period, in 1953, I enrolled in the University of San Marcos to study law and humanities. My family hoped that I would go to the Catholic University where the children of what were then known as 'decent families' went to study. But I had lost my faith between fourteen and fifteen and did not want to be a 'privileged boy'. I had discovered social problems in my last year at school, in the romantic way that a child discovers prejudice and social inequalities and I wanted to identify with the poor and be involved in a revolution that would bring justice to Peru. San Marcos, a secular, national university, had a tradition of nonconformity which attracted me as much as its academic opportunities.

The dictatorship had dismantled the university. There were lecturers in exile and, in the previous year, 1952, a big round-up had sent dozens of students to jail or into exile. An atmosphere of suspicion pervaded the lecture rooms, where the dictatorship had enrolled many policemen as students. Political parties were outlawed and the Apristas and the Communists, who were great rivals at the time, worked underground.

Soon after entering San Marcos, I became an activist in Cahuide, the name behind which the Communist party, which had been badly damaged by the dictatorship, was attempting to revive its fortunes. Our activism was quite inoffensive. We met in secret, in small cells, to study Marxism; we printed leaflets against the government; we fought with the Apristas; we conspired to make the university support working class struggles – our greatest achievement was to call a strike in San Marcos in solidarity with the tram workers – and we attempted to place our people in university bodies. It was the time of the absolute rule of Stalinism and, in the literary field, the official party aesthetic was socialist realism. It was this, I think, that first made me disillusioned with Cahuide. Albeit with some reservations, since I was also influenced by Sartre, whom I greatly admired, I became resigned to dialectical materialism and historical materialism. But I could never accept the aberrant dictates of socialist realism which ruled out all mystery and turned literary activity into a propaganda exercise. Our discussions were interminable, and in one of our debates in which I argued that *This is How Steel was Tempered* by Nikolai Ostrovsky was an anaesthetic novel and I defended *Fruits of the Earth* by the decadent André Gide, one of my comrades shouted at me: 'You are subhuman.'

And in a way I was, because I was reading voraciously, and with growing admiration, a number of writers considered by Marxists at the time to be 'gravediggers of Western culture': Henry Miller, Joyce, Hemingway, Proust, Malraux, Céline, Borges. But, above all, Faulkner. Perhaps the most enduring part of my university years was not what I learned in lecture halls, but what I discovered in the novels and stories that recounted the saga of Yoknapatawpha County. I remember how dazzling it was to read – pencil and paper in hand – *Light in August, As I Lay Dying, The Sound and the Fury* and the like, and to discover in those pages the infinite complexity of shade and allusion and the textual and conceptual richness that a novel could provide. Also to learn that to tell a story well required a conjuror's technique. The literary models of my youth have palled, like Sartre, whom I can no longer read. But Faulkner is still a major writer for me and every time that I read him , I am convinced that his work is a novelistic *summa*, comparable to the great classics. In the 1950s in Latin America, we read mainly European and North American writers and hardly looked at our own writers. This has now changed: readers in Latin America discovered their novelists at the same time as the rest of the world did so.

An important event for me in those years was my meeting with the chief of security of the dictatorship, the most hated man after Odría himself. I was then a delegate of the University Federation of San Marcos. There were many students in jail and we knew that they were sleeping on prison floors, with no mattresses or blankets. We organized a collection and bought blankets. But when we wanted to take them to the Penitentiary – the prison that was on the site now occupied by the Sheraton Hotel where, so the story goes, the souls of the victims tortured in the old dungeons still wander 'in torment' – we were told that only the Minister of the Interior, Don Alejandro Esparza Zañartu, could authorize the delivery. The Federation agreed that five delegates should ask for a meeting. I was one of the five.

I still remember very vividly the impression it made on me when I saw the feared character close up, in his office in the Interior Ministry. He was a small man of about fifty, wrinkled and bored, who seemed to be looking at us through water and did not listen to a word we said. He let us speak – we were trembling – and when we finished, he kept looking at us without saying anything, as if he was laughing at our confusion. Then he opened a drawer in his desk and took out some copies of *Cahuide*, a mimeographed little journal which we published clandestinely and in which, of course, we attacked him. 'I know which of you has written each of these articles,' he told us, 'where you meet to print it, and what you plot in your cell meetings.' And, indeed, he did seem omniscient, but, at the same time, deplorable, a pitiful mediocrity. He spoke in an ungrammatical way and his intellectual poverty was quite apparent. Seeing him in this interview, I had an idea for a novel that I would write fifteen years later: *Conversation in the Cathedral*. In it, I tried to describe the effects that a dictatorship like the eight-year period of Odría had on people's daily lives – their studies, work, loves, dreams and ambitions. It took me time to find a connecting thread for the mass of characters and episodes: a casual meeting between a former bodyguard and henchman of the dictator and a journalist, the son of a businessman who prospered under the regime, and their conversation, which runs through the entire novel. When the book came out, the ex-Interior Minister, who had now retired and was devoting himself to good works, observed: 'If Vargas

Llosa had come to see me, I could have told him more interesting things.'

Just as the Leoncio Prado Military School helped me to get to know my country, journalism also opened many doors for me and thanks to it, I explored all kinds of environments, social classes, places and activities. I began working as a journalist on the newspaper *La Crónica* when I was fifteen, in the fourth year school holidays, covering local affairs and, later, crime stories. It was fascinating to go to the police station at night to check what crimes, robberies, assaults and accidents had occurred and to investigate spectacular cases like the 'Nocturnal Butterfly', a prostitute who was stabbed to death in El Porvenir. This took me on a tour of the prostitution areas in Lima, the dives and the bars full of pimps and homosexuals. At that time, journalism and the underworld – or at least the shadier aspects of bohemian life – overlapped to some extent. When work was over, it was an obligatory ritual to go to some gloomy bar, usually with Chinese waiters, where the floor was full of sawdust to cover over the drunks' vomit. And then on to the brothels, where the crime reporters got preferential treatment, because of the trouble they could cause.

During my final years at university, I worked in the Panamericana radio station, preparing news bulletins. I had the opportunity to see close up, from the inside, the world of soap operas, that fascinating universe of sensibilities and truculence, wonderful coincidences and infinite affectation, that seemed a modern version of the nineteenth-century newspaper serials. They had such a following that it was said that a man in the street could listen to the episodes of *El derecho de nacer* [The Right to be Born] by Félix B. Caignet in any area in Lima since every household was listening to it. This effervescent and picturesque world gave me the theme for another of my novels, *Aunt Julia and the Scriptwriter*. On the surface, it is a novel about soap operas and melodrama; at a deeper level, it deals with something that has always fascinated me, something to which I have dedicated most of my life and which I have never managed to understand: why do I write, what is writing all about? Since childhood, I have always been beset by the temptation to turn into fiction everything that happens to me, to such a degree that, at times, I feel that everything I do and that is done to me – all of my life – is nothing more than a pretext for inventing stories. What lies behind this incessant transmutation of reality into fiction? Is it an attempt to save certain treasured experiences from the ravages of time? Or a desire to exorcise certain painful or terrible events by transfiguring them? Or is it simply a game, a drunken bout of words and fantasy? The more I write, the more difficult it is to find an answer.

I finished university in 1957. The following year, I submitted my thesis and received a scholarship for a doctorate in Madrid. To go to Europe – to get to Paris somehow – was a dream that I had cherished since first reading Alexandre Dumas, Jules Verne and Victor Hugo. I was happily packing my suitcase when, by chance, I was given the opportunity of a trip to the Amazon. A Mexican anthropologist, Juan Comas, was going to travel along the Upper Marañón River, where the Aguaruna and the Huambisa tribes lived, and there was one place left on the expedition, which I was given thanks to a friend of mine from San Marcos.

Those weeks spent in the Upper Marañón, visiting tribes, dwellings and villages, was an unforgettable experience and showed me another dimension of my country (Peru, quite clearly, is the country of a thousand faces). To go from Lima to Chicais or Urakusa was to leap from the twentieth century to the stone age, to come into contact with compatriots who lived half naked in conditions of extreme primitivism and who, furthermore, were exploited in a merciless way. Their exploiters, in turn, were poor merchants, barefoot and semi-literate, who traded in rubber and skins that they bought from the tribes at ridiculous prices. They savagely punished any attempt by the Indians to escape from their control. When we reached the settlement of Urakusa, the chieftain, an Aguaruna called Jum, came out to meet us and it was terrible to see him and hear his story because here was a man who had been recently tortured for having attempted to create a cooperative. In the lost villages of the Upper Marañón, I saw and touched the violence that the struggle for existence in my country could cause.

But the Amazon was not just suffering, abuse and the harsh coexistence of Peruvians of different mentalities and historical periods. It was also a world of prodigious exuberance and force, where someone from the city could discover untamed and untouched nature, the proud spectacle of the great swirling rivers and virgin forests, animals that seemed out of legends, and men and women living dangerous and completely free lives, like the protagonists of the adventure stories that were the delight of my childhood. I think that I have never made a more fertile trip than that one in 1958. Many of the things that I did, saw and heard later turned into stories.

On that journey I had my first intuition of what Isaiah Berlin calls 'contradictory truths'. It was in Santa María de Nieva, a small village where a mission had been set up in the 1940s. The nuns opened a school for girls of the tribes. But because they would not attend voluntarily, they were brought in with the help of the Civil Guard. After a spell in the mission, some of the girls lost all contact with their family world and could not go back to the life that they had been taken from. What happened to them, therefore? They were entrusted to the representatives of 'civilization' who came through Santa María de Nieva – engineers, soldiers, traders – who took them as servants. What was really extraordinary was that the missionary nuns did not realize the consequences of the whole operation, and that, furthermore, they demonstrated true heroism in order to carry it out. The conditions in which they lived were very difficult and they were almost totally isolated in the months when the river rose. That with the best intentions in the world, and at a cost of limitless sacrifice, they could cause so much damage is a lesson that I have never forgotten. It has taught me how vague the line is that separates good from evil and how prudent one must be in judging human actions and deciding the answers to social problems if one is to avoid the cure being worse than the illness.

I left for Europe and did not go back to live in my country for any length of time until 1974. I was twenty-two when I left and thirty-eight when I returned. Many things happened in that time and in many ways I was a completely different person when I got back. But as far as the relationship with my country goes, I think that it has not changed since adolescence. A relationship that can be defined through metaphors rather than concepts. For me, Peru is a kind of incurable illness and my relationship to it is intense, harsh and full of the violence of passion. The novelist Juan Carlos Onetti once said that the difference between him and me as writers was that I had a matrimonial relationship with literature whereas he had an adulterous relationship with it. I feel that my relationship with Peru is more adulterous than conjugal: it is full of suspicion, passion and rages. I consciously fight against all forms of 'nationalism', which I consider to be one of the greatest of human defects and has been an excuse for the worst forms of deceit. But it is a fact that events in my country exasperate or engage me more than events in other places and what happens or does not happen there concerns me in an intimate and inevitable way. It is possible that if I were to weigh everything up, then at the time of writing this article, the defects of Peru are uppermost in my mind. I have also been a severe critic (severe to the point of injustice) of everything that afflicts her. But I believe that beneath these criticisms, there is a profound solidarity between us. Although I have sometimes hated Peru, this hatred, in the words of the poet César Vallejo, has always been steeped in tenderness.

Lima, August 1983

# When Madrid was a Village

When I learned that I had been awarded a grant to study for my doctorate in Madrid, I felt an indescribable joy. Ever since, as a child, I had read Jules Verne, Alexandre Dumas, Dickens and Victor Hugo, to go to Europe, to live in Europe, was a long cherished dream which became almost a physical need when I was a student at university. The 'journey to Europe' seemed to me, as to many young people at the time in Latin America, an essential prerequisite for a good intellectual training. Europe held cultural sway over us, but I think that this is no longer so much the case for the new generations in Latin America.

My greatest ambition was to go to Paris – almost all my readings were in North American or French literature – but Madrid, as viewed from Lima, was not to be sneered at. Franco was there, of course (it was 1958), but I thought that it would be wonderful to see on stage those Golden Age plays that, in Peru, we only knew through books. And, furthermore, the University of Madrid, compared to the University of Lima, would be a centre of high culture in which I could fill the extraordinary cultural gaps in the education that I had received at the old San Marcos University (where, for example, the classes in medieval literature consisted of the lecturer reading us out pages from the Espasa Encyclopedia).

It turned out that the University of Madrid was not much better, at least in the field of literature. The lecturer in Spanish American literature only taught up to Romanticism since he was suspicious of everything from *modernismo* onwards. The books and authors put on the Index by the Vatican were removed from the faculty library; that year, the purged titles included work by Unamuno and the *Revista de Occidente*, edited by Ortega y Gasset, that I had begun to read between classes. The mood of sanctimoniousness and prejudice among the student body could also be surprisingly intense. One fellow student on the doctoral programme stopped saying hello to me when he found out that I had not been married in church. 'Stylistics' was the reigning critical orthodoxy and no other form of literary analysis apart from this linguistic approach was permitted or even known. Professor Leo

Spitzer, the author of laborious grammatical studies in search of (in the words of another critic, Dámaso Alonso) 'the ultimate moistness of the poem', was considered to be the canonical model of a literary intellectual, a scholar who had managed to master the 'science' of literature. But, surprisingly, almost none of my teachers or colleagues seemed to have heard of Sartre or Camus – whose books were banned by the censors – and on the subject of existentialism, which was then so fashionable in the rest of Europe, there was only a very cautious mention of the Catholic Gabriel Marcel.

Because of the mediocrity of the faculty, I spent a great deal of time reading romances of chivalry in the National Library, a big and gloomy building with very high ceilings where readers would freeze in winter. For some strange reason, many romances of chivalry, like Lancelot du Lac, were in the section called 'Hell' and could only be consulted with permission from the Curia. In order to obtain this permission, one had to present statements from teachers or academic institutions vouching for the 'scientific intentions' of the aspirant reader. Anyone who has made his way through the intricate forest of adventures of chivalric narrative in which, with very rare exceptions (the most famous of these is, of course, *Tirant lo Blanc*), the erotic scenes are normally very chaste, can imagine the really grotesque extremes that the control of thought in 1950s Spain could reach.

The newspapers and magazines were simply unreadable because they were old-fashioned and because the censorship not only banned articles that the regime thought dangerous or sinful, but also forced the press to present the news and other items that it let through in such a twisted and distorted way that any sense was lost. Only the most conservative foreign publications were allowed into the country, while, for example, *Le Monde* or the *Herald Tribune* were often banned, along with *L'Express* or *Le Nouvel Observateur.* To find out what was happening in the world and in Spain itself, the Spaniards listened to foreign radio stations. In the boarding house where I lived, in the Salamanca district, there was a fixed ritual every evening at dinner to tune into the Spanish language broadcasting service of French Radio-Television, where, by chance, I would end up working as an editor once my Madrid studies were over and I went to live in France.

I was not able to satisfy my desire to see, at long last, classic Spanish theatre on the stage. Or rather, the only Golden Age play that I saw in Madrid at that time was Lope de Vega's *La dama boba* (The Foolish

Lady), put on by a university company whose main actor was Ricardo Blume, a Peruvian! The poverty of the theatre being performed was terrifying: the listings were full of *sainetes* or pseudo-farcical, sickly nonsense – Alfonso Paso was the most successful dramatist – while the great modern playwrights of Spain, from Valle Inclán to García Lorca, were simply not staged. Censorship had removed one of the richest and most creative aspects of twentieth-century Spanish culture and had frustrated any attempt to bring the inhabitants of Madrid up to date with what was happening in theatre in the rest of Europe (the theatre of the absurd, the new English theatre, etc.). The anachronism of Spanish theatre in the 1950s was not just limited to the plays that were performed; the acting, the direction, the stage design and all the theatrical techniques and resources seemed to have remained petrified since the Civil War.

Cinema was worse. The films that the censors did not ban reached the screen horribly mutilated, to such an extent that they sometimes seemed like shorts. Apart from wielding their scissors, the censors also tampered with the dubbing, softening or altering the original dialogues to suit the dominant morality in such a radical way that the results were sometimes a source of great amusement (the most famous case of dubbing adulteration was when the lovers in *Mogambo* were turned into brother and sister). Visitors to Madrid today, who are impressed by its prosperity, its big city appearance, its cosmopolitanism and its intense cultural life, where every form of experimentation, every vanguard movement and even the wildest extravagances have a place, would find it difficult to imagine that provincial, quiet, asphyxiating city with its caricaturesque cultural life that I knew in 1958.

And yet, although I felt cheated in many respects, I came to have a deep affection for that village Madrid, and the year or more that I spent in its quiet little streets was one of the best times of my life. Because, despite Franco, censorship and all the other retrograde aspects, Madrid had innumerable attractions. With the $120 a month of my scholarship, I could live like a king in a good boarding house in the Salamanca district. I bought books, went to the bullfights, made trips throughout Castille and frequented the bars with their smell of fried food and shellfish. Old Madrid was very well preserved and, strolling in the mild autumn evenings, we could follow the itineraries of the novels of Pío Baroja dealing with turn of the century anarchists or compare with the original the descriptions that Pérez Galdós made of nineteenth-century Madrid in *Fortunata y Jacinta* (Fortunata and Jacinta), a novel that I read that year with passion. Apart from the Gijón, there were still many old cafés where poets as old as the cafés themselves still met, as in the days of those famous 'parties' or 'gatherings', which fill so many pages of Spanish literature, and where one could look at the illustrious writers. Furthermore, the warmth that everyone – high or low, from the country or the city – showed to a foreigner knew no bounds. Since then, I have lived in many cities in the old world and the new: I have never witnessed anything that even remotely resembles the overwhelming hospitality and generosity of the Spanish people towards foreigners. This virtue would go on increasing retrospectively in my memory in the following six years that I spent in Paris, a city which, curiously, can be characterized in two very different ways: it is the most bewitching and irresistible city for the rest of the planet and the most inhospitable towards the *métèque* (which I was at the time).

Lima, 1985

# Chronicle of the Cuban Revolution

I have just spent two weeks in Cuba, at a critical moment for the island, and I return convinced of two things that seem to me fundamental. First, the revolution is firmly established and could only be overthrown by a massive, direct invasion by the United States, an operation which would have incalculable consequences. Secondly, Cuban socialism is idiosyncratic, very different from the rest of the countries of the Soviet bloc, a fact that could have very important repercussions for the future of world socialism.

Within a few days of arriving in Havana, I witnessed an unusual spectacle. A film screening had to be interrupted in order to silence the audience, which had begun applauding and cheering Fidel Castro when his face appeared on the screen. 'Don't confuse this with the cult of personality,' a Cuban friend remarked when I told him about this incident. 'That cult is imposed from above; the affection for Fidel comes from below and can be seen in a spectacular way every time that the revolution is in danger. The night that Kennedy announced the blockade, everyone went out into the street, chanting "Fidel, Fidel". It's their way of showing their support for the revolution.' A few days later I went to a meeting in the García Lorca Theatre. Every time that the speakers wanted to fire up the audience, they would mention Castro; immediately, thunderous applause broke out. On another day, on a 'people's farm' some seven miles outside Havana, I asked the administrator, a *barbudo* from the Sierra Maestra with a scapular round his neck: 'If Fidel were to die, who would replace him at the head of the revolution?' 'No one,' he replied immediately, but then hastened to add: 'I mean, the revolution would continue, but it wouldn't be the same, something would be missing.' That 'something' is, at the moment at least, very important. All the differences of opinion that might exist within the revolution disappear when it comes to Fidel Castro. He is the most solid agglutinating force that the Cuban people possess, the factor that maintains cohesion and popular enthusiasm, the twin pillars of the revolution.

This support for Fidel is not just based on legend. Obviously the popular imagination has been caught by the odyssey of the young lawyer who attacked the Moncada barracks, disembarked with a handful of men from the *Granma* and fought an unequal battle against the regular army in the Sierra Maestra. But what has undoubtedly cemented this support is the relationship that Fidel has developed with the people in whose name he governs. This relationship cannot be reduced to any simple formula or label, it is something personal and friendly. It could be seen at the critical time of the blockade. The head of state suddenly appeared on 23rd Avenue, one of the streets in the centre of Havana, at the busiest time of the day. Passers-by congregated around him and he began to ask them questions. 'Let's see,' he said to someone, 'what do you think about the blockade? Do you think that the Russian missiles should be removed or should remain in Cuba?' And the following day, he turned up in the same surprising way in the university square, to talk to the students about current problems. In this way, the man in the street feels a direct link with the responsibilities of the state, feels that he is being personally consulted by Fidel at every important stage of the revolution. A journalist present at the conversation between Fidel and the passers-by told me that many people thought that the missiles should not leave Cuba, they were openly opposed to Nikita Khrushchev's offer to remove them, and chanted in front of Fidel: 'Nikita, Nikita, lo que se da no se quita' (Nikita, Nikita, what is given shouldn't be taken away). I am not trying to deny with all this that the revolution is Marxist-Leninist. Quite the opposite. It is clear from the press, the radio, the training courses and different publications that there is an official insistence on indoctrinating the masses. 'Social Books' published in Spanish in Moscow and the popular democracies circulate widely; in their speeches all the leaders proclaim themselves to be orthodox Marxists. But this campaign has not led to an exclusive ideological directorate, as happened in the popular democracies. I have seen Trotskyist and anarchist publications displayed in the windows of Havana bookshops. There is no censorship aimed at maintaining the ideological purity of the publications. Recently a rather quaint and improbable essay entitled *Espiritismo y Santería en la luz del marxismo* (Spiritualism and Santería in the Light of Marxism) appeared. A shop assistant recommended the book to me in the following way: 'It is a very interesting essay, comrade, of esoteric materialism.'

What I want to say is that the recognition of Marxism as the official philosophy of the revolution does not exclude, until now at least, other ideological viewpoints, which can be freely expressed. Castro's statement to the Congress of Cuban Writers – 'Within the revolution, everything; against the revolution, nothing' – is being put into practice in a rigorous manner. In art and literature this is very obvious: there is no official aesthetic. When I was in Havana, the National Council of Culture (where one of the best contemporary novelists in the Spanish language, Alejo Carpentier, works) was showing a retrospective of the surrealist Wilfredo Lam and a collective exhibition of young painters, all of whom were abstract. Literary publications have paid homage to William Faulkner, praised Saint-Jean Perse (*Pluies* (Rains) has just appeared in Havana) and have passionately discussed the objective novelists. The influence of Sartre is undeniable in three of the best young Cuban writers, Ambrosio Fornet, Edmundo Desnoes and Jaime Sarusky.

The prudence with which the revolution has acted concerning the freedom to publish can be seen clearly in the following example. I was very surprised to see in Cuba street stalls selling all kinds of pornographic books. It was very strange to find, displayed in the middle of the street, books that in any city of the world would be sold in a semi-clandestine manner: the *Kama-Sutra,* the *Ananga-Ranga,* Musset's *Gamiani,* the *Dialogues* of Aretino etc. I was with a Bulgarian engineer who was as surprised as me and also angry: 'This is a scandal,' he said. 'They should ban this trade: socialism and eroticism are incompatible.' Before the revolution, Cuba was not just a North American entrepôt, it was also the paradise of pornography. Many publishing houses specialized in exporting literature of this genre to the Spanish-speaking world. These enterprises no longer exist, but the books that remained on the island still circulate without any restriction. 'This trade will disappear by itself in time,' an official told me. 'The roots of the evil have been cut out and the leaves and branches will wither on their own. Look at what happened with prostitution and begging. Havana was the city that, proportionally, had the greatest number of prostitutes and beggars in the world. Both problems are being solved without any coercive measures, without violence. Instead of banning prostitution, the government made an offer to the women who worked in this area. It offered to teach them a trade and to give food and lodging to their families – parents and children – while they trained. At first, only a small number of prostitutes accepted, but then there was a real flood and new instruction centres had to be opened for them. They spend several months there and come out with a secure job. Today, prostitution has practically disappeared in Cuba.'

Cuba is not the only socialist revolution in which the creation of the revolutionary party came after the revolution itself. The 26 July was not really a party but rather a movement with quite a vague liberal and humanist ideology. The revolution has been shaping its political and economic doctrine in practice, in the exercise of power. This explains why, at the beginning, the revolution had the support of conservative groups and movements. As the young *barbudos,* faced with the open or covert aggression of the United States, became more radical and determined to save the revolution in any way possible from the economic stranglehold of Washington and became dependent on aid from the Soviet Union, all these sectors withdrew their support from the revolution. In the end, it was defended by just three movements: the 26 July, the Revolutionary leadership and the Popular Socialist Party (a Communist group). It has been said that the establishment of the Integral Revolutionary Organizations has placed the effective control of the revolution in the hands of the PSP. It is clear that there was a move made by a section of the PSP to place the key state posts in the hands of a group. Fidel Castro himself recognized this in his speech of 26 March against Aníbal Escalante. I think that the fight against sectarianism has been effective. The formation of a single party of the revolution is being carried out, at least, in an exceptional way. They are attempting, it seems, to create a party of 'exemplary men'. The nuclei of the party candidates are selected at the work place, in public assemblies, in which all the employees and workers in the enterprise participate. The 'exemplary workers' – those who have contributed greatly to production and have been designated as such by their fellow workers – are automatically candidates for party membership, unless they decide to the contrary. But – and this is the exceptional part – in these assemblies, the workers can make criticisms and even vote for the nomination of certain candidates. In some way, every member of the single party must be anointed and blessed by the masses. In his speech, Fidel Castro had insisted that the revolutionary party should be 'the vanguard of the workers'. The selection is carried out rigorously. In the province of Camaguey, in 525 work places, and out of a total of 76,439 workers, 4,605 candidates to the single party have been selected. Of these, only 25 per cent had previously been politically active. In the four Havana factories that I visited, the candidates to the party had recently been chosen in public assemblies. It is interesting to note the composition of these groups. In one of the factories, out of a total of 345 workers, twenty-seven were selected. Of these, five had been members of the PSP, three of the 26 July and the remaining nineteen had never been politically active. In the second, out of 150 workers, sixteen were chosen: two ex-PSP, four 26 July and the rest non-affiliated. In the third, out of 217 workers, the group was twenty-five: nine PSP, no one from the 26 July and the other sixteen non-activists. And in the last factory, out of 143 workers, the group was fourteen: no PSP, three 26 July and eleven non-activists.

The slowness with which this selection process is being carried out is another demonstration of the decision – expressed by Fidel Castro in his speech of 26 March – to make it an organization deeply rooted in the masses, in which they can 'recognize the best of themselves', a party formed 'without exclusivity or sectarianism'.

Paris, November 1962

# In a Normandy Village, Remembering
## Paúl Escobar

Paúl Escobar had spoken to me on several occasions about Montvilliers and I thought it was a city. It is only a village, hidden among the hills that roll down from Rouen to the sea. I had never imagined it to be so small, with such narrow streets, so damp or so loyal. I arrived before six and the sky was already dark and the light rain that was falling reminded me of the *garúa* in Lima. In the square, some women with umbrellas pointed the Lycée out to me and in the Lycée, a blackboard indicated that the meeting was not taking place there, but that I had to cross a field and a stream and go through a church to a large and ancient building which displayed a sign: 'entertainments room'.

Inside, the activities had begun. On a small rudimentary stage, some lads were singing and reciting to a solemn, provincial audience and from time to time a gentleman took the microphone and spoke of Paúl Escobar ('*Monsieur Escobar, notre cher confrère*'). I wondered whether those present had brought their own chairs, as they used to do in the sandy, open air Castilla cinema in Piura twenty years ago. Who were these moustachioed old men, these children, these well wrapped-up women? Had they known Paúl or were they there out of curiosity? Had they come to remember the teacher from that remote land who gave their children their first Spanish lessons or to kill the drowsy monotony of a winter's evening in the provinces? It was moving: for two years my friend had been an assiduous and beloved teacher (these were the words that the speaker had just used to describe him) and even though I saw Paúl throughout all that period, I had no idea about the life that he led for three days a week, outside Paris, here in the land of Flaubert, not far from the small Normandy town where, they say, Madame Bovary lived, dreamed and poisoned herself.

On the stage a woman with long arms was reading a poem by Vallejo in an atrocious translation and I thought of Madrid: there was a record player on the floor and around it a group of Peruvians trying to learn how to dance *huaynos, marineras* and *tonderos* in order to take part in a folk festival. For better or worse, we managed to form a group and we went to Extremadura and they even gave us a prize and took us to many towns where they made us dance in bullrings. Did Paúl dance well? He was short, plump, congenial and argumentative, with an eye for the girls, and in Cáceres, I now remember quite clearly, he got into a fight. Later, in Madrid, we began to see each other often and became friends. He lived poorly, studied a bit, though without much conviction, and was always telling jokes. I can't remember ever seeing him in a bad mood. He'd drop by the Jute, a bar near the Retiro park, at about six and would say, 'Are you still writing?' 'Yes, half an hour more.' 'No, that's enough, let's go for a stroll.' It was very pleasant to go for a walk with him, very amusing to see him eyeing up, following and complimenting the girls. One day he told me that he was going to Paris and I thought that we would probably not see each other again. In the second row, a little old woman with clogs has begun to knit, but she keeps her head raised and is listening. A group of musicians has gone on to the stage.

When I saw him again, months later, in Paris, I scarcely recognized him. He was married and was no longer the layabout, Bohemian joker of before, but a man breaking his back to survive. He kept up, I don't know how, his generous girth and his sudden, even somewhat naive, bursts of kindness. It was a difficult year, but what enthusiasm we had, what plans we made, what friendships we formed: Lucho Loayza was there, Jorge González, the Córdobas (Elsa as well, how horrible, she's just died), who else? An unpleasant person called, I don't know why, 'Pachito Eché'. What was Paúl doing and how was he living? Try to remember. He wandered around the Paris *quartiers* with suitcases. Was he a salesman? He had also begun to study and admire Sartre, he called his son Jean-Paul and I laughed at him, calling him sentimental. What was he studying? Something strange, to do with numbers, physics, chemistry or was it statistics? Remember that he sometimes went to classes in the centre of Saclay: engineering, something like that. He passed the first year and changed jobs, he found work that gave him time to study, looking after an old man. He dressed him, washed him and fed him and then told us about it and we laughed, it was like a cruel joke. He also passed the second year, but the old man died and Paúl had to find another job, as a cook. The restaurant was called Beautiful Mexico, yes, in the rue de Cannettes, is it true that the dishes he introduced (he invented) are still on the menu? Wander round there one day and see. The Peruvians and the Latin Americans all prowled hungrily round the rue de Cannettes when Paúl was there and he always managed somehow to give us all something to eat. He even managed to bring back to his friends in the hotel spicy morsels hidden in paper bags, poor Paúl. Now they have begun to applaud and the director is speaking once again. Paúl had organized a week of lectures on Latin America here at the Lycée in Montvilliers. When would that have been? He never mentioned it to you.

He also passed the third year and you told him, look at you then and look at you now, congratulations fatso, that's great. He was now a teacher, here, these were his pupils, these were his colleagues, the one speaking on the platform was his boss, *Monsieur le directeur.* Picture him in front of the blackboard with a piece of chalk in his hand, pronouncing slowly, *papá, mamá,* going through what all teachers of Spanish go through: roll your *r*s young man, roll your *r*s. Back then he often came to wake you up and we had lunch together in that cheap, packed restaurant in L'Odéon: La Petite Chaise. Are you getting your degree this year Paúl? No, he still had two years to go. What an appetite he had, how secure and mature he seemed, dressed in blue, with a briefcase under his arm and a ridiculous fur hat on his head (but it keeps me warm). You said, look how things have turned out, you've become a bourgeois. Then one morning, I'm off to Peru. Have you thought it through, fatso? Yes. You, you're going to fight? Yes, as if ashamed, yes, I am.

Now try to imagine that mound of flesh with a gun in his hand, try to see him panting in the mountains, climbing up slopes and hiding among the trees. It seems impossible, doesn't it? And yet it's true and it's also true that he is now a faceless corpse rotting somewhere in the mountains. What is it, what name can we give to that secret design that goes from a loafer to a salesman, to a cook, to a teacher, to a guerrilla fighter? But the meeting has now ended, the people are leaving and it is now time for you to return to Paris. Goodbye, dear Paúl.

Paris, 1965

Note: This small homage to Paúl Escobar, who died in 1965 in an engagement with the Peruvian army in Mesa Pelada – he was a member of the MIR guerrilla group led by Luis de la Puente – was sent in 1965 or 1966 to *Expreso* in Lima, a paper that I wrote for. The paper decided not to publish it. The text lay among my papers until May 1981, when I published it in Lima's *El Comercio.*

# Toby, Rest in Peace

You have to head out of the city by circling around the hill at Montmartre, going down the narrow avenue that separates Batignolles, the white Russian quarter, from the night time centre of Paris, until you get to the Porte de Clichy, then cross it and head into the northern suburbs. You have to go through the Communist enclave of Clichy along an avenue that has a Christian name (Jean Jaurès) and surname (Apostle of Peace), past the junction and lime trees of the Martyrs of the Resistance Square and ten minutes later you reach the bridge where Clichy ends and you find the factories, the rundown houses, the poor Algerians of Asnières. There, between two districts in the outskirts of Paris, on an island, like a motionless ship in the middle of the Seine, hidden by trees and ferns which make the gloomy landscape unusually refreshing, there lies that strange creation of human stupidity and tenderness, called The Dog Cemetery of Asnières.

It is also a beautiful place. A tumbledown stone pediment, three arched doors and some rusty bars are the border between this world and the city. When you cross it, the noise of the road abates and you hear the murmur of the river, the light is dappled by the thick crowns of the trees and there then appear, implausibly, the stones, the stelae, the tombs, the minuscule gardens full of flowers. A few yards from the entrance is a monument: at the foot of an Alpine village, surrounded by a rocky bank, carrying a child on his back, is the statue of Barry, a large Saint Bernard who, like the classical heroes, had a valiant existence ('he saved the lives of forty people') and a tragic end ('he was killed by the forty-first'). And a few steps away, something unexpected, intrusive: the tomb of Gribouille, 'a good, gentle and beautiful white pony who died aged thirty-five'. 'I mourn him,' adds the anonymous author on his tombstone, 'as one should mourn a servant and friend.' Alongside Gribouille, in the shade of some willows and erected by the Administration, according to a plaque, is the Tomb of the Unknown Dog, where a stray dog was buried that came to die at the doors of this place on the night of 15 May 1958. It was the forty thousandth animal to find its final resting place in The Dog

Cemetery, the plaque informs us bureaucratically. This does not mean that among the roots of the geraniums, carnations, plane trees and rubber plants of its gentle surface there lie mountains of bones: rather that this is a place of transition, for the living and the dead. There are no licences granted in perpetuity, the rent of the graves is renewed each year and since the memory and the affections of men are fragile, within a few years the living forget to renew the licence and the dead are exhumed and thrown into a common grave.

But there are exceptions. The occupants of the plot nearest to the entrance have been there for so long that, if it were not an irony, one could call them lifers. They are something like the aristocracy of this place, although there is nothing hierarchical about it: it is located in a suburb that seems out of a book by Louis-Ferdinand Céline and the people who maintain it are, for the most part, poor. On the graves along the avenue, which are elegant and sometimes luxurious, are stones of marble or metal, decorated with photos and inscriptions in different calligraphy, which say more about the relatives than about the dead that they are remembering. On the white stone of the little cat Follette (1910–1923), her owners, the Brismontier family, displayed a poetic inclination, writing these verses that I translate literally:

> Little one
> loving and loved in kind
> sleep, sleep.
> You will never be replaced
> Or out of our mind.

Not far from the cylindrical tomb of 'Gazon: small desert gazelle', there is a mound with a discoloured photo of a round old man with a twirled moustache and a lascivious mouth, cradling in his arms a black cat. The inscription reads: 'Here lies the cat of the famous polemicist Henri Rochefort'. No less vain and self-promoting is the inscription on the neighbouring tomb: 'Here lie the dogs of the famous music artist, Sybil Sanderson'. But a bit further on, near the slope that leads to the west bank of the island, in a cubic tomb half eaten away by ivy, there is someone really famous, a film star: Rin Tin Tin. Isolated from the others by a fence rests the Great Dane Drac (1941–1953), whom Queen Elizabeth of Romania calls in her epitaph 'a companion in the tragic hours, a precious friend in exile'. The contents of the inscriptions cover all shades of feelings; their form, all genres of rhetoric. Some are sober, like the one that illustrates the tomb of Kikí, a small monkey with mischievous eyes, caught by the photo in the moment of biting a banana: 'Rest in peace Kikí'. Others, refined lyrical constructions, mix lament and confessions and allow one to glimpse at dramas and personal involvement. The last paragraph of the stone to the puppy Pupú reads: 'You deserved a gentle death. Your cruel agony leaves me unconsolable for ever. I will cry for you, I will suffer greatly without you; rest, my love.' Richer in detail and dramatic energy is the pathetic inscription to Mopsik, the bulldog. 'Brave, affectionate and loyal Mopsik, so superior to us: to reward you for the treasures of your noble and tender heart, we had you killed. But you were old and ill and were suffering and you made us suffer. Forgive your ungrateful masters.' There are owners who, overcome by grief, disown their own species ('Dianette, your affection defended us against human ingratitude') and, unable to bear the definitive separation, become delirious ('Tobul, in your gaze there beat a thought more profound, more tender, than humankind') or metaphysically silly: 'I think that in the Perhaps and in the Beyond, good dogs wait for their masters. We will meet again Bobby!' But there are also happy, irreverent relatives lacking in funereal constraint, like the author of the stone of a triple tomb, who wrote this euphonic, ambiguous and brazen sentence: 'Here lie the three Ms: Maldoné, Mitzu and Madame.' There are inscriptions that are delicate ('To the sweet and beautiful Ismena'), intimate and confidential ('To you, Pulguita: from us'), gruff and factual as a military report ('To Kiki the cat, survivor of the exodus, died aged 21'), disconcerting ('Jasmin, beautiful girl'), tragic ('Muky: Forgive us! Your masters T. and F. Grall'), epic ('Here lies Atamo, the brave Great Dane'), and affected: 'Rest in peace, Anita de Marimbert'. One of the strangest funeral monuments, to Dick of the Trenches, is vaguely similar to the tomb of Napoleon and its inscription, in quartets, reveals the nihilistic grief of the owner:

> Dick of the Trenches, ever true,
> You were my only exemplary friend:
> Why did you leave? I love you
> And my memory will never, ever end.
>
> I was brutal with you and now regret it of course
> – I miss you so much my beloved dog! –

I hit you and I cry with remorse
I believe in nothing, my mind's a fog.

After the main avenue and on all sides are the poor graves; cardboard, wood, a square of tin are used as stones and the epitaphs seem
to be scribbled in chalk, ink, pencil or carved with a knife. They cover
the whole island and are semi-submerged by flowers. In summer and
winter, come rain or shine, a crowd of women, busy, contrite, methodical, lay people, bend over these graves, replace the withered wreaths,
water and clean the small plots, straighten up the photographs. There
are always couples who, from Clichy, Asnières, Saint-Ouen and even
Gennevilliers, go to The Dog Cemetery. They settle down beneath the
discreet branches of the river bank willows and their whispers and
murmurs are like the music of the place.

Paris, June 1964

# P'tit Pierre

He had been born in a small town in Brittany and (naturally) he must have had a mother and father, but I am sure that he did not know them or never remembered them and that, at some point, he began to see himself as self-generated, a child of chance, like certain wild organisms that seem like granite, resistant to all adversity and yet are very fragile inside. Although the translation of his name – P'tit Pierre – is Little Peter, in his case it should have been little stone (without the capital letters). Because that is what P'tit Pierre had been all his life when I knew him in Paris: a pebble, a rolling, wandering stone, without a surname, a history or any ambition.

He had always lived around the Latin Quarter, with no known address, virtually at the mercy of the elements, earning his living as a *bricoleur*. This word fitted him perfectly: a man for any job, a one-man orchestra, who could clean out pipes and chimneys, tile halls, repair roofs, mend old things and turn dilapidated attics into elegant *garçonnières*. But he was also unpredictable and very much his own man. He fixed the price of his services according to whether or not he liked his customers and he would think nothing of disappearing without warning in the middle of a job if he got bored with what he was doing. He didn't know the value of money and he never had any because everything he earned disappeared immediately paying the bills of his friends in a kind of potlach. Getting rid of everything he had as quickly as possible was, for him, something of a religion.

I got to know him through my friend Nicole, a neighbour of mine. The built-in shower in my garret was falling to pieces and in order to have a shower, I had to perform all manner of gymnastics and contortions every morning. Nicole said, 'P'tit Pierre is the answer.' She had got to know him recently and was very pleased because, with extraordinary skill and ingenuity, P'tit Pierre had begun to transform her small bathroom magically into a sumptuous palace for ablutions and diverse pleasures. P'tit Pierre came to my garret, examined my shower and humanized it with a sentence that summed him up completely: 'I'll cure her.'

We became friends. He was thin, shabby, with long curly hair that had never seen a comb, and roving blue eyes. Nicole lived with a Spanish boy who was in the cinema world, like her, and P'tit Pierre would wake them up in the morning with crisp croissants fresh from the baker's on the corner. He worked on Messalina's bathroom and then came to wake me up. We'd go down to Le Tournon for a sandwich and I'd begin to learn about his carefree lifestyle which consisted of sleeping wherever the night found him, in the landings, rooms, chairs and cushions of his innumerable friends, in whose houses he also left strewn around the few clothes and tools that were his capital.

While I wrote, he resuscitated my shower or rummaged through my things quite unselfconsciously or started doing sketches which he'd then tear up. He'd sometimes disappear for many days or weeks and when he reappeared, the same as ever, smiling and warm, I'd learn of the strange adventures that he had experienced, which he took for granted as the mere rituals of normal life. I found out that he had lived in a gypsy camp and that, on another occasion, he was locked up for swimming naked in the Seine at daybreak with a group of boys and girls who had formed a commune. But he was too much of an individualist for such promiscuous experiments and he did not stay with the group for long.

He had, on occasion, charitable love affairs with the owners of the houses that he painted, ladies whose maternal instincts, it seemed, were kindled by his absent-minded nature. He went to bed with them out of sympathy or pity and not in any self-interested way since, as I have already said, P'tit Pierre was a curious mortal, completely devoid of greed or calculation. One day he appeared with a girl who looked fresh out of a nursery. She was an old flame, so that when P'tit Pierre seduced her, she must have been in nappies (I exaggerate a little). They lived together and, some time later, she ran off with a Vietnamese. Now she had gone back to her parents and was finishing school. P'tit Pierre took her out from time to time to get some air.

When, after a few months, my shower was finally repaired, P'tit Pierre refused to charge me for his work. We continued to see each other in the bistrots of the Latin Quarter, sometimes with long gaps between our meetings. One afternoon I met my friend Nicole in the street. She blushed when she gave me the news: 'Did you know that I am living with P'tit Pierre?'

I was not as surprised as others were by this information since I had always suspected that P'tit Pierre was in love with the magnificent Nicole. How had the role swap come about? How had P'tit Pierre moved from being the bearer of croissants to Nicole and her Spanish lover to becoming the lover's replacement? My theory was that the decisive factor had not been the crumbling croissants but the bathroom, that marvel of marvels, a space of scarcely five square yards into which the imagination (and the love) of P'tit Pierre had concentrated mirrors, carpet squares, adornments, porcelain receptacles and cabinets, all with Babylonian refinement and Cartesian balance. All my friends in the *quartier* were sure that the relationship between that cultured, bourgeois and prosperous woman and the semi-literate and deliquescent artisan would not last long. With my incorrigible romantic imagination, I bet that it would.

I was wrong only in part since I was correct in assuming that this love affair would be unexpected and dramatic rather than conventional. I heard news of them in snippets and, after a time, by hearsay, because I left Paris soon after Nicole and P'tit Pierre began to live together. I went back after some years and in the course of a conversation with a casual friend about what had happened to people I knew, I learned that they were caught up in the labyrinths of a love passion: they separated then made up, only to split up again. Someone, somewhere, some time asked me: 'Do you remember P'tit Pierre? Did you know that he'd gone mad? He's been locked up for some time now in an asylum in Brittany.'

It was the part about being locked up — and his supposed violence — that left me sceptical. Because if madness is a break with normality, P'tit Pierre had never been a sane man. Since before the age of reason — like his ancestor, Gavroche, the urchin in *Les Misérables* — he had not complied with the accepted customs, the dominant morality, the dishonest values and probably even the law. But I could not conceive of him showing any trace of physical aggression towards another person. I had never known anyone more gentle, unselfish, helpful and kind-hearted than P'tit Pierre. No one could convince me that this man, for whom the attractive word nepheloid — a being lost in the clouds — seemed to have been invented, could become a furious madman.

Several more years had passed without news of him when, in a stopover between flights at Madrid airport, a shadow blocked my path, spreading its arms wide. 'Don't you recognize me? I'm your neighbour from the Latin Quarter.' It was the Spanish cinéaste who had lived with Nicole. He was so fat and white haired that I found it difficult to identify him with the weedy boy from León who, fifteen years previously, exploded with very Spanish prejudices every time his French lady gestured to pay the bill. We embraced and went to have a coffee.

He visited Paris from time to time but he wouldn't live there again for anything in the world, for the city was not a shadow of its former self. And did he see Nicole? Yes, sometimes, they were still good friends. And how was she? Much better now, fully recovered. Had Nicole been ill? What, didn't I know what had happened? No, I hadn't heard a word, I'd had no news of Nicole for ages.

So he gave me the news, of her and of P'tit Pierre against whom, he said, he had never harboured a grudge for having taken his woman away from him. The story about the asylum was true and also the rage. But not against others, because P'tit Pierre was not capable of hurting a fly. But he was capable of hurting himself. He'd been locked up for some time in Brittany when Nicole was told that he'd got hold of an electric saw and had mutilated himself horribly with it. Nicole's visits disturbed him and for that reason, until there was a marked improvement in him, the doctors forbade her from seeing him.

Weeks, months or years later, the clinic told Nicole that P'tit Pierre had disappeared. He could not be found. About then, I suppose, Nicole had — as they say — remade her life, improved her lot, found a new lover. I imagine that the day she decided to sell her flat in the Latin Quarter, P'tit Pierre would have been a distant memory. The fact is that one of the potential buyers decided to poke around in the huge attic above the bedroom, bathroom and kitchen of the apartment. Was it Nicole who saw it first? Was it the potential buyer? The body of P'tit Pierre was swaying among the spiderwebs and the dust, hanging from a beam. How did he manage to slip in there without being seen? How long had he been dead? Hadn't there been perhaps some smell that would have given the body away?

The plane was about to leave and I couldn't ask the Spanish cinéaste any of the questions that were pounding in my head. If I meet him again in some airport, I won't ask him then either. I don't want to hear another word about P'tit Pierre, that little stone from the Latin Quarter who mended my shower. I am writing this story to see if, by doing so, I can free myself from the wretched shadow of a hanging man that sometimes causes me to wake at night, in a sweat.

Lima, December 1983

# Hemingway: The Shared Feast

I read *A Movable Feast* for the first time in the middle of 1964, in the English edition that had just appeared. I identified immediately with the protagonist of this tender evocation. I was then also, like the Hemingway of the book, a young man serving his literary apprenticeship in Paris. I wrote the following review of the book at the time.

I

The newspapers have made us accustomed to confusing him with one of his characters. What is his biography? That of a man of action: journeys, violence, adventures and, at times, between a bout of drunkenness and a safari, literature. He had dedicated himself to literature as he had to boxing or hunting, brilliantly, sporadically: for him the most important thing was to live. Almost as by-products of his eventful life, his short stories and novels owed their realism and authenticity to his life. None of this was true, if anything it was the other way round, and Hemingway himself clears up this confusion and puts things straight in the last book he wrote, *A Movable Feast*. Who would have believed it? This genial good-natured globetrotter takes stock of his past at the end of his life and among the thousand adventures – wars, women, exploits – that he experienced, he chose, with a certain nostalgic melancholy, the image of a young man fired by an inner passion to write. Everything else, sports, pleasures, even the smallest joys and the daily disappointments and, of course, love and friendship, revolve around this secret fire, stoking it and finding there either condemnation or justification. It is a beautiful book in which he shows simply and casually how a vocation is both privileged and enslaving.

The passion to write is essential, but it is only a starting point. It is useless without that 'good and severe discipline' that Hemingway mastered in his youth in Paris, between 1921 and 1926, those years evoked in the book when he 'was very poor and very happy'. Apparently these were the years of his bohemian existence; he spent the day in the cafés, he went to the races, he drank. In reality, a secret order governed this 'movable feast' and the disorder was really a form of freedom, of being always open. All his actions converged on one point: his work. The bohemian life can, of course, be a useful experience (but no more or less than any other) as long as one is an experienced horseman who will not be thrown by his horse. Through stories, meetings, conversations, Hemingway reveals the rigid laws that he had imposed on himself to avoid shipwreck in the troubled waters through which he was sailing. 'My training was never to drink after dinner, nor before I wrote nor while I was writing. I would write one story about each thing that I knew about.' However, at the end of a good day, he treats himself to a glass of kirsch. He cannot always work with the same enthusiasm; at times he feels emptiness, depression, in front of the blank page. Then he would recite in a low voice: 'Don't worry. You have always written before and you will write now. All you have to do is to write a good sentence. Write the truest sentence you know.' To stimulate himself, he sets out fabulous goals. 'I will write a story about each thing that I know about.' And when he finishes a story he always feels empty, sad and happy at the same time, as if he had just made love.

He went to cafés, that's true, but he used them as his study. On those tables of fake marble on the terraces that overlook the Luxembourg Gardens, he did not go woolgathering or pontificate like the South American bohemians of the rue Cujas: he wrote his first books of stories and corrected the chapters of *The Sun Also Rises*. And if someone interrupted him, he was thrown out with a volley of insults: the pages where he narrates how he treats an intruder, in La Closerie des Lilas, are a thesaurus of curses. (Years later Lisandro Otero spotted Hemingway one night in a bar in Old Havana. Timidly and respectfully, he went up to greet the author whom he admired and Hemingway, who was writing standing at the counter, despatched him with a punch.) After writing, he says, he needs to read, so as not to stay obsessed by what he is telling. These are difficult times, there is no money to buy books, but Sylvia Beach, the director of Shakespeare and Company, gives him books. As do friends like Gertrude Stein in whose house he also finds beautiful pictures, a friendly atmosphere and delicious cakes.

His desire to *learn* in order to write is behind all his actions: it determines his tastes, his relationships. And whatever could be seen as an obstacle, like that intruder, is rejected without a second thought.

His vocation is a whirlwind. Let us take the example of horse racing. He befriended jockeys and trainers who give him tips for the races: one lucky day the horses allow him to dine at Chez Michaux, where he spots Joyce talking in Italian to his wife and children. The world of the races, furthermore (and he gives this as his main reason for going racing), provides him with material for his work. But one evening he discovers that this passion is wasting his time, has become almost an end in itself. He immediately suppresses it. The same occurs with journalism from which he earns a living; he gives it up, despite the fact that the North American magazines are still turning down his stories. Although literature is a constant, essential preoccupation of the young Hemingway, it is scarcely mentioned in *A Movable Feast*. But it is there, all the time, hidden in a thousand forms and the reader can feel it, invisible, sleepless, voracious. When Hemingway goes out to the quays and studies like an entomologist the customs and art of the fishermen of the Seine, during his conversations with Ford Madox Ford, while he is teaching Ezra Pound how to box, when he travels, speaks, eats and even sleeps, there is a spy hidden within him looking at him with cold and practical eyes, selecting and rejecting experiences, storing them. 'Did you learn something today, Tatie?', Hemingway's wife asks him every night when he returns to their apartment in the rue de Cardinal Lemoine.

In the final chapters of *A Movable Feast*, Hemingway remembers a colleague of his generation: F. Scott Fitzgerald. Famous and a millionaire thanks to his first book, written when he was a very young man, Fitzgerald in Paris is the writer who cannot control the reins. The bohemian steed drags him and Zelda down to the depths of alcohol, masochism and neurosis. These are pages similar to the last episode in *Farewell to Arms*, in which an icy current flows beneath the clear surface of the prose. Hemingway seems to hold Zelda responsible for the precocious decadence of Fitzgerald; jealous of literature, it was she who pushed him to excess and to this frenetic lifestyle. But others accuse Fitzgerald himself of the madness which led Zelda to an asylum and to death. Whatever the reason, one thing is evident: the bohemian life can only help literature when it is a pretext for writing: if the reverse occurs (as it does frequently), then the bohemian life can kill a writer.

Because literature is a passion and passion is exclusive. It cannot be shared, it demands every sacrifice and gives in to nothing. Hemingway is in a café and by his side there is a young woman. He thinks 'You belong to me and Paris belongs to me, but I belong to this notebook and pencil.' That is exactly what slavery means. The condition of the writer is strange and paradoxical. His privilege is freedom, the right to see, hear and investigate everything. He is authorized to dive into the depths, to climb the peaks: the whole of reality is his. What is the purpose of this privilege? To feed the beast within which enslaves him, which feeds off all his acts, tortures him mercilessly and is only appeased, momentarily, in the act of creation. When the words flow forth. If one has chosen the beast and carries it in one's guts, there is no alternative, one has to give it everything. When Hemingway went to the bullfights, visited the Republican trenches in Spain, killed elephants or fell over drunk, he was not indulging in adventure or pleasure, but he was a man satisfying the whims of this insatiable, solitary beast. Because for him, as for any other writer, the most important thing was not to live but to write.

2

Rereading it today, with all that we now know about the Hemingway who wrote it and about his relationships with the figures explored in its pages, *A Movable Feast* takes on a somewhat different meaning. In fact, the health and optimism that it displays are literary constructs which do not correspond with the dramatic reality of physical and intellectual decline that its author was suffering. He is right at the end of his literary career and he suspects it. He also knows that he would not now recover from the rapid diminution of his physical faculties that he was suffering at the time. None of this is mentioned in the book. But for today's reader, informed by the biographies of Hemingway that have appeared in recent years, this knowledge offers one of the keys through which, by reading between the lines of this testimony of the literary origins of a great writer that seems at first sight so clear and direct, he can discover the unhappy trauma that underlies it.

Rather than a nostalgic evocation of youth, the book is a magical spell, an unconscious attempt to return, through memory and the word, to the apogee of his life, the moment of his greatest energy and creative force, so as to recuperate that energy and lucidity which was now rapidly draining away. And the book is also a posthumous revenge, a settling of accounts with former companions in literature and in the bohemian world. A book of pathos, a swan-song – because it was the last book that he wrote – it conceals beneath the deceptive patina of his youthful memories a confession of defeat. The man who began in this way, in the Paris of the mad 1920s, so talented and so happy, so creative and so vital, who in a few months was capable of writing a masterpiece – *The Sun Also Rises* – at the same time as he drank in all the succulent juices of life – trout fishing and going to the bullfights in Spain, skiing in Austria, betting on the horses in Saint-Cloud, drinking the wines and spirits of La Closerie – is already dead, he is a ghost who is trying to cling on to life through that age-old conjuring trick invented by men to gain an illusory triumph over death: literature.

We now know that the book is full of pettinesses and spite against old friends and ex-friends and that, for example, some of his stories, perhaps the best – about Gertrude Stein and Scott Fitzgerald – are false. But these pettinesses do not cheapen what is admirable in the text: the fact that Hemingway was able to turn defects into virtues, to create a beautiful literary work out of loss and the limitations which, from that time on, prevented him from producing any memorable story or novel.

According to Mary, his widow, Hemingway wrote *A Movable Feast* between autumn 1957 and autumn 1960, with long interruptions in between. This was a moment of continual crisis for him, of nervous depression, of deep bitterness which rarely showed in his public appearances where he kept up the impression of being the happy and adventurous giant that he had always been, full of appetites and light. (That's how he seemed to me, in the summer of 1959 in the Plaza de Toros in Madrid, the one time that I saw him, at a distance, on the arm of another living myth of the age: Ava Gardner.)

In reality he was a wounded colossus, semi-impotent, incapable of the mental concentration of undertaking an important work, terrified by his loss of memory, a deficiency which for a man who plays at being a deicide – the novelist, who reinvents reality – is quite simply fatal. Yes, how can one invent a coherent fictional world in which the whole and the parts are vigorously linked in order to simulate the real world, the whole of life, if the memory of the creator is fading and the spell of the fiction is broken at every moment by incongruities and mistakes in the tale? Hemingway's answer to the question was this book: writing a fiction under the guise of memory, whose disconnected and fragmentary nature is concealed by the unity imposed on it by a narrator who remembers and writes the work.

Memory in *A Movable Feast* is a literary device to justify the vagaries of a memory which can no longer concentrate on the concrete or undertake the rigorous structure of a fiction, but which jumps, disorganized and free, from image to image, without any harmony or continuity. In a novel, this atomization would have been chaotic; in a book of memories it offers, instead, an impressionistic meandering through certain faces and places afloat in the river of time, unlike the innumerable other people who have been swallowed up by forgetfulness. Each chapter is a short story in disguise, a snapshot organized with the virtues of his best fictions: the terse prose, the taut dialogues which always suggest more than (and sometimes the opposite of) what they are saying and the descriptions whose stubborn objectivity seem to beg us to forgive them their perfection.

But alongside the real history, in each of these elegant snapshots there are more distortions than reliable testimonies. But what does that matter? It does not make them any the less persuasive or exciting for a lover of literature, that is, someone who expects a novelist to write books which are capable of telling him not necessarily the Truth, in capital letters, but rather his own particular truth, and in a way that is so convincing and clever that there is no alternative but to believe him. And in this final autobiographical fiction, Hemingway achieved this magnificently.

Furthermore, although he was not identical to the figure that he sketches in this portrait of his youth, some essential characteristics of his personality do appear in his book. His anti-intellectualism, for example. It is a pose that he always cultivated and which, above all in the final years, he took to extreme lengths. In this book also, authentic – not bookish – literature is presented as a physical skill, something that the consummate sportsman, the writer, perfects and controls through discipline and steadfastness, a healthy life and healthy body. The very idea that art or literature might in some way imply a retreat into the purely mental, a withdrawal from everyday life, a bathing in the wellsprings of the unknown or a challenge to the rational order of existence is energetically rejected and ridiculed. For that reason the sketch that the book offers of Ezra Pound, although lively and generous, does not even skim the surface of Pound's contradictory nature. And yet it is clear that Hemingway was not completely incapable of perceiving below or between the interstices of these permissible rituals of life, which sufficed for him, that other life, the life of the depths, of prohibition, of misconduct. It was a world that he feared and that he always refused to explore except in its most superficial manifestations (such as the cruel and fascinating ceremony of the bullfight). But he knew that it existed and could identify those damned souls who inhabited it, like Wyndham Lewis, who is badly treated in these pages. He inspired the best and the most disconcerting sentence in the book. 'Some people show evil as a great racehorse shows breeding. They have the dignity of a hard *chancre.*'

Another of his prejudices is also to be found in abundant measure: the *machismo* which, together with his passion for killing animals and the spell that violent sports held over him, constitute a morality and a code of life which is very different from our own, which is concerned with feminism and its truths, the conservation of nature and the struggle for freedom of sexual minorities. The conversation with Gertrude Stein, in which she tries to gain Hemingway's sympathy for lesbianism, with arguments that would today make a schoolgirl smile, and his reticence and replies are instructive in this respect. They show how far customs have evolved and how old-fashioned are many of the values that Hemingway extolled in his novels.

But, despite these anachronisms, this short book gives immense pleasure. The magic of his style, its Flaubertian insidious simplicity and precision, the passion for the elements and for physical prowess, the vivid recreation of the Paris of expatriate Americans in the period between the two world wars and an affirmation of the writer that the book symbolizes – a resolute affirmation of a vocation at a time when he could scarcely still write – blend to give a unique status to what would become his literary testimony. Although it contains as many additions and modifications to life as a novel, it remains an important autobiographical document and, with all the liberties that it takes with objective facts, it offers an incomparable picture of the times and the happy insouciance with which France stimulated art and excess, while, inside and outside its frontiers, its subsequent ruin was being brought about. But, above all, its pages, which are as clear and sonorous as a mountain stream, enable us to draw close, with the immediacy of successful fiction, to the secrets of art which allowed Hemingway to transmute the life he lived and the life that he only dreamed of, into this shared feast that is literature.

London, 23 June 1987

# A Visit to Buñuel

'Monsieur Buñuel?' The old lady behind the desk at the entrance of the Hotel L'Aiglon looked us up and down in an unfriendly fashion. 'He doesn't live here.' My friend told her that we had an appointment to see him and, with the same suspicious gaze, she picked up the phone, dialled a number and asked someone something. Yes, we could go up, Monsieur Buñuel was waiting for us on the fourth floor. In the lift, my friend asked me how I imagined Buñuel to be and I told him that I had seen him once, for just a moment, three years previously. I had been asked to escort Rafael Alberti to Radio Paris and when I came to collect him, at this same hotel, I found him saying goodbye to a man of similar age who, while he embraced him, repeated, 'Be careful of the cold, Rafael.' Alberti was replying, 'I'll see you soon, Luis,' in a booming voice. Afterwards I learned that this Luis was Luis Buñuel. 'He is quite deaf, he has got almost no hearing in his right ear,' my friend said. 'Try to sit on his left and speak very loudly.' A tall, blond, athletic young man, who spoke Spanish with a distinct English accent, opened the door. My friend explained that this was Buñuel's youngest son who had been educated in the United States; he wrote plays and had just returned from a motorbike trip to Turkey. While my friend and Buñuel's son exchanged a few words, I looked inside: the small, modern and elegant living room had a rug with black and white stripes ('a panther skin', Buñuel would later remark), a narrow passage led into another room, which must have been the bedroom, and on the other side of the room, a kitchen displayed its white walls and gleaming tiles. There, there was a man with his back to me, leaning over a sink with a tray of ice in his hand. He had not heard us come in and my friend had to cross the room and shout, 'Hello. Don Luis,' for him to turn round. He smiled, quickly left the ice and walked over to us drying his hands. He gave us a South American greeting: effusive claps on the back, energetic handshakes. 'Here he is,' said my friend. 'You'll see that he isn't as terrible as his films paint him.' A man of medium height, broad-shouldered, thinning grey hair, with enormous, bulging eyes and large, nervous and welcoming hands. Someone once said in my presence that, physically, Buñuel was a perfect Spanish peasant. Perhaps, with his blunt and rough features, the open expression, that stubborn conviction in his gaze and his voice, his brown and weather-beaten face, perhaps. 'Come in, come in,' he said, 'have a seat.'

We sat around a small glass table on which there was a luxuriously bound book: *The Universal Dictionary of Stupidity.* 'Do you want a whisky, a soft drink or a *buñuel*?' asked Buñuel, and he explained: 'It's an invention of mine; it isn't very strong, try it.' He went to the kitchen himself, brought glasses and ice, mixed some drinks, served them, and watched us anxiously as we took the first sip. 'How is it, good isn't it,' he smiled, relieved. 'I'm glad you like it.' He sat down and dragged his chair over very close to us. 'I always wanted to visit Peru,' he said. 'It's a pity that it's too late now. I'll never get to know your country now, you don't know how sorry that makes me.' I asked him why it was late and he shrugged dejectedly: he hated journeys, he hated leaving his house. 'I only do it when it is absolutely necessary,' he added, 'for work reasons, like now. But this will also be the last time. Last journey, last film. It's over, from now on I'll live in peace, without going out of the house.' My friend burst out laughing. 'I've heard you saying the same thing for ten years now, Don Luis, and in that time you've made how many journeys, how many films?' But Buñuel shook his head and gesticulated no: this time it was true, not one more film. Why make life difficult when one could live in peace. He had his rhythm of life, a perfectly regulated system, and if he kept to it, everything went perfectly: get up at six, prepare breakfast, have lunch at twelve on the dot, dinner at seven, in bed by nine, read a while, put out the lamp and sleep. Journeys, films, always mean a change of timetable, disorder. However much one tried to avoid it, one had at times to go to bed late, meet a lot of people, drink, sleep badly. Not that he hated people, of course not, he loved to have friends. It's just that – and he raised a hand to his ear in a gesture of cheerful melancholy – when you don't hear very well, to be with more than three people at once is a horrible torture. You can't understand anything, it's all an unintelligible, infernal noise, it feels as if your head is about to explode. No, no more journeys, no more films, all that was over for him.

I told him that he had found the ideal hotel, it seemed like limbo, you couldn't even hear the traffic along the Boulevard Raspail. 'That's why I came here fourteen years ago,' he replied, 'to this very room. I can describe it by heart, in all its details. Do you see that tree in the window?' There is the graceful crown of a chestnut tree, loaded with leaves that gleam fiercely in this sunny summer evening. 'I also know that by heart,' says Buñuel. 'I can say how many branches it has, how many leaves. When I was young, I was curious, I liked the new. Now I like what I know and nothing else.' He then tells us that Sartre's mother lives in this hotel and that Sartre himself has his secret refuge nearby, a small flat where he can work away from onlookers and journalists. He sometimes meets him, in a local bistro, at meal times. He tells us that, in addition, this neighbourhood has many memories for him. Here, in Montparnasse, he lived his best years and made innumerable friends. He is pleased that La Dome and La Coupole are close at hand, all those cafés where, in the 'mad years' between the two world wars, he met his surrealist friends and the Spaniards and Latin Americans that lived here then, like Alberti, Asturias, Vallejo and Carpentier. But now he does not go to the cafés any more. I ask him if he knows that all this neighbourhood is condemned to death, if he has heard that within a few years all these narrow streets and these old brothel houses will be replaced by skyscrapers, parks and wide avenues and he smiles; he thinks, of course, that I am joking. 'Paris is the best city I know,' he says, 'not only the most beautiful, but also the most open and welcoming. I have never had so many friends as here.' My friend and I tell him that things have changed a lot, that now Paris is a gigantic beehive where everyone lives imprisoned in the cells of their own minds, where it is very difficult to communicate and converse. Here nobody now lives spontaneously as in the mad years, Don Luis, there is now no place for creative leisure, and no one thinks that poetry will bring about the true revolution. Now the literary and artistic vanguard is funded by the state and bohemian life is not a sign of rebellion but of the most vile conformity. Do you remember how horrified the Paris bourgeoisie was when you organized those provocative performances, do you remember the scandal caused by the opening of *Un Chien andalou*, the anger at *L'Age d'or*? Now his films are shown in the best cinemas in Paris and, even if you don't like it, the bourgeois respect and admire you and flock to all your openings. Open any newspaper and you will see how critics are talking about the 'Buñuel Festival' in the Latin Quarter: even the ultra-right *L'Aurore* is saying that you are a genius. As long as their taxes don't go up, their comfort is not threatened and their houses, businesses and lands are not seized, then the bourgeois accept all forms of literary and artistic aggression, they even seek them out and think nothing of paying well for them. Buñuel's son tells us that he'd recently seen a screening of *L'Age d'or* at the Lincoln Center in New York; the audience enjoyed it immensely and did not seem in any way shocked. Buñuel is thoughtful for a moment, waves his thick right hand across his face, as if brushing away a fly: yes, he wasn't deceiving himself, times had changed. And he says that a few years ago, when he was in France filming *Le Journal d'une femme de chambre,* he met André Breton in the street in Clichy. They had not seen each other for a long time and they went off for a drink in the terrace of a café, to remember the old times. 'What a horrible age,' Breton had said nostalgically. 'People are no longer shocked by anything.' And, with disappointment and regret, he had added that even the best were selling out: it was the limit – even Max Ernst had accepted a prize at the Venice Biennale. 'But Breton is still incorruptible,' Buñuel says. 'He will not make any concession. If he knows that I have agreed to give an interview for *Blanco y Negro* in Madrid, he will be furious.' We told him no, that in any case Breton had written for *Le Figaro,* and had agreed to articles in *France Soir.* But Buñuel is talking about Paris again: the city has grown, but some neighbourhoods are still intact. He spends the mornings these days walking around the streets, from very early to midday, looking for locations for the movie that he is going to begin filming in October. It is a film based on a novel by Joseph Kessel. 'A bad novel,' says Buñuel. 'I would never agree to film a very good novel. You have to play to your strengths, you can always get a better film out of a bad novel, you can take liberties without having many scruples.' I ask him if he has seen the Russian version of *War and Peace* which is showing in Paris now and he looks at me in amazement: no, he never goes to the cinema. Or rather, he only goes when he has to. What's the last picture he can remember? Now then, let's think: yes, the Visconti film, *Vaghe stelle dell'orsa* (*Of A Thousand Delights*). That was a few months ago, in Mexico. There was something very good in that film, the gently incestuous relationship between the brothers, that had interested him, bothered him, he had forgotten all the rest. But now, in the evenings, he was watching fragments of films, a roll of this, two rolls of that, for work purposes: to find the companion for Catherine Deneuve in his next film. He hasn't decided on anyone yet; perhaps Jean Sorel, how curious, the young man in Visconti's film. He's not a bad actor, but I'd have to tell him to grow a beard, his face is too pretty for the character. My friend tells a story. A few years ago, he had dragged Buñuel to a popular Mexican cinema where they were showing *The Life, Passion and Death of Our Lord Jesus Christ*. At first, Buñuel was amused and made jokes; then he began to get upset and demand that they leave; finally he began to snort and started shouting angry and insulting remarks. They had to leave in a hurry to avoid being lynched. Buñuel looked at his watch; it was seven in the evening, did we mind going for dinner now, we had to forgive him, but he was used to retiring early. Round the corner from here was a very pleasant bistro, friendly people, home cooking, simple dishes, good wine.

We left the Hotel L'Aiglon and the sun was still burning down on the chestnut trees of the Boulevard Raspail; the terraces of the cafés are full of people reading the evening papers, *Le Monde* and *France Soir*, and buses pass by full of tourists — 'in these streets Giacometti spent his last years,' the guide must have been saying, 'that was his studio' — all looking avidly around, their faces pressed up against the glass; you can hear English and German being spoken. Buñuel's son points out a black motorcycle parked in front of the hotel: that was the one that had taken him to Turkey and back; splendid beast, it had behaved very well. The restaurant was rather elegant, disguised as a bistro at the entrance, and with a large room inside, where the tables were lit by very stylish lamps and the walls were adorned with landscapes and sea views. They know Buñuel, a woman comes out to greet him respectfully and tells him that the *patron* is not in, asks what table he wants and gives him a menu. Buñuel asks for an escalope and red wine and escapes from the woman's attentions quite brusquely. During the meal he is in excellent spirits and very talkative. He talks about Madrid, the Civil War and a plan he had to film a script by Lorca that did not come off. He says how moving it was to return to Spain in 1962 (to film *Viridiana*) after so many years of exile. Then he adds suddenly: 'Writers are lucky, they can write what they like; film makers are condemned to accept the instructions of the producer, they don't have freedom.' We say that this is not true in his case, for he had always done what he wanted, and that even his 'bad films' are full of his own obsessions and preoccupations. He contradicts us energetically: not so, he'd never had complete freedom. But no, he was exaggerating, his first three producers had given him *carte blanche*, and he could work comfortably. Who were his first three producers? An enormous, magnificent, mischievous smile lights up his face: his first producer was his mother, the second a French nobleman and the third a Spanish anarchist. He guffaws and we all feel very good. It had been his mother who had given him the money to film *Un Chien andalou,* the poor woman didn't even know what it was about, of course. Then one night, here in Paris, Jean Cocteau came to see him and told him that the Count of Noailles had seen *Un Chien andalou*; he was enthusiastic and wanted to propose that he make another film. 'But at that time I was uncompromising,' says Buñuel, 'and I asked Cocteau to tell the Count to go to hell, I didn't want to associate with noblemen.' But the Count was not put off and insisted until he obtained an interview with Buñuel. 'A splendid man, we became friends,' says Buñuel. 'He gave me the most complete freedom, he didn't intervene in any way. If it hadn't been for him, I would never have filmed *L'Age d'or.* Poor Count, he was very pleased with the film and I was told that he invited all his friends to the opening. The people left, offended, without saying goodbye to him.' And the Spanish anarchist had also been very understanding and respectful and had accepted the documentary *Las Hurdes* without any opposition. By contrast, afterwards, what battles he'd had to fight over each film. And he recalls that the producers of *La Fièvre monte à El Pao* had told him: 'We want a film on Latin America, Mr Buñuel, but not on what the French believe is Latin America.' Now, of course, he never completely gave in and each time he tried to put in his own ideas, even if he had to smuggle them in. For example, in all of his films he had put an instant of *morcillismo* and – he raises his glass, drinks, and there is a happy, perverse gleam in his eyes for a second – they had never been able to prevent this. What is *morcillismo,* Don Luis? Some thirty years ago in Spain, there was a mediocre painter called Morcilla, who always went around pestering celebrities to visit his workshop and look at his paintings. He got Manuel de Falla to visit him one evening. In a very ceremonial, affable and friendly manner, the musician went round praising each picture: 'This is a very pretty landscape', 'superb tonal qualities', 'this detail is excellent', and alongside him was Morcilla, contradicting him modestly and masochistically: 'What are you saying, Don Manuel, this landscape is a failure', 'the composition is wrong here, this colour isn't right here'. In this way, they came to a picture that the painter presented with a most crestfallen expression: 'This is the most defective of all my works, Don Manuel.' 'Well, yes, the conception of the painting is not very successful.' 'You are wrong,' roared Morcilla, in a rage, 'precisely the only successful part of the painting is the way in which it is conceived.' 'Do you see now what I mean by *morcillismo*?' asks Buñuel. And he recalls that in the story of satanic jealousy that he recounts in *El,* there is a conversation between Arturo de Córdova and Delia Garcés based on the exchange between Falla and the painter Morcilla. The couple are having a friendly conversation, in a lull in their tempestuous married life. What are my defects? he asks. You don't have any, she says. Yes, I must have some, he insinuates lovingly, seductively. 'Well, perhaps you're a little bit egotistical,' she ventures. 'The only thing I'm not is egotistical,' the husband shouts in a rage. 'Pure *morcillismo*,' says Buñuel. 'In all my films, there is a scene like that.'

We talk a moment longer over our coffee, but when the restaurant begins to be invaded by people coming for dinner, Buñuel jumps up as if bitten by a scorpion. He asks for the bill at the counter, scarcely listens to the thank yous and goodbyes of the owner and the waiters and bangs his way out. Now it has got dark, there is a stream of traffic going towards the Place Denfert-Rochereau and in the distance one can see, already lit up, the illuminated signs of the cabarets and bistros of Montparnasse. In the doorway of the Hotel L'Aiglon, Buñuel shakes our hands, bids us a polite farewell and we see him entering the place very quickly, as if he's running away. I look at my watch: it is three minutes to nine in the evening. Yes, he'll keep to his rigid timetable, despite being in Paris.

Paris, September 1966

# Luis Buñuel: A Festival of Excellent Bad Films

A cinema in Paris has had the clever and provocative idea of organizing a festival dedicated to the bad films of Luis Buñuel, the ones that do not usually appear in filmographies of the great Spanish director, and which biographers and critics omit or comment on very briefly, in discreet and benevolent terms. There are five movies, filmed in Mexico between 1946 and 1953: *Gran Casino* (1946), *El gran calavera* (The Great Carouser, 1949), *La hija del engaño/Don Quintín el amargado* (Daughter of Deceit, 1951), *La ilusión viaja en tranvía* (A Tram-ride of Dreams, 1953) and *El río y la muerte* (River of Death, 1954). The well-known and admired work of Buñuel predates and postdates these films – with the exception of *Los olvidados* (The Young and the Damned, 1950) – which are aggressively commercial and which all make, to a greater or lesser extent, generous concessions to what cretinous advertising calls popular taste: lacrimose sensitivity, folklore, comic *machismo*, chaste sexuality suitable for religious women and dull humour.

The film maker is the most unfortunate of creators because he has the least opportunity to do what he likes. Poets, painters, writers can find it difficult to disseminate their work if they dare to break the limits that the society they live in has placed on truth, but even if the publishers refuse to print their work or the galleries to exhibit their pictures, they have the relative privilege of creating in solitude, limited only by their own convictions and can keep their work for better times. Social censure is an obstacle that they have to face at a late stage, once the poem, the novel or the picture is already finished. The problem for the cinéaste is that the prejudices, the prohibitions, the social taboos are barriers that he has to contend with prematurely, before he begins to work. While a narrator, when he is working, has to struggle just with himself, that is with his neuroses and phantoms, the cinéaste is condemned to spread his energies between this interior struggle and also an exterior one, against the greed of the companies, the whims of producers and headstrong technicians and actors. In these conditions one wonders how a Bergman, a Losey or a Buñuel can have emerged. In the case of the latter, and after having taken a look at the festival of excellent bad films showing at Studio 43, it is possible to reply: thanks to a cunning as enormous as his genius.

Before taking refuge in Mexico, after the catastrophe of the Spanish Republic, Buñuel had directed three masterpieces (*Un Chien andalou*, 1928; *L'Age d'or*, 1930; *Las Hurdes*, 1932), but very few people were aware of this and the unknown exile could not yet lay down his own conditions. I imagine that he was then a 'pure' creator, not prepared to compromise in the area of his vocation and this would explain the long period of fifteen years that he spent without shooting one foot of film. Then, suddenly, he brings out *Gran Casino*, a Mexican super-production with half a dozen sacred monsters, Libertad Lamarque, Jorge Negrete, Meche Barba etc, a real apotheosis of vulgarity and bad taste. Had the inflexible artist finally decided to compromise? No, he had begun to put into practice a curious and very dangerous strategy which he would perfect two years later with *El Gran Calavera*, another work that reached the heights of crude sentimentalism.

This strategy, which at first might have gone unnoticed but now appears flagrant when one sees the 'bad films' of Buñuel one after the other, consists of not shrinking from the worst themes and ingredients of vulgar, sentimental cinema, but rather of making use of them all at once, resolutely, in such plentiful doses and in such crazy mixtures that he manages a real qualitative leap and the humour becomes bitter and the grief infinitely comic. Everything depends, of course, on the lens through which one watches these films. I remember seeing *El Río y la muerte* ten years ago in a Lima cinema and the audience at Marsano followed the interminable killings between Angianos and Menchacas with serious concern. We had what we had gone for: a real Mexican drama with pistol shots, tequila, tragic love and popular dances. In Studio 43 the other night, an audience made up mainly of students laughed until they cried throughout the whole film and applauded on many occasions: in that treacherous gunman priest, they recognized all of Buñuel's anti-clericalism; in the unctuous lecture by the paralytic doctor on the 'benefits of science' they could hear the sarcastic moralist. But what is extraordinary is that both publics were right and that *El Río y la muerte* is at once an impeccable melodrama and an unequivocal testimony of the multiple tics, obsessions and effrontery of Buñuel's essentially nonconformist spirit.

The beauty of these films lies in their clever duplicity, their ambiguous hermaphrodite status. It requires a special talent to bring off his sort of achievement, an extraordinary capacity for artistic simulation. It is an attempt, no less, to please both God and the Devil, to satisfy everyone. In the majority of cases, those who set out along this difficult path usually trip up and never get up again. There are countless directors debased by Hollywood, and here in France a talented director, Claude Chabrol, has also just committed hara-kiri. Angered by the contempt with which producers treated his projects, he decided to direct 'action' films for a mass public. The most recent is called *Le Tigre se parfume à la Dynamite* (*An Orchid for the Tiger*, 1965) and it is a horrible cocktail of exoticism, violence and comedy. There is nothing in this film to remind us of the elegant, decadent preciosity of *Le Beau Serge*, nor is it a good thriller because it does not obey the strict rules of the genre which demand that suspense be maintained, effective images, Flaubertian amorality and no trace of intellectualism. To make a good bad film, one has to respect the laws of the game and make a bad film which is *also* good.

*La Ilusión viaja en tranvía* is the story of Caireles and Tarrajas, two young employees of a tram company who are upset because the company has decided to scrap the old jalopy that they have driven for several years. After a tearful bout of drinking, they both decided to say farewell to the old tram by taking it on one last journey around the city. On the way, many different episodes occur, mainly comic, but also sentimental and dramatic. Seen with 'realist' eyes, the film is full of good social intentions, in its description of the life of the humble people of Mexico and the humour is simple, respectful and very orderly. With a touch of bad faith, however, and concentrating all one's attention on the details and not on the core of the tale, on the way in which the story is narrated and not on the story itself, the spectator can enjoy a surrealist film in which all the aspects of reality are described in an oneiric and marvellous way. Both readings are possible and valid and the greatest virtue of the film is this ambiguity.

Paris, January 1966

# Simone de Beauvoir: *Les Belles Images*

The existentialist novel had a brilliant albeit somewhat ephemeral life. It was born in 1938 with Sartre's *Nausea* and was for fifteen years the dominant tendency in French narrative. The date of its death can be put at roughly 1954, the year of the publication of the movement's best novel and also its swansong: *The Mandarins* by Simone de Beauvoir. This admirably describes the failure of a generation of lucid and honest intellectuals who believed in 'committed' literature which could have an immediate social function, and who were brutally disillusioned by the Cold War, McCarthyism, Korea, the colonial wars and the impotence of the left in the face of the conservative forces that have taken power in almost all of Europe. For fifteen years, the most gifted and serious French writers brought out plays and published novels, articles and essays trying to form a progressive consciousness, defending the generous ideals of the Resistance. This fine effort would come to very little and would be partially destroyed by the imperialist adventure of Suez and the barely disguised barrack room uprising that brought down the Fourth Republic. This generation was not only disillusioned but also divided by the time *The Mandarins* appeared: first the break between Sartre and Camus and then between Sartre and Merleau-Ponty weakened the formidable initial group of *Les Temps Modernes*. The novel was no longer the preferred genre of the existentialists: Sartre interrupted *Roads to Freedom* and the final volume would never appear; the narrative vein of Camus weakened pitifully after *The Outsider* and *The Plague* (his later stories and his third novel are exercises of style which do not reach any great heights); even Genet, who can just about be included within the ranks of the existentialist novelists, abandoned the genre after writing *Diary of a Thief*. Within a short period of time, a handful of apolitical and formalist novelists replaced the Liberation writers in the front rank of contemporary French literature. For ten years, nobody in France has contested the vanguard position of this disparate group which comprises, among others, Robbe-Grillet, Nathalie Sarraute, Butor and Beckett, despite the fact that their artful experiments show increasing signs of weakness.

The deaths of Camus and Merleau-Ponty reduce the leaders of French literary existentialism to two names (Gabriel Marcel, despite his attempts at drama, was never really a creator): Sartre and Simone de Beauvoir. Sartre is writing some plays but his main work in the future will be philosophical and political. Simone de Beauvoir wrote of her travels in China and the United States in books that are halfway between reportage and essays; then she brought out her memoirs: three solidly constructed volumes that describe intelligently and in depth the emancipation of a young woman from the bourgeois world that she was born into, her struggle to overcome the taboos and prejudices that a class stills holds over the 'second sex'. *Un Mort si douce,* a short account of the agony and death of Simone de Beauvoir's mother, is a type of appendix to these memoirs.

Thirteen years after *The Mandarins*, Simone de Beauvoir has now published a new novel (her fifth): *Les Belles images*. It is an excellent, tightly written text that dispels in its first pages the fears — set out by someone before the book appeared — that this novel, in the wake of the frantic desire for new forms and stylistic experimentation put in vogue by the authors of the *'nouveau roman'*, would damage the narrative prestige acquired by *The Mandarins* and would reveal Simone de Beauvoir as an old-fashioned novelist. Quite wrong. *Les Belles images,* although faithful in its contents to the existential postulates of 'commitment', is not traditional in its techniques, but is similar, in its writing and structure, to an experimental novel. This is perhaps its greatest merit: to have made use, in order to enhance an important narrative, of certain forms and expressive modes which seem artificial and irritating in other authors due to the poverty of the issues that they are dealing with.

*Les Belles images* is written in the present indicative, like a novel by Robbe-Grillet; it has the descriptive austerity — very short sentences, minimum allusion sufficient to present a landscape or a character — of a story by Marguerite Duras, and uses imagined dialogues, like Nathalie Sarraute, to reveal the subjectivity of its heroes (let's call them that). But although it is clear that Simone de Beauvoir has carefully read these authors and has used their techniques, it would be wrong to say that she imitates them. Her intentions are very different from, and even opposed to, these other writers. The main objective of *Les Belles images* is to show, through a fiction, the alienation of women in a large, modern, consumerist society; to describe the depersonalization of human beings, their subtle transformation into robots in the heart of a society in which what Marx called 'fetishes' — money, advertising and the like — have been transformed from instruments at the service of man into instruments that enslave man. Of course, Simone de Beauvoir is not the first person to deal with the theme of 'alienation' in industrial countries: literature and cinema are greatly concerned with this problem (which, for example, appears time and again in the films of Antonioni and Jean-Luc Godard). The difference is rather that while so many authors are content just to describe the symptoms or manifestations of this alienation and even jubilantly contribute to it with their own work, Simone de Beauvoir keeps her distance from the topic, is critical towards it and tries to fight it.

This danger, although real, is difficult to detect because of the pleasing forms that it adopts. The central character of *Les Belles images*, Laurence, is a young woman, married to an architect, who works in an advertising agency. She has a vague premonition of this danger, intuits that it is rooted in her life, but cannot identify it or rid herself of it. She feels that something, she does not know what, is every second gnawing away at her life which is apparently being led, without any major upheavals, in a comfortable environment made up of 'beautiful images' — an elegant apartment, social functions, travel — similar to those that she has to fabricate each day in order to win clients for her products. Her husband loves and respects her; she likes her work; her children are clever and entertaining; the family income allows her to live well. Why, then, is she not happy? To bring a bit of excitement and adventure to this very settled life, she has an affair; but she soon discovers that her relationship with Lucien, a colleague at work who is as well-mannered, affectionate and intelligent as Jean Charles, her husband, does not liberate her from tame matrimonial monotony but rather prolongs and duplicates it. Frustrated, Laurence breaks up with Lucien. She then seeks refuge in her father, who has a modest job in the Congress. His wife, Dominique, who has a good job in television, had left him years previously because of his lack of ambition. Laurence sees in her father, who lives shut away among his books and records, an example, something different from her conventional and empty world and is prepared to believe that her father is right when he accuses 'civilization' of having made men unhappy, of having snatched them from the simple happiness of primitive life.

But on a trip to Greece with her father, Laurence discovers that there is nothing healthy and pleasant about poverty, it is simply terrible. Furthermore, it is not true that literature and art are sufficient for happiness; the reconciliation between her father and Dominique, when she is abandoned by her lover, shows Laurence that he was tired of solitude and prepared to do anything – even accept a frivolous life – to escape from it.

'Why am I not like everyone else?' Laurence asks herself continually. Because she finds herself all the time saying things that she does not believe, acting without conviction, pretending to feel what she does not feel, showing to the world a personality that is not hers. When did this incomprehensible duplicity begin to appear in her life? Why was she not the woman she should have been and is now this being who is a stranger to herself? She tries to rebel but only very vaguely, because she does not clearly know how and against whom she should be rebelling: her blind swipes in the void only serve, in the long run, to aggravate her malaise. She would like 'to be a friendly presence for herself, a hearth radiating warmth', and instead she has the feeling that she is a sleepwalker moving in a 'smooth, hygienic and routine' world. At the end of the book, Laurence decides to educate her children in a way different from that demanded by the conventions of her world, to give them a chance to save themselves. 'What hope? She does not even know.'

Simone de Beauvoir ends the tragedy of Laurence with this gloomy sentence, the tragedy of a paradoxical world in which the greatest development of science and technology, the proliferation and abundance of goods, does not diminish but instead increases human unhappiness. Of course, the book is not an argument against progress, an obscurantist manifesto against machines. It is a plea in favour of man, who must always be the main object of progress, the master and beneficiary of these prodigious modern machines and not their victim.

For Latin American readers, the problem that Simone de Beauvoir describes in her novel is still somewhat indistinct, since the dangers that threaten a society which has achieved material well-being through technology do not yet hang over our countries, which are beset by more primary ills. But it is useful to keep in mind how deceitful these beautiful images are and to be aware of how derisory is progress which satisfies certain needs and forgets others. The progress of man, Simone de Beauvoir seems to tell us, must be at once material, intellectual and moral, or it will simply not be progress at all.

London, February 1967

# Sebastián Salazar Bondy and the Vocation of the Writer in Peru

Having fought against them unflaggingly, the irascible heroes of the romances of chivalry paid the most ceremonial honours to the brave adversaries that they killed in worthy or unworthy combat. Man or dragon, Moor or Christian, plebeian or of high rank, the valiant enemy was wept over, remembered amd glorified by the victors. Alive, the heroes pursued him implacably and had recourse to both God and the Devil — to physical force, intrigues, arms, poisons, spells — in order to destroy him. Dead, they defended his name, preserving it in their memory like a family member or a beloved friend and, on their travels through the world, proclaimed his merits and deeds to the four winds. This curious and somewhat cruel custom is also upheld today, although in a more cunning fashion; the changeable victors are the bourgeoisie, the victims rehabilitated after death are the writers. Humiliated, ignored, persecuted or scarcely tolerated, certain poets, certain narrators, now inoffensive in their tombs, are transformed into historical personalities and objects of national pride. Everything that once appeared reprehensible or ridiculous in them, is later forgiven or even celebrated by their former censors. Luis Cernuda wrote beautifully angry pages against this *a posteriori*, hypocritical assimilation of the creator by bourgeois society and denounced it in one of his best poems, 'Pájaros en la noche' (Birds in the Night).

The Peruvian bourgeoisie has very rarely adopted this hypocritical practice. More self-satisfied (and also more stupid) than the rest, it has never felt the moral obligation to honour writers, those recalcitrants who frequently emerge from its breast. Alive or dead, it condemns them to the same disdainful oblivion, to the same exile. There are few exceptions to this rule and one of them is Sebastián Salazar Bondy.

I was not in Lima when he died, but I learned through the newspapers and letters from friends that on the night of his wake, the Casa de Cultura was full of flowers and people, that his solemn funeral was attended by large numbers and that the whole of Lima wept for him. And I have read the homages that the press unanimously dedicated to him, the grief-stricken editorials, the obituaries, and I know that there were speeches in Parliament and that government officials and 'personalities' were part of the funeral cortège and showed their grief at this death that 'put Peruvian culture into mourning'. They were on the point, it seems, of flying the flags of the city at half mast.

Sebastián's attractive personality is not enough to explain these demonstrations of appreciation, nor is the work he leaves behind, although it is doubtless important, because this work can only be appreciated by Peruvians who read plays or go to the theatre and how many of these are there? Perhaps obscurely, those countless wreaths, that compact cortège, did not demonstrate the grief of Peru, of Lima, for the generous man who had departed, or their gratitude for the poems, plays and essays that will live on, but rather the admiration, the surprise of this country, this city, at someone who had dared over the years, to the last days of his life, to wage a bitter, harsh battle against this society. I would also like to praise that tough and doughty fighter Salazar Bondy by describing – briefly, superficially – that clandestine, and in some ways exemplary, quiet war that he fought.

A mysterious, invisible, extremely cruel war, but so subtly refined that we do not even know when it began. It must have been a long time ago, perhaps in his childhood, back there in Calle Corazón de Jesús, where he had been born in 1924, close to the house of another solitary warrior (though of a different sort), the poet Martín Adán. Did the crisis that brought his family to the capital, moving from a wealthy, high-ranking life in Chiclayo to modest circumstances and anonymity in Lima, have an influence on Sebastián's vocation? Did he begin to write when he was at the German School or when he went to San Agustín College? Certainly in 1940, when he entered the University of San Marcos, he was interested in literature, but not exclusively. In 1955, Sebastián confessed: 'If there had been the same theatrical activity in Lima ten years ago that there is today, I would have been an actor. I always felt drawn to the stage, but that ambition was frustrated due to the total lack of theatre life in Lima when I was at the age that one decides on a career.' As usually happens, literature slowly took him over in a surreptitious, gradual and, at first involuntary, fashion. Perhaps what proved decisive was his friendship at that point with a painter, Szyszlo, and two poets of his age, Sologuren and Eielson; perhaps Luis Fabio Xammar, the only teacher that he would later remember with affection, helped to instil in him the need to write. His first poems – 'Rótulo de la esfinge' (Letters of the Sphinx), 'Voz desde la vigilia' (The Voice from the Vigil) – appeared in 1943, when he was a university student. He completed his studies in the humanities faculty and began to teach in different schools, but it is clear that he never thought of a university career, because he never submitted his final graduation thesis. He would not be an actor or a professor. Why not a librarian? Sebastián never took his job in the National Library as a simple *modus vivendi*, he became involved in all aspects of its work. In 1945, he gave up the library job and took up politics, in the FDR (the Democratic Coalition) and journalism, writing for *La Nación,* a centrist paper. He also published new poems. When Salazar Bondy left for Argentina in 1947, a voluntary exile that would last for five years, there could be no doubt: he had chosen literature as his destiny.

What does this mean? That at twenty-three, almost without meaning to, despite himself, Sebastián had decided to confront the silent hostility of which we have spoken. He would not be an actor, a teacher, a journalist or a professional politician: the writer had developed in him as he adopted, fleetingly, these different roles, the writer had begun to take shape, putting all these other careers into second place. Sebastián had won a battle, but the war was just beginning and he must have known at the time that, sooner or later, this war would be *fatally lost*.

Because every Peruvian writer is defeated in the long run. Many things happen from the moment a Peruvian chooses to be a writer until his final defeat and it is in this space that Sebastián's heroic struggle took place.

The first battle was to pursue a career against which a society like ours is perfectly inoculated, a vocation that Peru attacks and eradicates in embryo through very powerful, albeit quiet mechanisms of psychological and moral dissuasion. Sebastián overcame that instinct for self-preservation which causes other young people to give up their literary aspirations as soon as they understand or intuit that here in Peru, to write implies leading the life of a pariah, a form of civil death. How could it be otherwise? In a society in which literature plays no role because the majority of its members do not know how to read or do not have the necessary conditions in which to read and the minority that have these opportunities do not read, then the writer is an anomalous being, without a precise place, a picturesque and eccentric individual, a sort of harmless madman who is allowed his freedom because, after all, the madness is not contagious – how can he harm others if they do not read? Yet, even so, he should be kept in a strait-jacket, at a distance, treated with caution, tolerated with systematic mistrust. Sebastián must have known, when he decided to become a writer, what the future held for him: an ambiguous, marginal, segregated position in society. Years later, in his essay 'Lima el horrible' (Lima the Horrible), Sebastián would describe the resistance that the Peruvian ruling classes have traditionally shown to literature and art: 'Aesthetic concerns encounter a tenacious obstacle in Peru: they are apparently gratuitous. Since it lacks use value for indoctrination or sensuality, beauty created by artistic talent has no function.' It is the same today. This did not prevent him from following his vocation. But, as we know, 'youth is idealistic and impulsive' and it is not difficult to make a bold decision when one is twenty: what is exceptional is to be loyal to it, against the odds, through time, to keep swimming against the current, at aged forty or more. Sebastián's great merit is that, unlike most Peruvian adolescents who hope to write, he was not a deserter.

It would not be right, of course, to condemn out of hand those young people who deny their vocation. Before this, we must examine the reasons that cause them to desert. In effect, what does it mean to be a writer in Peru?

'I am not at ease', says Carlos Germán Belli in one of his poems. Nobody in Peru who takes literature seriously will ever feel that they are at ease because society will force them to live in a state of anxiety. Taking the specific area of literature: although his contemporaries might not read him, although he has to overcome very great difficulties to publish what he writes, although it is only other poets and other narrators who are interested in his work, accept it and discuss it, and although he has the unfortunate sensation of writing for nobody, the young writer at least has the dubious consolation of being discovered, read and judged posthumously. But he knows that his daily life will be led in an asphyxiating cloister and will be a grey, irremediable series of frustrations. In the first place, it is clear that his vocation will not allow him to earn a living, will turn him into a meagre, *ad honorem* producer. But, in addition, the very fact of being a writer will be a hindrance to his earning a living. If a young person authentically feels the need to write, he also knows that his vocation is tyrannical and exclusive, that the solitary profession demands of its followers total commitment, and if he is honest and wants to follow his vocation in this way, how will he live? This will be his first defeat, his initial frustration. He will have to find another job, divorce his vocation from his daily activity, spread himself around, turn himself inside out: he will become a journalist, a teacher, a clerk, an unsettled worker in a variety of jobs. But, unlike other places, literature is not a strong letter of recommendation when it comes to applying for other jobs, it is a handicap. 'This is a part-time writer, a part-time poet,' people say, and what they mean is, 'this is a part-time clown, a part-time lunatic'. To be a writer means that many doors are closed, the young person is excluded from opportunities open to others, his vocation will condemn him not only to seek a living on the margins of literature, but also in badly paid jobs, miserable ways of earning a crust, that he will perform without any faith and often with disgust. But Peru is an underdeveloped country, that is, a jungle where one has to earn the right to survive through force. The writer will take on obligations which, at best, do not interest him deeply and will often go against his convictions, giving him a bad conscience. And this will also take up his time. He will dedicate more and more time to this 'other' job and, by force of circumstances, will read little and write less, and literature will end up as an activity for Sundays and holidays, a hobby.

Relegated in this way, turned into a casual pastime, almost a game, literature takes its revenge. Literature is a passion and passion does not allow itself to be shared. One cannot love a woman and spend one's life with another and then expect the former to show disinterested and limitless loyalty. All writers know that one has to win over and safeguard the solitary one through determined and intense attention. Because the writer, who is the freest person imaginable with respect to other people and the world, is a slave to his vocation. If one does not serve and nurture her daily, the solitary one becomes resentful and leaves. Those who do not want to expose themselves in this way, who realize the dangers of this vocation in the daily struggle to live, have no alternative but to give up the struggle in advance. For if they are afraid of being gradually distanced from that essential part of their life, they must become resigned to not having what people call a 'future'. But very few young people enter literature the way one enters a religious order: by making a vow of poverty. For is there any indication at all that the sacrifice entailed in accepting insecurity and poverty as a lifestyle can be justified? And what if this vocation, which makes so many demands for its survival, is not real and deep rooted, but rather a passing fancy, a mirage? And, even if it were authentic, what if the young person lacks the will, the patience and the madness necessary to be, at a later date, a true creator? The literary vocation is a bet in the dark and there are no guarantees, at the outset, that some day one will be a passable poet, a decent novelist, a good dramatist. One must give up many things – basic comfort and respectability – to embark on a journey which will perhaps lead nowhere or will be brutally cut short in a wasteland of disillusionment and failure.

Those who do not desert, those who, like Sebastián Salazar Bondy, dare to commit themselves to this lonely (hopeless) vocation must, from the outset, face up to innumerable difficulties. These brave souls must still find a way to prevent Peruvian reality from frustrating their ambitions in practice, they must find a way to remain true to themselves and write. Sebastián confronted this problem in an unusual and daring way.

At first sight, things seem quite simple. If Peruvian society has no room for him, the writer must, of necessity, turn his back on that society and make his own way on the margins; each, in his own domain, looking after his own concerns. For that reason a Peruvian writer who does not desert, who dares to be a writer, exiles himself. All our creators were or are in some way, at some moment, exiles. There are many forms of exile and, in this case, they all mean that the creator who is treated with contempt by Peru in turn feels contempt for Peru. First, there is physical exile. The writer in Peru has traditionally felt the temptation to escape to other worlds, in search of a milieu more compatible with his vocation, an environment of greater cultural complexity, or a more stimulating climate. It would take a long time to remember all the Peruvian poets and writers who produced their work partly or wholly abroad, in exile. How many of them died outside Peru. It is symbolic in this regard that the two most important writers in our literature, doubtless the only two with universal significance, Garcilaso and Vallejo, ended their days far fom here.

There is, however, another form of exile which has nothing to do with whether one remains in Peru or leaves. Literature is universal, of course, but the Peruvian contributions to this universe are so scarce and so poor that one can understand why the young writer can only satisfy the hunger of the solitary one for reading, by consulting foreign books and authors and must look for affinities, agreements, guidance and inspiration in non-Peruvian literature. Our cultural reality allows him no other alternative. If he were content to drink exclusively or by preference from the well of national literature, he would perhaps be a sort of patriot but also, with no perhaps, he would be culturally provincial and confused. Along this road one reaches, without wishing to, a form of exile that we might call interior. In short, it means protecting oneself against the poverty, the ignorance or the hostility of the environment, setting up a spiritual enclave as a retreat, a separate world of one's own, jealously guarded, erecting a small cultural citadel within whose walls the solitary one can grow, live and work. She accepts this cloistered existence and can even develop there in a splendid way. Salazar Bondy experienced all these different forms of exile in his life, but in the end he decided to live and die in Peru.

Let us remember what Peruvian literature was like fifteen years ago, in the early 1950s, when Sebastián returned to Lima, and what he achieved. There was almost nothing and he tried to do everything. All around him was a desolate emptiness and he set himself, body and soul, to fill it. There was no theatre and he was a playwright. There was no criticism or information and he was a critic and a theatre columnist. There were no schools of drama or companies and he sponsored the creation of a theatre club and was a teacher and even a director. There was no way of publishing dramatic works and he was his own publisher. There was no literary criticism and he set himself to review books that appeared abroad, to comment on poetry, short stories and novels published in Peru and to encourage, advise and help young authors. There was no art criticism and he was an art critic, lecturer and exhibition organizer. For a long time, and finally with allies, he personified the literary life of Peru. I remember this very well because ten years ago, for the reasons outlined above, his name and his presence fascinated me. Everything in Peru contradicted the vocation of the writer; in this milieu, such a vocation was a chimerical shadow, an unreal existence. But then there was this strange case, this man-orchestra, this living demonstration that, despite everything, someone had lived up to the vocation. Who of my generation could deny the decisive stimulus of Sebastián's example? How many of us dared to try to become writers because of his powerful, contagious presence?

In the second stage of his life as a writer, he added political involvement to his struggle for literature. He was a rebel, not only as a writer, but also as a citizen. Of course, every writer is a rebel, in disagreement with the world in which he lives, but this intimate rebellion inspired by literature is very diverse. Frequently the dissatisfaction that causes man to oppose verbal realities to objective reality escapes his reason. Almost always, the poet, the writer, is incapable of explaining the origins of his deep lack of conformity, whose roots are lost in an unknown infantile trauma, in a family conflict that appears unimportant, in a personal drama one thought resolved.

On to this obscure rebellion, this unconscious and particular protest that is called a literary vocation, there is almost always superimposed in Peru another rebellion, this time of a social nature, which is not the cause but rather the fruit of this vocation. To create is to hold a dialogue, to write is to have always in mind the *'hypocrite lecteur, mon semblable, mon frère'* that Baudelaire speaks of. Adam and Robinson Crusoe could not have been poets, narrators. But in the case of Peru, writers can almost be considered as Adams and Robinson Crusoes. When Sebastián began to write (it is the same today, although not so bad), literature was a clandestine activity, an enforced monologue. Everything seemed to point to the fact that Peruvian society could do without literature, had no need of poetry, theatre or the novel, that these were activities denied to that country.

Writers without publishers and without readers, with no audience to stimulate and make demands on them, or to force them to be rigorous and responsible, soon look to find the reason for this unfortunate situation. They then discover that there is blame and that this blame must be apportioned to certain people. The frustrated writer, reduced to solitude and the role of pariah, cannot, unless he is blind and stupid, attribute the neglect and the sorry condition of literature to men from the countryside and the suburbs who die without having learned to read and for whom, naturally, literature cannot be a vital or a superficial need because, for them, it does not exist. The writer cannot blame the lack of national culture on those who have never had the opportunity to create it because they live in conditions of constant oppression and suffocation. Their resentment, their fury, focuses logically on that privileged sector of society in Peru which knows how to read and yet does not read, on those families which have the resources to buy books and yet do not buy them, on that class which had the means to make Peru a cultured and decent country and did not do so. It is not strange, therefore, that in our country one can count on the fingers of one hand the writers of some value who have sided with the bourgeoisie. What writer who takes his vocation seriously can feel affinity with a class that punishes him with frustration, defeat and exile for wanting to write? By the very fact of being a creator here, one belongs within the ranks of the victims of the bourgeoisie. From there, it is only one step for the writer to become conscious of this situation, take responsibility for it and declare himself a supporter of the disinherited of Peru, the enemy of their masters. This is what happened to Salazar Bondy.

In addition to the courage that it took to be a writer in a country that does not need writers, Sebastián had the bravery to declare himself a socialist in a society in which the very word socialist provokes consternation and leads to persecution. It did not cause him to be imprisoned, as happened to others, but it did mean that he lived in constant economic anxiety, that he was deprived of work and vetoed for many possible openings, which made his daily struggle all the more difficult. Like his aesthetic convictions, his political ideas changed profoundly in the second stage of his life and he became more radical and more energetic. In the dramatic alternative posed today between capitalism and socialism, he clearly took the second option.

But it should also be said that while other writers, out of an explicable exasperation at the prostration of Peru and the injustices committed there, have decided to shape their vocation in accordance with revolutionary principles, Sebastián knew how to differentiate perfectly between his obligations as a creator and his responsibilities as a citizen. He avoided no risk as a man of the left, but he did not embrace the naive attitudes of those who subordinate literature to militancy and consider that, by so doing, they are serving society better. He had not sacrificed literature in order to gain admittance to his unjust society, he had not given up writing so as to become influential, rich and powerful one day. In the same way, he did not abandon literature in order to devote himself to revolutionary struggle as an exclusive and primordial concern, nor did he kill the solitary one by dedicating himself exclusively to fighting for a different country, freed from prejudices and anachronistic structures, where literature might be possible. He knew how to be politically committed while safeguarding his independence, his spontaneity as a creator. He knew that as a citizen, he could determine, calculate and rationally premeditate his actions but that, as a writer, his mission was to serve and obey the whims and obsessions of the solitary one, that mistress he voluntarily nurtured within him, whose commands were often incomprehensible to the creator and might have incalculable consequences. In the same way as he had defended his vocation against injustice and petty small-mindedness, he defended it against the temptations of idealism and social fervour. This is the only possible way for a writer to behave and all the rest is rhetoric: he must place the solitary one above all else and sacrifice good and evil for her. I do not know whether Sebastián would have agreed with this formulation or would have rejected it. Perhaps his incorrigible generosity would have made him say no, that in certain cases when the shortcomings, the defects or the wounds of a certain reality beckon him, then the writer must abandon partially or completely the service of the solitary one in order to take up more urgent and more immediately useful social tasks than literature. But even though he might not recognize it or might even deny it, an examination of his life and work, however summary, makes the point with extraordinary clarity: at all times, here in Peru or in exile, at the best or worst moments of his life, in all his many undertakings and adventures, when he was a journalist, a teacher or a militant, literature was always his main concern and cast its obstinate shadow over every other activity. Above all, despite his terrible goodness, his unquenchable curiosity for every aspect of life and his acute appreciation of human problems, Sebastián was that intransigent egotist, the writer, and of all the struggles that he undertook, the main one, that motivated all the others, was the one that maintained the solitary one as an ideal.

It is difficult to find among us writers of Sebastián's age when he died who are really writers, who are alive as creators. José Miguel Oviedo has accurately remarked on 'this sad law of Peruvian literature which has condemned its poets to premature death – that is, to silence – at the age of thirty'. Yes, Peruvians can be poets and writers when they are young. Then the milieu begins to change them: it reclaims and assimilates some, it defeats and abandons others, leaving them morally defeated, frustrated in their vocation, taking sad consolation in laziness, scepticism, bohemian behaviour, neurosis or alcohol. Some do not deny their vocation as such, but manage to shape it to the environment: they become teachers, they stop creating to teach and research, both necessary activities, but essentially different from those of a creator. But living writers of Sebastián's age? Living, that is curious, concerned, informed about what is written here and there, avid readers, creators in a state of constant and tormented restlessness, poisoned by doubts, appetites and plans, active, tireless: how many of them were there when Sebastián died, how many are there now in Peru? When they go to the grave, the majority of Peruvian writers have already been corpses for a long time and Peru is not usually moved by those victims that it destroyed ten, fifteen, twenty years before their death. In Sebastián, our city, our country found someone who put up much greater resistance. Death surprised him at the height of his powers, when he was not just resisting his numerous and subtle enemies, but attacking them with all his weapons to hand. The homages paid to him, the commotion that his death caused, the many different demonstrations of grief and mourning, these wreaths, these articles, these speeches, this compact funeral procession are the minute's silence, the forty-gun salute, the funeral honours that this stubborn and outstanding fighter deserved.

Lima, April 1966

# Literature is Fire

Lecture given in Caracas on 11 August 1967, on receipt of the Rómulo Gallegos prize.

Approximately thirty years ago, a young man who had read with fervour Breton's early works died in a charity hospital in the mountains of Seville, driven mad by rage. He bequeathed to the world a coloured shirt and *Cinco metros de poemas* ('Five Metres of Poems'), which have an extraordinary visionary delicacy. He had a sonorous, courtly, vice-regal name, but his life had been tenaciously obscure, stubbornly unhappy. In Lima, he was a hungry man from the provinces, a dreamer who lived in the Mercado district, in an unlit cave, and when he travelled to Europe, nobody knows why, he had been taken off the boat in Central America, locked up, tortured and left as a feverish ruin. After his death, his relentless misfortunes did not end, but rather reached their apotheosis: the canons of the Spanish Civil War erased his tomb from the earth and in the intervening years, time has been erasing his memory from the minds of the people who were lucky enough to know him and to read him. It would not surprise me if the rats are giving their attention to the copies of his only book which are buried in libraries that no one visits and that his poems, that now nobody reads, will very soon be transformed 'into smoke, into wind, into nothing', like that insolent coloured shirt that he bought to die in. And yet, this compatriot of mine had been a consummate wizard, a sorcerer of the word, a daring architect of images, a shining explorer of dreams, an exact and stubborn creator who had the necessary lucidity and madness to espouse his writer's vocation as one must: as a daily and furious immolation.

Tonight I summon up his furtive nocturnal shadow to spoil my own party, this party that is taking place thanks to the generosity of Venezuela and in the illustrious name of Rómulo Gallegos, because the award to a novel of mine of this magnificent prize, created by the National Institute of Culture and Fine Arts as a stimulus and a challenge to novelists of the Spanish language and as a homage to a great

American creator, not only fills me with gratitude towards Venezuela, but also strengthens my responsibility as a writer. And the writer, as you already know, is the eternal killjoy. The silent shadow of Oquendo de Amat here, at my side, should remind us all — but especially this Peruvian whom you wrenched from Kangaroo Valley, Earls Court in London, brought to Caracas and showered with friendship and honours — the sombre fate that befell, and still so often befalls, creators in Latin America. It is true that not all our writers have been tested in such an extreme way as Oquendo de Amat; some managed to conquer the hostility, the indifference, the contempt of our countries for literature and wrote, published, and were even read. It is true that not everyone could be killed by hunger, indifference or ridicule. But these fortunate ones are the exception. As a general rule, the Latin American writer has lived and written in exceptionally difficult circumstances because our societies have established a cold, almost perfect mechanism for discouraging and killing his vocation. This vocation is beautiful but it is also absorbing and tyrannical and demands of its followers complete dedication. How could these writers, surrounded by a majority of people who could not read or write, or by a minority who did not like reading, have made literature their exclusive destiny and activity? Without publishers, without readers, without a cultural milieu to stimulate him and make demands on him, the Latin American writer has gone into battle knowing from the outset that he would be defeated. His vocation was not accepted by society, scarcely tolerated; society gave him no means to make a living and turned him into a downgraded, *ad honorem* producer. The writer in our countries has had to turn himself inside out, separate his vocation from his daily work, split himself into a thousand jobs which took up the time needed for writing and were often unpalatable to his conscience and his convictions. Because apart from finding no room in their hearts for literature, our societies have always encouraged a constant feeling of mistrust towards this marginal, rather anomalous, being who has tried, against all logic, to pursue a profession which, in the context of Latin America, seems almost unreal. For that reason, dozens of our writers have become frustrated and have deserted their vocation or betrayed it, acting half-heartedly and furtively, without rigour or resolve.

But it is true that in recent years things have begun to change. Slowly, a more hospitable climate for literature is creeping into our countries. The number of readers is beginning to grow, the bourgeoisie is discovering that books matter, that writers are rather more than gentle fools, that they have a function to fulfil in society. But then, when justice is finally beginning to be done to the Latin American writer or rather, when the injustice that has weighed down on him is finally beginning to lift, another threat can arise, a diabolically subtle danger. Those same societies that once exiled and rejected the writer can now think that it is useful to assimilate him, integrate him, confer on him a kind of official status. For that reason it is important to remind our societies what to expect. Warn them that literature is fire, that it means nonconformity and rebellion, that the *raison d'être* of a writer is protest, disagreement and criticism. Explain to them that there are no halfway measures: that society must either suppress for ever that human faculty which is artistic creation and eliminate once and for all that unruly social element, the writer, or else embrace literature, in which case it has no alternative but to accept a perpetual torrent of attacks, of irony and of satire aimed at both the transitory and the essential aspects of life, and at all levels of the social pyramid. That is how things are and there is no escape: the writer has been, is, and will continue to be, dissatisfied. No one who is satisfied is capable of writing; no one who is in agreement with, or reconciled to, reality can commit the ambitious folly of inventing verbal realities. The literary vocation is born out of the disagreement between a man and the world, out of his intuition of the deficiencies, disparities and misery that surround him. Literature is a form of permanent insurrection and cannot accept strait-jackets. Any attempt to bend its angry, rebellious nature is doomed to failure. Literature might die but it will never be conformist.

Literature can be useful to society only if it fulfils this condition. It contributes to human improvement, preventing spiritual atrophy, self-satisfaction, stagnation, human paralysis and intellectual or moral decline. Its mission is to arouse, to disturb, to alarm, to keep men in a constant state of dissatisfaction with themselves: its function is to stimulate, without respite, the desire for change and improvement even when it is necessary to use the sharpest weapons to accomplish this task. It is essential that everyone understands this once and for all: the more critical the writings of an author against his country, the more intense will be the passion that binds him to that country. Because in the realms of literature, violence is a proof of love.

The American reality, of course, offers the writer a true surfeit of reasons to be rebellious and discontented. Societies where injustice is law, paradises of ignorance, exploitation, blinding inequalities, poverty, economic, cultural and moral alienation, our tumultuous lands offer us exemplary material to reveal in fictions, in a direct or indirect way, through facts, dreams, testimonies, allegories, nightmares or visions that reality is imperfectly made, that life must change. But within ten, twenty or fifty years, the hour of social justice will arrive in our countries, as it has in Cuba, and the whole of Latin America will have freed itself from the order that despoils it, from the castes that exploit it, from the forces that now insult and repress it. And I want this hour to arrive as soon as possible and for Latin America to enter, once and for all, a world of dignity and modernity, and for socialism to free us from our anachronism and our horror. But when social injustices disappear, this will not mean that the hour of consent, subordination and official complicity will have arrived for the writer. His mission will continue, must continue, to be the same: any compromise in this area will be a betrayal. Within the new society, and along the road that our personal ghosts and demons drive us, we will continue as before, as now, saying no, rebelling, demanding recognition for our right to dissent, showing in this living and magical way, as only literature can, that dogma, censorship and arbitrary acts are also mortal enemies of progress and human dignity, affirming that life is not simple and does not fit neatly into patterns, that the road to truth is not always smooth and straight, but often tortuous and rough, showing time and again with our books the essential complexity and diversity of the world and the contradictory ambiguity of human events. As yesterday, as today, if we love our vocation, we will have to continue fighting the thirty two wars of Colonel Aureliano Buendía even though, like him, we lose them all.

Our vocation has made writers the professionals of dissatisfaction, the conscious or unconscious subversives of society, rebels with a cause, the irredeemable insurgents of the world, the insufferable devil's advocates. I don't know if this is good or bad, I only know that this is how it is. This is the condition of the writer and we must revindicate it just as it is. In these years when Latin America is beginning to discover, accept and support literature, it must also recognize the threat that is closing in, the high price that it will have to pay for culture. Our societies must be on the alert: for, rejected or accepted, persecuted or rewarded, the writer worthy of his name will continue throwing in people's faces the not always pleasant spectacle of their miseries and torments.

By giving me this prize, for which I thank you most deeply, and which I have accepted because I consider that it does not demand of me even the slightest trace of ideological, political or aesthetic compromise and which other Latin American writers with more books and more merit than me should have received instead – I'm thinking of the great Onetti, for example, who has not received the recognition that he deserves in Latin America – and by showing me so much affection and warmth since my arrival in this city in mourning after the devastating earthquake, Venezuela has placed me overwhelmingly in her debt. The only way that I can repay this debt is by being, within the limits of my strength, more faithful and more loyal to this writer's vocation, which I never suspected would give me the satisfaction that I feel today.

Caracas, 11 August 1967

# Literature and Exile

Every time that a Latin American writer resident in Paris is interviewed, one question invariably crops up: 'Why do you live outside your country?' This is not simple curiosity; in the majority of cases, the question conceals either fear or a reproach. For some, the physical exile of a writer is literally dangerous, because the lack of direct contact with the way of being or the way of speaking (which is almost the same thing) of the people of his own country can impoverish his language and weaken or falsify his vision of reality. For others, the matter has an ethical significance: to choose exile is immoral, a betrayal of the fatherland. In countries whose cultural life is limited or non-existent, the writer – they think – should stay and fight for the development of intellectual and artistic activities to raise the spiritual level of the environment. If instead of doing so, he prefers to go abroad, then he is branded an egotist, an irresponsible person or a coward (or all three at once).

The writers' replies to this inevitable question are often very varied: I live away from my country because I find the cultural milieu in Paris, London or Rome more stimulating; or because distance gives me a more coherent and faithful perspective on my reality than being immersed in it; or simply because I want to (I'm talking here about literary, not political, exiles). In fact all of these replies can be summed up in one: because I write better in exile. *Better* in this case should be understood in psychological and not aesthetic terms: it means with 'more tranquillity' or 'greater conviction'; no one will ever know if what is written in exile is of better quality than what would have been written in one's own country. In answer to the fear that physical isolation from one's reality might prejudice one's work in the long run, the writer of fantasy might argue that the reality his fictions describe travels the world with him because his two-headed heroes, his carnivorous roses and his glass cities, emerge from his fantasies and dreams, not from any observation of the outside world. And he might add that the lack of daily contact with the language of his compatriots does not alarm him at all; he aspires to express himself in a language free of local colour, an abstract, even exotic, unmistakably personal language, which can be developed through reading.

The realist writer must resort to examples. If we take just the case of Peruvian literature, we can come up with a list of important books which describe the face and the soul of Peru faithfully and beautifully, written by men who had spent a number of years in exile, thirty in the case of El Inca Garcilaso's *Comentarios reales* (Royal Commentaries) and at least twelve in the case of Vallejo's *Poemas humanos* (Human Poems). In both these examples – perhaps the most admirable in the whole of Peruvian literature – distance in time and space did not diminish or disturb the vision of a concrete reality which is transposed in essence into that chronicle and into those poems. In Latin American literature, the examples are even more numerous. Even if the literary value of Bello's odes might be debatable, his botanical and zoological rigour is not in question and the flora and fauna that he rhymed from memory in London correspond to those of America. Sarmiento wrote his best essays on his country, *Facundo* and *Memorias de provincia* (Notes from the Provinces), far from Argentina. No one doubts that the work of Martí is profoundly national, although four-fifths of it was written in exile. And was the costumbrist realism of the final novels of Blest Gana, written several decades after his arrival in Paris, no less faithful to Chilean reality than the books he wrote in Santiago?

This is simply a list of examples and the statistics in this case are there to give an indication rather than to present a rounded argument. Is it an indication that exile does not impair a writer's creativity and that physical absence from his home does not imply a loss, or a deterioration of the view of reality that his books seek to transmit? Any generalization on this theme risks drowning in absurdity. Because it would doubtless not be difficult to give numerous opposing examples to show how, in a great number of cases, when writers left their country, they lost their creativity or wrote books that deformed the world that they were attempting to describe. To these counter-statistics – we are already in the realm of the absurd – one would have to reply with another type of example which would show the countless number of writers who, without ever having touched foreign soil, wrote mediocre or inexact books about their country. And what about the writers of proven talent who, without going into exile, wrote works that do not reflect the reality of their country? José María Eguren did not need to leave Peru to describe a world populated by

Nordic fairies and mysteries (like the Bolivian Jaime Freyres, and Julián del Casal who, while living in Cuba, wrote mainly about France and Japan). They did not go into exile physically, but their literature can be called 'exile' literature for the same reason as the literature of the exiled Garcilaso or Vallejo can be called literature 'rooted in a context'.

The only thing we've proved is that nothing can be proved in this area and that, therefore, in literary terms exile is not a problem in itself. It is an individual problem which takes on different characteristics with each writer and has different results. Physical contact with one's own rational reality means nothing from the point of view of the work; it determines neither a writer's themes, nor his imagination nor the vitality of his language. Exactly the same is true of exile. Physical absence from a country is sometimes translated into works that accurately reflect that reality and at other times into works that distort reality. Whether or not a work is an evasion or a reflection of reality, just as whether or not it is good, has nothing to do with the geographical location of its author.

That still leaves the moral criticism that some level at the writer who goes into exile. Surely the writers who desert their country show an indifference towards their own kind, a lack of solidarity with the dramas and people of that country? The question contains a confused and contemptuous idea of literature. A writer has no better way of serving his country than by writing with as much discipline and honesty as he can. A writer shows his discipline and honesty by placing his vocation above everything else and by organizing his life around his creative work. Literature is his first loyalty, his first responsibility, his primordial obligation. If he writes better in his country, he must stay there; if he writes better in exile, he must leave. It is possible that his absence might deprive his society of someone who might have been an effective journalist, teacher or cultural promoter, but it is equally possible that the journalist, teacher or cultural promoter is depriving society of a writer. It is not a question of knowing which is more important, more useful; a vocation (especially a writer's) cannot be decided in any authentic way by commercial, historical, social or moral criteria. It is possible that a young man who abandons literature to dedicate himself to teaching or fighting the revolution is ethically and socially more worthy of recognition than the other, the egotist, who only thinks about writing. But from the point of view of literature, a generous person is by no means exemplary or, in any event, he sets a bad example because his nobility and heroism are also a betrayal. Those who demand that a writer behave in a certain way (something that they do not demand, for example, of a doctor or an architect) are in effect expressing an essential doubt about the usefulness of his vocation. They judge the writer by his customs, his opinions or the place where he lives and not by the only thing by which he can be judged: his books. They tend to value these books according to the life the author leads and it should be the other way round. Deep down, they do not believe that literature can be useful and they hide their scepticism by keeping a suspicious (aesthetic, moral or political) watch on the writer's life. The only way to clear up these doubts would be by demonstrating that literature is worth something. The problem remains unresolved, however, since the usefulness of literature, although self-evident, is also unverifiable in practical terms.

London, January 1968

# Socialism and the Tanks

The military intervention in Czechoslovakia by the Soviet Union and its four allies in the Warsaw Pact is, purely and simply, an imperialist aggression which is a dishonour to the country of Lenin, a political blunder of dizzying proportions and an irreparable setback for the cause of socialism in the world. Its most obvious antecedent is not so much Hungary as the Dominican Republic. The sending of Soviet tanks into Prague to suppress a movement of socialist democratization is as much to be condemned as the despatching of American marines to Santo Domingo to stamp out by violence a popular uprising against a military dictatorship and an unjust social system.

The violation of the sovereignty of the Czech people by the USSR has been less bloody but no less immoral than that committed against the people of Santo Domingo. In both cases, the justifications used by Washington and Moscow – the famous argument that the interventions had been requested by the victims themselves and were intended to save 'democracy' or 'socialism' threatened by an outside power – reveal the same cynical contempt for the truth. The truth, in both cases, is that a great power, protected by the right of military superiority, has decided to trample over a small nation because the political direction that this nation has taken does not fit within its strategic global interests, and then it hides the intervention behind an ideological smoke-screen. What is at stake in the dramatic events that Czechoslovakia is living through today is not the struggle between capitalism and communism, but rather the destiny of those countries that make up the Third World. A terrible future seems to be darkening their historical horizon: to have to live perpetually at the mercy of the two great Colossuses, alienated between two forms of colonial servitude, never really to be independent and free.

What was threatened in Czechoslovakia was not 'socialism', nor was 'freedom' threatened in the Dominican Republic. What was in jeopardy in the Dominican Republic when the military intervention took place was the power of the large landowners, the plunder of the country's wealth by foreign companies and the greed of the local caste system.

What was threatened in Czechoslovakia was a robot socialism, remote-controlled by Moscow, press censorship, police abuse, the lack of internal criticism and a cancerous bureaucracy which had suffocated individual initiatives and allowed immorality to proliferate in its shadow. When they inform Dubček, Svoboda and Cernik that the presence of occupying troops, the destruction of freedom of expression and the banning of political organizations are the conditions of their survival, the Soviet leaders are not thinking of socialism but of preventing the development of any popular internal movement in East Germany, Bulgaria or the USSR itself that might seek to give socialism back a human face.

When the events in Hungary took place, divisions, uncertainty and confusion were still possible: it was the high point of the Cold War, the activities of counter-revolutionary forces could not be discounted and the Hungarian people seemed divided. None of this justified military intervention, but it was at least possible to have doubts, to think that this was a mistake that would later be corrected as far as it was possible. In the case of Czechoslovakia there can be no doubt, because all the elements with which we can judge the situation are crystal clear and none of them excuses the USSR, all of them instead accuse her.

Ten days after the intervention, Moscow cannot offer a shred of evidence to the world to show that the Dubček regime was endangering internal security or was about to leave the socialist camp to become part of the capitalist world. No factory had been seized from the workers, no international consortium had been undermining the socialist economy, the half a million occupying troops have not been able to capture one single 'agent of German militarism'. Furthermore, not even the most conservative elements of the Communist Party have dared to play the role of quislings and no one has ventured to claim authorship of this imaginary manifesto which purportedly asked the countries of the Warsaw Pact to carry out the invasion. Rather, the foreign occupation has shown the world the extraordinary unity of the Czech people behind their leaders, and their dignity and serenity in the face of the humiliation that has been inflicted on them. Whatever the outcome of this tragedy, and even if the outcome is the one that political morality and common sense dictate – the withdrawal of the occupying forces, to allow the Czech people the freedom to direct their socialism along whatever path they might choose, compensation for the damages sustained – one does not need to be a fortune-teller to know that the wound inflicted so disloyally by the USSR on Czechoslovakia will take a long time to heal and that, paradoxically, this action will only serve to sharpen and to strengthen precisely what it intended to snuff out: the Czech desire for national independence and freedom.

From an international point of view, the attitude of the USSR has gravely damaged the forces of the left. The right, of course, has already begun to use the Czech drama in its favour and the most immediate consequences will doubtless be the electoral victory of Nixon and the postponement of an end to the Vietnam war. Another equally serious consequence of the military intervention is that it has sharpened the international divisions within socialism. Almost all the European Communist parties have condemned the invasion in the strongest terms. Here, in London, the Labour Party tried to make electoral capital out of what had happened and called a protest meeting in Hyde Park. The Labour leaders on the platform had to speak above the jeers of ten thousand people who accused them of being hypocrites: how could one condemn the USSR over Czechoslovakia without condemning the US intervention in Vietnam? Those ten thousand demonstrators belonged, in the main, to left-wing organizations and when the meeting in Hyde Park was over, they marched in solidarity with the Czech people past the Russian Embassy shouting 'Dubček!', 'Svoboda!' and 'Russians go home!' and were addressed by the same student and trade union leaders who organize peace in Vietnam demonstrations. In France, the National Union of Students, which led the May revolution, was the first to encourage its members to go out on to the streets to protest against the military intervention in Czechoslovakia. One of the few positive things to have emerged from this tragic event has been the confirmation that these left-wing organizations do not operate in the same Manichaean ways as in former years, that the support for socialism does not now mean unconditional support for Soviet policy, and that the progressive forces are now more independent and more lucid.

In these circumstances, what should we make of Fidel's words justifying the military intervention? He is a leader who, until now, has shown himself to be very attentive to the problems of national autonomy and has exhaustively supported the rights of small nations to conduct their own policies without interference from great powers. How can he now support a military invasion aimed at stamping out the independence of a country which, like Cuba, was only asking to be allowed to organize its own society according to its own convictions? It is distressing to see Fidel reacting in the same conditioned and reflex way as the mediocre leaders of the Latin American Communist parties who rushed to justify the Soviet intervention. Doesn't the Cuban supreme commander understand that if he allows the USSR the right to decide the type of socialism suitable for other countries and to import its choice by force, then what has happened in Prague could happen tomorrow in Havana?

To many sincere friends of the Cuban revolution, the words of Fidel have seemed to us as incomprehensible and as unjust as the noise of the tanks entering Prague.

London, August 1968

# A Visit to Karl Marx

The street is very short and one can walk up and down it in ten minutes. It is no more than four hundred yards long and runs between Oxford Street and Shaftesbury Avenue. It seems like any other street in Soho, the frivolous night-life district of London: full of restaurants, clubs, bars, food shops, narrow side streets, stands selling newspapers, postcards and erotic books, brothels where rudimentary cards appear on the doors at night advertising 'rooms by the hour' and 'artistic models', small clubs where profligate and bored passers-by can see a striptease act or pornographic film for ten shillings. Exotic names flash in the windows and on the illuminated signs, advertising food from Hungary, Italy and Ceylon; the bars to some extent imitate the cafés of Saint-Germain-des-Prés and one of them is called Les Enfants Terribles. Dean Street does not have that popular, nineteenth-century, picaresque feel that other Soho streets have, with their fruit, flower and vegetable stalls, their strong smells and their noisy, semi-domestic, semi-noctambular clientele. There is no market in Dean Street; its pleasures are manufactured and industrial.

Although only one or two buildings in Dean Street seem recent and all the other houses — three or four storeys high, packed tightly together, their bricks blackened by the grime of time — could easily be one hundred years old, the physical appearance of the street must have changed a great deal in these one hundred years, since it no longer seems squalid or poor. It is difficult to imagine that in 1853 (according to a police report of the time), Dean Street was 'the worst, the cheapest, street in London', and it is also difficult to guess how it must have looked in 1850, when the Marx family, trapped by poverty, came to live here, in two inhospitable rooms, where they would spend the most difficult and, in some ways, the most important years of their lives. No plaque marks the house they lived in and because the street numbering that appears in the biographies is the original and has since been changed, inquisitive people or fetishists have to go to the Marx Memorial Library to locate in this quiet house flanked by side streets, the two small windows of the room that served as the living room/dining room/study/bedroom for Marx's children (the inner room was the parent's bedroom).

Winter has begun and if one stays too long outside, one's nose and ears freeze and the hands seize up, so I've plunged into a small, smoky, crowded bar where they don't serve coffee. I've had to ask for a glass of warm British beer, but then again I'm lucky because I've found a seat free next to the radiator, from where I can see, in front of me, the two small windows. What the hell am I doing in Dean Street? I haven't brought with me the two books I've been reading just now, which is a pity, since I would have liked to have taken another look at the pages which refer to the life that Marx led in Dean Street, to rekindle my surprise and fascinated admiration. The biography by Franz Mehring has apparently been superseded by contemporary historians and the essay by Edmund Wilson on the origins of socialism is doubtless debatable from many points of view, but the portrait that both books paint of that crucial period in Marx's life, the six splendid and terrible years in Dean Street, could hardly be bettered. Both give an image of epic proportions, a further demonstration of the victory of the rebel hero in his solitary battle against society or against evil, which appears in so many classic poems and narratives. I feel frustrated; I've come here quickly, anxiously, to find some remnants, some trace of that memorable battle, only to discover that the place where it was fought is an artificial area, an elegant place where the local bourgeoisie and tourists with money come to enjoy exotic food, to drink and to buy sex. It is disturbing, paradoxical, that this district, this street in which, in a certain way, the most angry and effective opponent of the bourgeoisie was born, is now the most affected and decadent pleasure spot for the bourgeoisie in London. In Marx's day, without doubt, a bourgeois never set foot in Dean Street.

All manner of misfortunes had befallen the Marx family in the months that preceded their move to London. Expelled from Germany, they had taken refuge in a working-class suburb in Brussels and one day, Marx was captured by the police and exiled to France. When she went to look for him, Jenny Marx was detained in the street by the gendarmes, accused of vagrancy, locked up in a cell and forced to share a bed with a prostitute. In Paris, despite living under a false name, the Marx family was discovered by the police and sent to England. But they still had some money left and for the first few months in London, they lived in some comfort, renting a furnished flat in Camberwell. In 1850, the money was spent and the landlord evicted them. It was then that they moved here and things got very much worse. Since they could not pay their food bills in local shops, all the family belongings – including the beds and the children's toys – were impounded and sold. The youngest male child, who was a few months old and had been born in the middle of these persecutions and exiles, fell ill; he could not be looked after or fed properly and died. For many months, the only food the Marx family ate was bread and potatoes, and in the first winter, the parents and children caught flu. The youngest girl had no resistance to it and died soon after. Almost at the same time, there was an epidemic of cholera in Soho and most of the residents left the neighbourhood, but the Marxes had to stay through lack of money. The following year, their few remaining items were impounded, including their clothes (the children's shoes and Marx's overcoat were sold). One night, the police came to the house and Marx was locked up, accused of theft: a neighbour in Dean Street had supposed that the glass ornament that sparkled in one of the Marxes' rooms (the only family memento that Jenny had tried to preserve) was stolen. In 1855, the surviving male child also died and, among all the innumerable blows suffered in those six years, this seems to have been the one that affected Marx most deeply. 'I have suffered all manner of adversity,' he wrote to Engels, 'but now, for the first time, I know what misfortune means.' It was when the Marxes had been reduced – here, in Dean Street – to the most extreme poverty that Engels decided, heroically, to return to Manchester, to the hated family industrial centre, so that he could support his friend economically. He agreed to write, under Marx's name, the articles that Marx sent to New York, to *The New York Times* and the *New York Tribune*, so that these commitments, that kept the family fed, would not distract Marx from his study of economics. It was here, in Dean Street, that the policeman came to investigate Marx's living conditions and his report, written in 1853, is a precious document:

There is not one clean or decent piece of furniture in either room, but everything is broken, tattered and torn, with a thick dust over everything . . . manuscripts, books and newspapers, besides the children's toys, bits and pieces from his wife's sewing basket, and cups with broken rims, dirty spoons, knives, forks, lamps, an ink-pot, tumbler, some Dutch clay pipes, tobacco ash, all in a pile. . . . On entering Marx's room, smoke and tobacco fumes make your eyes water to such an extent that . . . you seem to be groping about in a cavern . . . sitting down is quite a dangerous business. Here is a chair with only three legs, there another, which happens to be whole, on which the children are playing at cooking.

And the same scrupulous policeman informs us that, 'As a husband and father, in spite of his restless and wild character [Marx] is the gentlest and mildest of men.'

Here in Dean Street, Marx's political activity diminished considerably, but his intellectual and creative work acquired superhuman force and virulence. Here, despite the hardships, the family tragedies and illnesses, he imposed on himself, and kept implacably to, a timetable of eight hours of daily study in the British Museum. It isn't difficult to imagine his journey each day, leaving at nine in the morning and returning at seven thirty at night, followed by a further three or four hours (which sometimes became five or more) of private study in his room, there, behind the small windows. It was here, in the year of the epidemic, that he completed his admirable essay, *The Class Struggle in France*, and wrote his book, *The 18th Brumaire of Louis Bonaparte*, the following year, while his children, brandishing a whip, played at horse riding, whinnying and snorting around the table. Here he wrote his first books of notes for *Das Capital* and discussed, in long daily letters to his friend Engels, his economic interpretation of history and the situation of the European working classes. Here, in these six years, he learned languages, composed books, devoured whole sections of libraries, wrote hundreds of articles and found the time to invent a story for his children about an imaginary character called Hans Rockle, 'who had a magic shop but always went around without a penny in his pocket'.

How and from where did he summon up the will and sufficient energy to carry out such a lofty and ambitious undertaking in such difficult circumstances? In the book by Edmund Wilson, there is a quotation from Marx that struck me deeply. It is a text that he wrote when he was still a quarrelsome student, terribly sarcastic and brilliant, at a time when he was reading Hegel with passion and sending Jenny ardent romantic poems. 'The writer', he says, 'can make money in order to be able to live and write, but in no circumstances should he live and write in order to make money. In no circumstances should the writer consider his work to be a means. For him, his work is an end in itself; and it is so definitely not a means for him that, if necessary, the writer is prepared to sacrifice his existence for his work. To a certain extent, as the priest does with religion, the writer embraces this principle: "Obey God before men", when dealing with the human beings among whom he is confined by his desires and human needs.'

I have reread this paragraph several times and now, in this bar, which is overrun by young people with long, curly hair, tailored suits, blue and pink shirts, flowery ties and cloaks – what is happening in Puritan London is something that might be termed 'the revenge of Oscar Wilde' – I have it once again very much in mind. Could not Flaubert have signed the same text, without changing a comma? Did not the titanic and painstaking Flaubert, the solitary man from Croisset, set down his definition of the creator and his work in very similar terms?

It has now grown dark in Dean Street and, because it is Saturday, a dense crowd is walking up and down the pavement, slowly and inquisitively, looking at the windows of the exotic restaurants, the pornographic book stands, the disguised brothels and the cinemas and striptease joints. I have stopped in front of the twin windows and immediately three or four passers-by also stop and stare anxiously: what terrible images would they like to see? But the shutters of the house are closed and they move away, disappointed. I also leave and I now no longer think it regrettable that no one has thought to put up a plaque commemorating Marx's stay in Dean Street.

London, November 1966

# Joyce's *Dubliners*

Good literature saturates certain cities, covering them with a patina of mythology and images that are more resistant to the passing of the years than their architecture and history. When I got to know Dublin, in the mid 1960s, I felt betrayed: that lively and friendly city, full of exuberant people who stopped me in the middle of the street to ask me where I was from and invited me for a beer, did not seem much like the city portrayed in the books of Joyce. A friend patiently acted as a guide as we followed the footsteps of Leopold Bloom through those protracted twenty-four hours in *Ulysses*; the names of the streets and many locations and addresses were the same, but yet it lacked the solidity, the squalor and the metaphysical greyness of Dublin in the novel. Had the same city once displayed both these aspects?

Of course, it was never like that. Because although Joyce shared Flaubert's mania for documentation and although he (who was the lack of scruples personified in everything other than writing) took scrupulousness in description to such precise lengths that he would ask in letters from Trieste and Zurich which flowers and which trees could be found on which precise corner, did not describe the city of his fictions: he invented it. And he did so with such art and force of persuasion that the city of fantasy, nostalgia, bitterness and (above all) of words that was his, remains in the memory of his readers with a power far greater in terms of dramatic quality and colour than the ancient city of flesh and blood – or rather of stone and clay – that was its model.

*Dubliners* marks the first phase of that duplication. The overwhelming importance of *Ulysses* and *Finnegans Wake*, literary experiments that revolutionized modern narrative, sometimes causes us to forget that this book of stories, which at least appears to be more traditional and subsidiary (its use of naturalistic realism, even for the date when it was published, 1914, was somewhat archaic), is not a minor work of apprenticeship, but rather the first masterpiece that Joyce wrote. It is an organic work, not a compilation of texts. Read straight through, each story complements and enriches the others and, by the end, the reader has a vision of a compact society which he has explored in its social complexities, in the psychology of the people, its rituals, prejudices, enthusiasms, disputes and even its lewd underside.

Joyce wrote the first story of the book, 'The Sisters', in 1904, when he was twenty-two, at the request of the publisher friend George Russell, who paid him a pound sterling and published the story in the Dublin newspaper *Irish Homestead*. Almost immediately he conceived of the plan to write a series of stories that he would entitle *Dubliners*. They would, as he said to a friend in July of that year, 'betray the soul of that hemiplegia or paralysis which many consider a city.' The betrayal would be more subtle and far-reaching than he could have imagined when he wrote those lines; it would not mean attacking or denigrating the city in which he had been born, but rather removing it from the objective, transitory and circumstantial world of history, to the fictional, atemporal and subjective world of great artistic creation. In September and December of that year, 'Eveline' and 'After the Race' appeared in the same newspaper. Other stories, with the exception of the last, 'The Dead', were written in Trieste, from May to October 1905, when Joyce was scraping a living giving English classes in the Biarritz School, borrowing money from everyone to keep Nora and their recently born son, Giorgio, and to pay for the sporadic bouts of drunkenness which would leave him, literally, in a comatose state.

By then, distance had smoothed some of the rough edges of his youthful feelings against Dublin, lending to his memories a nostalgia which, albeit very contained and diffuse, appears from time to time as an iridescence of landscape or as a soft background music to the dialogues. At that time, he had already decided that Dublin would be the protagonist of the book. In his letters from the period, he states his surprise that the city had been ignored for so long: 'When you remember that Dublin has been a capital for thousands of years, that it is the "second" city of the British Empire, and that it is nearly three times as big as Venice, it seems strange that no artist has given it to the world.' (letter to his brother Stanislaus, 24 September 1905). In the same letter, he indicates that the structure of the book will correspond to the development of a life: stories of childhood, of adolescence, of maturity and, finally, stories of public or collective life.

The final story, the most ambitious and the one that would embody that idea of the 'public life' of the city, 'The Dead', was written somewhat later – in 1906 – to show an aspect of Dublin which, as he remarked to his brother Stanislaus, would not appear in the other stories: 'its ingenuous insularity and its hospitality, the latter "virtue" so far as I can see does not exist elsewhere in Europe' (letter of 25 September 1906). The story is a real tour de force because we leave its pages with the impression of having embraced the collective life of the city and, at the same time, of having glimpsed its most intimate secrets. In its pages, among the varied society that comes to the annual dance of the Misses Morkan, we find on display the great public themes – nationalism, politics, culture, encompassing the local customs and practices in dances, meals, clothes, the rhetoric of the speeches – and also the affinities and disputes that bring people together or keep them apart. But, in an imperceptible way, all that crowd is narrowed down to just one couple, Gabriel Conroy and his wife, Gretta. The story ends by exploring the most buried emotions and feelings of Gabriel, as we share with him the disturbing revelation of the love and death of Michael Furey, a sentimental episode in Gretta's early life. In its perfect blending of the collective and the individual and in the delicate balance that it achieves between the objective and subjective, 'The Dead' already prefigures *Ulysses*.

But despite all the narrative skill that it displays, 'The Dead' is not the best story in the book. I still prefer 'The Boarding House' and 'A Painful Case', and their peerless mastery places them alongside certain texts by Chekhov, Maupassant, Poe and Borges as among the most admirable examples of that genre – so brief and intense, as only poetry can be – which we call the short story.

In fact, all the stories in *Dubliners* reveal the hand of a consummate artist, not the novice writer that Joyce then was. Some, like 'After the Race' and 'Araby', are not stories as such but rather prints or snapshots which capture for eternity some of its inhabitants: the empty frivolity of certain wealthy young people or the awakening of an adolescent to the adult world of love. Others, by contrast, like 'The Boarding House' and 'A Painful Case', condense in a few pages stories that reveal all the psychological complexity of a world and, in particular, the emotional and sexual frustrations of a society that has metabolized its religious restrictions and many prejudices into institutions and customs. However, although the vision of society which the short stories of *Dubliners* displays is most severe – by turn sarcastic, ironic or openly furious – this is a secondary concern of the book. Beyond these documentary and critical aspects, an artistic intention always prevails. What I mean is that the 'realism' of Joyce is closer to Flaubert than to Zola. Ezra Pound, who was wrong in many things, but always right in aesthetic matters, was one of the first to recognize this. When he read, in 1914, the manuscript of the book that had been passed from publisher to publisher for some nine years, without anyone making a commitment to publish it, Pound pronounced that the prose was the best being written at the time in the literature of the English language – comparable only to Conrad and to Henry James – and that what was most notable about it was its 'objectivity'.

This observation could not be more accurate and the definition applies to Joyce's art as a whole. And where this 'objectivity' first appears, organizing the world of the narrative, giving coherence and specific movement to the style, establishing a system of involvement and distance between the reader and the text, is in *Dubliners*. What do we mean by 'objectivity' in art? A convention or an outward appearance which, in principle, presupposes nothing about the success or failure of the work and is, therefore, as legitimate as its opposite: 'subjective' art. A story is 'objective' when it appears to be projected exclusively on to the exterior world, avoiding the intimate, or when the narrator becomes invisible and what is narrated appears in the eyes of the reader as a self-sufficient and impersonal object, not tied or subordinated to anything outside itself, or when both techniques are combined in the same text, as occurs in the stories of Joyce. Objectivity is a technique or, rather, the effect that a narrative technique can produce when it works well, without awkwardness or other flaws that might detract from its effectiveness and make the reader feel that he is the victim of rhetorical manipulation. In order to achieve this magic, Flaubert suffered indescribably for the five years that it took him to write *Madame Bovary*. Joyce, by contrast, who suffered with the titanic effort that *Ulysses* and *Finnegans Wake* demanded of him, wrote these stories quite quickly, with a facility that is astonishing (and demoralizing).

The Dublin of the stories is described as a sovereign world, without ties, thanks to the coldness of the prose which outlines, with mathematical precision, the gaunt streets where ragged children play, the boarding houses of the dingy clerks, the bars where the bohemians get drunk and arm wrestle, and the parks and back streets which are the setting for casual love. Variegated, diverse, human fauna enliven its pages and sometimes certain individuals – mainly children – talk in the first person, recounting some failure or passion, or in other parts, someone, who might be everyone or nobody, narrates with a voice that is so unobtrusive, so discreet, so attached to those beings, objects and situations that it describes, that we constantly forget it, we are too absorbed in what is being narrated to notice that it is being narrated to us.

Is it a seductive, desirable world? Not at all. It is squalid, filled with pettiness, rigidity and repression, over which the Church maintains a tight, intolerable control and where nationalism, however explicable it might appear to us as a reaction against the semi-colonial status of the country, breeds warped cultural values and a certain mental provincialism in some of its inhabitants. But in order to notice all these defects, we have to *leave* the world of the narrative and make an effort to reflect critically on it. Because, when we are immersed in its magic, the squalor could not be more beautiful or the people – however contemptible and wretched – more fascinating. The attraction is not moral, or of a social nature: it is aesthetic. And the fact that we can make this distinction is, precisely, a feat of Joyce's genius. He is one of a very small number of contemporary authors who have been able to endow the middle class – an unheroic class *par excellence* – with an heroic aura and with an outstanding artistic personality; in this, he is once more following the example of Flaubert. Both accomplished this very difficult feat: the artistic dignification of ordinary life. Through the sensibility with which it is recreated and through the cunning with which the stories are told us, the everyday existence of the Dublin *petit bourgeois* takes on, in the book, the dimensions of a very rich adventure, of a redoubtable human experience.

Joyce's 'naturalism', unlike Zola's, is not social; its only intention is aesthetic. This caused certain English critics to accuse *Dubliners* of being 'cynical' when it first appeared. Since they were used to a realist technique which adorned its stories with reforming intentions and edifying sentiments, they were disturbed by these fictions which did seem to have a testimonial and historical basis and yet did not make explicit any moral condemnation of the iniquities and injustices that they described. Joyce – who called himself a socialist when he wrote these stories – was not interested in any of this, at least not when he sat down to write: he did not want to give information or opinions on a specific reality, but rather recreate this reality, reinvent it, endowing a purely artistic existence with the dignity of a beautiful object.

And that is what characterizes and differentiates the Dublin of Joyce from the other, the fleeting, the real, Dublin: a society in a state of ferment, seething with dramas, dreams and problems which has been metamorphosed into a beautiful mural of the most refined forms, colours, tastes and music, into a great verbal symphony in which nothing is out of tune, where the shortest pause or note contributes to the perfect harmony of the whole. The two cities are similar, but this similarity is a subtle and prolonged deception, for although the streets bear the same names, as do the bars, the shops and the boarding houses, and although Richard Ellmann, in his admirable biography, has been able to identify almost all the real models for the characters in the stories, the distance between the two is infinite, because their essences are different. The real city lacks that perfection which only the artistic illusion of life – never life itself – can achieve. The ceaseless, dizzying clamour of real life, life in the making, can never achieve that finished, spherical form. The Dublin of the stories has been purged of imperfections or ugliness or, and this amounts to the same thing, they have been transformed, by the magic wand of style, into aesthetic qualities. It has been changed into pure form, into a reality whose essence is made up of that impalpable, evanescent matter which is the word; into something that is sensations and associations, fantasy and dream, rather than history and sociology. To say, as some critics have, that the city of *Dubliners* lacks a 'soul' is a tolerable formulation as long as no criticism is implied. The soul of the city where the boys of 'An Encounter' avoid the attentions of a homosexual, where the little shop-girl Eveline wavers between fleeing to Buenos Aires or remaining enslaved to her father and where Little Chandler broods on his melancholy as a frustrated poet, is all on the surface. It is that most elegant, sensory, outward appearance which imposes an arbitrary grandeur on the misfortunes of the city's humble inhabitants. Life, in these fictions, is not the deep, unpredictable force which animates the real world, causing its intense precariousness, its unstable swings of fortune, but rather a sort of glacial brilliance, a still flash, with which the objects and characters have been suffused by means of verbal conjuring.

And there is no better way to illustrate this point than to stop and contemplate, with the calm and insistence that a difficult painting demands, those scenes in *Dubliners* which seem to pay homage to a Romantic aesthetic of sentimental convulsions and narrative cruelty. The sudden decision of Eveline, for example, not to run away with her lover, or the beating that the drunken Farrington inflicts on his son Tom in 'Counterparts', as a way of taking his frustrations out on someone, or the grief of Gabriel Conroy, at the end of 'The Dead', when he discovers the youthful passion of the consumptive Michael Furey for his wife Gretta. These are episodes which in any Romantic tale would lead to rhetorical effusions and an emotional and mournful overload. Here the prose has chilled them, giving them a plastic quality and stripping them of any trace of self-pity or emotional blackmail towards the reader. Whatever confusion or delirium these scenes might contain has disappeared and, through the workings of the prose, has become clear, pure and exact. And it is precisely that coldness enveloping these excessive episodes that excites the sensibility of the reader. Challenged by the divine indifference of the narrator, the reader reacts, enters the story emotionally and is moved by it.

It is true that Joyce developed first in *Ulysses* and then in *Finnegans Wake* (although this novel takes his experimental audacity to unreadable lengths) the skill and talent that he had shown earlier in *Portrait of the Artist as a Young Man* and in *Dubliners*. But the stories of his first attempt at narrative already express what those masterpieces would later confirm in abundant measure: the supreme ability of a writer, through use of detailed memories of the small world of his birth and through his extraordinary linguistic facility, to create a world of his own. Both beautiful and unreal, it is a world capable of persuading us of a truth and an authenticity which are nothing more than the result of intellectual juggling, of rhetorical fireworks, a world that, through the act of reading, enriches our own, showing us some of its keys and helping us to understand it better. Above all, it makes our lives more complete, adding something which, on their own, they could never have or never experience.

London, 23 June 1987

# The Other Oscar

We were having breakfast in the small kitchen of the Earls Court house when we saw, peeping out from under the sideboard, the unmistakable face of a mouse. I ran to complain to the owner of the house. Mrs Spence's eyes lit up. 'Ah! Oscar!' And she insisted that I should leave out for the morning visitor the cheese with holes in that the mouse loved; that's what her children used to do. It took me a great deal of effort to make her understand that we did not find Oscar's presence amusing, that we hated even the platonic idea of a mouse. Mrs Spence bid me goodbye with the observation that when he realized that he was so unloved, Oscar would probably move off and find a more welcoming house.

A few days later, getting back from the cinema and turning on the kitchen light, we saw, jumping happily out of a basket of fruit on to the floor, Oscar, Oscar's father, his mother, and one of his little brothers. Dawn broke to find me mounting guard outside Mrs Spence's door. This time the owner yielded and gave me some instructions. I had to report the invasion to an office in Kensington Town Hall which answered to the appropriate name of 'The Rodent Department'. I explained my problem over the telephone. An impassive voice asked me the address and told me to wait.

The gentleman who visited us the following afternoon seemed an eccentric out of an English short story. He was tall and bony, dressed in a black coat, striped trousers and a bowler hat. He carried a suitcase that seemed like a sarcophagus. He came in, took off his hat and coat and we discovered that he had false cuffs which were attached to his arm by a small sleeve with ties, like a cashier. He subjected me to a pragmatic interrogation. Where had they first appeared? How many were there? What size and colour were they? Were they noisy in the night? He put down my replies in a notebook that was also spectral, with a pencil that was lost in his fingers.

When he completed the information, he began to work. The suitcase, when opened, was an artistic spectacle, immediately reminiscent of Joseph Cornell. There were countless bottles full of different coloured powders, fanatically ordered, and a stack of small cardboard plates. On his hands and knees, moving around the kitchen like a duck, the man from the Rodent Department embarked on a meticulous operation which took him a long time. He poured different powders on to the cardboard plates and smoothed them carefully with a brush before placing them in strategic places that he had marked in a plan of the kitchen sketched in his notebook. He stipulated that nobody should move the plates from their place or disturb the powder. He said that some of them were poisoned and the rest were just sand, which increased our curiosity. Before leaving, he murmured that it would be better to keep the kitchen closed for a time.

He came back a week later and from then on he returned every week, with astral punctuality, for a year. We did not manage to become friends because he was not susceptible to such weaknesses and we did not even speak very much. As soon as he arrived, I interrupted my own work to watch his, and the phlegmatic way he went about it. I very soon understood the function of the inoffensive white sand. It was not to choke the mice or disconcert them, but to keep a record of their deposits. The gentleman picked up with metal tweezers the diminutive black pellets that Oscar and his friends evacuated on to the plates and placed them in tubes which departed with him in the funereal suitcase. On the subject of the poisons, every week he examined the tell-tale traces, time and again he passed his circumspect gaze over the furrows, channels, footprints and hollows that the intruders had left. I learned that the variety of colours had to do with the different doses of the lethal composition, because mice generate antibodies that immunize them so quickly that the gentleman, with those weekly changes of powder, tried to be swifter and more astute than the metabolism of Oscar and his kind.

He never explained anything to me and when, overwhelmed by curiosity, I asked a question, he had a perfect strategy for demoralizing me even more: he made out that he did not understand my English. What were the results from the analysis of the droppings? Yes, yes, it is sure to rain, he'd reply. What were his impressions at this stage of the campaign? With all those pounds of powder in their system, would the species be deteriorating, disappearing? Yes, Chelsea Football Club were the champions.

Apart from the stomach residues, he also took away with him the fresh bodies that he found. He picked them up with a glove, observed them clinically for a moment, without hate or love, buried them in little plastic bags and, into the suitcase! Many died, it's true, but our family had the contradictory and fantastic impression that at the same time as they exterminated the mice, the multicoloured powders reproduced them. Life was becoming rather difficult. True, they had never crossed the boundaries of the kitchen, but to have the kitchen closed meant cooking on a primus, eating in the bedroom and turning the bathroom into a washing-up area. It was impossible not to hate them, they were so obstinate, but seeing them die ended up giving us a bad conscience. They would suddenly appear, bloated by their homicidal banquet, dragging themselves in slow motion across to our feet where they would remain without moving, breathing in very weak gasps, until they died with a bubble of froth on their mouths. To throw them in the rubbish bin became a horrible task, causing nightmares and nausea. While I wrote, gave classes at the university, read or talked to people, I could think of nothing but them and the gentleman with the bowler hat.

There were periods when the war seemed to be won: seven, fourteen days without a single victim. We became excited, drank toasts. The man from the Rodent Department continued, undaunted, placing plates and powder in the corners of the kitchen and taking notes in his book. And he knew best because one morning we would see once again the little black pellets on the sand and the dust on the floor tiles. I beleaguered him so often, asking why, instead of adopting this almost infinite method, he did not fumigate the house, that one day in that terrible year he explained to me: as in the nineteenth century, a fumigated house had to remain in quarantine for I don't know how long. Therefore we had no alternative but to wait for him to defeat them in his own way.

I could not wait. I found work outside London, outside England. I left, putting between them and us countries, oceans, continents. But I liked London so much, it was a city where people and things always surprised me, that two years later I returned. Miraculously, the little house in Earls Court, in Kangaroo Valley, was once again vacant. We rented it once more. On the night we moved in, we joked with friends from the neighbourhood that only They were missing for everything to be as it was before. When our friends left and we began to unpack, a slight feeling of foreboding made us both look towards the bedroom door at the same time. Just like the end of Truman Capote's short story, 'Myriam', there on the red carpet, with scarcely half his head peeping into the room, small, rubicund, bidding us welcome, forecasting new tortures for us, was Oscar.

Lima, March 1979

# Doris Lessing: *The Golden Notebook*

When I came to London, in 1966, *The Golden Notebook* had already been published for four years, but people still spoke about it a great deal. It was the object of passionate recrimination and praise and both its admirers and its detractors agreed that the novel symbolized an age. The feminists had adopted it as a manual and in certain literary circles it was considered the most daring experiment in novelistic form since Malcolm Lowry's *Under the Volcano*. A woman colleague at Queen Mary College recommended it to me: 'Read it,' she said, 'if you want to know what the feminine condition is.' I read it and on that first reading I was quite sceptical. I commented to my colleague that Doris Lessing's novel reminded me of Simone de Beauvoir's *The Mandarins* and she became angry. Rereading it, I think that she was right and that I was on the wrong track. *The Golden Notebook* is a better book than *The Mandarins*, it is less pretentious and it treats the same themes with greater depth as well as exploring other themes that do not appear in the French novel. Both are, it's true, a novelistic documentary of postwar Europe.

*The Golden Notebook* has many merits. It is an ambitious novel which sets out to explore such diverse areas as psychoanalysis and Stalinism, the relationship between fiction and life, sexual experience, neurosis and modern culture, the war between the sexes, women's liberation, colonialism and racism.

I do not think that in modern English literature there is a more 'committed' novel in the Sartrean definition of the term. That is, one more rooted in the debates, myths and violence of its time; more aggressively critical of the rites and values of society and also more compelled to participate, through its art, in collective struggles, in history.

The intellectualism of its first few pages is deceptive. It makes us initially nervous that we are dealing with one of those postwar Sartrean novels which now slip out of our fingers through boredom. But very soon, as we begin to enter the confusing game of mirrors which is set up in the book between the (apparently) objective story — 'Free Women' — and the different coloured notebooks, we realize that this rationality has feet of clay; it is a harmonious device that hides a chaotic landscape. And, gradually, the reflexive lucidity of the narrator and the character Anna Wulf (we will discover that both might be the same person) begins to splinter and eventually dissolves into madness, in which the protagonist takes refuge — at least according to her literary testimony — after losing her brave but useless fight against the different forms of alienation that threaten women in modern industrial society.

I do not know why this novel became a feminist bible. Read from that standpoint, its conclusions are so pessimistic that they bring one out in goose bumps. Both Anna and Molly, the two 'free women', fail catastrophically in their attempt to achieve total emancipation from the psychological and social servitudes of femininity. Molly's capitulation is pathetic because she opts for a bourgeois marriage for the most bourgeois of reasons: a quest for security. And Anna is walled up in a mental world in which the exploration of madness (the golden notebook) is more than a dangerous game: it reflects the frustration of her attempt to have a fulfilled life. The independence and freedom that they both enjoy do not protect either of the two friends against emotional collapse, emptiness and suffering. Nor do they gain the intellectual maturity that would allow them to overcome their failures by establishing an ironic distance from their own lives. Anna, who wrote a successful novel as a young woman, now suffers — at forty — from artistic sterility and she assures all her lovers that she will never again pick up a pen (although that might be a lie, as we discover at the end).

After their respective divorces, Molly and Anna became free of the family, that great *bête noire* for certain feminists, who argue that this institution always reduces women to passive and inferior roles. They both have lovers at will but these relationships, above all in Anna's case, are unusually bitter: they leave her wounded, with an increasing feeling of emotional deterioration. Furthermore, one has the impression that both Anna and her alter ego in the diaries ('She') hope instinctively that each one of these sexual adventures will become a permanent relationship, a 'marriage'. Both seem incapable of making sex a mere diversion, a physical pleasure with no involvement of the heart. In the novel this ability remains exclusively the domain of men, who always come, fornicate and go.

In reality, *The Golden Notebook* does not pretend to be an edifying book or an antidote to the alienation of women in contemporary society. It is a novel about the lost illusions of an intellectual class which, from the war up until the mid 1950s, dreamed of transforming society according to the guidelines laid down by Marx, and of changing life, as Rimbaud had argued. They ended up realizing, however, that, in the long term, all their efforts – naive in some cases, heroic in others – had not amounted to much. Because history, which kept on moving throughout these years, did so in directions that were very different from what idealistic intellectuals and dreamers had hoped for. Although the novel is related from the perspective of a woman, it is not the feminine condition in abstract which appears as a central theme of the book, but rather the failure of utopia experienced by an intellectual, who is *also* a woman.

From this perspective, *The Golden Notebook* is a rigorous autopsy of the political and cultural alienation of the avant-garde European intelligentsia. With this book, Doris Lessing was ahead of her time because it would take until the 1970s for progressive thinkers in the rest of Europe to dare to criticize their own ideological mystifications and the revolutionary power of literature.

2

The fragmentary nature of the book is not gratuitous. Nor is its kaleidoscopic structure, in which stories form and de-form each other. This structure corresponds to the tangled emotional and social reality as it is lived and analysed by the protagonist, Anna, herself.

In theory, the novel is divided as follows: an objective story – 'Free Women' – which consists of five sections and is interspersed with the secret notebooks that Anna writes. They are in five different colours and, also in theory, each of them contains material of a different sort. In the black, everything concerning Anna as a writer appears; in the red, her political experiences; in the yellow, Anna invents stories based on her own life and the blue purports to be a diary. The golden notebook at the end should be the synthesis of the others, a document which will put together, in a vision of unity and coherence, the Anna who has been torn apart in the other notebooks.

This organization is undermined in practice. Anna cannot maintain the boundaries that she has fixed for each notebook and the reader discovers that inventions often appear in the diary, that politics is a topic of conversation throughout and that Anna's craft, literature, permeates the political notebook. All this shows in a very graphic way, at the level of form, what Anna discovers in the course of the novel: that life cannot be contained in an exclusively rational scheme, be it in a political doctrine like Marxism, in a therapy that purports to have an overall philosophy, like psychoanalysis, or in the symmetries of the structure of a novel. The rational and the irrational are bound up in an inseparable reality, ensuring that human life is fundamentally unpredictable. The significant incongruities in the novel's construction revealed in Anna's notebooks are not the only surprises in store for the reader of *The Golden Notebook*. The greatest surprise is the magical moment at the end when the reader realizes – through a remark made to Anna by the American Saul Green, in a page of her diary – that 'Free Women', a story that had seemed autonomous until then, written by an omniscient narrator, could in fact be the novel that Anna would write *after* completing the final diary, that it is the book with which she would finally break through the psychological block that had caused her to waste so many years as a writer.

It is one small turn of the screw, which leaves one more ambiguity floating in the mind of the reader, in this book which is so full of enigmas. It is important to emphasize the baroque nature of the structure to show how, in this 'committed' novel, the richly inventive form is on a par with the complexity of the content.

## 3

Yet to focus too much on the subtleties of the form would be to misrepresent *The Golden Notebook*, whose main aim is not artistic experimentation, but rather the discussion of certain moral, political and cultural issues that can be summed up in the question: what could progressive intellectuals do between the Second World War and the end of the fifties to improve the world and themselves?

Anna, who spent the war years in Southern Rhodesia, was an activist in a small Marxist group made up of Royal Air Force pilots, all of whom were white. Theirs was an unreal commitment, full of good intentions but with nothing to show for them, which left everyone, at the end of frenetic drinking bouts in the country hotel of Mashopi, with a bad taste in the mouth, the sense of acting out a farce. But Anna becomes aware of the racism that pervades the whole of life in that colony and of the ignominious conditions in which the natives live — all of this the work of a country which, paradoxically, was fighting against Nazi totalitarianism in those years in the name of freedom.

In England after the war, Anna writes a novel based on her African experiences: *The Frontiers of War.* From the summary of the book contained in her diaries — the love of an Englishman for a black woman — it appears to be a severe critique of colonialism. But the great commercial success that it achieves defuses the book politically. It becomes an object of consumption, just for the entertainment of a public which does not associate literature with 'problems' of any sort. Perhaps this is why Anna has stopped writing. Perhaps this is why she rejects every plan to make a screen adaptation, since she sees that the producers are always trying to adulterate the book, to make it more accessible to a public alienated by conformity.

Her desire to escape in some way from the dead hand of British life and culture leads Anna to enrol in the Communist party, where she remains as an activist for several years. She does this without many illusions, conscious of what is happening in the USSR — the great crimes of Stalin are already in the public domain — with the vague hope that things might change through 'fighting from within'. This is another of her painful failures: to discover that the ideological dogmatism and vertical structure of the party are impermeable to change and capable of 'absorbing all contradictions'. Neither the social revolution nor the great moral change that she seeks will come from that quarter.

Giving up collective ideals, Anna tries to organize her intellectual life in accordance with certain principles and norms which are authentically moral and nonconformist. She tries to overcome her crisis with the help of psychoanalysis (another utopia of the age, almost as exciting for intellectuals as revolution). What she discovers, however, through the quiet advice of her psychoanalyst — the enchanting Mother Sugar, who is the most sympathetic character in the book, even though she only appears tangentially — is that therapy is pushing her relentlessly towards what she had been attempting to escape: 'normality', a life based on the customs and values of the establishment.

Her private life, like her public life, is a series of failures. With the exception of a very brief but intense relationship with Paul in Africa —

while she was Willi's lover – Anna has never known a great love. She had a husband fleetingly, whom she did not love, and a daughter, Janet, by him. After that, numerous lovers who sometimes gave her pleasure for a time, without ever making her happy. Perhaps the greatest failure of all is Anna's attempt to organize her daughter's future. Following an obscure instinct for self-defence, the girl tries to be different from her mother and wants, at all costs, to become part of that alienated, prejudiced, conformist society that Anna has been trying to get away from. Through her own wishes, Janet goes to that bastion of British class society – a public boarding school for girls – and the reader imagines that Janet might well end up as a beautiful lady, indifferent and neurotic.

Is it surprising that, with this build-up of frustrations, Anna should have a bitter and pessimistic view of the world? One of the criticisms made of the novel is that the male characters are all repulsive or contemptible. But are the women any better? Not even Anna, the character we know most intimately, with whom we might feel the greatest affinity, manages to seduce us. Her life reveals an excessive, self-imposed sterility, due to her debatable ideological principles, and an inability to adapt which, however admirable this might be as an artistic image – the hero or heroine opposed to the world always makes our hearts flutter – is also a guarantee of individual unhappiness and social ineffectiveness. Although she has fought so insistently against convention, she can also succumb to certain stereotypes, such as when she passes judgement on men in the United States or mythifies, to an unrecognizable degree, the guerrilla fighters in the Third World.

But although it is a book without heroes or heroines, *The Golden Notebook* lives in the memory as only successful novels can. Dozens, hundreds of fictions from the 1950s and 1960s tried to capture the spirit of the age, with its great illusions, its terrible failures and the profound historical transformations that also came about, though not always in the ways that the lovers of the apocalypse might have wished. In *The Golden Notebook*, Doris Lessing succeeded in doing so. It is not her fault if the spectacle is not agreeable or stimulating.

London, November 1988

# Letter to Haydée Santamaría

Compañera Haydée Santamaría
Director, *Casa de las Américas*
Havana
Cuba

Barcelona, 5 April 1971

Dear Compañera

I am sending you my resignation from the Committee of the journal *Casa de las Américas*, to which I have belonged since 1965, and also my decision not to travel to Cuba in January to give a course, as I promised you on my last visit to Havana. You will understand that this is the only course of action open to me after Fidel's speech upbraiding 'Latin American writers who live in Europe', to whom he has forbidden entry to Cuba 'for an indefinite and infinite period of time'. Was he so irritated by our letter asking him to clarify the situation of Heberto Padilla? How times have changed. I remember very clearly that night we spent with him four years ago when he listened willingly to the observations and the criticisms which a group of 'foreign intellectuals', that he now calls 'swine', made to him.

In any event, I had decided to resign from the Committee and not give the course when I read Heberto Padilla's confession and the bulletins of Prensa Latina on the meeting of UNEAC in which the Compañeros Belkis Cuza Malé, Pablo Armando Fernández, Manuel Díaz Martínez and César López made their self-criticism. I know all of them sufficiently well to realize that this unfortunate spectacle was not spontaneous but had been prefabricated like the Stalinist trials in the 1930s. To force comrades, with methods repugnant to human dignity, to accuse themselves of imaginary betrayals and sign letters in which even the syntax seems to be that of the police, is the negation of everything that made me embrace, from the first day, the cause of the Cuban revolution: its decision to fight for justice without losing respect for individuals. This is not the example of socialism that I want my country to follow.

I know that this letter might be greeted with invective – but it will be no worse than what I have received from reactionary elements for having defended Cuba.

Yours sincerely,

Mario Vargas Llosa

# Albert Camus and the Morality of Limits

Twenty years ago, Albert Camus was a fashionable author and his plays, essays and novels helped many young people to live. Since I was very influenced by Sartre at that time and followed his ideas passionately, I read Camus without enthusiasm and even with a certain impatience at what I considered to be his intellectual lyricism. Later, with the posthumous publication of the *Notebooks* (1962 and 1964), I wrote a couple of articles in which, with a superficiality which now makes me blush, I stated that the work of Camus had suffered what, in the words of Carlos Germán Belli, we might call a 'premature greyness'. And, based on Camus's attitude towards the drama in Algeria – a position that I did not know well and had learned from the caricature that his opponents made of it and not through his original texts – I allowed myself a few ironic jibes at the image of the just man, the lay saint, that some of his devotees had formed around him.

I did not read Camus again until a few months ago when, by chance, following a terrorist attack in Lima, I reopened *The Rebel*, his essay on violence in history that I had completely forgotten (or had never understood). It was a revelation. This analysis of the philosophical origins of the terror that characterizes contemporary history astonished me with its lucidity and contemporary relevance and with the answers that it gave to many doubts and fears that I felt about the reality in my country. I was also heartened to discover that on several difficult political, historical and cultural questions, I had, on my own account, after a number of lapses, come to exactly the same conclusions as Camus. In these past few months I have kept on reading him and this rereading, despite inevitable disagreements, has changed what was previously reticence into appreciation, my former scorn into gratitude. In a few crude brushstrokes, I would like to outline the new image that I have of Camus.

I think that in order to understand the author of *The Outsider*, it is useful to remember his threefold condition as a provincial, a man of the frontier and a member of a minority. All three, for me, contributed to his way of feeling, writing and thinking. He was a provincial in the strict sense of the term because he was born, educated and grew up far from the capital, in what was then one of the most remote areas of France: Algeria, North Africa. When Camus moved definitively to Paris, he was almost thirty; that is, he was already in essence what he would be for the rest of his life. He was a provincial for better or worse, above all for better in many respects. First, because, unlike the experience of men in large cities, he lived in a world where landscape was the primordial presence, infinitely more attractive and important than cement and asphalt. The love of Camus for nature is a permanent aspect of his work: in his first books – *Between Yes and No*, *Noces* (The Wedding), *L'Eté* (The Summer), *Minotaure ou halte d'Oran* (The Minotaur or the Shop in Oran) – the sun, the sea, the trees, the flowers, the harsh earth or the burning dunes of Algeria are the raw material for description or the starting point for reflection, they are the obligatory reference points of the young essayist when he attempts to define beauty, celebrate life or speculate on his artistic vocation. Beauty, life and art blend, in these brief and careful texts, into a sort of natural religion, a mystical identification with the elements, a consecration of nature which often makes me think of José María Arguedas, in whose novels something similar occurs. In Camus's later work, the landscape – and, above all, his favoured Mediterranean landscape – is also present, often as an atrocious desire or as a terrible nostalgia: Marthe and her mother, the robbers and killers in *The Misunderstanding*, kill the travellers in the inn so that one day they will be able to set themselves up in a little house by the sea, and Jean Baptiste Clemence, the protagonist of *The Fall*, exclaims, at a desperate moment in his monologue: 'Oh sun, beaches, islands of trade winds, memories of youth that make us despair!' In Camus, the beauty and beneficial warmth of the landscape not only satisfy man's body; they also purify him spiritually.

All his life he remained true to the conviction that man fulfils himself completely, lives a total reality, insofar as he is in communion with the natural world and that the divorce between man and nature mutilates human existence. Perhaps it is this conviction, the experience of someone who grew up at the mercy of the elements, which kept Camus apart from the intellectuals of his generation. For all of them, Marxists and Catholics, liberals or existentialists, had something in common: the idolization of history. Sartre and Merleau-Ponty, Raymond Aron and Roger Garaudy, Emmanuel Mounier and Henri Lefebvre agreed at least on this one point: that man is an eminently social being and that to understand his misery and sufferings and propose solutions to his problems is something that can only take place within the framework of history. Enemies in everything else, these writers shared the most widespread dogma of our time: that history is the key to the human question, the area where the *whole* fate of man is decided. Camus never accepted this modern decree. Without ever denying man's historical dimension, he always maintained that a purely economic, sociological or ideological interpretation of the human condition was incomplete and, in the long run, dangerous. In *L'Eté*, 1948, he wrote: 'History explains neither the natural universe that existed before it, nor the beauty that is above it.' And in the same essay, he objected to the hegemony of the cities, which he associated with historical absolutism and which later, in *The Rebel*, he would see as the origins of the modern political tragedy, the era of dictatorships which took as their philosophical justification the demands of history.

In contrast to this man of the city, which modern thinkers have turned into a mere historical product, which ideologies have stripped of flesh and blood, this abstract and urban being, separated from the the land and the sun, non-individualized, severed from his original unity and turned into an archipelago of mental categories, Camus talked of natural man, linked to the world of the elements, proudly asserting his physical being, who loves his body and tries to please it, who finds the harmony between the landscape and matter to be not only a full and satisfying form of pleasure but also the confirmation of his greatness. This man is elemental not only because his pleasures are simple and direct but also because he lacks social refinements and guile: that is, the respect for conventions, a capacity for deception and intrigue, a spirit of accommodation and an ambition for power, glory and wealth. These are things that he does not even despise: he does not know that they exist. His virtues – frankness, simplicity, a certain preference for the Spartan life – are those traditionally associated with life in the provinces and, in another way, with the pagan world. What happens when this natural man tries to exert his right to be part of the city? A tragedy: the city crushes him, destroys him. This is the theme of Camus's best novel: *The Outsider*.

For a long time it was repeated that this was a novel about injustice in the world and in life, a literary illustration of the philosophy of the absurd that Camus had tried to describe in *The Myth of Sisyphus*. Read today, the novel appears above all to be an argument against the tyranny of convention and the lie that social life is based upon. Mersault is, in a certain way, a martyr to truth. What leads to his imprisonment, sentencing and presumably his execution is his ontological inability to disguise his feelings, to do what other men do: play a part. It is impossible for Mersault, for example, to affect at his mother's funeral more grief than he actually feels, and say the things that, in these circumstances, it is expected that a son should say. Nor can he – despite the fact that his life depends on it – show the judge more repentance than he actually feels for the death that he has caused. He is punished for this, not for his crime. From another standpoint, the novel is also a declaration in favour of the superiority of this life above any other. Mersault – the elemental man – is educated, laconic, mild-mannered (his crime is really the work of chance), and he only loses control of himself and becomes irritated when people talk to him about God, when someone – like the judge or the prison chaplain – refuses to respect his atheism (or rather his paganism) in the same way that he respects the faith of others. Catechizing, sectarian and domineering attitudes exasperate him. Why? Because everything that he loves and understands is exclusively on this earth: the sea, the sun, the sunsets, the young flesh of María. With the same animal indifference with which he cultivates the senses, Mersault tells the truth: this causes those around him to think that he is a monster. Because truth, that natural truth that flows from the mouth like sweat from the skin, is at odds with the rational forms that make up social life, the community of men in history. Mersault is in many ways an alter ego of Camus who also loved this world with the same intensity that mystics love the other world, who also had the vice of telling the truth and who, in the name of this truth – above all in politics – did not hesitate to flout the conventions of his time. Only a man from afar, unfamiliar with the latest fashions, impervious to the cynicism and enslavement of the city, would have been able, at the height of the belief in systems, to defend, like Camus, the thesis that ideologies lead irremediably to slavery and crime, to argue that morality is a superior demand to which politics should submit, and to be the champion of two maidens so discredited at the time that their very names had become an object of derision: freedom and beauty.

Camus's style is somewhat anachronistic, solemn and mannered, reminding one of those gentlemen from the provinces who shine their shoes and put on their best suit every Sunday to walk around the square and listen to the band. In the best sense of the word, his prose demonstrates a constant affectation. Its gravity, complete lack of humour and stiffness are all very provincial. His normally short sentences are polished, purified and refined to the essential, and every one of them is as perfect as a precious stone. But the movement or dynamism of the whole is often quite weak. His is a statuesque style which, apart from its admirable conciseness and the effectiveness with which it expresses an idea, seems somewhat *naïf:* it is a stuffy style, old-fashioned, smelling of starch. It is a paradox that the modern writer who has celebrated with the most persuasive arguments the natural and direct life was, in his prose style, one of the most 'artistic' (both highly wrought and also artificial) prose writers of his time.

Apart from these literary concerns, there are also values that Camus cultivated and defended which had already been exiled from the city, from the world of solitary and cynical people: those of honour and friendship. These are individualistic values by definition, resistant to any purely social conception of man, in which Camus saw two forms of redemption for the species, a way of regenerating society and a superior and privileged type of human relationship.

Camus was a man of the frontier because he was born and lived in that tense, rough border between Europe and Africa, the West and Islam, industrialized society and underdevelopment. That experience of the periphery gave him, as a European, a complex view of his own world. On the one hand he felt a greater adherence to this culture than those who live in the centre and cannot judge or appreciate the significance of the culture to which they belong. On the other hand, he felt a much stronger anxiety, sense of danger and concern for the weakness of the bases of society than someone who, because he is far from the frontier, can forget about these problems and even dig up, in suicidal fashion, the ground that supports him. I am not accusing Camus of ethnocentrism, of contempt for cultures in the rest of the world, for he was profoundly European in the universal sense of the term. But it is a fact that Europe and the problems of Europe were the central preoccupation of his work; this does not diminish the work but it frames it within precise limits. When Camus became involved with Third World concerns – like the suffering of the Kabyles or the colonial repression in Madagascar – he did so from a continental perspective.

He denounced events which – and this was the gravest accusation that he could make – *dishonoured* Europe. The Europe that Camus defends, the one that he would like to preserve, invigorate and offer as a model to the world is the Europe of a modern and southern pagan, who feels that he inherits and defends values derived from classical Greece: the cult of artistic beauty and the dialogue with nature; restraint, tolerance and social diversity; the balance between the individual and society; a democratic arrangement of both rational and irrational factors in life and a rigorous respect for freedom. Christianity and Marxism have been banished from this relative utopia (as he called it). Camus was always opposed to both of them because, in his view, they both, for different reasons, diminished human dignity.

To say that Camus was a democrat, a liberal, a reformist, would not be very useful or, rather, it would be counter-productive because these concepts – and here, we must recognize, is one of the greatest victories of totalitarian ideologies – have come to define, at best, political naivety and, at worst, to signify the hypocritical masks of reactionaries and exploiters. It is more useful to try to define what these terms meant to Camus. Basically, he completely rejected totalitarianism as a social system in which the human being is no longer an end and becomes an instrument. The morality of limits is a state in which the antagonism between means and ends disappears, in which the means justify the ends and not vice versa. The theme of totalitarianism, of authoritarian power, the extremes of madness that can be reached when man violates this morality of limits, obsessed Camus throughout his life. It inspired three of his plays, *Caligula, State of Siege* and *The Just Assassins,* his best essay, *The Rebel,* and his novel, *The Plague.* It is enough to look at reality today to realize to what extent the obsession of Camus with state terrorism and modern dictatorship was justified and prophetic. These works are complementary, describing and interpreting different aspects of the same phenomenon.

But it would be unjust to believe that Camus's reformism did no more than proclaim political freedom and a respect for the rights of the individual to disagree, forgetting that men are also victims of other 'plagues', as atrocious or more atrocious than oppression. Camus knew that violence has many faces, that it is also inflicted, most cruelly, through hunger, exploitation and ignorance, that political freedom is worth little to someone who lives in poverty, without culture, and works like an animal. And he knew all this through very direct and personal experience since, as I have said, he was the member of a minority group.

He had been born a *pied noir*, one of a million Europeans who formed a privileged minority among seven million Algerian Arabs. But this community of Europeans was not homogeneous. There were rich, middle income and poor people and Camus belonged to the lowest stratum. The world of his childhood and adolescence was very poor. His father was a worker and when he died, his mother had to earn a living as a servant. His guardian uncle, the first person who taught him how to read, was an anarchist butcher. He was able to study through grants and when he caught tuberculosis, he was nursed in charity institutions. Words like 'poverty', 'defencelessness', 'exploitation', were not for him, unlike many progressive intellectuals, terms learned in revolutionary manuals, but rather everyday experiences. For that reason, it is totally wrong to accuse Camus of being insensible to social problems. The journalist in him on many occasions denounced economic injustice, discrimination and social prejudice with the same clarity with which the essayist fought against authoritarian terror. This is shown in the articles that he wrote in 1939 under the title *La Misère à Kabilie* (The Misery of Kabylia), which revealed the terrible situation of the *kabilas* in Algeria and which led to his expulsion from the country. Furthermore, in Camus's thought the economic exploitation of man is implicitly condemned with the same rigour as his political oppression. And for the same reasons: through his humanistic belief that the individual can only be an end, not a means, that the enemy of man is not only the person who represses him but also the one who exploits him for gain, not just the person who puts him in a concentration camp, but also the one who turns him into a production machine. But it is true that when he settled in France, Camus concentrated more on political and moral oppression than on economic oppression. This was because the first of these was a more acute problem for him (he was, as I have said, a European whose main point of reference was European reality), in particular at the time he was living. In the postwar years, when faced with the rising tide of Marxism, historicism and ideologies, which tried to reduce everything to a social problem, Camus's work became an important counterbalance, emphasizing what these movements scorned or ignored: morality.

But we should also remember that this severe critic of revolutions carried out in the name of ideologies was himself a rebel, and that his thought completely legitimates, on moral grounds, the right of man to rebel against injustice. What difference is there, therefore, between revolution and rebellion? Do not both lead inevitably to violence? For Camus, the revolutionary is a person who places man at the service of ideas, who is prepared to sacrifice the man who is living for the one who is to come, who turns morality into a process governed by politics, who prefers justice to life and who believes in the right to lie and to kill for an ideal. The rebel can lie and kill but he knows that he has no right to do so and that if he behaves in this way, he threatens his cause. He does not agree that tomorrow should take preference over today; he justifies the ends by the means and he puts politics at the service of a higher cause – which is morality. Is this 'relative utopia' simply too remote? Perhaps so, but it does not make it any the less desirable, and it is certainly more honorable than other models of current action. The fact that these other models triumph more quickly is not a guarantee of their superiority because the truth of a human endeavour cannot be measured through its effectiveness. But if one can question the precise limitation that Camus places on the act of rebellion, one cannot deny that, in theory and in practice, he was a nonconformist, an opponent of the established order.

I would like to end by referring to an aspect of Camus's thought with which I feel a great affinity. I also consider that it is particularly relevant to this day and age in which the inflation of the state, that monster which is gaining ground all the time, invading territories that were believed to be safe and protected, suppressing differences, establishing an artificial equality (eliminating differences, like Caligula), is also affecting many artists and writers, who succumb to the mirage of good salaries and certain perks and become bureaucrats, instruments of power. I am referring to the relationship between the creator and the principles that govern societies. Like Breton and Bataille, Camus also warns that, at the end of the day, there is an unbridgeable gap between the two, for the function of the creator is to moderate, correct and counterbalance these forces in society. For power, any power, even the most democratic and liberal in the world, contains within it the seeds of a desire for self-perpetuation which, if it is not controlled and fought, grows like a cancer and leads to despotism and dictatorship. In the modern era, with the development of science and technology, this is a mortal danger: our age is the age of the perfect dictatorships, of policemen with computers and psychiatrists. Against this threat that is incubating within all power structures, a small but obstinate foe stands up, like David against Goliath: the creator. For him, by the very nature of his office, the defence of freedom is not so much a moral duty as a physical need, because freedom is an essential prerequisite of his vocation, that is, his life. In 'The Banishment of Helen', Camus wrote: 'The historical spirit and the artist, each in its own way, want to remake the world. The artist, through his very nature knows the limits that the historical spirit does not know. This is why the latter ends in tyranny while the passion of the former is for freedom. All those who fight for freedom today come to do battle, in the last instance, for beauty.' And in 1948, in a talk in the Salle Pleyel, he repeated: 'In this age in which the conqueror, by the logic of his attitude, becomes an executioner or a policeman, the artist is obliged to be a recalcitrant. In the face of contemporary political society, the only coherent attitude of the artist, unless he prefers to renounce his art, is unconditional rejection.' I believe that today, here in Latin America, here in our own countries, it is difficult but imperative for everyone who paints, writes or composes, that is everyone who, by the nature of his office, knows that freedom is the main condition of his existence, to preserve his independence and remind those in power, at every moment and by every means at his disposal, of the morality of limits.

It is possible that this voice of Camus, the voice of reason and moderation, of tolerance and prudence but also of courage, freedom, beauty and pleasure, might be less stimulating and attractive for young people than the voices of those prophets of violent adventure and apocalyptic denial, like Che Guevara or Frantz Fanon, which move and inspire them to such a degree. I consider that this is unjust. As things are today in the world, the values and ideas – at least many of them – that Camus postulated and supported have become as necessary for life to be liveable, for society to be really human, as those values that Che and Fanon turned into a religion and for which they gave up their lives. Modern experience shows us that to separate the struggle against hunger, exploitation and colonialism from the struggle for the freedom and dignity of the individual is as suicidal and absurd as dissociating the idea of freedom from that of true justice, which is incompatible with the unjust distribution of wealth and power. To bring all this together into a common action, a single goal, is of course a very difficult and risky adventure, but it is only through this adventure that a society can come about which really embodies in this world the paradise that believers trust will be theirs in another world. As Camus wrote: 'Life will be free for everyone and just for all.' As we enlist in this struggle and attempt to carry it through until victory, despite the enormous incomprehension and hostility that we are exposed to from entrenched positions from both sides, the reading and rereading of Camus will be invaluable to us.

Lima, 18 May 1975

# Bataille or the Redemption of Evil

The way into Bataille's anthropology is through his notion of Evil. In his terms, this concept is stripped of any supernatural connotations, it is 'atheological' (that is how he baptized his philosophy in one of his most recent texts, the 'lectures on non-knowledge'), exclusively human. By it he means everything that contravenes the laws that society has imposed on itself in order to endure, to make life possible, to struggle against death. These laws, or list of prohibitions, make up the world of reason, of work, of coexistence and of purpose. The paradox of human life lies in the fact that, in order to allow beings to endure, so that life does not come to an end, society must constrain man, hem him inside a wire fence of taboos, force him to suffocate the non-rational part of his personality – that spontaneous and negative aspect of his being which, if left unchecked, would destroy order and communal life and sow confusion and death. Although it is repressed and denied by social life (Good), this *maudit* (damned) aspect of the human condition is, however, still there, hidden but alive, coming out of the shadows, insinuating itself, fighting to reveal itself and exist. Only when this *maudit* dimension manages to express itself, causing violence against Good (placing the laws of the city in danger) can man achieve his sovereignty. 'Thus', says Bataille, 'we must not be surprised if the quest for sovereignty is accompanied by the breaking of one or more prohibitions. This means that, to the degree that humanity tries to achieve it, sovereignty requires us to place ourselves "above the essence" of society. It also means that deep communication is only possible on one condition; that we resort to Evil, to the violation of a prohibition.'

Evil, according to Bataille, does not negate but rather completes human nature, it gives it fullness and is the praxis through which man can recover that part of himself that reason – Good, the city – *must* cut off in order to defend social existence. Evil is made possible through liberty. 'Perhaps liberty is based on rebellion as well as lack of submission,' he remarked in 1949. And in *Literature and Evil* (1957), he stated: 'Liberty is always a way into rebellion.' We can see how fundamental the concept of 'rebellion' is for Bataille. On the one hand, it is a praxis determined by the quest for sovereignty. Since this is achieved by infringing the law and prohibitions ('Sovereignty is the power to raise oneself, indifferent in the face of death, above the laws that assure the maintenance of life'), rebellion is the only attitude that allows man to achieve 'totality', his highest intensity, his greatness, insofar as he replaces his sense of self-preservation and attachment to life with tolerance and a search for death. For this reason, I have called Bataille's message 'funereal'. For him, death is not only acceptable, it is the very price of human integrity. Torn between reason and lack of reason, between the desire to endure and the desire to live 'supremely', man, that miserable paradox, 'should not allow himself to remain enclosed within the limits of reason', but nor can he abolish these limits for fear of causing his own destruction: 'First he must accept these limits, must recognize the need for calculating his interests; but he must know that there exists within him an irreducible part, a sovereign part that escapes the limits, that escapes that need which he recognizes.' What defines human nature is 'the fact of introducing into life, damaging it as little as possible, the greatest possible number of elements that contradict it'.

This is the explanation and justification of eroticism for Bataille. Eroticism (he defines it gloomily as 'the approval of life even in death'), a sexual practice freed from reproduction, an activity which is essentially sterile, gratuitous, profuse, wasteful, is one of those 'tumultuous', 'excessive' movements which is opposed to reason, to Good, to the activity of work. That is, it is one of those privileged areas of 'Evil and the diabolical', through which man, by approaching death, can exercise his freedom, rebel and reach fullness. Erotic activity, in Bataille's analysis, has little to do with animal, joyful pleasure, the celebration of instinct that an Aretino or a Boccaccio might describe. It is more akin to the mathematical nightmares of a Marquis de Sade. The pleasure that man extracts from 'vice' is, for him, macabre and mental: it consists of a challenge to death (causing it and flirting with it), and a sense of committing wrong. Quoting Sade ('There is no better way of familiarizing oneself with death than by associating it with a libertine idea'), he asserts that the practice of eroticism leads towards crime, that the attraction of death is fundamental to it.

Sanctity is another excessive form of behaviour which, by violating the calculation of self-interest and the laws of coexistence, allows man to attain a form of sovereignty. The mystic, like the libertine, challenges the law of duration, violates the precepts that govern collective existence, his endeavour is also sterile in 'productive' terms and his behaviour places death before life. It is this mutual indifference in the face of death that, for Bataille, connects the saint and the voluptuary, not sex. It is surprising to find in *Eroticism* this materialist, satanic atheologist commenting, with great sympathy, on a volume of the Carmelite Fathers entitled *Mystique et Continence* (Mysticism and Continence) and rejecting with distaste the sexual interpretation of mystical life offered by some psychoanalysts.

Just as the existence of Good is indispensable for Evil, the Devil indispensable for God, so for the man who achieves sovereignty by subverting the rules and transgressing the taboos, it is absolutely necessary that rules and taboos exist. This *maudit* writer could not be further from defending a tolerant society without barriers or sexual prejudices. Those who have been attracted by the 'dark' prestige of Bataille and have thought to use him to fight against 'repressive society' are very wrong: 'I am not someone who thinks that forgetting certain sexual problems is a way forward. I think, in fact, that human possibility depends on these prohibitions: that we cannot conceive of that possibility without those prohibitions.' It is essential to remember that the Marquis de Sade was an energetic opponent of the death penalty, he wrote a pamphlet against it and voted against it during the Terror. It is also worth recalling that Roger Vaillant (a theoretician and practitioner of eroticism more superficial than Bataille, but who wrote some good novels), argued in *Le Regard froid* (The Cold Gaze) that modern women were no longer suitable for a life of voluptuousness because of the excessive freedom with which they had been educated. What made the women of the eighteenth century so fit for the life of the libertine? Vaillant seriously considered that the answer could be found in the severity of their convent education. There is an underlying coherence in this seemingly contradictory attitude. For rebellion to be authentic and involve risk, there must be something to rebel against. From Bataille's individualistic viewpoint, the existence of prohibition, the rules of taboo guarantee the possibility of transgression, that is the possibility of achieving sovereignty, one's own totality. This alternative, or way of overcoming animality, of reaching a higher form of humanity, is attributed, by definition, to individuals or minorities. This, for me, is one of the most demoralizing conclusions of this aspect of Bataille's thought. It excludes the possibility that a civilization, a society, *of any kind,* might reach wholeness globally, might develop a sovereign life for all the inhabitants that make up the group. It condemns the majority of every community always to live separated from an essential part of their being. The social body will always obey the rule that it has created, will not rebel, or, if it does so, it will be in order to create new rules and prohibitions, so that the *majority* will be a diminished and mediated humanity, qualitatively inferior to the few who dare to embrace Evil. This gloomy conviction is implicit in statements like the following: 'Humanity has two aims, one negative, to preserve life (avoid death) and the other, positive, to increase intensity. These two aims are not contradictory. But intensity has never been increased without danger. The intensity desired by the majority (or the body of society) is subordinated to the desire to preserve life and its works, which undoubtedly takes preference. But when it is pursued by minorities or individuals, it can be pursued without hope, outside the desire to endure.' Elitist, minoritarian, aristocratic: this is an accusation often lodged against Bataille's theory. But, in the end, he does not propose a 'programme of action' but rather a reading of something that he sees written in reality. Furthermore, it is not so simple to establish a hierarchy between these two forms of behaviour. Should one reach human fulfilment by embracing death as early as possible or live separated to some degree from one's being, only to die in any event in the long run? These are the options that man debates in this tragic philosophy, which justifies death in the name of life and Evil in the name of Good.

Rebellion, sovereignty, irrationality and Evil are embedded in Bataille's conception of literature. It is here that I feel closest to him, that I respect him the most. The idea at the heart of this conception of literature seems to be the following: Literature can express *all* of human experience, but it fundamentally expresses the *maudit* part of that experience. It is the most effective and accurate, the least deceitful, way that this aspect of existence, which is besieged and deformed by society, can be expressed and understood. Literature exists because man is unhappy and feels hemmed in, yet, deep within him, rejects this condition. This intimate rejection of social life's coercive nature is what Bataille calls the will to sovereignty, the call of Evil: 'The lessons of *Wuthering Heights,* of Greek tragedy – in fact of any religion – is that there exists a state of divine intoxication that the world of calculation cannot endure. This impulse is contrary to Good.' It is this impulse that finds expression in all authentic literature. Thus the heart of literary creation is an act of rebellion, a desire to restore the hidden part of life: the irrational, instinctive, excessive, mortal face of Evil. Only literature is capable of 'uncovering the mechanism for transgressing the law (without transgression the law has no purpose), independent of any order that might be created.' Literature enjoys this privilege because it is an individual activity and because of the decisive influence that the irrational plays in creation (in it, obsessions are more important than convictions). It is a spontaneous concern, not entirely governable by the calculation of interest, an egotistical enterprise, that is disinterested in social terms. It has nothing to lose (it expresses anger or grief at what man *has lost*); therefore it is in a position to say *everything* and, in particular, what society – the empire of reason, of duration, of Good – does not want it to say. For this reason, in any society, authentic literature is always a threat: 'Literature is also, like the transgression of moral law, a danger. Since it is inorganic, it is irresponsible. Nothing weighs on it. It can say everything.'

One can understand, in the light of these ideals, how difficult it is to carry out an activity based on rebellion, on the irrational and on the individual in a society built fundamentally on rational and collective ideas, like a socialist society. I believe that no one has explained better than Bataille (in his essay on Kafka), the tyranny that has characterized until now the relationship between socialist power and literature:

Apparently, effective activity, raised to the discipline of a system based on reason, which is Communism, is the solution to every problem. But it cannot either condemn completely, or tolerate in practice, the purely autonomous, sovereign, attitude by which the present moment is detached from all the other moments that will come later. This presents a great difficulty for a party which only respects reason, and which cannot see in irrational values – through which the abundant, useless and infantile aspects of life are born – anything beyond the the particular interest they conceal. The only sovereign attitude admitted within the framework of Communism, albeit in a minor way, is that of a child. It is accepted that children cannot aspire to the seriousness of an adult. But an adult who gives a primordial meaning to the infantile, who engages with literature as if he were dealing with a supreme value, has no place in Communist society.

There is without doubt a strong element of Romanticism in Bataille's idea of literature. It becomes very evident – because this tendency is accentuated – when he talks about poetry. Bataille would have accepted without hesitation the Platonic formula that the poet does not know what he is saying. For him, the poet was the negation of reason, of responsibility; in other words, he was Evil (or innocence) in pure form. Thus, nothing could be further from Bataille's ideas than the notion of socially 'committed' poetry or of the poet as a 'constructive' political militant. Quite the reverse: for him, the poet is the opponent, the contradiction of power. He says so clearly in a comment on Blake: 'For the life of the poet to conform in general with reason would go against the authenticity of poetry. At least it would deprive the work of an irreducible quality, a sovereign violence, without which poetry is mutilated. The authentic poet is in the world like a child; he can, like Blake or a child, make undeniably good sense, but the authorities will have no confidence in him.'

The ideas of Bataille on literature – expressed, in the main, in *Literature and Evil*, a collection of excellent essays on a series of *maudit* writers (de Sade, Baudelaire, Blake, Genet) and others that he read in this way (Emily Brontë, Michelet, Kafka) – seem to me very lucid and I agree with them almost entirely. I think that their ideas take us to the heart of literature, arguing as they do that a feeling of rebellion is part of every literary vocation and saturates all authentic literature, that the influence of the irrational is decisive in creation and that literature above all communicates negative experiences or, as Bataille would say, *maudit* experiences. My only discrepancy is that this final observation had too restrictive a meaning for Bataille and seemed to contain a kind of modesty. It is true that, in the main, literature expresses Evil, but Bataille, in practice if not in theory, seemed convinced that it could *only* express Evil. I consider that in addition to this *maudit* aspect, all authentic literature contains a similarly strong feeling, which is the urge to commit deicide, to remake reality critically, to contradict creation in its integrity, to hold up to life a verbal image which expresses and denies it *totally*. This representation is almost always drawn from that mass of experiences that Bataille calls Evil (obsessions, frustra-tions, pain, vice), but it is broader and deeper in the sense that it man-ages to get closer, through the negativity that sustains it, to the totality of human experience, and gives a more complete vision of life, which is both individual and social (both Good and Evil).

What limits Bataille's conception of literature appears, in a glaring way, in the fiction that he wrote. In this, the desire to transgress and to destroy is stronger than the desire to create and to construct (and in the novel, rebellion consists of destroying by constructing, of denying by affirming, of capturing the irrational within a rational structure), and his vision of the tree is so hypnotic and exclusive that the wood often disappears. The result is always (even in his best constructed novel, *The Blue of Noon*) a world in which man is as limited as the mass – man in society – only from the other side of his nature – and in which the representation of life, however disturbing, is minimal and even somewhat fallacious. I am trying to say that Bataille was an inter-esting, but not an important, novelist. He put into practice as a creator, with great scrupulousness, what as a critic he had always explored in literature: the expression of the *maudit* in humanity. I am not criti-cizing him for doing this, but for doing it *exclusively*, because since his testimony of life, albeit original and brave, only deals in his stories with the prohibited and the atrocious, it appears fragmentary and even parodic. Man is made up of outrage, latent misery, a death wish, unhap-piness and solitude but at the same time he is also made up of reason and feelings, enjoyment and generosity, feelings of solidarity and an instinct for life.

He wrote his first novels when he was still to some extent linked to surrealism which, let us remember, had an Olympian contempt for the genre of the novel (even this is an example of Bataille's rebellious spirit). From the start, they make the reader uneasy at the level of 'form' due to their stylistic poverty, the crudeness of their construc-tion, the appearance they give of being primitive fictions, narratives in brute form. This was obviously intentional, so that no 'literary' pleasure would detract from the infernal material of these texts into which Bataille poured, with the greatest purity and objectivity, his subjectivity: his obsessions, his madness. The oneiric, the erotic and the absurd dominate these stories, which always take place in irrational locations, rarefied by foul air, and which are full of the themes and props of 'dark' literature, in particular the English Gothic novel. They are short, anguished and narrated in the first person by a desperate and narcissistic narrator. Their intellectualism cannot disguise their diligent rhetorical poverty and their desired rudimentary structure. When I read them, I feel that the light of day, the tacit consent of the city, is damaging to them. They should be read in secrecy in sinful garrets or in the infernos of libraries. When he wrote *The Story of the Eye*, under the pseudonym of Lord Auch, he was a responsible employee in the National Library: to write these horrors (or to read them), courted the risk of such a loss of prestige that this fact, in itself, gave prestige to the undertaking. Times have changed and in this era (I am talking, of course, of countries without censorship), when it acquires the freedom of the city, the terrible is no longer terrible, and horrific gestures, repeated by everyone, become frivolous mimicry. I feel that from the rich tree of Bataille's work, the novels will be the first branch to wither.

In his tales, sexual madness is usually as important as blasphemous frenzy and homicidal fury. But in his first, *The Story of the Eye*, my favourite, this excess is relieved by a youthful freshness, a certain cheerful dynamism (this is the only work in the whole of Bataille's oeuvre to which the adjective cheerful can be applied) in the protagonists, whose vicious ferocity also contains a desire for enjoyment, a love of life, which redeems and humanizes them to a certain extent.

The best of Bataille is found in his essays. There is no better way to demonstrate the Satanic sharpness of his intelligence and the creativity of his theories when embodied in a concrete theme than to study his affinity to Gilles de Rais. It is one of the most fortunate encounters in modern literature, as if both had been born to coincide at some moment. In this apocalyptic character of the Middle Ages, Bataille found some of his theses, in flesh and blood and carried to their most extreme limits. Here is an extraordinary case in which those who populate the human prison, the angels and the demons, can be observed, touched and measured in all their human ambivalence. Gilles de Rais was an absolute monster only in legend; in reality he was also a feared Maréchal, who fought for France alongside Joan of Arc, a sensitive man who could be moved to tears by the Gregorian chant, a Catholic who, even in the moments of his most bloody bestiality, kept his faith, and whose repentance of his crimes, before death, was not only spectacular but almost certainly sincere. For here is an example of what occurs when a man has the power to transgress the prohibitions of the city, to knock down the doors of the kingdom of reason and allow the animal enclosed there to escape: lines of children, kidnapped, sodomized and butchered; dizzying orgies; grotesque midnight ceremonies in woodland clearings, summoning up the devil. Bataille's analysis is not moralizing, but rather didactic and scrupulously clear: no one could accuse him of manipulating the story of Gilles de Rais to illustrate his beliefs in a better light. Above all, he shows in great detail the historical context without which the crimes of the Maréchal would be incomprehensible. ('The crimes of Gilles de Rais are the crimes of the world in which he committed them.') He lived in a world in which nobility conferred a semi-divine superiority, an almost limitless right to turn desires into reality. And the forms of life of those times – wars, tournaments – stimulated precisely those desires for blood and crime. When Gilles de Rais fought alongside Joan of Arc, he could commit more atrocities than he did later, for his own individual pleasure, and be celebrated and rewarded for them. War must have established the custom of killing, aligning it to a previous custom, that of pederasty, and a great Breton nobleman of the fifteenth century had the means to turn fantasies into reality. One of the most chilling facts of Bataille's study is that the only thing that caused de Rais's downfall was his becoming bankrupt; other crimes, perhaps worse than his, committed by people who kept their fortunes to the end of their days, would never be unearthed.

But Bataille's essay also shows the limits of an exclusively social interpretation. The historical context is essential for explaining the case of Gilles de Rais, but at the same time, insufficient. Of all the noblemen who went to war, who had power and riches, only one followed the rough course of the Lord of Machecoul. There is an aspect of this person that the reality of his time does not manage to illuminate, because it was not the product of historical praxis or the reflection of the dominant system, but belonged instead to the dark side of humanity, that permanent redoubt, common to the species, where its terrible singularity lies. Man's congenital desire to reach wholeness, sovereignty and total freedom can only be fully assuaged at the price of carnage in which life itself would be extinguished. How then can one achieve the legitimate aim of perpetuating existence and, at the same time, enriching it, 'intensifying' it? Bataille's answer seems to be: through a precarious, polemical balance between the social whole and the individual, by which society controls, but does not kill, the spirit of rebellion and the desire for rupture – for waste, for excess – because this would imply man's return to an animal state. This spirit can live on in man, fighting to achieve sovereignty, without ever fully achieving it, because to achieve it would bring with it the holocaust. This is the implacable warning contained in Bataille's work: in each of us, muzzled and tied by the conventions of the community that surrounds us, there lurks, panting at the boys with golden locks, brandishing a dagger, one hand on his flies, a secret Gilles de Rais.

Barcelona, April 1972

# Sartre, Fierabrás and Utopia

Many Latin American cities have what we might call an Adamic complex, or a fear of the old. The colonial areas, where the powerful men of the past built churches and mansions to display their vanities, their fears and their faith are now systematically deserted by the powerful of today who, instead of preserving these neighbourhoods, prefer to develop others, living in new houses and buildings. Preservation, restoration, reconstruction are concepts that instinctively disgust them, as if they were ashamed of their tradition. This attitude, which is so different from Europe – where the old in housing is what is valued and indicates good taste – has meant that most of the old districts in Latin American countries have fallen into decline or into irreparable ruin.

This has happened in Lima and it is also happening in Bahía de San Salvador de Todos los Santos (known to everyone as Bahía). The historical centre, a four-sided labyrinth, bristling with palaces, convents, squares and balconies, which dominates the majestic bay from up on the cliffs, is still very beautiful. But a hundred years ago, it must have been one of the world's most extraordinary architectural settings. Now, despite the efforts that one can see here and there to repair a site or to roof a church, there is no doubt that its decline is as inevitable and rapid as that of old Lima. It is very clear that in this district, the only inhabitants are those that have no alternative but to live here.

Poverty has invaded the splendid houses, the proud apartments whose facades still gleam with chipped tiles from Portugal. Where once one family lived, fifty or a hundred people have now packed in, dividing and subdividing the rooms with tin and cardboard sheets, turning the building into beehives. Wretched prostitutes work day and night on the street corners and every small square is a market, with swarms of vendors, street clowns and even snake charmers. Everywhere the poverty is horrific. But it is not squalid. It is masked by the fantastic brightness, the views of the sea and the islands which appear at every few steps, the vegetation that explodes in the waste ground, on the pavements and the roofs, climbing across the house fronts, becoming entwined in the rusty window bars and clambering into the dilapidated balconies. But above all, it is masked by the vibrancy and vitality of the people who seem to dance as they walk, sing as they speak and to have stepped out of a fancy dress ball.

I have spent some time trying to write a story set in the interior of Bahía, at the time of the messianic rebellion of Antonio the Counsellor — a civil war that led to the writing of one of the most hypnotic books that I have read, *Os sertões* (Rebellion in the Backlands) by Euclides da Cunha — and one of the things that surprised me in my study of the life of Bahía in the previous century was to learn that medieval romances were popular in the archaic and isolated society of the inhabitants of the *sertão*. That wandering troubadours entertained by singing of the adventures of Charlemagne, The Twelve Peers of France, Princess Magalona and Robert the Devil. The romances of chivalry were an early love of mine and the knowledge that in the remote territory of Canudos a tradition lived on that had already died out everywhere else, perhaps contributed to my fascination with this world of mystics and *cangaçeiros* (social bandits). On my first Sunday in Salvador, I was very impressed to come across, at the doors of the cathedral, a sleepy mulatto who was selling, among the stories of the martyrdom and the flagellations of the saints and the adventures of the bandit Lampião, a broadsheet entitled *The Battle of the Knight Oliveros with Fierabrás (episode of the Round Table)*. It is a romance that can be read at one go, a flood of octosyllables with non-stop action, which takes place in a fantastic geography, where Brazilian locations are mixed in with the French. It is a genuinely popular recreation, a literature which — as Borges has explained in an essay on gauchesque literature — is very different from that written by populist writers: it is a sumptuous, adorned literature, sparkling with daring action and absurdity.

The character of the Counsellor is not popular in Salvador. He never was: Canudos is hundreds of miles from here. In the markets, his ascetic figure wrapped in a blue habit never appears among the dozens of statues of heroes and saints that are on sale. When I asked in the Santa Barbara market if there was an image of him, a very quick-witted black woman tried to foist a brand new St Francis on me, swearing that this was the Counsellor. The imposing wooden sculpture of him by Mario Cravo is half hidden in the patio of a restaurant. To speak about Canudos, one must talk to the historians and intellectuals of the city or delve into the dusty newspapers of the period in the libraries.

But I did come face to face with this messianic utopianism which the Counsellor seems to have embodied, through a most unexpected source. It was after an unsuccessful attempt to question the Capuchin monks of the Convento de la Piedad about one of their ancestors, Fray Juan Evangelista del Monte Marciano, who had the privilege of knowing Canudos before the war and who wrote a tract against it, accusing it of fanaticism and subversion. I was having an ice cream (they are excellent here), when I saw in a publication with the enchanting title of *O inimigo do rei* (The Enemy of the King), which is indeed a libertarian journal, a reference to *The Political Testimony of Sartre*.

It was a summary of the book, but there was enough there to guess the rest. Sartre is a man who has aged well: now he is younger, freer and more agreeable than he was at forty or fifty. Then his intelligence so dominated everything else that when one read him one had the impression that, for him, thinking was an exclusive activity incompatible with other areas like loving, suffering and pleasure. Now it is the other way round: he is daring to be passionate and even irresponsible. I read these four pages of *O inimigo do rei* on the edge of my seat. Who would have thought that Sartre was capable of such boundless elation, impetuous idealism and apocalyptic thunderbolts. It is a sign of vitality that, instead of ending his days as an academic, he persists in being a youthful hellraiser.

This 'frontal attack on religion, the family, the government and property' is moving, above all for its furious utopianism, for having been written without regard for the only thing that, at the end of the day, is important for measuring the validity of a political philosophy: its feasibility. Sartre begins with a premise that half the world would accept: every government is conservative. From there he concludes with something that seems impeccable as a theory: the advantages of having no governments. And? How would we achieve this? What resources would we use to fashion this fantastic design? What would we put in the place of these 'steamrollers' once we have eliminated them? Because if, as Sartre states, 'egoism is the essence of man', how will this conglomeration of egoisms be organized and function with a minimum of coherence, without the checks and balances that make up society? It is true that the family is an imperfect institution, that it contains seeds of authoritarianism and that it opposes desires. But would the problem be solved by abolishing it and establishing universal promiscuity by decree? I suspect that the cure would be worse than the illness. In this great outburst of free instincts that Sartre proposes, it is probable that there would soon emerge privileges and forms of slavery much worse than those which currently exist in the domain of sex. Have cats and dogs, which are promiscuous, achieved some form of equality and equity in the field of desire?

But it is his argument against religion that contains the most surprises. 'Onward! The sickle against the confessionals! The hammer against the church! Let us burn the habits! Let us tear down, destroy, wipe out and burn to the ground the divinities, cults and altars, the sacred texts, temples and priests.' This is not the language of freedom but rather the language of religion. All those who have tried to abolish religion by these means – fire and bullets – have ended up substituting one form of fanaticism with another, putting in place even worse forms of intellectual obscurity.

We must mistrust utopias: they usually end in holocausts. It is a strange fact that in politics mediocre solutions tend to be the best solutions. We cannot abolish governments but we can, on the other hand, weaken them, restrain them, counterbalance them, so that they cause as little damage as possible. We cannot put an end to armies, religion, the family and property through an apocalyptic explosion. But we can democratize and neutralize these institutions, making them more flexible and relative so that they have less control over human freedom and do not stand in the way of progress towards equality. In politics, the only solution is to be a realist. This is not true of literature and for that reason literature is a freer and more lasting activity than politics.

Bahía, August 1979

# The Mandarin

Of all the writers of my time, there were two that I preferred above all others and to whom I was most indebted in my youth. One of them, William Faulkner, was well chosen for he is an author that any aspirant novelist should read. He is perhaps the only contemporary novelist whose work can be compared, in volume and in quality, with the great classics. The other, Sartre, was less well chosen: it is unlikely that his creative work will last and although he had a prodigious intelligence and was, on balance, an honest intellectual, his ideas and his position on issues were more often wrong than right. Of him we can say what Josep Pla said of Marcuse: that he contributed, with more talent than anyone else, to the confusion of our times.

I

I read him for the first time in the summer of 1952 when I was working as a copy editor on a newspaper. It is the only time that I led what many people still believe that writers lead all the time: a bohemian life. When the edition was put to bed, late at night, the journalistic fauna rushed to the bars, the low-life night clubs and the brothels and that, for a boy of fifteen, seemed a great adventure. In fact, the real adventure began one of those early mornings in a bar when my friend Carlos Ney Barrionuevo lent me *The Wall*. These stories, together with *Nausea*, the plays – *The Flies, Huis Clos, The Respectable Prostitute, Dirty Hands* – the first volumes of *Roads to Freedom* and Sartre's essays enabled many of us to discover modern literature at the beginning of the fifties.

They have aged terribly; today we can see that there was little originality in these works. Incommunication, the absurd, had been expressed in Kafka in a more tremulous and disturbing way; the technique of fragmentation came from John Dos Passos, and Malraux had written about political topics with a vitality that one never feels, even in the best story of that sort that Sartre wrote: 'The Childhood of a Leader'.

What could these works offer to a Latin American adolescent? They could save him from provincialism, immunize him against rustic views, make him feel dissatisfied with that local colour, superficial literature with its Manichaean structures and simplistic techniques – Rómulo Gallegos, Eustacio Rivera, Jorge Icaza, Ciro Alegría, Güiraldes, both Arguedas, even Asturias after *The President* – which was still our model and which repeated, unwittingly, the themes and fashions of European naturalism imported half a century previously. Apart from stimulating us to move away from a regionalist literary framework, we realized, albeit secondhand, through reading Sartre that narrative had undergone a revolution, that the range of its themes had diversified in all directions and that the modes of narration were both freer and more complicated. To understand what was happening in *The Age of Reason, The Postponement* or *Death in the Soul,* for example, there was no alternative but to know what an interior monologue was, how to differentiate between the points of view of the narrator and the characters, and become used to the fact that a story can change place, time and levels of reality (from consciousness to facts, from lies to truth) with the speed with which images change in a film. We learned, above all, that the relationship between a narrator and a character could not be, as before, that of puppet master and his puppet: it was necessary to make those strings invisible at the risk of the reader's incredulity. (Sartre demolished François Mauriac in an essay for not bothering to hide these strings, and consigned his novels to where they belong: the past.)

Sartre could also save us from aestheticism and cynicism. Thanks to Borges, literature in our language would acquire, in those years, a great inventive subtlety, an extraordinary originality. But, as an influence, the originality of Borges could be fatal: it produced Borges clones, who tried to copy his grammatical boldness, his exotic erudition and his scepticism. Disbelief had allowed him to create an admirable oeuvre: but for those who learned from Borges to believe in adjectives and mistrust everything else, the experience could be inhibiting and lead to minor works or to silence. Less of an artist than Borges and with a more impoverished view of literature, Sartre could none the less be more stimulating if one became imbued with his conviction that literature could never be a game and that, instead, writing was the most serious thing in the world.

Sartre's limitations were also legion. One of them was to turn his disciple against humour, to make him think that laughter was forbidden in any literature that sought to be profound. He never said as much, but did not need to: his stories, plays, novels were mortally serious. Another, more important, limitation was to make his disciple uninterested in poetry, which Sartre never liked and never understood. This is something that I discovered at the time when I was most under his influence, when I realized that in his essays on Baudelaire or on black poetry, he quoted poetry as if it were prose, that is, only for the rational concepts that it expressed. This lack of understanding of poetry meant that he was unfair towards surrealism, which he saw as nothing more than a strident manifestation of bourgeois iconoclasm, and he scorned the impact that the movement had on the art and sensibility of our time. But perhaps what was most limiting of all was the fact that Sartre's fiction lacks mystery: everything in it is subject to the empire – in his case dictatorship – of reason. There is no great art without a certain measure of unreason, because great art always expresses the whole of human experience, in which intuition, obsession, madness and fantasy play their part as well as ideas. In Sartre's work, man seems to be made of ideas alone. Everything about the characters, including their passions, is an epiphenomenon of intelligence. Because his own intelligence was so powerful – he was compared, accurately, to a thinking machine – he was able to write, from a standpoint of ideas alone, narratives and plays which at first were attractive because of their power of reason and their intellectual vigour. At a distance, they were less effective and our memory does not retain a great deal of these narrative or dramatic fictions because the creative literature that endures is that in which ideas are embodied in the actions and the feelings of the characters, while in Sartre's case, it was the other way round: ideas devoured life, disembodied the characters, the world seemed a mere pretext for formulating ideas. That is why, despite his dedicated involvement in the problems of his age – the essence of his theory of commitment – his novels and his theatre now seem somewhat unreal.

And yet there is a lateral, elusive vein in his literature which seems to come out of a deep wellspring and it is there despite the overwhelming rationality of the rest of the work. An unhealthy, provocative, scandalous vein which can be seen in his themes and characters – men and women who prefer masturbation to making love or who dream of castration, semi-incestuous brothers, individuals who zealously cultivate paranoia – but above all in a sickly, acidic language. Sartre said that his characters were upsetting because they were too lucid, but this is not true since Malraux's characters are also too lucid and they do not bother us. What is uncomfortable about them is that they do not know how to enjoy life, they lack enthusiasm and naivety, they never give in to simple impulses, they are not irresponsible, even when they sleep, and they think too much. But what prevents them from being mere entelechies and makes them human is the fact that they almost always have vices, that they are tortured souls, drawn to the dark side of life. Faced with Sartre's fiction, a receptive reader could intuit that, despite what the master was trying to do, it was absolutely impossible to prevent literature from expressing experiences which, in all other realms of social existence, men are not aware of or deny their existence.

2

The essay is the intellectual genre *par excellence* and it was in this genre that Sartre the writing machine excelled. To read his essays was always an extraordinary experience, a performance in which ideas had the strength and vitality of a good adventure novel. They had another quality which is rare: whatever the topic, the essays went straight to the essential point – the problems that obsess those who emerge from the comfortable blindness of childhood and begin to doubt, to ask what they are doing in the world, what is the meaning of life, what is history and how are the fates of individuals decided.

Sartre suggested answers to these questions which were more rational and persuasive than those of religion and less schematic than those of Marxism. Whether or not his theses were correct is another question. I now know that they were not as original as they appeared to so many of us at the time. What was important was that they were useful: they helped us to organize our lives, they were a valuable guide to the labyrinths of culture and politics and even to the most private aspects of work and the family.

Freedom is the axis of Sartrean philosophy. As soon as he comes into this world, man is entirely free within himself, he is a constant process which develops according to the choices that he makes among the multiple daily options with which he is confronted (all the options, both important and trivial). Man is always free to choose – abstention is, of course, a choice – and for this reason he is responsible for the errors and achievements that make up his life, for its moments of misery or happiness. Man is not an immutable essence (a 'soul') which precedes and continues after its bodily incarnation, he is an existence which, according to how it develops in time and history, gradually acquires its own intransferable essence. Men exist, human nature does not.

The fact that man is master of his destiny does not mean, of course, that all men can choose their lives under equal conditions, among equivalent options. The 'situation' of a worker, a Jew, a millionaire, a sick person, a child, a woman is each distinct and that presupposes a raft of totally different alternatives for every person in all aspects of experience. But in all cases, even in the case of the most underprivileged, the worst victim, it is possible to choose among different forms of behaviour and each choice implies a general human undertaking, a conception of society, a morality.

Sartre's best essays – the pages caught fire in one's hands, nights spent reading them were too short – are those in which he describes so accurately how certain men chose to lead their lives within their particular situation: geniuses like Baudelaire, terrible men like Genet or self-denying people like Juan Hermanos, Henri Martin or Henri Alleg. Or those essays, like 'Reflections on the Jewish Question', in which, through a concrete case, anti-Semitism in this instance, he expounded his conception of human relations, that fearsome interdependence which is condensed in the celebrated phrase of *Huis Clos,* 'Hell is other people.' The 'other' is a projection of oneself, someone that we see in a certain way and thus form in that way. It is the prejudices of the non-Jew that create the Jew, the whites that create the blacks, man that has created woman. 'Others' make and remake us continually and we also do the same to them. The freedom of certain men – groups or classes – endowed with a certain power, has allowed them to reduce or distort the freedom of others, conditioning them to certain functions which they have ended up adopting as an essential condition of their lives. But this is a lie, there are no 'essential' functions. To be a colonizer or colonized, a worker or a boss, white or black, man or woman, are 'situations', facts forged by history and thus transformable.

These ideas covered hundreds of pages and – in a book or in an article – they were always magisterially developed, nuanced, illustrated, in a solid, rough-hewn prose that is sometimes so dense as to leave one breathless. His *bêtes noires were the tricheur* and the *salaud,* that is, those who cheat at the moment of choice, seeking moral justifications for their cowardice or baseness, and those who 'become committed' to a wrong cause, choosing to support injustice.

It now seems clear to me that, when explored in depth, the famous Sartrean theory of commitment was quite confused, but in the 1950s it seemed luminous to us. His greatest merit, therefore, was to offer a young man with a literary vocation, who had discovered social problems, a way forward politically which did not emasculate him intellectually, as often happened to those who opted for the other theory then at hand: socialist realism. 'Commitment' meant assuming the responsibilities of the age in which one lived and not the dictates of a party; avoiding gratuitousness and irresponsibility when writing, and also not believing that the function of literature was to spread certain dogmas and become pure propaganda. It also meant retaining one's doubts and asserting the complexity of human experience even in those extreme situations – like racism, colonialism and revolution – in which the border between justice and injustice, the human and the inhuman, seemed clearly demarcated.

When applied to literature, the theory of commitment could be interpreted in two different ways and Sartre himself alternated between these interpretations according to his political shifts and intellectual preferences at the time. In a broad sense, every writer with talent was committed because the 'epoque', the 'time', is such a vast concept that all imaginable themes can be included in it if they are connected in some way to human existence (and in literature, they are always connected). Thus Sartre could, at times, 'make committed' creators as elusive as Mallarmé, Baudelaire, Francis Ponge or Nathalie Sarraute. This generalized the idea of 'commitment' in such a way that it was no longer an illuminating or an operable concept. In a strict sense, to become 'committed' was to do so in the political sphere, participating in the social struggles of the age, in support of those actions, classes and ideas that represented progress. For a writer, this struggle had to be waged simultaneously as a citizen and as a writer since the pen, if put to good use, could be a weapon: 'words are acts'.

In its broader sense, 'commitment' was a formula that embraced so much – all of literature – that in the end it embraced nothing. In its restricted sense, it left out of literature an enormous number of writers who had been indifferent to political reality (like Proust, Joyce and Faulkner) or who had chosen 'badly' (like Balzac, Dostoievsky and Eliot) or else it gave importance to writers who had chosen well but who were mediocre creators (like Paul Nizan). There is no better example of the ineffectiveness of the theory of commitment than Sartre's views on Flaubert. In 1946, he attacked him harshly, accusing him of being responsible for the crimes committed by the bourgeoisie against the communards in Paris, 'for not having taken up his pen to condemn them'. Did that mean that to be a political sceptic was a hindrance to the writing of a great literary work? To prove that was the case, Sartre began to write a book, *The Idiot of the Family*, that would take him a quarter of a century to complete, in the course of which it would not be Flaubert but the theory of commitment which would be debunked by Sartre himself when he concluded that the author of *Madame Bovary* was the best writer of his time and, together with Baudelaire, had founded modern sensibility.

Because although he was often wrong, Sartre had the courage to contradict himself and to correct his errors as often as he considered necessary.

### 3

Until after the war, Sartre was apolitical. The accounts of his colleagues at the Ecole Normale, of his students at the Lycée Le Havre, where he taught, and of Simone de Beauvoir on the early years of their friendship, in the 1930s, give an image of a young man completely absorbed by intellectual passions: philosophy at first — he had a scholarship in Berlin and his discovery of the phenomenology of Husserl and the thought of Heidegger was decisive in his life — and, immediately after this, literature.

The war changed this man of thirty-five who, according to his own confession, 'until 1940 lacked political opinions and did not even vote'. Enlisted in the army, captured during the invasion, he spent some months in a prison camp and left there converted to political concerns. But although he belonged to Resistance intellectual groups, during the years of the Occupation this new preoccupation cannot be seen in any explicit way in what he publishes (*The Imaginary, Being and Nothing, Huis Clos*, the literary essays) except, perhaps, in *The Flies*, which has been seen, somewhat stretching the point, as an allegory against absolutism. (Malraux once harshly observed: 'When I was fighting against the Nazis, Sartre was putting on his plays in Paris which were approved by the German censors.')

Sartre's political activity really begins at the time of the Liberation, with the foundation of *Les Temps Modernes* in October 1945. He threw himself into politics with gusto and from then on, politics would condition everything that he wrote. But, paradoxically, his declarations, manifestos and actions would achieve, in the long term, more notoriety and perhaps greater effectiveness in the political field than his works of intellectual creation inspired by politics. I mean, for example, that while his public stance in favour of Algerian independence caused many young Frenchmen to fight against colonialism, few, by contrast, read *The Critique of Dialectical Materialism,* an ambitious attempt to make Marxism less schematic and revitalize it with borrowings from existential philosophy, none of which had any resonance, especially among those for whom it was written: Marxist intellectuals.

It is difficult to draw up a balance of Sartre's thought and political history over these thirty-five years, because it is so close to us and so complex. One could say that he was full of contradictions, that his passion often caused him to be unjust and yet, at the same time, there was always a basic generosity and moral honesty in his attitudes and ideas that made him, with all his mistakes and political naivety, respectable. His dialectical genius was, in this case, a double-edged sword because it allowed him to cloak with a force of persuasion and an appearance of truth everything that he upheld, including his wildest remarks (like the celebrated, 'Every anti-communist is a dog'). All this is perhaps true, but it is not enough. In his case the whole will always be more important than any synthesis.

No one could ever question the selflessness and integrity with which he upheld all his positions. These were coherent and consistent in some areas, like anti-colonialism, for which he fought with great courage when Indochina was still French and when almost no one on the European left dared speak out in favour of the independence of the North African or other African colonies. He was also coherent and lucid in his attempt to understand the Third World and fight Eurocentrism, to show the French that Africa, Asia and Latin America were worlds in upheaval, that some of their poverty was caused by the old colonizing powers or the current neo-colonial powers and that their cultures deserved to be recognized and respected. (Many years before the Third World became fashionable, *Les Temps Modernes* published articles on the problems in these countries and I remember, for example, that I discovered in its pages, in 1954 or 1955, the existence of the Cuban Alejo Carpentier.

But these were sideline aspects of Sartre's political project. The central concern was his conviction, formed at the time of the Liberation and maintained until his death, that socialism is the only solution to social problems and that the intellectual has the duty to work for the triumph of socialism. 'Socialism' today means a number of different things and, throughout his life, Sartre supported different variants including, at the end of his days, Scandinavian social democracy which, after so many years of reviling contemptible bourgeois reformism, he recognized as having gone further than any other system in reconciling social justice with the freedom of the individual.

Pro-Soviet, pro-Chinese, pro-Castro, Trotskyite sympathizer or defender of urban guerrilla groups, he never joined the Communist Party. He was always what was known as a 'fellow traveller'. In his case this did not mean, as it did for other intellectuals, an opportunistic docility, a loss of independence, becoming a mere instrument. When the moment came, he distanced himself from and severely criticized the party of the USSR, for example, over the intervention in Czechoslovakia or the trials of Siniavsky and Daniel. Because he kept his distance on these occasions, the Communists launched the strongest attacks ever written against him, despite the fact that he had spent a good deal of his political life making a bold intellectual and moral effort never to appear to be against them even though he was not one of them. This dramatic position, which defines progressive intellectuals in the fifties and sixties, was formulated by Sartre in an essay from 1960: 'Collaboration with the Communist Party is, at once, both necessary and impossible'.

Why necessary? Because socialism is the only radical response to human problems and because the struggle for socialism is embodied in the working class. Why impossible then? Because, although Marxism is the 'insuperable philosophy of our time', the Communist Party is dogmatic, bound hand and foot to the policies of the USSR, and because although the USSR is the home of socialism and 'the only great country where the word progress has any meaning', that country has witnessed profound ideological deformations which have led it to commit abuses, injustice and even great crimes in the name of socialism.

If this sounds like a caricature, it is due to my clumsiness, for I do not intend it to be so. Because this, in short, is the desperate dilemma which – with his habitual shining intelligence – Sartre developed in his political essays for at least twenty years, in *The Communists and Peace, The Phantom of Stalin,* innumerable articles and in his polemics with those who were once his friends and allies and who, because they could not follow him in all the daily detours that this most difficult position forced him to take, broke with him: Camus, Aron, Etiemble, Koestler, Merleau-Ponty and many other less well-known figures.

In the end, it is this dilemma that is the most difficult to forgive. That he convinced those of us who admired his intellectual power so greatly, with rational arguments that he made irrefutable, to accept something that was, purely and simply, an act of faith. Or, to use his terminology, bad faith. That he made us believe, those of us who had to a great extent broken free from the Church and Rome and the realm of exclusive truths, that there was another exclusive truth, another Church and Rome, which had to be criticized, sometimes very severely, but in the knowledge that, outside it, there was no real moral or political salvation and, for that reason, if one wanted to remain a progressive, there was no alternative but to live with the knowledge of being one of the damned.

4

It will be as difficult for readers in the future to have an exact idea of the importance of Sartre to this era as it is for us to understand exactly what Voltaire, Victor Hugo or Gide meant to their age. He was, like them, that curious French institution: the intellectual mandarin. That is, someone who is seen as a teacher, beyond what he knows, what he writes or even what he says, a man on whom a huge public confers the power to legislate on matters ranging from the largest moral, cultural and political questions to the most trivial. Wise man, oracle, priest, mentor, *caudillo,* teacher, father – the mandarin influences his time with ideas, gestures, attitudes and expressions which start out as his own, or which are perceived to be his own, but then become public property, assimilated into the life of others. (Mandarin status is typically French because, although in other countries there are occasionally figures that fulfil that function – like Ortega y Gasset in Spain and Tolstoy in Russia – in France, at least since the eighteenth century, all of intellectual life has developed in this way, revolving around writers who were popes of sensibility, taste and prejudices.)

It will be difficult for those who know Sartre only through his books to understand to what extent the things that he said or did not say, or what it was thought he might have said, had an impact on thousands of people and became transformed into forms of behaviour, 'vital choices'. I'm thinking of my friend Michael, who fasted and went out half-naked into the Paris winter until he got tuberculosis so that he would not have to fight in the 'dirty' Algerian war, and of my garret crammed with Algerian FLN propaganda which I hid there because 'one had to be committed'. For Sartre we put our hands over our ears so as not to hear, at the appropriate moment, the political lessons of Camus; but also, thanks to Sartre and *Les Temps Modernes,* we could cut through the complexity of the Palestine–Israel conflict, which was heartrending. Who was right? Was Israel, as most of the left maintained, simply an artificial construction of imperialism? Should we believe that the injustices committed by Israel against Palestine were morally identical to those committed by the Nazis against the Jews? Sartre saved us from adopting schematic and unilateral views. Here was one of the issues where his position was always consistent, lucid, courageous and illuminating. He understood that there could be two positions that were equally right and yet contradictory, that both Palestinians and Jews had legitimate rights to a homeland and that, for this reason, one had to defend the view – which then seemed impossible but which now, thanks to Egypt, seems less so – that the problem would only be resolved when Israel consented to the creation of a Palestinian state and the Palestinians, for their part, recognized the existence of Israel.

My disillusionment with Sartre occurred in the summer of 1964 when I read an interview that he gave to *Le Monde,* in which he seemed to go back on everything that he had believed – and had made us believe – on the subject of literature. He said that, compared with a child dying of hunger, *Nausea* was useless, worthless. Did this mean that to write novels or poems was useless or, worse still, immoral, while social injustices existed? It seemed so because in the same article he advised writers from the new African countries to give up writing for the time being and concentrate instead on teaching and other more important tasks in order to construct a country where literature would be possible at a later date.

I remember having thought and thought about that article with the depressing sensation of having been betrayed. The man who had taught us that literature was something so important that it could not be played with, that books were acts that changed lives, was suddenly telling us that it was not true, that, at the end of the day, it was not that important when compared to serious problems; it was a luxury that could only be permitted in prosperous and just societies, but not in poor and unjust societies like mine. At that time, there was no argument in the world that could make me give up literature, so the article instead freed me from Sartre: the spell was broken, that irrational link that binds his followers to the mandarin. I remember very clearly the consternation that I felt when I realized that the most intelligent man in the world could also – albeit in a moment of depression – talk rubbish. And yet in a way it was refreshing after so many years of respectful silence to argue with him in my mind and to debunk him with my questions. What coefficient of proteins per capita did a country have to achieve before it was ethical to write novels? What indexes of national income, education, mortality, health had to be reached for it to be moral to paint a picture, compose a cantata or make a sculpture? What human endeavours can withstand the comparison with dead children more successfully than the novel? Astrology? Architecture? Is the palace of Versailles worth more than a dead child? How many dead children are the equivalent to quantum theory?

Following the polemic that his declaration provoked, Sartre softened and modified these views. But, deep down, they reflected something that he felt: a disillusionment with literature. This was, of course, quite understandable. But it was his fault for asking of literature something that it could not provide. If one thinks that a novel or a play is going to resolve social problems in a more or less visible or concrete way, it is probable that one will end up disillusioned with literature or any artistic activity since the social effect of a work of art is indirect, invisible, mediated, always very difficult to measure. Does that mean that they have no *use*? Although it cannot be demonstrated the way one demonstrates a theorem, of course they are useful. I know that my life would have been poorer without the books that Sartre wrote.

Albeit at a distance and with a certain reticence that never left me, I always maintained an interest in everything that he said, did, or wrote. And probably, as must have happened to everyone who, in one way or another, was influenced by him, at the time of every polemic, crisis or break up, if I wanted to know if things had turned out well or badly, I always thought of Sartre. I remember how happy I felt when I sat next to him in the Mutualité in 1967, at a meeting which called for the release of Hugo Blanco, and the moral tranquillity that I felt during the so-called Padilla Affair, when he and Simone de Beauvoir were the first people in France to sign our protest manifesto.

With him there has died a certain way of understanding and working within culture which was a fundamental part of our age; with him, there ends the reign of a mandarin and he will probably be the last, since the mandarins of his generation who have outlived him are very academic or very abstruse, with a feeble entourage, and of the younger generation there is no one who seems capable of filling that striking gap that he leaves.

Someone has told me that these notes I have written are sharper in tone than one might have expected from someone who has confessed to owing him so much. I do not think that this would have bothered him; I am sure that it would have upset him less than the implacable celebrations – homages, dithyrambs, shows – with which the country against which he had ranted, official France, has buried him. We must remember that he was a man completely lacking in that sort of vanity, who found homages unacceptable and who had a horror of sentimentalism.

Washington, May–June 1980

# Isaiah Berlin: A Hero of Our Time

## A discreet philosopher

Many years ago, I read in Spanish translation a book on Marx which was so clear, suggestive and unprejudiced that I spent a long time looking for other books by its author, Isaiah Berlin. I later discovered that until recently his work had been difficult to find since it was scattered, if not buried, in academic publications. With the exception of his books on Vico and Herder, and the four essays on freedom, which were available in the English language world, most of his work led the quiet life of the library and the specialist journal. Now, thanks to a former student of his, Henry Hardy, who has collected together his essays, these are now available in four volumes: *Russian Thinkers, Against the Current, Concepts and Categories* and *Personal Impressions.*

This is an important event since Isaiah Berlin — a Latvian, brought up and educated in England, where he has been Professor of Social and Political Theory in Oxford and President of the British Academy — is one of the most exceptional minds of our time. He is a political thinker and essayist of extraordinary breadth whose work provides a rare pleasure in its skill and brilliance as well as offering an invaluable guide for understanding, in all their complexity, the moral and historical problems faced by contemporary man.

Professor Berlin believes passionately in ideas and in the influence that these ideas have on the behaviour of individuals and societies, although, at the same time, as a good pragmatist, he is aware of the space that usually opens up between ideas and the words that seek to express them and between the words and the deeds that purport to put them into practice. Despite their intellectual density, his books never seem abstract to us — unlike, for example, the work of Michel Foucault or the latest books of Roland Barthes — or the result of a speculative and rhetorical virtuosity that has, at some moment, cut its moorings with reality. Instead, they are deeply rooted in the common experience of the people. The collection of essays, *Russian Thinkers,* is an epic fresco of nineteenth-century Russia in intellectual and political terms, but the most outstanding characters are not people but ideas: these shine, move around, challenge each other and change with the vigour of heroes in an adventure novel. In that other beautiful book on a similar theme – *To the Finland Station* by Edmund Wilson – the thoughts of the protagonists seem to transpire from the persuasive and varied portraits that the author draws of his characters. Here, by contrast, it is the concepts that they formulated, the ideals and arguments with which they confronted each other, and their intuitions and knowledge which define the figures of Tolstoy, Herzen, Belinski, Bakunin and Turgenev, which make them plausible or reprehensible.

But even more than *Russian Thinkers,* it is the collection *Against the Current* that will doubtless remain as the major contribution of Professor Berlin to the culture of our time. Each essay in this magisterial work reads like a chapter of a novel whose action takes place in the world of thought and in which the heroes and the villains are ideas. Thanks to this scholar who never loses a sense of balance and who can clearly see the wood for the trees, Machiavelli, Vico, Montesquieu, Hume, Sorel, Marx, Disraeli and even Verdi are seen to have a great contemporary significance and the things that they believed, put forward or criticized illuminate in a powerful way the political and social conflicts that we wrongly considered to be specific to our age.

The most surprising thing about this thinker is that he appears, at first sight, not to offer ideas of his own. It might seem nonsense to say this, but it is not nonsense because when one reads him, one has the impression that in these essays, Isaiah Berlin achieves what, after Flaubert (and because of him), most modern novelists have tried to achieve in their novels: to erase themselves, to make themselves invisible, to offer the illusion that their stories are self-generated. There are many techniques for 'making the narrator disappear' in a novel. The technique that Professor Berlin uses to make us feel that he is not behind his texts is 'fair play'. This is the scrupulous moral purity with which he analyses, exhibits, summarizes and quotes the thoughts of others, considering all their arguments, weighing up the extenuating circumstances, the constraints of the age, never pushing the words or ideas of others in one direction or another to make them appear similar to his own. This objectivity in the transmission of the inventions of others gives rise to the fantastic impression that, in these books which say so many things, Isaiah Berlin himself has nothing of his own to say.

This is, of course, a rigorously false impression. 'Fair play' is only a technique which, like all narrative techniques, has only one function:

to make the content more persuasive. A story that seems not to be told by anyone in particular, which pretends to be making itself, by itself, at the moment of reading, can often be more plausible and engrossing for the reader. A thought that seems not to exist by itself, that reaches us indirectly, through what certain eminent men from different epochs and cultures thought at specific moments in their life, or one that professes to be born not out of the creative effort of an individual mind, but rather out of the contrast between the philosophical and political conceptions of others and the gaps and errors in these conceptions, can be more convincing than a thought that is presented, simply and arrogantly, as a single theory. The discretion and modesty of Isaiah Berlin are, in fact, a wily stratagem.

He is a 'reformist' philosopher, a defender of individual sovereignty, convinced both of the need for change and social progress and of the inevitable concessions that the latter demands of the former. He is a believer in freedom as an alternative undertaking for individuals and nations, although he is aware of the obligations that economic, cultural and political conditions bring to bear on this option for freedom and is a clear defender of 'pluralism', that is, of tolerance and of the coexistence of different ideas and forms of life, and a resolute opponent of any form of despotism, be it intellectual or social. This all obviously says something about the man, but it is also, to some extent, a way of depriving the reader of the pleasure of discovering these ideas through that lingering, subtle and indirect method – a novelist's method – that Professor Berlin uses to expound his convictions.

A few years back, I lost my taste for political utopias, those apocalypses that promise to bring heaven down to earth: I now know that they usually lead to injustices as serious as those they hope to put to right. Since then, I have thought that common sense is the most valuable of political virtues. Reading Isaiah Berlin, I have come to see clearly something that I had intuited in a confused way. That real progress, which has withered or overthrown the barbarous practices and institutions that were the source of infinite suffering for man, and has established more civilized relations and styles of life, has always been achieved through a partial, heterodox and deformed application of social theories. Social theories *in the plural,* which means that different, sometimes irreconcilable, ideologies have brought about identical or similar forms of progress. The prerequisite was always that these systems should be flexible and could be amended and reformed when they moved from the abstract to the concrete and came up against the daily experience of human beings. The filter at work, which separates what is desirable from what is not desirable in these systems, is the criterion of practical reason. It is a paradox that someone like Isaiah Berlin, who loves ideas so much and moves among them with such ease, is always convinced that it is ideas that must give way if they come into contradiction with human reality, since if the reverse occurs, the streets are filled with guillotines and firing-squad walls and the reign of the censors and the policemen begins.

Of the authors that I have read in the past few years, Isaiah Berlin is the one who has impressed me the most. His philosophical, historical and political opinions seem to me illuminating and instructive. However, I feel that although perhaps few people in our time have seen in such a penetrating way what life is – the life of the individual in society, the life of societies in their time, the impact of ideas on daily experience – there is a whole other dimension of man that does not appear in his vision, or does so in a furtive way: the dimension that Georges Bataille has described better than anyone else. This is the world of unreason that underlies and sometimes blinds and kills reason; the world of the unconscious which, in ways that are always unverifiable and very difficult to detect, impregnates, directs and sometimes enslaves consciousness; the world of those obscure instincts that, in unexpected ways, suddenly emerge to compete with ideas and often replace them as a form of action and can even destroy what these ideas have built up. Nothing could be further from the pure, serene, harmonious, lucid and healthy view of man held by Isaiah Berlin than this sombre, confused, sickly and fiery conception of Bataille. And yet I suspect that life is probably something that embraces and mixes these two enemies into a single truth, in all their powerful incongruity.

Washington, DC, November 1980

# Faulkner in Laberinto

A quarrel has broken out in the bar but it spills immediately on to the street. I hear the noise and go out to investigate. A man in his underpants is being punched and stoned by three or four individuals. He must have started the fight since one of the attackers has a cut face and is bleeding profusely. In the midst of the dust, the cursing and the blows, a child is screaming and trying to clutch on to the legs of the bleeding man. When the man being attacked decides to run away and all the onlookers go back into their cabins to continue getting drunk, the child's wailing persists, like an out of tune drizzle falling on the palm-leaved roofs and wooden walls of the houses of Laberinto.

It is impossible not to think of Faulkner. This is the heart of Amazonia, far away, of course, from the Mississippi. The language, the races, the traditions, the religion and the customs are different. But the citizens of Yoknapatawpha County and those of this settlement in the department of Madre de Dios, by the bank of the wide river of the same name, which gold fever has transformed in a short space of time into a sort of ragged millionaire, have a lot of things in common: violence, heat, greed, an untameable nature which seems to reflect instincts that people do not try to keep in check; in short, life as an adventure in which the grotesque, the sublime and the tragic are enmeshed as inextricably as branches of trees in a wood.

On the plane from Lima to Puerto Maldonado and in my lodgings in this place (here, by the light of a rancid candle), I have been reading *Intruder in the Dust*, Faulkner's third novel, his first masterpiece and the beginning of the saga. Its complete version was only published in 1973. The novel published in 1929 entitled *Sartoris* had been stripped of a quarter of its pages and reordered by Ben Wasson, Faulkner's literary agent. Eleven publishing houses rejected the manuscript, considering it confused, and the house that finally plucked up the courage to publish it did so on condition that these cuts and amendments — which were supposed to simplify the story — were made. Today, we can lament the dominant standards of taste in narrative at the end of the 1920s, which were so poor that the readers of eleven publishing houses could not recognize what they had in front of their eyes: a masterpiece that would change in a profound way the very nature of modern fiction.

But it is easy to make this type of *a posteriori* criticism. The novelty was, in fact, too great and, furthermore, New York was as far away in time and space from Jefferson, the land of the mythical characters — Bayard, John Sartoris, Jenny du Prés and the pig, Byron Snopes — as Lima is from Laberinto. Faulkner's America is underdeveloped and primitive, filled with rough and uncultured, prejudiced and gallant people, capable of extraordinary meanness and nobility, but incapable of breaking free of their visceral provincialism which makes them, from the moment they are born until their death, men of the periphery, wild and old-fashioned, pre-industrial, branded by a history of wicked exploitation, bloody racism, chivalric elegance, pioneer daring and lost wars. The world out of which Faulkner fashions his universe is not that of New York, Boston, Chicago or Philadelphia. He held up a mirror in which the America of ultra-modern machines and financial conglomerates, of specialized universities and cities bristling with skyscrapers and of intellectuals bewitched — like T. S. Eliot or Ezra Pound — by the spiritual refinement of Europe, did not like to see itself. In this America, the novels of Faulkner took time to be accepted: they represented a past and a present that it wanted to forget at all costs. It was only when Paris discovered Faulkner and authors like Malraux and Sartre proclaimed his genius to the four winds that the southern novelist gained the right to citizenship in his own country. His country then accepted him for reasons similar to those of the French, as a brilliant, exotic product.

Faulkner's world was really not his alone. It was ours. There is no better way of illustrating this than by coming to this lost settlement in the jungle of Madre de Dios which, because of the bends and swirls in the river that runs through it, has been baptized with the beautiful name of Laberinto. The population that give it personality and colour do not live here in these couple of dozen huts choked by vegetation but, as in Jefferson, they are scattered around it. They are searching and panning for gold, just as the inhabitants of Yoknapatawpha grew cotton and reared horses. But on Sundays they all come to town to do their business, stock up with provisions and enjoy themselves (which means getting drunk).

People from the sierra who scarcely speak Spanish and who are stunned by a heat which they have never experienced in their homes in Cuzco or Puno, which they have left to become miners; young men from Miraflores in Lima who have exchanged surfboards and motor racing for the heavy boots of the explorer; foreigners thirsty for adventure and instant wealth; hardened prostitutes who have come from the brothels of Lima to work as 'visitors' in the camps, where they charge by account and, in their free time, also try their luck scratching in the gravel banks for the precious metal; sweaty policemen overwhelmed by the size of their responsibilities, which are too much for them: if they could read, or took time to read, these men and women in Laberinto would feel very much at home in the novels of Faulkner and would be amazed to know that someone who had never been here, who had no way of knowing that one day fate would propel them all here and make them share so many hopes and difficulties, had been able to describe so well the exuberance of their life and their souls.

This is Faulkner's world. People are known by their names and industrial civilization, that impersonal society in which people communicate through things, is still far off. It is true that here everything is elemental and archaic and that lack of comfort, dirt and brute force predominate. But at the same time, nothing here seems predetermined: everything to be done is being done and one has the exhilarating impression that with a bit of luck and a great deal of courage and resilience any man or woman can magically change his or her life. There is that warm, immediate, healthy contact with natural elements – that air, that water, that earth, that fire which people in the city do not know – and the feeling that the food one eats, like the hut in which one lives, is produced by one's own hands.

Violence is always simmering beneath the surface and breaks out at any pretext. But at least it is an open, physical, natural violence, that has a certain minimal dignity, like the violence between animals, which attack and kill each other obeying the the first rule of life: the law of survival. It is not the disguised, city, civilized violence, institutionalized in laws, codes and systems, against which there is no defence since it does not have a body or a face. Here it has a name and features, it is individualized and, however horrible it might appear, it is still human.

It is not strange that at the time when the cultured media of his own country strongly resisted Faulkner's work, depriving him of readers, here in Latin America his work was immediately and unanimously proclaimed. The reason for this can be found not only in the enchantment of these turbulent lives of Yoknapatawpha County or in the formal accomplishment of these fictions built like beehives. It was that in the turbulence and complexity of the world 'invented' by Faulkner, we readers in Latin America discovered, transfigured, our own reality and we learned that, as in Bayard Sartoris or Jenny du Prés, that backwardness and marginality also contain beauty and virtues that so-called civilization kills. He wrote in English, but he was one of our own.

Lima, April 1981

# William Faulkner: The Sanctuary of Evil

According to his own testimony, Faulkner wrote the first version of *Sanctuary* in three weeks in 1929, immediately after *The Sound and the Fury*. The idea of the book, he explained in the second edition of the novel (1932), had always seemed to him 'cheap' because he had conceived it with the sole intention of making money (up to then, he had only written for 'pleasure'). His method was 'to invent the most horrific tale that I could imagine', something that someone from the Mississippi could take as a topical theme. Aghast at the text, his editor told him that he would never publish such a book since, if he did so, both of them would go to prison.

Then, while he was working in a power plant, Faulkner wrote *As I Lay Dying*. When this book came out, he received the proofs of *Sanctuary* which the editor had finally decided to publish. On rereading his work, Faulkner decided that the novel was indeed unpresentable as it stood and made many corrections and deletions, to such an extent that the version which appeared in 1931 differed considerably from the original. (A comparison of both texts can be found in Gerald Langford, *Faulkner's Revision of Sanctuary,* University of Texas Press, 1972.)

The second version is no less 'horrific' than the first: the main horrifying events of the story occur in both versions, with the exception of the discreetly incestuous feelings between Horace and Narcissa Benbow and Horace and his stepdaughter Little Belle, which are much more explicit in the first version. The main difference is that the centre of the first version was Horace Benbow, while in the new one, Popeye and Temple Drake have grown and have relegated the honest and weak lawyer to a minor role. With regard to structure, the original version was much clearer, despite the temporal complexities, since Horace was the perspective from which nearly all the story was narrated, while in the definitive version the tale continually changes point of view, from chapter to chapter, and sometimes even within a single paragraph.

Faulkner maintained his negative opinion of *Sanctuary* throughout his life. A half century after that self-critical prologue, in his *Conversations* at the University of Virginia (Vintage Books, New York, 1965), he once again called his story — at least in its first version — 'weak' and written with base intentions.

In fact, *Sanctuary* is one of his masterpieces and deserves to be considered, after *Light in August* and *Absalom, Absalom*, among the best novels of the Yoknapatawpha saga. What is certain is that with its harrowing coarseness, its dizzying depiction of cruelty and madness, and its gloomy pessimism, it is scarcely tolerable. Precisely: only a genius could have told a story with such events and characters in a way that would be not only acceptable but even bewitching for the reader. This almost absurdly ferocious story is remarkable for the extraordinary mastery with which it is told, for its unnerving parable on the nature of evil, and for those symbolic and metaphysical echoes which have so excited the interpretative fantasy of the critics. For this is, without doubt, the novel of Faulkner that has generated the most diverse and baroque readings: it has been seen as the modernization of Greek tragedy, a rewriting of the Gothic novel, a biblical allegory, a metaphor against the industrial modernization of the culture of the South of the United States etc. When he introduced the book to the French public in 1933, André Malraux said that it represented 'the insertion of the detective novel into Greek tragedy', and Borges was surely thinking of this novel when he launched his famous *boutade* that North American novelists had turned 'brutality into a literary virtue'. Under the weight of so much attributed philosophical and moral symbolism, the story of *Sanctuary* tends to become diluted and disappear. And, in truth, every novel is important for what it tells, not for what it suggests.

What is this story? In a couple of sentences, it is the sinister adventure of Temple Drake, a pretty, scatterbrained and wealthy girl of seventeen, the daughter of a judge, who is deflowered with an ear of corn by an impotent and psychopathic gangster — who is also a murderer. He then shuts her away in a brothel in Memphis where he forces her to make love in front of him with a small-time hoodlum whom he has brought along and whom he later kills. Woven into this story is another, somewhat less horrific: Lee Goodwin, a murderer, an alcohol distiller and bootlegger who is tried for the death of a mental defective, Tommy (who was killed by Popeye), condemned and burned alive despite the efforts of Horace Benbow, a well-intentioned lawyer, to save him. Benbow cannot make good triumph.

These horrors are a mere sampling of the many that appear in the book, in which the reader encounters a strangling, a lynching, various murders, a deliberate fire and a whole raft of moral and social degradation. In the first version, furthermore, the character endowed with a moral conscience, Horace, was caught in the grip of a double incestuous passion. In the final version this has been softened to the extent that it remains as scarcely a murky trace in the emotional life of the lawyer.

In every novel it is the form – the style in which it is written and the order in which it is told – which determines the richness or poverty, the depth or triviality, of the story. But in novelists like Faulkner, the form is something so visible, so present in the narration that it appears at times to be a protagonist, and acts like another flesh and blood character, or else it appears as a *fact*, like the passions, crimes or upheavals of its story.

The effectiveness of *Sanctuary*'s form stems above all from what the narrator hides from the reader, putting the facts in a different place in the chronology, or leaving them out altogether. The yawning gap in the novel – the barbarous deflowering of Temple – is an *ominous* silence, an expressive silence. Nothing is described, but from that unexpressed savagery a poisonous atmosphere seeps out and spreads to contaminate Memphis and other places in the novel, turning them into a land of evil, regions of ruin and horror, beyond all hope. There are many other hidden pieces of information, some of which are revealed retrospectively, after the effects that they cause – like the murder of Tommy or Red or the impotence of Popeye – and others which remain in the shadows, although we do learn something about them, enough to keep us intrigued and for us to surmise that in this darkness something murky and criminal is lurking, like the mysterious journeys and shady affairs of Clarence Snopes and the adventures of Belle, the wife of Horace.

But this manipulation of the facts of the story, which are withheld momentarily or completely from the reader, is more cunning than these examples might indicate. It occurs at every stage, sometimes in every sentence. The narrator *never* tells us everything and often throws us off the scent: he reveals what a person does, but not what he thinks (Popeye's private life, for example, is never revealed), or vice versa, with no prior warning, he depicts actions and thoughts of unknown people, whose identity he reveals later, in a surprising way, like a magician who suddenly makes the vanished handkerchief reappear. In this way, the story lights up and fades; certain scenes dazzle us with their illumination while others, almost invisible in the shadows, can only be glimpsed.

The pace of the narrative time is also capricious and variable: it speeds up and goes at the pace of the characters' dialogues, which the narrator recounts almost without commentary – as for example in the trial. In Chapter 13, the crater chapter, time is filmed in slow motion, almost stops and the movements of the characters seem like the rhythmic development of a Chinese shadow theatre. All the scenes of Temple Drake in the house of the old Frenchman are theatrical, they move at a ceremonial pace which turns actions into rites. In this tale, with some exceptions, the scenes are juxtaposed rather than dissolving into each other.

All this is extremely artificial, but it is not arbitrary. Or rather, it does not seem arbitrary: it emerges as a necessary and authentic reality. The world, these creatures, these dialogues, these silences could not be otherwise. When a novelist succeeds in transmitting to the reader that compelling, inexorable sensation that what is being narrated in the novel could only happen in that way, be told in that way, then he has triumphed completely.

Many of the almost infinite number of interpretations of *Sanctuary* stem from the unconscious desire of critics to come up with moral alibis which allow them to redeem a world which is described in the novel as so irrevocably negative. Here once more we come up against that perennial view – which, it seems, literature will never be able to shake off – that poems or fiction should have some kind of edifying function in order to be acceptable to society.

The humanity that appears in this story is almost without exception execrable or, at the very least, wretched. Horace Benbow has some altruism, which makes him try to save Goodwin and help Ruby, but this is offset by his weakness and cowardice which condemn him to defeat when he tries to face up to injustice. Ruby also shows some spark of feeling and sympathy – she does at least try to help Temple – but this does not have any useful outcome because she has been inhibited by all the blows and setbacks and is now too cowed by suffering for her generous impulses to be effective. Even the main victim, Temple, causes as much repugnance as sympathy in us because she is as vacuous and stupid – and, potentially as prone to evil – as her tormentors. The characters who do not kill, bootleg, rape and traffic – like the pious Baptist ladies who have Ruby thrown out of the hotel, or Narcissa Benbow — are hypocritical and smug, consumed by prejudice and racism. Only the idiots like Tommy seem less gifted than the rest of their fellow men in this world when it comes to causing harm to others.

In this fictional reality, human evil is shown, above all, in and through sex. As in the fiercest Puritans, an apocalyptic vision of sexual life permeates all Faulkner's work, but in no other novel of the Yoknapatawpha saga is it felt more forcibly. Sex does not enrich the characters or make them happy, it does not aid communication or cement solidarity, nor does it inspire or enhance existence. It is almost always an experience that animalizes, degrades and often destroys the characters, as is shown in the upheaval caused by Temple's presence in the Old Frenchman's house.

The arrival of the blonde, pale girl, with her long legs and delicate body, puts the four thugs — Popeye, Van, Tommy and Lee — into a state of excitement and belligerence, like four mastiffs with a bitch on heat. Whatever traces of dignity and decency that might still survive within them vanish when faced with this adolescent who, despite her fear and without really being conscious of what she is doing, provokes them. Purely instinctive and animal feelings prevail over all other feelings such as rationality and even the instinct for survival. In order to placate this instinct, they are prepared to rape and to kill each other. Once she is sullied and degraded by Popeye, Temple will adopt this condition and, for her as well, sex will from then on be a transgression of the norm, violence.

Is this animated nastiness really humanity? Are we like that? No. This is the humanity that Faulkner has invented with such powers of persuasion that he makes us believe, at least for the duration of the absorbing reading of the novel, that it is not a fiction, but life itself. In fact life is never what it is in fiction. It is sometimes better, sometimes worse, but always more nuanced, diverse and predictable than even the most successful literary fantasies can suggest. Of course, real life is never as perfect, rounded, coherent and intelligible as its literary representations. In these representations, something has been added and cut, in accordance with the 'demons' — those obsessions and deep pulsations that are at the service of intelligence and reason, but are not necessarily controlled or understood by these faculties — of the person who invents them and bestows on them that illusory life that words can give.

Fiction does not reproduce life; it denies it, putting in its place a conjuring trick that pretends to replace it. But, in a way that is difficult to establish, fiction also completes life, adding to human experience something that men do not meet in their real lives, but only in those imaginary lives that they live vicariously, through fiction.

The irrational depths that are also part of life are beginning to reveal their secrets and, thanks to men like Freud, Jung or Bataille, we are beginning to know the way (which is very difficult to detect) that they influence human behaviour. Before psychologists and psychoanalysts existed, even before sorcerers and magicians took on the role, fiction helped men (without their knowing it) to coexist and to come to terms with certain phantoms that welled out of their innermost selves, complicating their lives, filling them with impossible and destructive appetites. Fiction helped people not to free themselves from these phantoms, which would be quite difficult and perhaps counterproductive, but to live with them, to establish a *modus vivendi* between the angels that the community would like its members exclusively to be, and the demons that these members must also be, no matter how developed the culture or how powerful the religion of the society in which they are born. Fiction is also a form of purgation. What in real life is, or must be, repressed in accordance with the existing morality – often simply to ensure the survival of life – finds in fiction a refuge, a right to exist, a freedom to operate even in the most terrifying and horrific way.

In some way, what happened to Temple Drake in Yoknapatawpha County according to the tortuous imagination of the most persuasive creator of fiction in our time, saves the beautiful schoolgirls of flesh and blood from being stained by that need for excess that makes up part of our nature and saves us from being burned or hanged for fulfilling that need.

London, December 1987

# John Dos Passos: *Manhattan Transfer*

The protagonist of *Manhattan Transfer* is New York, a city that appears in its pages as a cruel and frustrating ant-hill, where egotism and hypocrisy hold sway and where greed and materialism suffocate the altruistic sentiments and the purity of the people. In this powerful and cold novel which at all times appeals to the intelligence of the readers – not to their heart or their feelings – there are dozens of characters but none of them is attractive, no one who might merit envy or respect. Those who do well are professional rogues or repugnant cynics and those who fail are weak and frightened people who have already defeated themselves through their lack of conviction and laziness, before the city in turn squashes them.

But although the particular individuals of *Manhattan Transfer* are too blurred and rapidly sketched to live on in the memory – not even the two most recurrent and best drawn characters, Ellen Thatcher and Jimmy Herf, escape this rule – the great collective character of the city of New York is admirably portayed through the vignettes and cinematographic sequences of the novel. Turbulent, impetuous, full of dynamism, of strong smells, life and violence, a modern Moloch which feeds off the lives that it swallows without trace, New York with its garb of reinforced cement, its caravans of clattering vehicles, its rubbish, its tramps, millionaires, cheery women and crooks, is depicted as a modern Babylon. Babylon out of man's control, propelled by its own dynamism along an unstoppable path towards something that we foresee can only be a disaster. The flight of Jimmy in an unknown direction at the end is almost a premonition of the catastrophe which, sooner or later, awaits what he calls the 'city of destruction'.

When John Dos Passos wrote *Manhattan Transfer* at the beginning of the 1920s, it was his intention to criticize, in a raw, realist novel, the capitalist system and its putative child – urban, industrial civilization – in the city that symbolized all of these aspects. His intention is very clear in the diligent rationalism of the book, in its lack of spontaneity, sentimentalism and mystery. But outside this conscious will of the author, a different impulse emerged, the novel took another turn and it became in the end a pointilliste and somewhat mythical work in which, in an atmosphere laden with pessimism, the stage of concrete and steel becomes humanized, takes on an intensity of life and an underlying personality which it seems to have absorbed from the paltry and inconsistent marionettes whom it also displaces as the main protagonists in the narrative. Written under the strong influence of Joyce, who had made Dublin a city-character, *Manhattan Transfer* is one of the few novels which, like *Berlin Alexanderplatz* by Alfred Döblin, deserve to be called collective. In this novel, the hero is not an individual, but a crowd, a gregarious being, made up of many faces and events which the narration, thanks to its skilful and effective technique, brings together as parts of an indissoluble form.

Now, after fifty years of being used by countless novelists, the techniques employed by Dos Passos seem familiar and even conventional to us. But when he published *Manhattan Transfer* in 1925, they were daring, imaginative and were a real revolution in narrative form. One of his most industrious disciples, Jean-Paul Sartre – who, without *Manhattan Transfer* and the USA trilogy *The 42nd Parallel, 1919* and *The Big Money*, would not have written *Roads to Freedom* the way he did – said of its author, quite correctly: 'Dos Passos has invented just one thing: an art of narration. But this is enough to create a universe.'

The art of Dos Passos consists of a series of techniques aimed at making the realist illusion persuasive, communicating to the reader the sensation of being directly confronted with life, the objective world of what is narrated, without the mediation of literature and of the author. The whole of the novel is made up of a series of pictures, some very brief, like fleeting film images, which combine in a great mosaic: the protoplasm of New York. Each vignette is a slice of life of some character, which begins and ends arbitrarily without the whole episode coming to an end, so that the reader feels at once close to but also distanced from the men and women that file incessantly through the book. Unable to concentrate on or get inside any of the characters, the reader feels somewhat bewildered and confused by the lively, dispersed nature of the tale which conceals a very rigorous order and intention: to describe not the parts, but the whole, that great plural being in which the parts give glimpses of the whole.

Collage had been invented years before in painting but Dos Passos was the first to make it into a narrative technique in *Manhattan Transfer*. The method would later be perfected in the USA trilogy. Headlines and fragments of newspapers, advertisements and street signs, slip into the narrative, to fix the historical moment, to outline the social context of an episode and, in certain cases, to reveal the final outcome of some character whose good or bad fortune has given him the doubtful honour of appearing as a mention in a newspaper.

The novel starts at the beginning of the century and ends in the middle of the 1920s. The reader feels this quarter century pass without any sense of continuity, like a long and intricate panoramic shot of subtly worked images. These were also the years in which cinema had, for the first time, become a major influence and Dos Passos was one of the first narrators to make skilful use of certain filmic narrative resources and techniques in literary narrative (although curiously in *Manhattan Transfer*, where the whole of New York appears, there is not a single scene that takes place in a cinema). This can be seen in the visual nature of the descriptions, the pliable, sensuous feel of the whole book and, above all, in the structure of montage, which is very similar to that of a film. The treatment of time in the novel comes out of a cinematographic rather than a literary tradition; there is a delicate transposition from one genre to another which Dos Passos achieved with total success. In each scene, there are temporal and spatial 'silences', which occur without warning, moments and places silenced by the narrator, violent hiatuses of minutes or hours, of a few yards or long distances, which are not narrated, not mentioned, in the way that a film cuts from one image to the next and the characters can have changed age or setting without the spectator becoming confused or the narration losing its fluency. These jumps in time or in space are worked into the narrative of *Manhattan Transfer* with great mastery so that the reader scarcely notices them. But he does notice, on the other hand, how well they work in the narration: the pace that they set, the sensation of movement, of life developing, of time without pauses, and also the condensation that this technique permits, the density and the authenticity of life that is being narrated.

Dos Passos's novel also gives the impression of being a symphony because within it, as in a vast and ambitious musical composition, certain beings and themes are hinted at, disappear and then reappear, connected to other themes within an integrated and synthetic movement which, at a given moment, is presented to us as a compact and self-sufficient world. In this world, noise and music play a major part. Speech defines the origins and the education of the characters, with their rich ethnic diversity, their slang and their professional and social codes. Fashionable songs and dances appear from time to time as landmarks which define the period of the scenes, enliven the atmosphere and help to strengthen the impression that the 'real' world is being presented.

The objectivity of the narration is almost absolute. Dos Passos, who was a great admirer of Flaubert, once stated that he also had a passion for the *mot juste* and in this novel, the precision of the language is almost infallible and is one of the ways in which the impersonal appearance, the self-sufficient nature, of the fiction is achieved. I say 'almost' because in some episodes there is at times too brusque a change of point of view in the narration – we notice that the perspective changes from one character to another – which, for an instant, jeopardizes that Flaubertian imperative of the invisibility of the narrator. (It is enough for the attention of the reader to be distracted for one second from *what* the novel is narrating to *how* it is being narrated, for the obstructive and disappointing shadow of the narrator to appear.) But these are scarcely furtive shadows within an extraordinary novelistic construction in which both the language and the organization of the tale mutually support and enrich the composition of the fictional world.

Few modern novels demonstrate as clearly as *Manhattan Transfer* the propensity of narrative fiction to offer a 'total' vision of the world. This is a desire to extend itself, to grow and multiply through descriptions, characters and incidents in order to exhaust all the possibilities, to represent its world on the largest and also the most minute scale, at all levels and from all angles. A successful novel is like an iceberg: only part of it is revealed, but in such a way that the reader's own imagination can complete the picture. But a few novels, the greatest achievements of the genre, works like *War and Peace, Madame Bovary, Ulysses, In Remembrance of Things Past, The Magic Mountain*, seem to us, thanks to their extraordinary ambition, their fantastic scope, to have achieved that utopian design inherent in the art of the novel, of having described a world, a story, in a *total* way, both intensively and extensively, qualitatively and quantitatively. This novel by Dos Passos belongs to this illustrious list of omnivorous works.

The vastness of the world that unfolds before our eyes is sometimes dizzying. The hundred or so characters that move through its one hundred and thirty episodes represent crowds, humanity itself fighting – usually in vain – to get on, to become rich, to attain some form of happiness or simply to exist in a powerful and indifferent city which is also, for them, a great prison of steel and asphalt. Bankers, union men, lawyers, actresses, thieves, murderers, businessmen, journalists, tramps, doormen, rub shoulders, meet and part company on its pavements, as if in an immense kaleidoscope which shows us the seething life of the city. The novel keeps us mainly on a surface reality, showing us the scenes, what people are doing and hearing, what they are saying, but from time to time it also introduces us to the intimate life of their thoughts, their fantasies, their dreams and visions. These brief incursions into subjectivity are welcome because they add touches of delicacy and poetry, even of madness, to a text whose realist harshness and dryness sometimes leaves us breathless. Fantasy often invades the characters before some catastrophe, like the vision that assails the parricide Bud Kopening before he commits suicide or the dream of the poor seamstress Anna Cohen – of the revolutionary Red Guard parading down Fifth Avenue – before the fire consumes and disfigures her.

A novel fails or is successful on its own terms – through the strength of its characters, the subtlety of its plot, the elegance of its construction, the richness of its prose – and not because of its view of the real world. However, all fiction, however self-sufficient and resistant to exterior reality, has powerful and unbreakable links with that other life, the one that is not created by the magic of fantasy and the literary word, but life in the raw, lived and not invented. In artistic terms, one does not need to compare 'fictional' and 'real' reality, because in order to judge if a novel is good or bad, a work of genius or mediocre, it is not necessary to know if it was faithful or unfaithful to the real world, if it reproduced or invented it. It is the intrinsic power of persuasion and not its documentary value that determines a fiction's artistic worth.

However, a book like *Manhattan Transfer* cannot be judged solely from a literary perspective, as the polished artistic product that it undoubtedly is. Because the novel, as well as being a beautiful lie that distances us from the real world, is also a parable that is determined to elucidate and educate us in a critical fashion, not about the world we are reading, but about the world that we inhabit in our reality as readers. This book is the best example of what Lukács called critical realism, fiction which is an instrument of analysis, a dissection of the real world and a denunciation of the myths, fraudulence and injustices of history.

What remains, almost sixty-five years after its publication, of the accusations and warnings that *Manhattan Transfer* made about New York? Capitalism went through the crisis that the novel anticipates — the crash of 1929 — and survived it, just as it survived the Second World War, the Cold War and the disintegration of the European empires and it is today in better health than ever. It is not capitalism but socialism which seems in decline today on a world scale. But the book was not wrong in pointing to the Achilles' heel of industrial capitalism, that it makes men more prosperous but not happier. It suppresses poverty, ignorance, unemployment and manages to ensure a decent standard of living for most people. But today, as in the years that preceded the Great Depression, when Dos Passos wrote his novel, in New York, London, Zurich or Paris, in all the citadels of industrial development, the prodigious development of science, opportunities and comfort have not made women less tense or anguished than Ellen Thatcher in the novel nor have they rid innumerable men of the same corrosive feeling of emptiness, of spiritual frustration, of leading an insufficient, petty, directionless life that torments Jimmy Herf and causes him to run away.

Will modern civilization, which has conquered so many challenges, be capable of overcoming this one? Will it also find a way of enriching men spiritually and morally so that not only the great demons of material need are defeated but also egotism, solitude and ethical dehumanization which are continual sources of frustration and unhappiness in societies with the highest standards of living on this planet? While industrial and technological civilization does not give a positive answer to these questions, *Manhattan Transfer*, as well as being one of the most admirable works of modern fiction, will continue to be a warning hanging, like a sword, above our heads.

London, 22 May 1989

# The World Cup, Spain 1982

### Before the orgy

Albert Camus has written that the best lessons in ethics were taught him not in university lecture rooms but on football grounds. I am sure that Camus who, like Henri Montherlant, was a reasonable player and an enthusiastic football fan, would have loved to have visited the Nou Camp stadium in Barcelona, as I did this morning, on the eve of the opening of the World Cup.

As soon as I set foot in the friendly chaos of the Press Office – with its computers and pretty hostesses in baggy trousers, bermudas and jockey caps, who were giving out to the visiting correspondents elegant leather bags containing the latest budget of the Generalitat of Catalonia, written in Catalan alexandrines, and other civic literature of the same sort – I was assailed by questions about my compatriots, the sorcerers. What sorcerers? The ones the Peruvian team had brought with them to cancel out the evil powers of the witch doctors travelling with the Cameroon team, their first opponents in La Coruña.

It seemed to me pointless to disappoint my colleagues by explaining to them that the Peruvian sorcerers were almost certainly representatives of the national picaresque tradition who had found a flamboyant and a cheap way of attending Spain '82 and I informed them that they were sorcerers from the most important witchcraft region in Peru, the highlands of Ayabaca, where girls learn to fly on broomsticks before learning to walk and boys learn to turn themselves into toads, snakes and guinea pigs and then change back again. I was besieged by questions. Did Peruvian sorcerers practise black or white magic? I opted for ambiguity, stating that they were experts in *cholo* magic, that is mestizo magic, and I predicted that with all these extra-football ingredients, the Peru–Cameroon game would be really bewitching.

I met my old friend Andrés, who has the dreadful honour of doing battle with the four thousand accredited journalists and the ten thousand fraudulent ones who had come to Spain '82. He was swamped by a crowd worthy of Babel, which, in all known languages – including Latin, papiamento, braille and telepathy – was asking him for passes, typewriters, telexes, travel tickets, hotels, secretaries, masseuses and complaining that the Generalitat had not included, among the literature so gracefully offered to the visitors, the budgets for the previous year, the year before that and the forthcoming year. Everyone threatened him with personal and family catastrophe and imminent death, and the most aggressive were not the Scots but the French. One of them, heedless of cacophony, kept on reciting: 'Ce n'est l'organisation, c'est l'inorganisation, Monsieur.'

An infamous calumny, of course. In fact, everything is running wonderfully, but it's taking its toll on the staff. To judge by my friend Andrés, who was thin before and is now all skin and bone, the organizers of the World Cup have reduced their life expectancy and gained innumerable grey hairs preparing for this extraordinary event.

When I saw him under siege, I hardly dared approach him with my tiny problem – how to get to La Coruña after the World Cup opening ceremony in Barcelona – but as soon as he saw me, Andrés, who is the friendliest man in the world, broke free of the press-assassin pack with a benevolent smile, took me by the arm and led me on a comprehensive tour of the new installations in Nou Camp.

I ended up amazed and exhausted. I almost did not recognize the stadium where, ten years before, I had come to cheer on Barsa – whose team included another sorcerer compatriot, el Cholo Sotil – since it was now so much bigger and more elegant. It is clear that they have thrown everything at it to stun and amaze the 120,000 fans who will be filling the stands.

While he showed me, with legitimate pride, the aerodynamic press rooms, with machines with every keyboard imaginable for the ungrateful journalists, the press conference rooms, the clinics, the four-star dressing rooms, the five-fork restaurants, the misty saunas, made me try out the soft, brand new seats and breathe in the aroma of the fragrant Virgilian grass on the pitch, my friend Andrés also gave me a few lessons on the erotic nature of football.

I will synthesize clumsily some of his disturbing allegories and worrying metaphors. A goal is an orgasm through which a player, a team, a ground, a country, all of humanity, suddenly discharge their vital energy. Every country plays football the way it makes love. The tactics and techniques of the players on the field are nothing more than a translation into football of national erotic customs and fantasies. The Brazilian footballer, for example, is lingering and sensual, he caresses the ball tenderly rather than kicking it, he does not like to part with it and, instead of putting the ball into the net, he prefers to put himself into the net with it. The Russian footballer, by contrast, is sad, melancholic and violent, prone to unpredictable and contradictory outbursts, and his relationship to the ball brings to mind the relationships of those Slav lovers with their girlfriends, full of poems and tears, that end up in pistol shots. And, without beating about the bush or being coy, is the grass on a football field just that, or is not rather a grand pubic area, a green, inviting down?

When I said goodbye to my friend Andrés, I understood at last why Camus had said those things about football grounds and I was so excited imagining the extraordinary orgies that awaited us in the World Cup that I did not even notice that the beautiful assistant who had been delegated to get me to Galicia after the opening event, had got me tickets for Santiago (in Chile, alas).

Barcelona, 12 June 1982

## The empty pleasure

A couple of years ago, I heard the Brazilian anthropologist Roberto da Matta give a brilliant lecture in which he explained that the popularity of football – which is as strong today as ever – expresses people's innate desire for legality, equality and freedom.

His argument was clever and amusing. According to him, the public sees football as a representation of a model society, governed by clear and simple laws which everyone understands and observes and which, if violated, brings immediate punishment to the guilty party. Apart from being a just arena, a football field is an egalitarian space which excludes all favouritism and privilege. Here, on this grass marked out by white lines, every person is valued for what he is, for his skill, dedication, inventiveness and effectiveness. Names, money and influence count for nothing when it comes to scoring goals and earning the applause or the whistles from the stands. The football player, furthermore, exercises the only form of freedom that society can allow its members if it is not to come apart: to do whatever they please as long as it is not explicitly prohibited by rules that everyone accepts.

This is what, in the end, stirs the passions of the crowds that, the world over, pour into the grounds, follow games on television with rapt attention and fight over their football idols: the secret envy, the unconscious nostalgia for a world that, unlike the one they live in which is full of injustice, inequality and corruption, gripped by lawlessness and violence, offers instead a world of harmony, law and equality.

Could this beautiful theory be true? Would that it were, for there is no doubt that it is seductive and that nothing could be more positive for the future of humanity than to have these civilized feelings nestling in the instinctive depths of the crowds. But what is probable is that, as always, reality overtakes theory, showing it to be incomplete. Because theories are always rational, logical, intellectual — even those that propose irrationality and madness — and in society and in individual behaviour, unreason, the unconscious and pure spontaneity will always play a part. They are both inevitable and immeasurable.

I'm scribbling these lines in a seat in Nou Camp, a few minutes before the Argentina–Belgium game that is kicking off this World Cup. The signs are favourable: a radiant sun, a clear sky, an impressive multi-coloured crowd full of waving Spanish, Catalan, Argentine and a few Belgian flags, noisy fireworks, a festive, exuberant atmosphere and applause for the regional dancing and gymnastic displays which are a warm-up to the game (and which are of a much higher standard than is normal on these occasions).

Of course this is a much more pleasant and appealing world than the one left outside, behind the Nou Camp stands and behind the people applauding the dances and the patterns made by dozens of young people on the pitch. This is a world without wars, like those in the South Atlantic and the Lebanon, which the World Cup has relegated to second place in the minds of millions of fans throughout the world who, in the next two hours, will be thinking, like those of us here in the stands, of nothing else except the passes and the shots of the twenty-two Argentine and Belgian players who are opening the tournament.

Perhaps the explanation for this extraordinary contemporary phenomenon, the passion for football — a sport raised to the status of a lay religion, with the greatest following of all — is in fact a lot less complicated than sociologists and psychologists would have us suppose, and is simply that football offers people something that they can scarcely ever have: an opportunity to have fun, to enjoy themselves, to get excited, worked up, to feel certain intense emotions that daily routine rarely offers them.

To want to have fun, to enjoy oneself, to have a good time, is a most legitimate aspiration, a right as valid as the desire to eat and work. For many, doubtless complex, reasons, football has taken on this role in the world today with more widespread success than any other sport.

Those of us who like, and get pleasure from, football are not in any way surprised at its great popularity as a collective entertainment. But there are many who do not understand this fact and, furthermore, deplore and criticize it. They see the phenomenon as deplorable because, they say, football alienates and impoverishes the masses, distracting them from important issues. Those who think like this forget that it is important to have fun. They also forget that what characterizes an entertainment, however intense and absorbing, and a good game of football is enormously intense and absorbing, is that it is ephemeral, non-transcendent, innocuous. An experience where the effect disappears at the same time as the cause. Sport, for those who enjoy it, is the love of form, a spectacle which does not transcend the physical, the sensory, the instant emotion; which, unlike, for example, a book or a play, scarcely leaves a trace in the memory and does not enrich or impoverish knowledge. And this is its appeal: that it is exciting and empty. For that reason, intelligent and unintelligent, cultured and uncultured people can equally enjoy football. That's enough for now. The King has arrived. The teams have come out. The World Cup has been officially opened. The game is beginning. That's enough writing. Let's enjoy ourselves a bit.

Barcelona, 13 June 1982

## Maradona and the Heroes

Because he had a lifeless game in the opening match against Belgium, many people were asking where the myth of Maradona came from and why it still endured. After the Argentina–Hungary game, which the little star lit up from beginning to end with the fireworks of his skill, there are no longer any doubts: Maradona is the Pelé of the 1980s. More than that: he is one of the living deities that men create in order to worship themselves through these deities.

For a period that will be fatally brief – for this is the most absolute and transient of reigns – the Argentinian is now, for millions of people throughout the world, what Pelé, Cruyff, Di Stéfano, Puskas and a few others once were, also for the briefest imperial moment: the personification of football, the hero who is the emblem of the sport. The thousand million pesetas which, it is rumoured, Barcelona has paid to sign him up, is a clear proof that Maradona has already assumed this mantle, and to judge by the way he played against the Hungarians, this World Cup will show that Barsa has made a good investment. Ten million dollars is a lot of money to pay for a simple mortal who kicks a football, but nothing if what they are buying is a myth.

Maradona is a myth because he plays marvellously, but also because his name and his face are immediately engraved on the memory and because, for some indecipherable reason that has nothing to do with reason, he seems at first sight intelligent and pleasant. Has this impression something to do with his size? In the game against Hungary, watching him operate against those tall and muscular Magyar defenders, who were pathetically unable to contain him, one had the agreeable impression that there is innate justice; that in football, as well, it is true that skill is more important than force, that what counts when it comes to kicking a football is not strength, but imagination and ideas.

However, despite his small size, Maradona does not give the impression of being frail. He seems solid and strong, perhaps because he has powerful legs, with bulging muscles, which can withstand, without injury, the heavy tackles of the opposing defenders, however big and strong. That face of his, with its dreaming, child-like naivety, seemingly full of good intentions, is a great asset when it comes to wheedling what he wants out of the demoralized bipeds who have to mark him, for it is true that when he needs to attack and play tough, he can do so with a strength that seems incompatible with his physique.

It is not easy to define Maradona's game. It is so complex that each adjective used to describe it needs to be given an extra shade of meaning. He is not brilliant and histrionic, like the lordly Pelé, but he is so effective when he hits those powerful shots at goal from the most unlikely angles or when, with a short pass as precise as a theorem, he sets in motion an irresistible attack, that it would be unjust not to call him spectacular, a player who turns a game into an exhibition of individual genius (or into a 'recital', as one critic wrote very aptly about his game against Hungary).

Maradona complicates the division that we thought to be valid between a scientific, typically European football and an artistic, Latin American football. The Argentinian forward is both these things at once and neither of them in particular; he is a curious amalgam, in which intelligence and intuition, calculation and inventiveness, are always in play. As has happened in literature, Argentina has produced a style of football which is the most European expression of being Latin American.

If, in the next games, Maradona plays as he played against Hungary, organizing his team's attacks with the same effectiveness, fighting for the ball with the same energy, shooting and heading at goal with the same strength and precision and even going back to help out his defence, there is no doubt that however well Argentina does in the final reckoning, he will be the hero of the championship (and of years to come).

People need contemporary heroes, beings that they can turn into gods. No country escapes this rule. Cultured or uncultured, rich or poor, capitalist or socialist, every society feels this irrational need to enthrone idols of flesh and blood and burn incense to them. Politicians, military men, film stars, sportsmen, crooks, playboys, saints and ferocious bandits have been elevated to the altars of popularity and turned into a collective cult, for which the French have a good image: they call them 'sacred monsters'. Well, footballers are the most inoffensive people on which one can confer this idolatrous function.

They are, it is quite clear, infinitely more innocuous than politicians or warriors, in whose hands the idolatry of the masses can become a fearful weapon, and the cult of the footballer is not infected by the miasma of frivolity that always surrounds the deification of a film star or society's low life. The cult of a football star lasts as long as his talents last and fades when these fade. It is ephemeral because football stars soon burn out in the green fire of the stadia and the followers of the religion are implacable: on the terraces, applause soon gives way to jeers.

It is also the least alienating of cults since to admire a footballer is to admire something very close to pure poetry or abstract painting. It is to admire form for form's sake, without any rationally identifiable content. The virtues of football – skill, agility, speed, virtuosity, power – can not easily be associated with pernicious social attitudes or inhuman behaviour. For that reason, if we need to have heroes, then long live Maradona.

La Coruña, 19 June 1982

# The Story of a Massacre

When he got off the plane that had taken him from Lima to Ayacucho that morning – Tuesday 25 January 1983 – the photographer from *Oiga*, Amador García, was bursting with pleasure. At last he had been given what he had been requesting for months: an important assignment instead of bland photographs of fashions or sporting fixtures. 'You're going to Ayacucho,' the editor of the magazine had said. 'You get to Huaychao and find out what happened between the Indians and the guerrillas. Send me the photos on the Thursday plane, because I want to use them for the cover. Good luck.' Amador knew that it would be devilishly difficult to get an exclusive, because ever since the events in Huaychao had been made public, Ayacucho had been swarming with reporters. But he was sure that he could do better than his colleagues. He was a shy, tenacious man, who had earned his living as an itinerant photographer before getting a job on the magazine. He was married with two children, seven and two years old.

His heart must have been beating fast that morning, as he passed past the sentries armed with machine guns who were guarding the airport at Ayacucho. Because Amador was going back home. He had been born in Ayacucho thirty-two years earlier and spoke Quechua, which would surely be very useful to him up in Huaychao where very few peasants would understand Spanish.

That morning, Amador had telephoned an editor at *Oiga* from the airport in Lima to remind him to ask the authorities for cooperation. Heading for the centre of Ayacucho, Amador noticed the changes in the city – the once quiet, narrow, old-style streets, full of churches and colonial houses, now had their walls daubed with revolutionary slogans in praise of the armed struggle, were subject to a curfew from ten in the evening to five in the morning, and had armed patrols on street corners. Meanwhile, in Lima, the editor at *Oiga*, Uri Ben Schmuel, spoke to the commander of the Civil Guard at the Ministry of the Interior, Eulogio Ramos, and got him to promise to ring the Ninth Police Headquarters at Ayacucho. Commander Ramos would later say that he could not keep his promise because there was a fault on the line, but that he had sent a radiogram giving details of Amador's trip. According to the military command in Ayacucho, this radiogram did not arrive and Amador García did not report to the Ninth Police Headquarters.

Why didn't he report in? Perhaps because by the time he had reached the Plaza de Armas of his native city, he had realized what his colleagues from Lima already knew: that if he wanted to get to Huaychao, the worst thing to do would be to ask the military authorities for help. They were very wary of journalists, if not downright hostile, and had refused almost all their requests to be taken to the areas where there was fighting. So far, nobody had managed to obtain permission to go up to Huaychao which, in any event, was a difficult place to reach. It is in the province of Huanta, some 12,000 feet high on top of the mountains, and the only way of reaching it is up steep slopes, where you run the risk of meeting the guerrillas or the *sinchis* (the anti-subversion troops of the Civil Guard) who might confuse you with the enemy. For this reason, many journalists had given up on the idea of going to Huaychao. Amador learned all this from a Lima colleague, the reporter from *Gente*, Jorge Torres, whom he met in the Plaza de Armas. But Amador was not going to be so easily defeated by these difficulties. Instead of being put off, he argued his case with such conviction that in a few minutes it was he who had convinced Torres that they should go to Huaychao, whatever the obstacles. Wouldn't it be wonderful to discover, with our own eyes and with our own cameras, what had happened? Jorge Torres went with Amador to the Hostal Santa Rosa, where the journalists who had come to Ayacucho to get information about the guerrillas and a number of policemen who had arrived to fight these guerrillas were all staying. In the hotel, Amador García met several colleagues from Lima – some were just getting out of bed – who also wanted to go to Huaychao, but, given the problems, had not made the trip.

Sitting on the patio of the hotel, in the pleasant heat of the morning – the nights are always cold and the mornings warm in the Andes – and gazing at the peaks, sharply outlined in the clear air, which encircle the old city, outside whose walls the troops of Simón Bolívar fought the battle that sealed the independence of Latin America, Amador García and Jorge Torres talked to half a dozen colleagues. In the end, they all agreed to go to Huaychao together.

Shortly before midday, a group of them – including the corpulent

Jorge Sedano from *La República* and Amador García – went to the Plaza de Armas and hired a taxi for a journey outside the city early the next morning. The driver, Salvador Luna Ramos, agreed to take them as far as Yanaorco – on the Tambo road, an hour from Ayacucho – for 30,000 *soles* (roughly $50). The journalists did not tell him that their final destination was Huaychao. Did they keep this from him for fear that the information would be passed on to the military authorities, who would prevent them from making the journey? However, that morning and afternoon they discussed their travel plans out loud in the Hostal Santa Rosa, and other clients, as well as the manager, saw them consulting maps and planning their itinerary. The journalists gave the taxi driver 15,000 *soles* and they agreed that he would come to pick them up as soon as the curfew was lifted.

The route they decided upon was mainly planned by two journalists from Ayacucho who had become involved with the project: the director of the newspaper *Noticias,* Octavio Infante, and the Ayacucho-based correspondent for *Diario de Marka,* Félix Gavilán. Infante's mother's family, the Argumedos, lived in Chacabamba, a small settlement at the foot of the mountain where Huaychao was located. They decided to go on the Tambo road to the Tocto lagoon, Toctococha, which was very near Yanaorco. From there they would walk to Chacabamba to ask Infante's half-brother, Juan Argumedo, to take them to Huaychao.

With the travel plans made, some of them went to the market to buy trainers, pullovers and plastic capes for the rain, while others – de la Piniella and Félix Gavilán – went to the cinema. They could all sleep peacefully, because that night there were no explosions or gunshots in Ayacucho. Although they were doubtless excited, they had no inkling of the very great risk that they were about to run. Except, perhaps, Félix Gavilán who, that night, asked his wife to pack in his travelling bag a white sheet which could be used as a flag of peace in case they met the *sinchis* or the *terrucos* (terrorists) on the way.

Salvador Luna went to the hotel at five twenty in the morning. Jorge Sedano, washed and dressed, was there to meet him. There was a change of plan: Jorge Torres had decided not to go. But he came down to say goodbye and saw his companions piling into the car and the long face of the driver who had not expected so many passengers. The travellers joked with 'All Mouth' Torres and one of them made the macabre remark, 'Come on, you idiot, take a last photo of us.' But,

Torres recalls, none of his colleagues was really nervous. They were all in excellent spirits.

### A general pleased to be reporting good news

Why did the journalists want to get to this village which does not appear on the maps? Why was the name Huaychao on the lips of every Peruvian?

Because, three days earlier, General Clemente Noel, head of the Political and Military Command of the Emergency Zone, had made a sensational announcement in Ayacucho: that the peasants of Huaychao had killed seven Sendero Luminoso (Shining Path) guerrillas. They had stripped them of arms, ammunition, red flags and propaganda. The diminutive general glowed with pleasure. Normally a laconic man, he spoke at length, praising the courage of the Indians of Ayacucho for standing up to the people that he always referred to as 'subversive criminals'. The response of the villagers, he said, was a reaction against those 'cruel men who go into villages to steal animals, kill the authorities, rape the women and abduct the young'.

The general's happiness was due to the fact that the killings in Huaychao were the first piece of 'good news' that he had been able to give since taking charge of the fight against Sendero Luminoso five weeks before. Until then, although the military communiqués sometimes spoke of encounters with Senderistas, the impression was that the forces of General Noel could not get to grips with the guerrillas, who slipped through their fingers thanks to the support, active or passive, of the peasant communities. Proof of this was the way in which the Senderistas kept on blowing up bridges and power lines, blockading roads, and occupying villages, where they beat or executed thieves, spies, and the authorities put in place after the municipal elections of 1980. The seven dead in Ayacucho were in some ways the first genuinely defeated guerrillas that the head of the Political and Military Command could show to the country. It was also the first incident which, since the beginning of the insurrection two years previously, seemed to indicate that Sendero Luminoso did not count on the support of the peasantry or at least, their neutrality.

How had the events in Huaychao occurred? General Noel was evasive when asked for precise details. He said that some peasants had gone to the police station in Huanta to report the matter. A patrol, led by a lieutenant of the Civil Guard, had gone up into the mountains to Huaychao – a journey of twenty hours through ravines, precipices and desolate plains – and had verified the killings. The submachine guns of the dead Senderistas had been stolen in several attacks on police stations in the interior of Ayacucho.

Many people thought that General Noel knew more than he was saying. The general had no luck with journalists. It was obvious that he had not been trained to deal with people who, unlike the rank and file in the barracks, were not satisfied with what they heard, asked impertinent questions and even had the audacity to question what they were told. In fact, General Noel was ill-prepared for Peru's return to democracy in 1980, after twelve years of military dictatorship. When the government of Belaúnde took up office, the newspapers and television and radio stations that had been expropriated by the dictatorship were returned to their owners, other newspapers were founded and the freedom of the press was re-established. These freedoms had, on occasion, been taken to such disconcerting lengths that General Noel's lack of confidence was not completely incomprehensible, especially with regard to newspapers like *Diario de Marka* (which had a Marxist orientation) and *La República* (founded by bureaucrats of the former government), which ran stories strongly attacking the counter-insurgency forces, accusing them of crimes and abuses.

Did General Noel keep quiet because he did not want to give the opposition press any more ammunition with which to attack the *sinchis*? What seems clear is that the general only talked in generalities because by that Sunday, 23 January, he did not have any more information. Not even the lieutenant in charge of the patrol that went up to Huaychao had a complete picture of what had happened. He, and the guards under his command, came from other parts of Peru and only one of them could speak Quechua. On the way to Huaychao, they saw large numbers of Indians on the mountain tops, with white flags. These massed peasants, who were in a very agitated state, alarmed them. But there were no incidents. In Huaychao they found the bodies of the seven guerrillas. The peasants asked to keep their weapons, but General Noel had given orders not to leave them behind since he felt that these weapons would be a much stronger source of attraction to the 'subversive criminals' than any desire to avenge their dead. The *varayocs* (the traditional authorities in the community) stated, through an interpreter, that they had killed the *terrucos* by tricking them.

When they saw them approach, the people of Huaychao went out to meet them, waving red flags and cheering for the Communist Party of Peru (the official name of Sendero Luminoso) and the armed struggle. Chanting the songs and slogans of the 'militia', they herded the guerrillas to the community house. When they had them totally surrounded, they fell on them and killed them in a few seconds, with axes, knives and stones hidden under their ponchos. Only one Senderista managed to escape, badly wounded. This was all that General Clemente Noel knew at the time of his jubilant press conference on 23 January. He was not even aware that three of the seven guerrillas who had been killed were boys of fourteen and fifteen years of age, who had disappeared from their parents' houses some months before. What had happened in Huaychao was the tip of the iceberg of some extraordinary events that had taken place, simultaneously, in many communities in the heights of Huanta. These would only become known in the following days and weeks.

How did Peru greet the news of the killings in Huaychao? The government, the democratic parties and independent public opinion felt the same as General Noel. What a relief! The peasants are not identified with the terrorists, they are fighting them. That means that Sendero Luminoso will not last long. Let's hope that other communities follow the example of Huaychao and put an end to these people who blow up electricity pylons and kill mayors. While the democratic sectors were reacting in this way, the extreme left refused to believe that the peasants were responsible for this act and declared in Parliament and in *Diario de Marka* that the real executioners of the guerrillas were the *sinchis* or paramilitary forces disguised as peasants.

Nobody, however, stopped to think about the legal and moral questions posed by the killings in Huaychao, or the dangerous precedent that had been set. For it was not just the military and the journalists that were out of practice in behaving democratically in a country that had suffered a long dictatorship. This ill had spread to every citizen.

But, while some applauded and others placed a question mark over the identities of those responsible for the massacre at Huaychao, nobody was satisfied at the small amount of information available. Everyone wanted to know more. For that reason, dozens of reporters had gone out to Ayacucho. And for that reason, those eight reporters, on that morning of 26 January, had squeezed into Luna Ramos's taxi.

## Through the high sierra

The cobbled streets of Ayacucho were deserted and it was still cold when the taxi left the hotel and, passing bleary-eyed soldiers, went to Bellido Street to pick up Octavio Infante, the director of *Noticias*, who had spent the night at his printing office and had not even told his wife about the journey. The car made another stop in the Ovalo de la Magdalena for the travellers to buy cigarettes, lemons, biscuits, sugar, condensed milk and fizzy drinks. It left Ayacucho, crossing the police check-point at Magdalena. The driver stopped in the queue of traffic and when the guard came up, the passengers showed him their identity cards. He did not check them, but just said 'Go on'. That was the only check-point that they came across on their trip.

There would later be a controversy as to whether or not the authorities knew about the expedition. General Noel insists that they knew nothing about it. In any event , they could not have found out about it at the check-point, because nobody spoke to the travellers there. If the Political and Military Command had heard of the expedition, it might have been through someone at the hotel (where, as we have said, some policemen were staying). What is likely is that the plan for the journey was known to minor officials, who attached no importance to it. Journalists had made journeys like this before, to far-flung, dangerous places, without the authorities taking any special precautions.

Despite being so uncomfortable — with five in the back and four in the front including the driver — the journalists never stopped telling jokes and Luna Ramos found the journey entertaining. The taxi skirted the Pampa de la Quinua — the site of the battle of Ayacucho — where they had hoped to have breakfast, but the small houses that offer food, lodging and handicrafts were shut. They took the road to Tambo, which winds up to a height of 12,000 feet, with sheer drops. As they made the ascent, the trees thinned out and the landscape was covered with black rocks and clumps of cactus. They began to see red flags bearing the hammer and sickle on several mountain tops or waving over the ravines. Along this road, Sendero Luminoso had made a number of attacks on small farms and their columns often stopped vehicles to demand a 'revolutionary quota'. There was very little traffic. They seemed to be the masters of this majestic location.

Who were the journalists? With the exception of Amador García from *Oiga*, a weekly that supported the regime, the other seven were from opposition papers. Two of them – Willy Retto and Jorge Luis Mendívil – worked for *El Observador*, a moderate centre left newspaper. Willy Retto, twenty-seven years old, had journalism in the blood, since he was the son of a well-known photographer from *Ultima Hora*, and Jorge Luis Mendívil was twenty-two, but with his slight form and smooth face, he looked like an adolescent. They were both from Lima and this landscape and the Indians in sandals and coloured ponchos that they glimpsed herding flocks of llamas were as exotic to them as to anyone coming from abroad. In the few days that they had spent in Ayacucho, Willy Retto had been involved in an incident where the police had confiscated a roll of his film. The previous evening, he had scribbled a few lines to a woman in Lima. 'There are many things going on here that I never thought I would see and experience at such close range. I see the poverty of the people, the fear of the peasants, and the tension that we all feel is the same for the PIP [the Investigating Police], the GC [The Civil Guard] and the army as it is for Sendero and for innocent people.' Unlike Retto, who was not a political activist, Mendívil was a member of a left-wing organization, and he had insisted that his newspaper send him to Ayacucho. He had just moved from the international section to the Sunday supplement and he wanted to mark his debut with a report on Ayacucho.

Jorge Sedano was also from the coast, a stranger to the world of the sierra. At fifty-two, he was the oldest member of the group and also the fattest: his sixteen-stone frame was squashing the others on the seat. He was an outstanding photographer on the staff of *La República*, and one of the most popular newsmen in Lima, renowned for his photographs of motor races, his overwhelming good humour and his Rabelaisian appetite. A great cook, he bred cats and swore that he had invented a finger-licking cat stew. His love of the profession had brought him here. His editor had said, 'If you want to go to Ayacucho, lose some weight', but he had been so insistent that, in the end, he was sent out.

Eduardo de la Piniella, Pedro Sánchez and Félix Gavilán were from *Diario de Marka*, a cooperative publication of all the different Marxist groups. The most militant of the three, de la Piniella – thirty-three years old, tall, with light coloured eyes and hair, a sportsman – was a member of the Communist Revolutionary Party, a Maoist group. He was interested in literature and among his papers in Lima was a half-finished novel. Pedro Sánchez was recently married and since his arrival in Ayacucho he had spent a great deal of time photographing the city's homeless children. In contrast to the journalists already mentioned, Félix Gavilán — a member of the MIR (Movement of the Revolutionary Left) — knew the Andes. He was from Ayacucho, a former student of the School of Agronomy and he featured on a radio programme, broadcasting to the peasants in Quechua. He had spent a large part of his life working in Indian communities, as a journalist and an agricultural adviser. One of these communities had presented him with an owl, Pusha, which Félix had trained and he and his three children played with the owl every day. Octavio Infante was also from the region. Before becoming the owner of *Noticias,* he had been a worker, a rural teacher and a government employee. Also of the left, he seems to have been the least enthusiastic about the expedition. It could be that he was there more out of friendship towards his colleagues than for any journalistic reasons.

What did they hope to find in Ayacucho? Amador García: new material. Jorge Sedano: spectacular photos and all the better if the photos helped *La República's* line of embarrassing the government. The journalists doubted — or completely disbelieved — the story that the peasants had executed the seven Senderistas. They thought that those responsible for the killing were *sinchis* or that, perhaps, the seven dead were not guerrillas, but innocent peasants murdered by drunken or overbearing guards, as had happened on occasion. With variations depending on their more moderate or more radical political view-points, they were going to Huaychao to confirm certain truths that seemed to them self-evident: the abuses committed by the forces of order and the lies of the government concerning what was happening in the countryside of Ayacucho.

But the gravity of these matters was not reflected in their behaviour as they crossed the high plateau. Luna Ramos remembers that they did not stop laughing and joking and that, for example, they told Eduardo de la Piniella, who was wearing a green jacket, that, dressed as he was, anyone might mistake him for a *terruco* or a *sinchi.*

An hour out of Ayacucho, they stopped at Pacclla, half a dozen ramshackle huts between the road and a stream. There they finally found something to eat. While his passengers stretched their legs by the hut of a woman who agreed to make them a chicken broth, Luna Ramos went to the stream to get water for the radiator. When he got back, he found the journalists taking photographs. To get a group shot,

Willy Retto had clambered on to a rock. The journalists invited him to have some broth and did not let him pay. They stayed half an hour in Pacclla.

From their conversation on the journey, the driver knew that they intended going to Huaychao. They were also interested in Yanaorco because, when they saw the microwave radio tower still intact, one of them exclaimed, 'They lied to us. I bet they also lied to us about what happened in Huaychao.' They asked the driver to take them to the tower, on the Yanaorco turn-off. But Luna Ramos did not want to go, because the road was bad and because he thought it was dangerous, since the tower had been attacked on several occasions.

They did not mind him saying no and asked him to go past the Tocto lagoon and stop about seven hundred yards further on. Luna Ramos was surprised that they had got out of the car on that desolate plain. There was no road, only a faint path that people of the area used to get to Chacabamba, Balcón or Miscapampa without having to go through Tambo. That way, they would save an hour's walk. Octavio Infante took this route when he visited his family. But it had been a year since he had been to Chacabamba.

After taking the 15,000 *soles* for the fare, Luna Ramos turned his car around to go back to Ayacucho. He saw them for the last time, loaded with cameras and bags, beginning to climb up the mountain in single file. He silently wished them good luck, because the area they were entering had been declared a 'liberated zone' by Sendero Luminoso.

### The fourth sword of Marxism

Most Peruvians heard of Sendero Luminoso for the first time towards the end of the military dictatorship, one morning in 1980 when the people of Lima were confronted with the macabre spectacle of dogs hanging from street lamp posts. The animals bore placards with the name of Deng Xiaoping, accusing him of having betrayed the Revolution. This was the way Sendero Luminoso announced its existence. Senderistas still hang dogs as symbols of their phobias. They do this in certain villages to show – to a peasantry that does not know what China is – their contempt for the 'dog' Deng Xiaoping for causing the failure of the Cultural Revolution.

Sendero Luminoso was then a small faction, with few followers in Lima or elsewhere in Peru, with one exception: Ayacucho, in the south-east Andes. In this city of 80,000 inhabitants, the capital of one of the regions with the least resources and the highest figures of unemployment, illiteracy and infant mortality in the country, it was the most powerful political organization in the university. This was due to the charisma of its leader, who was born in Arequipa in 1934 and became a lecturer at the university there in 1963, after having graduated in humanities with a thesis on 'The Theory of the State in Kant'. His name has the ring of a biblical prophet: Abimael Guzmán.

Shy, somewhat obese, mysterious, elusive, the ideologue of Sendero Luminoso was an activist in the Communist Party from the 1950s and in 1964 he was one of the supporters of the Maoist tendency that formed the Red Flag Communist Party. He and his followers split with Red Flag and founded an organization which would be known as Sendero Luminoso, after a phrase of the ideologue José Mariátegui who argued that 'Marxist–Leninism would open up the shining path of the revolution', although its members only call themselves the Communist Party of Peru.

The strength of Sendero Luminoso in Ayacucho was the work of this lecturer, who married a middle-class woman from Ayacucho, Augusta La Torre, and turned her small house into a meeting place where groups of fascinated students came to listen to him. A puritan, with a real obsession for secrecy, nobody remembers having seen him give a speech or attend the street demonstrations organized by his disciples. Unlike other leaders of Sendero Luminoso, it is not known if he has ever been to China or if he has left Peru. He was imprisoned only once, in 1970, for a few days. In 1978, he went underground and there has never again been news of his whereabouts. He suffered a skin disease and was operated on in 1973, so it is unlikely that he is leading the guerrilla struggle in person. What is certain is that Comrade Gonzalo, his *nom de guerre*, is the undisputed leader of Sendero, the object of a religious cult. He is called The Fourth Sword of Marxism (the first three were Marx, Lenin and Mao), and he is said to have restored a doctrinal purity to Marxism which had been lost in the revisionist betrayals of Moscow, Albania, Cuba and, now, Beijing. Unlike other insurrectionary groups, Sendero Luminoso spurns publicity because of its contempt for the bourgeois media. No journalist has yet managed to interview Comrade Gonzalo.

His theories are surprising, both for their schematic quality and for the fanatical conviction with which they are applied. According to him, the Peru described by José Carlos Mariátegui in the 1930s is in essence the same as the Chinese reality analysed by Mao in the same period – a 'semi-feudal and semi-colonial society' – and would achieve liberation through an identical strategy to that of the Chinese revolution: a prolonged, popular war which, with the peasantry as its backbone, would 'assault' the cities.

The violence with which Sendero attacks the other left parties – calling them 'parliamentary cretins' – is perhaps even greater than that shown to the right-wing parties. The models of socialism that they support are Stalin's Russia, the Cultural Revolution of 'the gang of four' and Pol Pot's regime in Cambodia. This demented radicalism has seduced many young people in Ayacucho and other provinces in the Andes, perhaps because it offers a release for the frustration and impotence felt by university students and schoolchildren who see their future as a dead end. Given the current conditions in Peru, most young people in the interior of the country know that they will not find work in the saturated markets of their home towns and that they will have to emigrate to the capital, with the prospect of sharing the horrible life of internal migrants in the slums.

In 1978, the Senderistas began to disappear from the University of Ayacucho and, some months later, the acts of sabotage and terrorism started up. The first of these, in May 1980, was the burning of ballot boxes in the community of Chuschi, during the presidential elections. Nobody paid much attention to these first explosions in the Andes because westernized and modern Peru – half of its eighteen million inhabitants – was euphoric at the end of dictatorship and the re-establishment of democracy. Belaúnde Terry, deposed by the army in 1968, returned to the presidency with a strong majority (45.4 per cent of the vote) and his Popular Action party, with its allies, the Christian Popular party, had an absolute majority in Parliament.

The new government sought to minimize the importance of what was happening in Ayacucho. In his previous term of office (1962–8), Belaúnde Terry had to confront the insurrections of the MIR and the ELN (National Liberation Army) which had established guerrilla bases in the Andes and in the jungle with young people trained in Cuba, China and North Korea. The government put the army in charge of the anti-subversion campaign and the military repressed the rebellion brutally and effectively, summarily executing most of the rebels. But the military leaders of the anti-guerrilla movement also led the coup of 3

October which set up a *de facto* government for twelve years. For that reason, when Belaúnde Terry once again assumed the presidency, he tried at all costs to prevent the armed forces from leading the fight against Sendero Luminoso. He wanted to forestall a future coup and avoid the inevitable excesses of a military campaign.

For its first two years in office, the government buried its head in the sand with regard to Sendero Luminoso. It argued that the press was exaggerating its importance, that one could not talk of 'terrorism' but rather of 'Petardism' and that since the actions were taking place in only one department – less than 5 per cent of national territory – there was no reason to distract the Armed Forces from their specific function, which was the defence of the nation. The incidents were ordinary crimes, and the police could take care of them.

A batallion of *sinchis* of the Civil Guard ¬ the Quechua word means brave, daring – was sent to Ayacucho. Their ignorance of the region and its inhabitants, combined with insufficient training and poor equipment, meant that their efforts were largely ineffectual. More serious still, the police are often the slowest to adapt to the rule of law and give up the expediences of dictatorships. While the *sinchis* barely made a dent in the Senderistas, the acts of indiscipline in their own ranks and the abuses they committed multiplied: arbitrary arrest, torture, rape, robbery, woundings and even killings. This created a climate of fear and resentment in the poorer sectors which in turn helped Sendero Luminoso, since it tended to neutralize what might otherwise have been a rejection of their own activities.

These activities revealed a 'technological' efficiency and a cold, unscrupulous mentality. Beside blowing up electricity pylons and attacking mining camps to get hold of explosives, Sendero Luminoso destroyed the small agricultural properties of Ayacucho (the large properties had been redistributed by the Agrarian Reform in 1969), killing or wounding the owners. The most absurd of these operations was the total destruction of the Allpachaca Farm, run by the Agronomy Programme of the University of Ayacucho. The Senderistas killed all the animals, set fire to the machinery and caused 500 million *soles'* worth of damage. The reason that they gave was that Allpachaca had received North American aid (which was untrue). The real reason was Sendero's desire to cut all communication between the countryside and the city, which was seen as a centre of bourgeois corruption which one day the popular army would come to regenerate. Dozens of police stations in the rural areas were attacked. In August 1982, Sendero Luminoso boasted of having carried out '2900 successful operations'.

Among these were a large number of killings: eighty civilians and thirty-eight policemen and soldiers up to 31 December 1982. In the first four months of 1983, the figure rose to more than two hundred civilians and about one hundred soldiers and policemen, while the Political and Military Command claimed to have killed some five hundred Senderistas in the same period. Guards and police were killed in the street, as were local authorities, in particular elected mayors. The mayor of Ayacucho himself, Jorge Jáuregui, miraculously survived two bullets in the head fired by some young people on 11 December 1982. In the peasant communities, the 'people's courts' sentenced the real or supposed enemies of the guerrillas to execution or beatings.

The tactics of the rebels caused the collapse of civil power in the interior of Ayacucho: mayors, sub-prefects, governors, judges and other officials fled *en masse*. Even parish priests made their escape. The police stations which were blown up were not reopened. Convinced that it was too dangerous to keep squads of three or five men in the villages, the Civil Guard regrouped its forces in the cities, where they could protect themselves better. And what happened in the meantime to the peasant communities left to the mercy of the guerrillas? It is senseless to ask whether or not they received Sendero's indoctrination willingly or unwillingly, since they had no alternative but to support or, at least, to coexist with, those who had assumed real power.

It was into one of these zones that the eight journalists were now walking, among the brambles and clumps of *ichu* (brushwood). The region is divided into the lowlands, a valley where the most prosperous and modern settlements could be found (compared with the overall poverty and backwardness of the region) and the highlands, in which some twenty peasant communities of the same ethnic family, the Iquichanos, are scattered. The land is poor, the area is almost completely isolated and the customs are archaic. The lowlands were subject to almost constant attacks in 1980 and 1981 and all the police stations – in San José de Secce, Mayoc, Luricocha – were abandoned. Sendero Luminoso declared it a 'liberated zone' halfway through 1982.

This process had gone on almost unnoticed in the area of Peru that the journalists came from. They were better informed about the actions of Sendero Luminoso in the cities. The press had concentrated above all on the operations that had some repercussion in Lima, like the daring attack on the prison in Ayacucho on the morning of 3 March 1982, in which Sendero freed 247 prisoners and demonstrated to the government that 'Petardism' had increased enormously. But as to what was happening in these regions of the sierra, where journalists never go and where no news ever filters out, they had only a vague and general idea. Perhaps for that reason they were so unsuspecting when, on the top of the mountain, they saw the green and wooded slopes of Balcón and Miscapampa and the rectangular fields of Chacabamba. Octavio Infante pointed out to them his mother's small plot.

### In Chacabamba, with the Argumedo family

Doña Rosa de Argumedo, Octavio's mother, was grazing her animals on the fertile land and the fruit trees of the Chacabamba gorge when she caught sight of the eight men. Visitors to this place where Doña Rosa had spent her whole life were very rare, so the woman – in her sixties, barefoot, with elementary Spanish – scrutinized the travellers. When she recognized her son, she ran out to meet him, crying with joy.

Octavio Infante explained that his friends were journalists who were going to Huaychao to investigate 'that killing'. Doña Rosa saw that most of them were not from the mountains. And, what a state they were in! The fat one, Jorge Sedano, could scarcely speak for tiredness and altitude sickness and in that summer shirt, he was dying of cold. While the young boy, Jorge Luis Mendívil, had torn his trousers. They were on edge and thirsty. Doña Rosa led them to her small house made of mud, wood and corrugated iron and offered them lemons so that they could make a drink. They were soon joined by her children, Juana Lidia and Juan Argumedo, and Juan's wife, Julia Aguilar, who came from her house a hundred yards further up the mountain. The journalists talked to the family while they got their strength back. They lent Jorge Sedano a jacket and Mendívil a pair of trousers. Eduardo de la Piniella, notebook in hand, enquired about conditions there and asked Julia Aguilar, 'How do you get your children to a school?'

In the meantime, the director of *Noticias* asked his half-brother to be their guide and to hire them out some animals to carry their bags and cameras and also Jorge Sedano, who otherwise would find it very difficult to get up to Huaychao. Juan Argumedo agreed to rent them a horse and a mule and asked Juana Lidia to saddle them up. He agreed to guide them only as far as the Huachhuaccasa peak where, he said, he would come back with the animals.

From Chacabamba to Huaychao there is no visible path and, without a guide, the journalists could easily have become lost in those rocky, icy, slopes. However, the Argumedos had been to Huaychao on different occasions and also to the Iquichano village before it, Uchuraccay. They used to go to these communities in October, for the feast day of the Virgen del Rosario and in July, on the day of the Virgen del Carmen, to sell brandy, clothes, medicine and coca leaves, which the Indians chew with chalk to help them put up with hunger and cold. Juan Argumedo, Doña Rosa, Juana Lidia and Julia knew some of the villagers and had even established spiritual kinship links with them as godparents to their children.

Within the stratified social structure of the Andes, the Argumedos, although they are simple farmers, poor and uneducated, are a privileged and rich sector in comparison to the Indians of villages such as Uchuraccay and Huaychao, which are the poorest of the poor. The farmers of the valley, like the Argumedos, with their *mestizo* culture and their ability to speak in Quechua to the peasants and in Spanish to the people of the city, have been the traditional link between the Iquichanos and the rest of the world. Despite this, contact was sporadic and limited to those feast days or to the occasions on which the peasants from Huaychao and Uchuraccay went through Chacabamba on their way to the markets at Huanta or Tambo. Relations had been peaceful in the past. But that changed with the appearance of Sendero Luminoso and the *sinchis*. Communications were cut between the valley and the uplands and there was tension and hostility between the two areas. That was why the Argumedo family had not been up to sell their produce on the feast days of Rosario and del Carmen for two years.

Does that explain why they were so ill-informed about what was happening up there? Information in this region is transmitted by word of mouth and the perpetrators of the bloody events in the mountains were not interested in publicizing them. It is therefore possible that, despite being so close to the Iquichano communities, the Argumedo family knew as little about the events as General Noel, the government in Lima and the journalists who, after a brief rest, put out their cigarettes, picked up their bags and cameras and took some photos with the Argumedos before leaving. As a sign of gratitude, they gave the three women some biscuits and chewing gum. Their good humour was restored and they were, according to Julia Aguilar, 'happy and content'.

Octavio Infante asked Doña Rosa to lay out some blankets for them in the barn and prepare a meal, since they would try to get back that same night. The reason for the hurry was Amador García, who had to send his photos back on the Thursday plane. Their calculations were over optimistic. It is ten miles from Chacabamba to Uchuraccay and a further five miles to Huaychao and it would take them twice as long as local people, who can get from Chacabamba to Uchuraccay in two or three hours. Knowing that it would be difficult for them to get back in a day, Doña Rosa gave them the name of a woman she knew in Uchuraccay, Doña Teodora, the widow of Chávez, who could be useful to them if they spent the night in the community. Félix Gavilán wrote down the name in his notebook.

It was not yet midday when they set out on the final leg. The sun was shining in a sky that showed no sign of rain. Julia Aguilar offered them some milk in the doorway of her house and watched them disappearing up the pass. Jorge Sedano was on a mule and Juan Argumedo was pulling on the reins; behind was the horse with the bags and the cameras and, in the rear, the journalists. 'They were laughing,' Julia recalls.

## The Iquichanos

In the meantime, what was happening in the highlands of Huanta, in the twenty or so Iquichano communities that number some 20,000 inhabitants? In the depressed region of Ayacucho, the Iquichanos are among the most destitute of groups. Living in those inhospitable lands since pre-Hispanic times, with no roads, no medical or technical assistance, without water or light, they have only known, since the beginning of the Republic, the exploitation of large landowners, the demands of the tax collector and the violence of civil wars. Although the Catholic faith took deep root there, it has not replaced the old beliefs like the cult of the *apus* or mountain gods. The most famous of these is Rasuwillca, in whose belly a horseman with light skin and a white horse lives in a palace full of gold and fruit; his prestige dominates the whole region. For these men and women, who are mainly illiterate and speak only Quechua, who are condemned to live on a meagre diet of beans and potatoes, survival has been a major challenge in a world where death through hunger, illness or natural catastrophe stalks their every step.

The eight journalists, guided by Juan Argumedo, were about to encounter another historical time, since life in Uchuraccay and Huaychao has remained almost unchanged for two hundred years. In the houses at Huanta, the families still speak with alarm of the possibility that the Iquichano Indians will come down from the mountains, like that time in 1896, when they captured the city and killed the sub-prefect, in a rebellion against the imposition of a salt tax. Because, throughout history, each time the communities of Iquicha have left their lands, it has been to fight. There is a constant in the outbreaks of violence of these peasants; they still react to the fear that their way of life will be disturbed, that their ethnic identity is being threatened. During the Colonial period, they fought with the royalist troops against the two most important indigenous rebellions of the eighteenth and nineteenth centuries: those of Túpac Amaru and Mateo Pumacahua. Their isolation from other Andean ethnic groups was also shown in their rejection of Independence: between 1826 and 1839, they refused to accept the Republic and fought for the King of Spain. This same desire to defend their regional sovereignty can be seen in their nineteenth-century uprisings.

The few studies that have been made of them show them to be jealous defenders of customs and practices which might be archaic, but which are all that they have. They tolerate the occasional merchant or traveller but, in the 1960s, they expelled a group of anthropologists from the University of Ayacucho and refused to deal with officials of the Agrarian Reform in the 1970s.

The relationship between the Iquichanos and the more modern and westernized villages of the valley has always been tense. This is a feature of the Andes, where the *mestizo* inhabitants of the lowlands despise the Indians of the highlands, calling them *chutos* (savages). The Indians, in turn, hate them.

This was the climate in the region when Sendero Luminoso began its operations. In 1981 and 1982, the guerrillas were strong throughout the lowlands. But while the Senderistas indoctrinated the peasants and recruited young people in San José de Secce, Luricocha, Mayoc, Chacabamba and Balcón, they do not seem to have made any effort to win over the Iquichanos. Was this because their isolation, the severity of the climate and the terrain and their primitivism did not make them an attractive proposition? Throughout those two years, Sendero Luminoso only used the highlands as a corridor that allowed them to move from one end of the province to the other in relative safety and to disappear after their attacks on Huanta, Tambo and other places.

The Indians of Uchuraccay, Huaychao, Carhuarán and Iquicha hear these 'militias' passing through, almost always at night, and when they speak about these strange, disturbing apparitions, the strangers take on a phantasmagoric form, or become the projections of unconscious terrors. The fact that their rivals in the valley help the Senderistas, whether they want to or not, would be reason enough for predisposing the Iquichanos against them. But there are other reasons as well. On their marches, the guerrillas want food and shelter and when the communities try to stop them butchering their animals, disputes occur. In an incident of this sort, at Uchuraccay a few weeks previously, a detail of Senderistas had killed two shepherds, Alejandro Huamán and Venancio Aucatoma. This theft of animals caused resentment in the communities, which have minimal resources. For that reason, when the villagers of Uchuraccay speak of them, they call them *terrorista-sua* (terrorist thief).

But what precipitated the break between the Iquichanos and Sendero Luminoso was the attempt by the revolutionaries to apply a policy of 'economic self-sufficiency' and control of production to the 'liberated zones'. Their objective was to cut off the cities and to inculcate work patterns among the peasants that conformed to their own ideological model. The communities were ordered to plant only enough for their needs, with no surplus, and to end all trade with the cities. With each community feeding itself, the money economy would disappear. Sendero Luminoso imposed this policy by force. At the beginning of January, they closed the Lirio market at gunpoint and blew up the road, cutting off the traffic between Huanta and Lirio. The Iquichanos went down to Lirio to sell their surpluses and to stock up with coca, beans and corn. This ending of all possibility for trade, decreed for reasons that were incomprehensible to them, seemed like an intrusion that endangered their very existence and throughout their history, the Iquichanos have always reacted with ferocity to such situations.

In the middle of January, the *varayocs*, the leaders of the Iquichano communities, called two meetings in Uchuraccay and Carhuarán (the

same places where, a century and a half before, they had met to declare war on the new Republic). There they decided to oppose Sendero
Luminoso.

The government and the forces of order knew almost nothing about
these events. The army had only been ordered by Belaúnde Terry to
direct operations at the end of December, and General Clemente Noel
had scarcely begun to realize how complicated his task was going to
be. A company of marines, an infantry batallion and a detachment of
army commandos had just arrived in Ayacucho to support the Civil
Guard. But only the *sinchis* had been in Uchuraccay.

The schoolteacher Alejandrina de la Cruz saw the first *sinchi* patrol
arrive in May 1981. There were no incidents between the guards and
the villagers, unlike what had happened in Paria, where a peasant was
beaten. In 1981, the *sinchis* went through Uchuraccay about once every
two months in their fruitless search for the Senderistas. But, in 1982,
Alejandrina de la Cruz did not see any patrols right up to 18 December,
when she left Uchuraccay. However, the inhabitants of Uchuraccay
said that the *sinchis* came once again after the teacher had left, in a
helicopter. When they asked the *sinchis* to stay and protect the village,
the *sinchis* replied that they could not, but that if the *terrucos* came,
they should 'defend themselves and kill them'.

In any case, this is what the Iquichanos had decided to do in the
meetings at Carhuarán and Uchuraccay. They began to take action
immediately, in various places at once. Senderista columns and real
or suspected accomplices were ambushed, beaten and executed
throughout the whole Iquichano district. The seven dead in Huaychao
that General Noel announced was only one of the killings that the
exasperated Iquichanos were carrying out at the time. But, unlike the
deaths in Huaychao, the others were not reported to the authorities. In
Uchuraccay, five Senderistas had been killed on 22 January, and the
number of *terrucos* put to death in the whole region was at least two
dozen and perhaps many more.

The journalists did not know this nor, apparently, did Juan Argumedo. But the zone that they were entering was in turmoil and the
villagers were in a state of rage and panic or, as they call it, in a state
of *chaqwa* (disorder, chaos). They were convinced that, at any moment,
the Senderistas would return to avenge their dead. The fear and rage
of the peasants were heightened by their feeling of being at a disadvan-
tage since they had no firearms. The element of surprise, which had

stood them in good stead for the first killings, was no longer a possibility. This was the mood that prevailed in Uchuraccay, where some three hundred villagers were holding a meeting, when the shepherds or sentries came to warn them that a group of strangers was approaching the community centre.

## In the mouth of the wolf

That night, in Chacabamba, Doña Rosa, Juana Lidia and Julia Aguilar waited in vain for Juan Argumedo to return. Although they doubted that Octavio Infante and the journalists would get back that night, Doña Rosa prepared them a meal and laid out some blankets. It did not greatly surprise them that the group had not appeared, but why wasn't Juan back since he was only going part of the way with them? The women went to bed worried.

The following morning, Thursday 27 January, a boy, Pastor Ramos Romero, appeared in the village shouting that something terrible had happened up there, that in Uchuraccay they'd killed some men who'd been with Don Juan. Terrified, Doña Rosa and Juana Lidia gathered up a small bundle of potatoes and coca leaves and set off for Uchuraccay. Julia Aguilar had gone on ahead. When she heard the boy, she had jumped on to a horse and spurred it up the stony gorge.

Julia reached the outskirts of Uchuraccay about noon. As soon as she saw the first huts with their straw roofs and small stone corrals, she realized that something was wrong, because a large number of Indians were standing on the hills armed with slings, staves and axes. Among them were people from other communities: Huaychao, Cunya, Pampalca, Jarhuachuray, Paria. Some were waving white flags. A group surrounded her menacingly and, without giving her time to ask about her husband, they began to accuse her of being an accomplice of the *terrucos* and told her that they would kill her just as they had killed them. They were excitable, nervous and violent. Julia tried to talk to them, to explain that the strangers were not terrorists and neither was her husband, but the peasants called her a liar and became even more aggressive. In response to her pleading, instead of killing her, they imprisoned her in the Uchuraccay community hall. When she was taken into the village, she saw that the community was in 'a frantic state' and it seemed to her that there were 'several thousand' peasants from other communities.

In the hall she found her sister-in-law and mother-in-law, crying and terrified, also under guard. They had had a similar experience to hers, but they also had some information about what had happened the previous night. In the outskirts of the village they were able to talk for a moment to Roberta Huicho, who told them that the villagers had killed some terrorists, but that Juan Argumedo was not with them when they were killed. The guide had fled with his animals down the Huachhuaccasa mountain. Villagers on horseback had gone after him and caught him in a place called Yuracyaco. They had taken him prisoner, but Doña Rosa and Juana Lidia could not ask her anything else because they were surrounded by furious villagers calling them *terrucos*. The women swore on their knees that they were not terrorists and in an attempt to calm the villagers, they gave out the potatoes and coca leaves that they had brought. On the way to Uchuraccay, Doña Rosa and Juana Lidia came across the horse and mule of the journalists, both dead.

They were kept prisoner until the following afternoon, their lives hanging by a thread. In the dark hall, with its earth floor and blackened walls, that served as their jail, there were thirteen other prisoners, all badly beaten. They had been brought there from Iquicha, accused of being collaborators of Sendero Luminoso. One of them was the government representative, Julián Huayta, who was bleeding from the head. They had tied a red flag to his neck and were accusing him of having flown that flag in Iquicha. That evening, that night and the following morning, Doña Rosa, Juana Lidia and Julia saw the people from Uchuraccay and from other communities – they say that there were 'four or five thousand', which seems an exaggeration – judge the thirteen prisoners in an open council, according to ancient practices. Nine were cleared of the charge of helping the *terrucos*. Were the other four sentenced to death? The Argumedos do not know; they only know that the Uchuraccay villagers handed them over to representatives of another community, who took them off. But it is quite possible that the killings of the previous day continued after the meeting. Once they had taken the decision to become involved in the war between Sendero Luminoso and the *sinchis*, the Iquichanos felt that they had to kill first or die, without stopping to think that there might be accidents on the way.

The Argumedos were tried on Friday afternoon. Time and again, they heard that the villagers had killed some terrorists and nobody took any notice of the women when they tried to explain that the group were not terrorists but journalists, on their way to Huaychao. Do Iquichano Indians know what a 'journalist' is? Only a few do and then in a very vague way. During the trial, an Iquichano, a godson of Doña Rosa, Julio Gavilán, vigorously defended the women before the *varayocs*, swearing that they did not belong to the 'militia'. Doña Rosa, Lidia and Julia begged to be released and gave the *varayocs* the 3000 *soles* that they had brought with them and the rest of the potatoes and coca leaves.

Why this insistence on treating the women as accomplices of the *terrucos*? Surely many villagers knew the Argumedos from Chacabamba? Perhaps that was the reason, for the three women came from an area where Sendero Luminoso had sympathizers. A persistent but unverifiable rumour circulating in the region maintained that Juan Argumedo was a protector and a friend of the Senderistas. His family deny it. Yet it is true that they live in a region which Sendero Luminoso controlled and where the inhabitants, out of solidarity or out of fear, collaborated with the guerrillas. Perhaps Juan Argumedo was not a collaborator but, for the highland peasants, he might well have been the tangible proof of the arrival in the village of the Sendero detachment that they were expecting. Was Juan Argumedo the decisive factor in the misunderstanding that provoked the killing? This is something that we might never know because, although they admit to the crime against the journalists, the peasants in Uchuraccay are totally silent about Juan Argumedo. While they were imprisoned, his mother, his wife and his sister heard different versions of what had happened to him: that he had been locked up with another peasant and that then both of them had been killed; that he had been handed over to the custody of another Iquichano village. But, up to now, the peasants of Uchuraccay maintain that they did not know him and had never seen him and, despite the many searches, his body has never been found. The three women were luckier than he was. The *varayocs* eventually gave in to their pleas and to those of Julio Gavilán. Before releasing them, the tribunal made them solemnly swear, on the staff of a crucifix – the staff of the senior *varayoc* – that they would remain completely silent as to what they had seen and heard since they set foot in Uchuraccay.

When the grief-stricken women returned to Chacabamba on Friday night, two military patrols were combing the area, looking for the journalists. The previous evening, General Noel had heard of the expedition from journalists who were alarmed that they had had no news of their colleagues, and had ordered the posts at Huanta and Tambo to look for them. The first patrol to reach Uchuraccay was from Tambo, led by a marine, First Lieutenant Ismael Bravo Reid. They entered the village on Friday night, in torrential rain, after a ten-hour march. The Indians were in their homes and it was only on the next day that Bravo Reid could speak to them through an interpreter. The peasants told them that they had killed 'eight terrorists who came to Uchuraccay, holding a red flag and shouting "Death to the *sinchis*".' They showed them the graves and gave them a red flag, a telephoto lens, twelve rolls of film (which turned out to be unused) and some identity cards. 'And their weapons?' asked the official. 'They didn't have any.'

And so the authorities in Ayacucho and Lima learned of the death of the journalists on Saturday night. On Sunday, the whole of Peru watched on television the exhumation of the corpses, the gruesome sight of eight bodies mutilated by sticks, slings, stones and knives. Not one of them had any bullet wounds.

The Commission of Investigation set up by the government to investigate the killings – which included the writer of this article – did not find it difficult, after visiting the locations, reading official documents and questioning dozens of people, to reconstruct the essential facts, although some details remained unclarified. It did not find it difficult to conclude that the journalists, exhausted after their five-hour walk, were killed by a mob of men and women whom fear and anger had imbued with a ferocity that was uncommon in their daily life and their normal circumstances. There was no doubt that the Iquichanos killed them because they took them for Senderistas.

We were told all this by the peasants of Uchuraccay, in an open meeting that we held there on 14 March. They did so naturally, without any sense of guilt, both intrigued and surprised that people had come from so far away and that there was so much commotion over something like this. Yes, they had killed them. Why? Because they had made a mistake. Isn't life full of mistakes and deaths? They were 'ignorant'. What worried the people of Uchuraccay, that 14 March, was not the past but the future, that is, the Senderistas. Would we ask the *sinchis* to come to protect them? Could we ask 'Mr Government' to send them at least three guns? At the beginning of the meeting, at the suggestion of the anthropologists who were advising the Commission, I had poured brandy on the ground, drunk to the tutelary mountain god, Rasuwillca, distributed coca leaves and tried to explain, through translators, to the dozens and dozens of villagers around us that the laws of Peru forbid killing, that we have judges to pass sentence and to judge and we have authorities to enforce the laws. And while I was telling them these things and looking at their faces, I felt as absurd and unreal as if I were indoctrinating them on the authentic revolutionary philosophy of Comrade Mao betrayed by the counter-revolutionary dog Deng Xiaoping.

### The massacre

How did the murder of the journalists take place?

The Uchuraccayans refused to give us the details. We assumed that they had attacked them suddenly, without any word, from the mountains that surround the village, using their *huaracas* (slings), with which they can shoot stones so quickly – they demonstrated this proudly to us – that they can bring down a *vizcacha* running at full speed. We thought that there had been no dialogue because the Iquichanos thought that the 'Senderistas' were armed and because, if they had spoken, the journalists who knew Quechua – Octavio Infante, Félix Gavilán and Amador García – could have calmed the hostility of their assailants.

But the facts were colder and more cruel. They came to light four months later when a patrol, which was escorting the judge appointed to investigate the events, found in a cave in Huachhuaccasa, near Uchuraccay, the camera of Willy Retto – a Minolta, serial number 4202368. It had been uncovered, it seems, by *vizcachas* digging around in the ground where the villagers had buried it. The young photographer of *El Observador* had the presence of mind to use his camera in the moments just before the massacre, perhaps when his friends were already being cut down. The photos show the journalists surrounded by the villagers. In one, Jorge Sedano is on his knees next to the bags and cameras that someone, who might be Octavio Infante, had just placed on the ground. In another, Eduardo de la Piniella has his arms raised and in another young Mendívil is waving his hands, as if imploring everyone to calm down. In the last pictures, Willy Retto photographed an Iquichano bearing down on him. This chilling document proves that dialogue had been to no avail and that, despite seeing them unarmed, the Iquichanos had attacked the strangers, convinced that they were enemies.

The massacre had magical and religious as well as political and social overtones. The horrible wounds inflicted on the bodies seemed ritualistic. The eight were buried in pairs and face down, a way the communities bury people they consider 'devils' or those like the scissors dancers whom they believe have made a pact with the devil. At the same time, they buried them outside the village boundaries, to emphasize the fact that they were strangers. (In the Andes, the devil merges with the image of a stranger.) The bodies were particularly battered around the mouth and eyes, because there is a belief that the victim must be deprived of his sight so that he cannot recognize his killers, and of his tongue so that he cannot inform against them. Their ankles were broken to prevent them coming back to seek revenge on their killers. The villagers took off the dead men's clothes, washed them and then burned them, in a ceremony of purification called *pichja*.

The crime of Uchuraccay was horrendous and to know the circumstances in which it occurred does not excuse it. But it makes it more comprehensible. The violence astonishes us because it is an anomaly in our daily lives. For the Iquichanos, this violence is the atmosphere they live in from the moment they are born until their death. Scarcely a month after we had been in Ayacucho, a new tragedy confirmed that the panic which the people of Iquicha felt at the possibility of Sendero Luminoso reprisals was not unfounded. It happened in Lucanamarca, some 130 miles from Uchuraccay. The villagers there had collaborated with Sendero Luminoso but then had disputes with the *terrucos* over food. They then captured some guerrillas and handed them over to the police in Huancasancos. On 23 April, four Senderista detachments, together with hundreds of peasants from a rival community, entered Lucanamarca on a punishment expedition. Sixty-seven people were murdered in the main square, some with bullets, but mostly with axes, machetes and stones. Among the decapitated and mutilated bodies were four children.

When our meeting was over, and very moved by what we had seen and heard — the graves of the journalists were still open — we were preparing to leave when a tiny woman from the community began to dance. She was murmuring a song that we could not understand. She was an Indian, as small as a child, but with the wrinkled face of an old woman, and the scarred cheeks and swollen lips of those who live exposed to the cold in the mountains. She was barefoot, wore several coloured skirts and a ribboned hat and while she sang and danced, she struck us gently on the legs with a bunch of nettles. Was she saying farewell to us in some sort of ancient ritual? Was she cursing us for also being one of those strangers – 'Senderistas', 'journalists', 'sinchis' – who had brought to their lives new reasons for anguish and fear? Was she exorcizing us? In the previous weeks, when I had been interviewing soldiers, politicians, policemen, peasants, journalists, reading through despatches, articles, judicial statements, trying to put together what had happened, I had lived in a state of enormous tension. I was awake at night, trying to judge the truth of the statements and the hypotheses, or I had nightmares in which the certainties of the day became once more enigmas. In those weeks, as I was uncovering the story of the eight journalists – I knew two of them and I had been with Amador García just a few days before his trip to Ayacucho – it seemed that I was also uncovering a new and terrible story about my own country. But at no time had I felt so sad as on that evening in Uchuraccay, with its threatening clouds, as we watched this diminutive woman dance and strike us with nettles, a woman who seemed to have come from a different Peru from the one in which I live my life, an ancient and archaic Peru, which has survived among these sacred mountains despite centuries of isolation and adversity. This fragile little woman had undoubtedly been one of those who threw the stones and swung the clubs, since Iquichano women have a reputation for being as belligerent as the men. In Willy Retto's posthumous photos, you can see them in the front row. It was not difficult to imagine that community transformed by rage or fear. We sensed it in the meeting when, suddenly faced with difficult questions, the passive audience, led by the women, began to bellow 'chaqwa, chaqwa', ('enough, enough') and the air was filled with evil omens.

If the essential facts of the death of the journalists have been clarified – who killed them, how and why – there are some that still remain obscure. What happened to Juan Argumedo? Why did the Iquichanos not confess to his killing? Perhaps because Juan was a 'neighbour', someone from a rival region, but one with which they are forced to coexist for reasons of commerce and travel. To admit that they killed him would be tantamount to a declaration of war on the farmers of the valley. This precaution, in any event, has not proved successful because, since that time, there have been several bloody confrontations between the Indians of Uchuraccay and the inhabitants of Chacabamba and Balcón.

Another unresolved aspect is the red flag. General Noel said that the journalists were murdered because they went into Uchuraccay with a Communist flag and the villagers said the same thing to the Commission. But it is clear that there are no grounds for this assertion, as the photographs of Willy Retto reveal. Why would the journalists have carried with them a flag which could only have put them at risk? Probably this was a version invented by the community when they realized their mistake, to give greater weight to their claim that they mistook the strangers for Senderistas. The red flag that they gave to First Lieutenant Bravo Reid was, doubtless, the one that flew in Iquicha and which was tied round the neck of the government representative of that village.

Even more dramatic than the blood that flows through this story are the misunderstandings that caused it to flow. The peasants killed some strangers whom they thought were coming to kill them. The journalists thought that the *sinchis* and not the peasants had killed the Senderistas. It is quite possible that they died without knowing why they were being killed. A wall of disinformation, prejudices and ideologies separated each group, making dialogue impossible.

Perhaps this story helps us to understand the reason for the dizzying violence that characterizes guerrilla activities in Latin America. Guerrilla movements are not, in these countries, 'peasant' based. They grow up in the cities, among intellectuals and middle-class activists who, with their plans and rhetoric, are often as foreign and exotic to the peasant masses as Sendero Luminoso was to the men and women of Uchuraccay. What tends to win them peasant support are the abuses that other strangers commit (the counter-insurgency forces), or simply the way in which those who believe themselves to be the masters of history and absolute truth coerce the peasantry. The fact is that the war between the guerrillas and the armed forces is a settling of accounts between 'privileged' sectors of society, in which the peasant masses are used with cynicism and brutality by those who say they wish to 'liberate' them. It is these masses who always suffer the greatest number of victims: 750 in Peru since the beginning of the year alone.

The story of the eight journalists shows the vulnerability of democracy in Latin America and the ease with which it dies under military or Marxist–Leninist dictatorships. The achievements of democracy – freedom of the press, elections, representative institutions – are things that cannot be defended with conviction by people who are not in a position to understand them, much less to benefit from them. Democracy will not be strong in our countries while it remains the privilege of one sector and an incomprehensible abstraction for everyone else. The double threat – the Pinochet model or the Fidel Castro model – will continue to haunt democratic regimes for as long as there are people in our countries who kill for the reasons that the peasants of Uchuraccay killed.

Lima, 7 June 1983

# Freedom for the Free?

## A polemic with Günter Grass

Some time back I read an interview with Günter Grass in which the German novelist – who was on a visit to Nicaragua – said that Latin American countries would not solve their problems until they followed 'the example of Cuba'. This solution to our problems is proposed by many European and Latin American novelists, but I was surprised to hear it coming from the author of *The Tin Drum* (if the report is correct).

Günter Grass is one of the most original contemporary novelists. If I had to take the books of only one living European novelist on to a desert island, I would take his. My admiration for him is political as well as literary. The way he has behaved in his own country, defending the democratic socialism of Willy Brandt and Helmut Schmidt, campaigning for this opposition in the elections and energetically rejecting any form of authoritarianism and totalitarianism, has always seemed to me to be a model of good sense. Also a healthy counterweight – which was reformist, viable and constructive – to the apocalyptic position of so many modern intellectuals who, through blindness, opportunism or naivety, end up supporting dictatorships and justifying crime as a political instrument. I remember a few years ago a polemic in Federal Germany between Grass and Heinrich Böll over a bouquet of flowers that Böll had sent to a hardened woman revolutionary who had struck the German Chancellor in public. Günter Grass explained that, unlike Böll – a Christian and a good-natured man who, judging by his bloodless stories, one would not expect to find defending violence – he did not think that the best way to resolve political differences was through blows and that the Germans should have learned from recent history about the dangers of accepting force as an ideological argument. This genuinely democratic and progressive position seems to me to give more moral weight to the declarations of a Günter Grass against the dictatorships and crimes of Pinochet and those in Argentina and Uruguay than the statements of writers who think that brutality in politics is bad only when it is used by its opponents.

How to square all this with the 'Cuban solution' that Günter Grass recommends for the countries of our continent? It is an interesting double standard, an instructive schizophrenia. What it implies is that what is suitable and good for the German Federal Republic is not good or suitable for Latin America, and vice versa. For Germany and, by extension, Western Europe and the developed world, the ideal is a democratic and reformist system, representative elections and institutions, freedom of expression and freedom to organize political parties and unions, open society, respect for individual sovereignty and no control of culture or censorship. For Latin America, however, the ideal is revolution, the violent seizure of power, the establishment of one party, enforced collectivization, the bureaucratization of culture, concentration camps for dissidents and feudal control by the USSR.

What can have brought an intellectual like Günter Grass to make such a statement? Probably experiencing Latin American poverty at first hand – this spectacle, that is almost inconceivable for a Western European, of the iniquitous inequalities that disfigure our societies, the insensibility of our privileged classes, the exasperation one feels at seeing the slow death that the multitudes of the poor in our countries seem condemned to suffer and the savagery displayed by our military dictatorships.

But one expects an intellectual to try to be lucid, even at moments of great intellectual turmoil. A Marxist–Leninist dictatorship is not a guarantee against hunger and can, in fact, add to the horror of under-development the further horror of genocide, as the regime of the Khmer Rouge clearly demonstrated in Cambodia, or lead to an oppression that is so asphyxiating that hundreds of thousands and perhaps millions of people are prepared to leave everything that they have and take to the sea, braving the sharks, in order to escape from the regime, as we have seen in Vietnam or in Cuba itself (during the Mariel exodus). An intellectual who thinks that freedom is necessary and possible for his society cannot decide that it is superfluous and secondary for other societies, unless he has come, deep down, to the unfortunate conclusion that hunger, lack of culture and exploitation make men unsuitable for freedom.

And here, I think, is the nub of the problem. When a North American or European intellectual, journal or liberal institution proposes options and methods for our country that would never be permitted in their own society, it reveals an essential scepticism about the capacity of Latin American countries to adopt systems of coexistence and freedom which have made Western countries what they are today. In most cases it is an unconscious prejudice, an inchoate feeling and a sort of visceral racism that these people – who usually have impeccable liberal and democratic credentials – would reject indignantly if they were really aware of them. But in practice, that is, in what they say, do or do not do, and above all in what they write about Latin America, this essential doubt as to the ability of our countries to be democratic crops up all the time and explains their incongruities and inconsistencies when they give information about us or interpret our history and our problems. Or when, like Günter Grass, they propose as a solution to our problems a type of regime that they would find intolerable in Federal Germany. (All this inevitably reminds me of how I felt when I discovered in Spain at the end of the 1950s that the Franco regime, which applied a careful 'moral' censorship to all types of publication, including scientific works, allowed Spanish houses to publish pornographic books as long as they were for export to Spanish America. The mission of the censors, then, was to save native-born souls; Spanish American souls could go to hell.)

Perhaps this helps us to understand more clearly cases like the offensive, denigratory and lying information that the western media disseminate about democratic Latin American regimes, painting them as behaving as badly as, or worse than, the dictatorships themselves. There is the case, which is unfortunately not exceptional, of *The Times* in London and its Latin American 'specialist', Mr Colin Harding, a diligent slanderer of Peruvian democracy. The most prestigious newspapers of the Western countries, like *Le Monde* in France, *The New York Times*, or *El País* in Spain, bulwarks of the democratic system, which are clearly not in league with those who support totalitarian ideas in their respective countries, none the less often report on Latin America with the same discrimination as Günter Grass and for the same reasons. To judge by what they write one would say that in Latin American countries only the worst can be true. This is a policy that includes not just countries suffering from dictatorships, which would have a certain justification, but also countries which have emerged from dictatorship and are trying to consolidate democracy. It would seem that the only important things to show are the mistakes and the horror (even if these are fictional).

The violations of human rights which lamentably occur in these democracies when they are forced to respond to guerrilla actions or terrorism are always highlighted, while it is difficult to find in the pages of these newspapers equivalent information about the violations of human rights by those who kill in the name of revolution and proclaim that guns and bombs – not votes – are the criteria for political truth. The worst lies and calumnies which, under the mantle of freedom of the press, are spread against democratic governments by their internal opponents, find a favourable echo, a receptive attitude outside, without any responsible attempt to check the truth, while any denial or official version is presented as something suspicious, an alibi for the guilty or the propaganda of power.

With its attacks, murders and blowing-up of electricity pylons, Sendero Luminoso and its handful of followers – a few hundred or, at most, a few thousand people – have achieved an infinitely greater publicity in the press of the Western world than, say, all the inhabitants of the Dominican Republic who, for a decade or more, have been setting an admirable example in Latin America in terms of governing with democratic political parties, political coexistence and freedom, civilized disagreements and, what is even more striking in this time of crisis, making progress in the fight against underdevelopment. That a country which has suffered the most terrible dictatorship and, later, a foreign intervention and a civil war, has been able, in a relatively short period of time, to establish a democratic system, is of absolutely no interest to the great newspapers of the West. The slightest abuse committed by a democratic government in its fight against terrorism, by contrast, is usually published.

Why does this happen? Because these abuses confirm a pre-established image and the Dominican phenomenon contradicts this stereotype, which is deeply rooted in the subconscious of the West, that sees us as barbarians and uncivilized, essentially incapable of freedom and condemned, for that reason, always to choose between the Pinochet model and the Fidel Castro model. One does not have to be a fortune teller to know that if, to its great detriment and to that of the whole of Latin America, the Dominican Republic should fall victim, like the Peruvian regime, to armed insurrection and terrorism, the Colin Hardings of the great Western newspapers would be quick to show – even at the price of magnifying or distorting the truth – that the democracy was not a democracy at all, but rather a sham, a mere masquerade behind which, as in dictatorial regimes, there lies a struggle between corrupt and authoritarian power and the rebellion of the oppressed.

Am I exaggerating to make my point clearly? Perhaps. But I challenge any researcher to study the articles on Latin America published by the great democratic newspapers that I have mentioned. The balance will show, without the slightest doubt, that the articles tend to corroborate this scepticism and put forward arguments which, instead of correcting this miserable image of Latin America, tend instead to reinforce it.

It is important to keep this in mind because it is one of the most extraordinary paradoxes of our time. We Latin Americans, who think that the solution to our problems is to break out of the sinister cycle of dictatorships, either from the left or the right, must realize that, among the obstacles we still have to face in order to establish and defend democracy, we will find not only the plots of reactionary castes and revolutionary insurrections, but also the lack of understanding – even contempt – of those we take as models and we believe to be our allies. This does not mean, of course, that we should lose hope. But we should certainly give up certain illusions. We Latin Americans will have to fight and win by ourselves the battle against totalitarian countries which would like to have us in their sphere of influence and, as surprising as it might seem, against certain organs of information and a number of democratic intellectuals in the free world.

Lima, August 1983

# Nicaragua at the Crossroads

On the morning of 23 December 1972, an earthquake destroyed 53,000 of the 70,000 dwellings in Managua, burying under the rubble ten thousand people and injuring a further twenty thousand. The centre of the city became a waste ground, with sporadic buildings or half-destroyed houses which remain to this day in these eccentric poses, without doors, windows or floors, looted, split apart and twisted, like monuments to the cataclysm or totems to ward off a new devastation.

The Rubén Darío Theatre, built in the last years of the Somoza dictatorship, has been closed for two years since the air conditioning has broken and the government does not have the $200,000 which, they say, it would cost to repair. The Sandinista revolution has built a National Theatre among the ruins of the Grand Hotel, one of the victims of the earthquake. There, on 9 January 1985, on an improvised stage over what was once the swimming pool, Daniel Ortega introduced a folklore spectacle for the foreign delegations that had come for his presidential investiture, to be held the next day. The guide assigned to me by the government – the novelist Lizandro Chávez Alfaro, director of the National Library – was fanatical about punctuality and made me arrive an hour early for each engagement. It was fortunate this time because, while the rest of the guests were arriving, the wife of Comandante Ortega, Rosario Murillo, the general secretary of the Union of Workers in Art and Culture, took me on a tour of all the rooms and corridors of what had once been the Grand Hotel and now also housed a Museum of Modern Art. It was an excellent choice to show abstract, surrealist and primitive paintings among those ruins that seemed to be designed, *ex profeso,* by an architect with a daring imagination.

That happened on the third day of my visit to Nicaragua. I was there for a month, until the beginning of February, to write this article. I never found the ruins of the Grand Hotel again. Every time that I set out to walk through the ghostly 'centre' of Managua – which was not rebuilt after the earthquake – I searched for it in vain and could never get there on my own by following the directions I was given. It always seemed a miracle to me that the taxi drivers could locate it. Until then,

I'd thought that Tokyo was the most labyrinthine city in the world. It is not: Managua is.

Its vast, uninhabited spaces cause agoraphobia. In what is supposedly the 'centre' there are crops being sown and cows grazing. The streets of the capital of Nicaragua are all side streets and they have no names and the houses have no numbers. Directions are real conundrums, full of humour, anachronisms and history. A typical direction: 'From where the little tree used to be, seventy *varas* up and twenty down'. What 'little tree' are they talking about? A tree that once existed in the past – nobody knows when – in a place where there is now nothing, and yet the inhabitants of Managua can identify it. *Vara* is a Medieval Spanish unit of length, roughly a yard, which now no one uses in the world apart from the Nicaraguans. And how to interpret 'up' and 'down'? Predictably, I was given different explanations. According to some, 'up' meant east, coming from the airport, where the planes 'go up' into the sky and 'down', the west, the direction of the cemetery, where one 'goes down' into the ground. But for others, both denominations date from the pre-Hispanic Indians: 'up', where the sun rises and 'down' where the sun sets.

On my journey to Managua, I stopped off in Venezuela. A Venezuelan friend was surprised. 'You, in Managua! The country's almost like Cuba. With your reputation as a right winger, it might be a problem for you. Take care!' (For a reason as mysterious as the street directions in Managua, the defence of freedom of expression, elections and political pluralism gain one the reputation, among Latin American intellectuals, of being right wing.)

In fact, I didn't take any care, and instead of badly, everything went so well that I almost breathed my last in Nicaragua, out of pure exhaustion from the hospitality shown me by both the Sandinistas and those in opposition to the regime. The Vice President, Sergio Ramirez, a novelist and a friend of mine from before the revolution told me one day, over dinner at his house: 'I suppose you realize that the hospitality that the Sandinistas and the reactionaries are showing you is because we both want you to write nice things about us in your articles. And bad things about our opponents.' Ramirez is a cultured man, forty-three years old, with a fine sense of humour. He lived in West Berlin and ran a university publishing house in Costa Rica before the revolution. He is married to a beautiful society lady who stated one night, in one of her characteristic phrases: 'I am studying Marx and I

am inclined to believe everything except when he picks on religion.'
Sergio's opponents say that in public he takes his radicalism to
extremes so as not to lose face with his Sandinista comrades but that,
at heart, he is one of the most moderate of the regime.

It was an intense, passionate and schizophrenic month during which
I spoke to hundreds of people, I travelled around almost the whole of
the country and I had some unforgettable experiences. One of these:
seeing the variety and beauty of the Nicaraguan countryside, dotted
with lakes, volcanoes, rich plains for flourishing cattle farming, sheer
mountains and — on the Atlantic coast — jungles through which rivers
like Rio Escondido run, which flows from Bluefields to Rama — some
four hours in a motor launch. Here one came into contact with nature
which is scarcely touched by man.

Except on the Atlantic coast, where one needs an official permit to
travel, due to the clashes between the government and the Miskito
Indians, a third of whom (there are some seventy thousand of them)
have gone into exile in Honduras, one can travel freely in the rest of
the country, including the northern frontier with Honduras where the
campaigns against the Contras are widespread. I made some of these
journeys accompanied by the good-natured Lizandro Chávez Alfaro —
himself a native of Bluefields — and some on my own, without ever
being bothered. I was surprised by the lack of vigilance and the normality of life, even in the zone of Estelí and Jinotega, where the traces
of the war (empty villages, destroyed cooperatives, burnt-out vehicles)
are clearly visible. The only area where I felt a certain nervousness at
the level of the man in the street, was in Bluefields and its environs.
The attacks and actions of the rebel Miskitos are, however, less frequent there than on the frontier with Honduras.

Lizandro organized the interviews with leaders of the regime and I
organized those with the opposition. That was in the first few days.
Because, after the second week, my problem was not how to get interviews with all of them, but how to find the time to be able to speak to
even a third of the ministers, businessmen, farmers, journalists,
priests, feminists, evangelicals, poets and even madmen who offered me
'fundamental data' for my article, or to accept one tenth of the social
invitations extended to me. At the same time my room in the Interconti-
nental Hotel (in the penthouse room of the hotel, so the story goes, the
ghost of Howard Hughes roams: he was living here when the terrible
earthquake occurred) was filling up with so many books, papers,

journals, bulletins, letters, fliers that I would have needed a trunk to take them with me. Nicaraguan hospitality was symptomatic of the importance that both the regime and its opponents give to what is said abroad about Nicaragua. They both know that the fate of Sandinismo is being decided not only inside the country but also outside it (especially in the United States).

## The civic opposition and the Contras

Is Nicaragua a Marxist–Leninist state? Is it on the way to becoming a second Cuba? In its fifth year, the Cuban revolution was already a vassal of the Soviet Union: its economic and military survival depended on the USSR; all forms of opposition had been suppressed; the private sector was on the way to extinction, the bureaucracy of the single party spread its tentacles throughout the country and the ideological regimentation was absolute. In Nicaragua, five and a half years after the fall of Somoza, the private sector, although under strong state control, is still in a majority in agriculture, cattle raising, commerce and industry; despite the severe censorship, one can talk of media pluralism, albeit minimal: in *La Prensa*, the weekly *Paso a Paso* and two or three radio stations, one can still hear timid criticism; and there are opposition political parties, with their own offices and internal bulletins which express their hostility to the regime from the outside – the Democratic Coordinator – and from within, in the recently elected National Assembly. It is true that these opposition groups seem to be tolerated because they are not very effective and because the area of operation that the regime permits them does not allow them to compete in terms of true equality with Sandinismo, as was demonstrated during the November elections, but it is no less true that the opposition is not subjected to the terror and paranoia that threatens all dissidence in a totalitarian state. The Soviet Union, Cuba and the countries of the Eastern bloc give military and technical aid to Nicaragua, and send visible and invisible advisers. But it would be a distortion of the truth to say that Nicaragua is a fiefdom of the Soviet Union, like Cuba. This is not the case. Perhaps not through any decision of the Sandinistas themselves – who would have been happy to place themselves under the protection of Moscow – but through the unwillingness of the Soviet Union to take on the onerous burden of a second Cuba and the risk of a direct confrontation with the United States that this would imply. (President Lusinchi of Venezuela told me that he had asked the Soviets if they were planning to put MiG fighters in Nicaragua. They had replied through their ambassador: 'We are not that stupid!') That is the only way to explain the speech of Fidel Castro announcing what everyone already knew – that Cuba would maintain a prudent neutrality if Nicaragua were invaded – and his exhortations to the Sandinistas to come to a negotiated agreement with the United States within the framework of the Contadora group.

The evidence that they could only count to a limited extent on the support of Moscow, in addition to the internal resistance against the establishment of a Marxist regime, the economic difficulties caused by expropriation and state control in the first few years and the back-lash that the terrorism and the sabotage of the Contras caused, all of this has moderated the initial Communist project of the Sandinistas. In its place is a model as yet unformed, vaguely neutralist, nationalist and socialist – one that they believe will be more likely to ensure the survival of the regime and to achieve internal peace. The Comandantes have become pragmatic as they discovered that their messianic dreams of radical revolution were leading them to the edge of a crisis and provoking discontent that could have ended disastrously. For that reason they boldly announced that they would sign the Contadora agreement, they have devalued the currency, withdrawn subsidies on transport and certain basic products and announced a moratorium on the purchase of arms and the withdrawal of one hundred Cuban military assessors, and have increased their declarations assuring that the regime is 'now aligned with a mixed and pluralist economy'. This is, at present, a half truth. But it could become a reality if, in exchange for it, they obtain peace and guarantees against an intervention. In the month that I was in Nicaragua, I heard almost all the officials of the regime with whom I spoke repeat the *leitmotif* 'the experience has made us realists'. What that means is that they are prepared to make many concessions, except one: to hand over power.

The desire to hold on to power in the name of generous ideals or out of a pure desire for power itself – and there are both these aspects to Sandinismo – is not exclusive to totalitarian regimes; it also character-izes military dictatorships or, for example, the discreet dictatorship of the PRI in Mexico. A Nicaraguan – the conservative, ophthalmologist, sceptic, political guru and fine ironist, Don Emilio Alvarez Montalbán, whom it was pleasant to meet under the stars of Nicaragua in that frenetic month – told me one night: 'This revolution is smelling less and less of Moscow and more of Mexico City.' That is, it is a revolution which will discreetly turn into something different from what it now appears to be. I tend to agree with him.

When they heard me say such things, the Nicaraguans of the opposition parties responded angrily. In meetings attended by dozens of people hostile to the regime – some, like the meeting with CONAPRO (The National Confederation of Professionals), with more than one hundred and fifty people present – in order to prove to me the totalitarian nature of Sandinismo, they gave examples of abuses of human rights, the legal mockery of the Anti Somoza Popular Tribunals, the harassment of free trade unions, the banning of the right to strike, the closure of 24 radio stations and papers, the uncertainty of the businessmen when faced with confiscation and the proliferation of contradictory decrees, and the indoctrination of young people in schools and in the army. Nobody minced his words and some, after giving their name and surname, made ferocious (and unverifiable) accusations against the Comandantes: that they had stolen the best houses, that they had a brothel on kilometre 14.5 of the southern highway; that they had turned the Sacuansoche Restaurant into a place where Cubans, Soviets, Bulgarians and other Communist advisers could have orgies. When I insinuated that in the totalitarian countries that I know, such a meeting would be inconceivable and it would be even more inconceivable to have someone making such a statement and going unpunished they reproached me for my naivety. Didn't I realize that the 'tactical' tolerance of the system was coming to an end? To speak as they had spoken, they were risking their freedom and perhaps their lives.

I always came away from the meetings admiring the courage of these people but also somewhat sceptical as to their effectiveness in changing the course of events in Nicaragua. How large, in numbers, are the parties that make up the so-called civilian opposition? The statistics from officials or the opposition always seemed to me to be rather fanciful, without much connection to reality. Probably they represent little more than their own leaders. There are juntas of élites. Through their own fault and through the Machiavellian nature of the regimes, they have become divided and almost all of them – the Democratic Conservative Party, the Liberal, the Christian Socialist and the Social

Democrat parties – have a branch, or rather a splinter, that collaborates with the government.

In the case of the party with probably the most supporters, the Conservative, there are three-way divisions. Among the leaders there are capable and cultured men, but in general terms, their political action is unpractical. They do not admit that they made a mistake by abstaining in the November elections which, however fraudulent they might have been – and they were no more fraudulent, in any case, than Mexico's ritual elections or the most recent in Panama – would have given them a great visibility at a national level and a platform from which to criticize the official excesses and errors and to have a democratizing influence on the system. They refuse to see that the changes undergone by Nicaraguan society in the last five years and the type of regime that they are fighting means that they need to be very inventive, clear thinking and daring if they wish to save what freedom still remains, without sacrificing legitimate reforms and social progress. They preach an orthodox legalism and a liberal democracy that Nicaragua has never experienced and – unfortunately of course – is not likely to experience in the near future. They have thus put themselves between a rock and a hard place and can only say to themselves, and try to convince others, that Nicaragua is already, or is about to become, a totalitarian state, a satellite of the USSR, which at the end of the day reduces its strategy to a catastrophe policy: waiting for the Contras, aided by the 'Marines', to correct this intolerable situation. Such an assessment is wrong in my opinion.

Who are these Contras that the Sandinistas call 'mercenaries' and President Reagan calls 'freedom fighters'? Most belong to the FDN (the Nicaraguan Democratic Front) led by Adolfo Caleo Portocarrero, the ex-President of the Conservative Party, and they operate in the north, out of Honduras. There is another group, ARDE, on the southern border with Costa Rica, led by the ex-Sandinista Edén Pastora (there are some 700 of them, it seems). According to the regime, all the officers of these 'bands' are ex-members of Somoza's National Guard. 'If the Contras win,' President Daniel Ortega told me, 'one of the first victims will be *La Prensa*. The Contras do not want democracy, they want to restore the old order, which that newspaper opposed so fiercely.'

The opposition ridicules these statements. According to them, 'Somocismo' died with Somoza and, if one wants to dig up political precedents, then the Sandinista government has as many ex-collaborators of the dictatorship as the Contras (each group has its own list). The versions that the government and its opponents give of almost everything are so contradictory that anyone trying to be objective often becomes totally bewildered. But at least I reached one conclusion about this war: those who are fighting it, on both sides, are poor. The 'bourgeois' are not to be found on the winding front. Like the wounded Sandinista soldiers that I saw in the Germán Pomares Field Hospital in Jinotega, some five hundred miles from Managua, the Contras are also humble people, mainly peasants.

The testimonies of the Sandinistas are conclusive in this respect. The Vice Minister of Defence and head of the army staff, the young Comandante Joaquín Cuadra (who belongs to an aristocratic family and whose father is the director of the Central Bank), assured me that, 'All the Contras who fall into our hands are peasants. Up to now, we have captured only one professional, a doctor who had gone to Costa Rica.'

I asked the Interior Minister, Tomás Borge, how he explained the fact the peasants were taking up arms against the regime. 'Many of them were initially taken by the Somocistas to their camps in Honduras,' he replied. 'And there they became emotionally involved with the Contras and then their families and friends began to help them. For sentimental rather than political reasons. But we must also recognize that we made many mistakes which provoked hostility in the countryside. Many lumpen elements joined the militias, cruel, vicious people who stole, raped and abused people. Although we severely punished those responsible, this conduct has helped the Contras.'

In any event it is a paradox that in the five and a half years since the victory of the revolution, those who kill and are killed in the war on the border are poor people on both sides, many of whom have an unclear idea of what is at stake. Some think that they are fighting against the territorial greed of Ronald Reagan. Others, to judge by the leaflets of the Contras that I saw in the office of Comandante Manuel Morales Ortega in Estelí, who took me to see the peasant cooperatives that had been attacked by the FDN, that there is a crusade against the Devil in the name of Mary the Most Pure.

(One night at dinner in a bourgeois household, I witnessed a lively exchange between a North American diplomat and a Nicaraguan who was reproaching Washington for being undecided about sending in the Marines. The diplomat replied: 'None of you here tonight has your sons fighting with the Contras. You have sent them to Costa Rica, Guatemala and the United States so that they can avoid military service. And you want the Marines to come in and solve the problem. You've got a nerve!)

The Contras can cause the Sandinista regime great damage. Perhaps greater than the damage they have already inflicted: 7,698 victims in five years, according to Daniel Ortega (which would be the proportional equivalent of half a million people in the United States). But they will not be able to overthrow the regime. They have support among some peasant and bourgeois sectors, but not enough to provoke a generalized uprising like the one that got rid of Somoza. Although they are Nicaraguans, their military and economic dependence on the CIA and the United States causes suspicion, even in groups hostile to the Sandinistas, but who do not not forget the troubled past relations between the two countries: the many North American interventions and occupations in Nicaragua, including the one that lead to the Somoza dynasty. (One of the most respected opposition figures, the Catholic poet and writer Pablo Antonio Cuadra, who is co-director of *La Prensa*, told me: 'The covert aid of the CIA to the Contras has been an error.')

To overthrow the Sandinistas would require a massive and bloody North American military intervention which would bring not democracy but dictatorship, the only regime capable of imposing order on a wounded society with terrorism and guerrilla groups operating on all sides. This unlikely invasion is not an alternative if one is trying to preserve some kind of democratic option in Nicaragua. In the present circumstances, this democratic option – which is, of course, a small ray of hope – can only be achieved through some sort of understanding with the regime. Although the regime has taken many steps along the road to totalitarianism, it is faced with many challenges and difficulties that make it open to compromise. By not understanding this, the opposition political parties are, to a degree, marginalized from Nicaraguan political reality.

## The Church

Nicaragua is one of the most Catholic countries I have known. When I was travelling through the department of Estelí, visiting cooperatives devastated by the Contras, I came across processions of peasants in their Sunday best who were walking – many barefoot, to honour a vow – to the Sanctuary of Our Lord of Esquipulas in El Sauce, about forty-five miles away. Every Nicaraguan village has its saint and celebrates its patron saint day in a festival that often lasts days and involves colourful processions and rituals.

Religion in Nicaragua today is inseparable from politics. And perhaps the most decisive debate in the country is the confrontation between, on the one hand, the Church and the government and, on the other, the disagreements within the ranks of the Church itself.

Many Catholics fought with the Sandinistas against Somoza and nearly all the leaders of the FSLN, including those most influenced by Marxism like Tomás Borge or Carlos Fonseca Amador, were brought up as Catholics. In Jinotega, in a Territorial Army battalion, they pointed out to me a Jesuit, Comandante Sanginés, who hung up his clerical garb to become involved in the revolution and is now fighting the Contras. The Catholic hierarchy stood up to Somoza repeatedly and, after the victory, gave the Sandinistas their blessing in a pastoral letter (7 November 1979) which stated: 'The revolution is a propitious moment to make the dedication of the Church to the poor a reality.' But the honeymoon did not last long. The radicalization of the regime saw to this and also the growing importance within Nicaragua, with the regime's support, of the theses and personalities of the movement which proposes a synthesis of Marxism and Christianity. This asserts that the first duty of Christians is their commitment to the revolution and identifies sin with 'the unjust social structures of capitalism' and that in its most extreme version – take for example the version of the poet priest, Ernesto Cardenal, recently suspended *a divinis* for not resigning from his post as Minister of Culture – proclaims that 'Marxism is the only solution for the world'. Nicaragua became a paradise for socialist Catholics, radical theologians, apocalyptic prophets and Marxist–Leninist priests from all over the world. The Sandinista regime, who had in its government four revolutionary priests, promoted this Popular Church, believing that it would give the revolution a Christian aura without limiting its radicalism. This was a wrong calculation. But, in my opinion, it had a positive effect, since it has helped to prevent Nicaragua from falling into pure totalitarianism.

When one speaks of a dispute between the Popular Church and the Catholic hierarchy one has the idea that the former represents the humble masses of the faithful and their pastors, while the latter is made up of a phalanx of teratological bishops and a handful of ultramontane and integralist Catholics blind and deaf to the winds of history. In fact the Popular Church is not very popular. It is made up of priests and laymen whose intellectual disquisitions and sociopolitical work lie outside the scope of the ordinary, run-of-the-mill Catholic. Above all, the poor. Its Centre and Institutes publish some suggestive journals – like *Pensamiento propio* (Thinking for Oneself) by INIES (The National Institute of Economic and Social Research) directed by the Jesuit Xavier Gorostiaga and *Amanecer* (Dawn) from the Antonio Valdivieso Ecumenical Centre founded by the most conspicuous dignitary of the Popular Church, the Franciscan Uriel Molina. But its efforts to denounce the historical role that the Church has played at the service of the dominant powers, to clothe the class struggle and anti-imperialism with evangelical symbolism and to show, through biblical exegesis, that the fight for socialism is the most important debate among Christians, only has a resonance in intellectual and committed sectors of the middle classes, who are already converts. The bulk of Nicaraguan Catholics, as in the rest of Latin America, do not profess to that reflexive, intellectual and critical religion proposed by the Popular Church, but rather to an intuitive, disciplined and ritual faith which has always been the motor force of the Church among us: the faith of the simple man. This tendency is what the hierarchy and their indomitable leader, Archbishop Monsignor Obando y Bravo, represent, preach and defend against those who threaten it.

The Solidarity Mass, celebrated by Father Uriel Molina in the Santa María de los Angeles Church in the Rigueiro neighbourhood where he has been a parish priest for many years, takes place in a circular chapel, without any religious images, except for one of the Virgin Mary, surrounded by revolutionary murals in which one can see Christ, dressed as a Nicaraguan peasant, and ignominious Yankee imperialists and adipose soldiers shooting young people brandishing Sandinista flags. 'The Peasant Mass' by the composer Carlos Mejía Godoy is punctuated by revolutionary songs set to pleasant music. In his sermon, Father Uriel gives us a lesson on the 'process of revolutionary transformation of society' which must be lived by Christians through their faith. He calls out the Sandinistas who have fallen in action in recent days and asks us to give the response 'Present' after each name. At the moment of the kiss of peace, the mass becomes a political meeting. More than half of the congregation are North American 'internationalists' who, with the television cameras rolling, fall on Comandante Tomás Borge, who is beside me, to kiss him, photograph him and ask for his autograph. (I whisper in his ear 'The revolution is in trouble: this is like Hollywood!')

In the Church of Las Sierritas, in Altos de Santo Domingo, by contrast, there are no foreigners. The people that pack into the church are Nicaraguans, waving Vatican and Nicaraguan flags, greeting Monsignor Obando with applause (it is his birthday) and cheering the Pope. Beneath the traditional appearance of the church and its decorations, everything, including the exaggerated enthusiasm of the faithful is also, as in the Rigueiro neighbourhood, politically loaded. Ever since the events that occurred during the visit of John Paul II to Nicaragua, the Pope is a password: to cheer him means protesting against the regime. In his sermon, Monsignor Obando talks of Mary taking Jesus to the temple, of her grief as a Mother, which makes her understand the grief of all those mothers who have their sons wrenched from them (everyone understands that he is talking about the recruitment of young men into the Patriotic Military Service).

The Antonio Valdivieso Ecumenical Centre, a house in the centre of Managua, is a cosmopolitan place. Progressive theologians, both Protestant and Catholic, come from all over the world to its seminars and it publishes articles by heterodox luminaries such as the German professor, Hans Küng, Karl Rahner, or the famous bishop of Cuernavaca, Méndez Arceo (who exhorted the faithful to 'go on a pilgrimage to Cuba, as one would go to Lourdes or Fatima'). 'We are not a parallel church, but rather a movement for renewal which tries to live in solidarity with the poor,' José Argüello, the director of *Amanecer*, tells me. 'For us, the problem is not whether the revolution is becoming Marxist. It is whether it will survive. The alternative would not be democracy, but something similar to Guatemala or El Salvador. And for a Marxist, living people is preferable to a dead people.'

According to Father Uriel Molina, 'all this about the Popular Church is an invention of the Medellín Cardinal López Trujillo. Certain publications of Liberation Theology horrify me. We want the Church to maintain its credibility among the people, the credibility that our bishops have lost by not condemning North American aggression.' He says that in the present circumstances, censorship is justifiable, but as a transitional measure. The revolution has given the Nicaraguan people its identity back 'which is nurtured by folklore, by poetry, and by all our traditions. Thanks to this identity, our people now have a pride in themselves that dictatorships and secular exploitation had stripped away from them. By opposing the revolution, the hierarchy has lost its moral authority. Its declarations and actions serve the transnationals and the CIA.' He defends the right of the four minister-priests to continue in their posts despite the prohibition of the Vatican. 'They want to force them to resign, to break with what they symbolize: the solidarity between Christians and the revolution.' To prove that he is no blind apologist of the regime, Father Molina reminds me that he has protested against the abuses of human rights and, also, against the expulsion of priests. How does the Nicaraguan clergy line up? 'Of the four hundred priests in Nicaragua, about one hundred are with us and the other three hundred with Monsignor Obando,' he says.

When he hears these figures, the Archbishop of Nicaragua smiles. 'The Nicaraguan priests that follow Uriel can be counted on the fingers of two hands. It is true that these numbers are boosted by the foreign clergy that the government brings in. On the other hand, the government denies visas to nuns and priests who wish to come on purely apostolic grounds. Recently it denied a visa to seven Salesian teachers and the Vice Chancellor of the Order.' (The Salesians resolutely supported the bishops and have thus incurred the hostility of the government. Jesuits, Franciscans and Dominicans tend to support the other group.) 'As you will have discovered, these manoeuvres didn't do them much good. Most Nicaraguan Catholics are faithful to the bishops and to the Pope.'

I think that he is right. I saw this in the Festival of San Sebastián, in Diriamba, where a boisterous crowd applauded every time that Monsignor Bosco Vivas, the officiating bishop, mentioned Monsignor Obando or the Pope and I heard the ovation that an old priest received at the beginning of the procession, when he seized the microphone and shouted against 'the Communists who are responsible for this war and who are making our boys enlist to fight it'. And I have seen, above all, the excitement that Monsignor Obando generates in his public appearances. For Monsignor Obando, at fifty-eight, is a charismatic character. His purple robes cannot disguise his rugged Indian looks and his small, strong peasant body. When he was an auxiliary bishop in Matagalpa, he founded the first rural union in the countryside and he became very popular as he moved tirelessly from one village to another in that mountainous region. The story goes that when he was told of his promotion to archbishop he was on a donkey during one of those hard journeys that he still makes in these difficult times. Unlike his opponents, Monsignor Obando has no intellectual pretensions. He is a conservative, in the mould of John Paul II (with whom, it is clear, he gets on very well): that is, a man who combines commitment to traditional and ecclesiastical authority with a sense of justice and a noteworthy capacity for communicating a spiritual message to humble people.

The pastoral letters of the bishops of Nicaragua criticizing the regime have touched on the most sensitive issues. The tense relationship between the Sandinistas and the Miskito Indians on the Atlantic coast was due, according to the Church, to violent acts committed by the government. The bishops also questioned the law of Patriotic Military Service, arguing that the Sandinista army was a party, not a national organization, and requesting the right of 'conscientious objection' for those not wishing to serve an ideology opposed to their religion. But the pastoral letter that provoked the greatest furore was issued on 22 April 1984 and called for a dialogue between the government and the Contras. From the pulpits, bishops and priests that support these letters frequently attack Marxism and denounce any signs of totalitarianism, atheism or religious persecution. Has the campaign been exaggerated, hypersensitive? Have the bishops, at times, been seen to have little understanding of the difficulties that the revolution has faced and has it undervalued its efforts to help the poor? That's possible. But this frontal attack by the Church – perhaps more than the economic crisis or external pressure – has placed a brake on any totalitarian moves that the government might have countenanced. Recently, the Sandinista leadership started up a dialogue with the Episcopal Conference. While I was in Nicaragua, two private meetings took place, one between Monsignor Obando and President Ortega and another between Ortega and the president of the Episcopal Conference, Monsignor Pablo Antonio Vega.

## Is the Virgin anti-Sandinista?

The village of Cuapa is in the department of Chontales, in the centre of the country. One night in 1980, Bernardo the sacristan went into the church and saw a radiant light emanating from the Virgin, which lit up the whole chapel. The phenomenon disappeared when Bernardo turned on the electric light. One morning three weeks later, when he was fishing by the river bank, the sacristan was suddenly filled with happiness. All around him, the landscape began to change: the sun was in eclipse, he heard warbling and the whisper of leaves and saw gentle flashes of lightning. A cloud alighted on a pile of stones beside a cedar tree. A beautiful barefoot young woman, her hands clasped, wrapped in a cape embroidered with jewels and with a crown of stars on her head, appeared on the cloud. She had chestnut hair, honey-coloured eyes and a bronzed skin. She opened her hands and warmth flooded through the sacristan. 'What is your name?' he stammered. 'My name is Mary.' 'Where do you come from?' 'From heaven. I am the mother of the Lord.'

This first apparition took place on 8 May. There were another four, in June, July and September, always on the eighth of the month. The sacristan was also summoned on 8 August, but he could not go because the swollen waters prevented him from crossing the river. In the final apparition, it was not the young woman who appeared, but an eight-year-old girl.

In the first apparition, the Virgin asked the Nicaraguans to say the rosary with their families and exhorted them to love one another, to carry out their obligations and to make peace. She let slip, at the same time, statements that had political reverberations. 'Nicaragua has suffered greatly since the earthquake and will continue to suffer if you do not change. If you do not do so, you will hasten the coming of the Third World War.' After the second vision, the message was unequivocal. Bernardo asked her what she thought of the Sandinistas. She replied: 'They are atheists, Communists, and for that reason I have come to help the Nicaraguans. What they promised has not been fulfilled. If you do not observe what I ask, Communism will spread throughout America. But you must not leave the country, you must not turn your back on your problems. If you listen to my pleas, Nicaragua will be the light of the world.'

Bernardo tells me this in a soft voice, in the garden of the seminary where he is being kept, adding that he cannot yet reveal all that Mary said. He is a calm man and he also has that quiet look of a believer that I find fascinating but also makes me nervous. He replies, however, even to my most impertinent questions. He tells me that when the bishop of Juigalpa, Monsignor Pablo Antonio Vega, authorized him to reveal the miracle and crowds of pilgrims began to come to Cuapa, three government officials visited him to offer him, as a present, a farm on good land and some cows. There was one condition: he had to say that the

Virgin was a Sandinista. He explained to them that he had to tell the truth. They compromised: it would be enough to omit the fact that she was anti-Sandinista. 'I cannot betray her,' he replied. Then the official newspapers, *Barricada* and *Nuevo Diario*, and the television began a campaign accusing him of being mad, hysterical and suffering from hallucinations. A woman called Sandra began to come up to him and whisper lustful suggestions in his ear like, 'I want to see you at midnight'. The faithful that were protecting him discovered photographers lying in wait for him. Early one morning, the police invaded his house and tried to kidnap him, but the faithful who were sleeping in the house came to his rescue. A couple of years ago, to keep him safe, the Church brought him to this seminary where he looks after the garden and regales the seminarians with his stories.

When Bernardo was moved to Managua, the Virgin of Cuapa was well on her way to becoming an object of devotion in Nicaragua. Tens of thousands of the faithful often visit the place, led, on occasion, by Monsignor Vega and Monsignor Obando. *La Prensa,* censorship permitting, always publishes news of these pilgrimages and defends Bernardo. The hierarchy let it be known that 'the petitions of the Virgin were not opposed to the teaching of the Church'. The efforts of the Popular Church to eradicate 'bourgeois Marianism' have, to now, been to no avail. When asked to give a blessing on the day of the presidential investiture of Comandante Ortega, in front of hundreds of guests and the millions watching on television, the president of the Episcopal Conference, Monsignor Vega, made a clever reference to the Virgin of Cuapa. When the Valdivieso Ecumenical Centre tried to counteract this 'Marianism charged with potential counter-revolutionary politics' with a novena to the Virgin, proposing instead a progressive and revolutionary image of the Mother of Christ, the hierarchy declared the novena impious and condemned the Centre for anti-Christian activities. I ask Monsignor Obando if the miracles have been ratified by the Church. 'To have miracles ratified takes some time,' he replies. 'We have confined ourselves for the moment to verifying that the message Bernardo received does not contradict orthodoxy.'

This is not a medieval story. It is happening today in Nicaragua and its political importance is considerable. To believe or not to believe in the Virgin of Cuapa places people ideologically and lines them up on one side or the other of the internal conflict.

## The quiet Sandinista

It often occurs in revolutions that, before their triumph, their dynamism and appeal is focused on a libertarian impulse – hatred of the tyrant, repression, censorship. Once in power, another impulse, egalitarianism, takes over. Inevitably, at some point, these two impulses come into conflict, as has happened in Nicaragua. Because it is a tragic fact that liberty and equality are harshly antagonistic. True progress cannot be achieved by sacrificing one of these impulses – social justice without liberty for example, or liberty with exploitation and unspeakable inequality – but by finding a tense balance between these two ideals which are intimately repellent. But, until now, no socialist revolution has achieved this balance.

In Nicaragua, the revolutionaries who took power after struggling bravely against a dynastic dictatorship believed that they could do everything, without legal restrictions. (Didn't they repeat that 'the revolution is the source of law?') They thought that they could redistribute land, achieve full employment, develop industry, lower the price of food and transport, end inequality, uproot imperialism and help neighbouring countries in their fight for revolution. The tenets of Marxism that guided them – which were quite general, to judge from the texts of Carlos Fonseca Amador, the most venerated figure among the founders of the FSLN – had convinced them that history can easily be shaped if one knows its laws and acts 'scientifically'. Five and a half years later they are beginning to discover – some more, others less, but I doubt that anyone is still blind to the fact – that to transform a society is more difficult than to set ambushes, attack barracks or rob banks. Because the supposed laws of history fall apart when faced with the brutal conditions of underdevelopment, the diversity of human behaviour and the fateful limitations on the sovereignty of poor and small nations which stems from the rivalry between the two superpowers. In the conversations that I had with Sandinista leaders, above all in informal meetings, where the good humour and friendliness of the Nicaraguans flourished, I often noticed that they appeared gradually to be learning the bourgeois art of compromise. And the one among the nine leaders of the National Directorate who, according to all the rumours, has learned this the best is Comandante Daniel Ortega.

I am told that Violeta Chamorro once said of the new President: 'He is the best of them all.' He is also the quietest, so much so that he appears shy. I accompanied him on a tour of the Northern front, where he visited widows and war orphans and soldiers wounded in Contra ambushes, adolescents of fifteen, sixteen, eighteen years old, with their faces, hands and legs blown away. The last day I was in Nicaragua, he invited me to have lunch with him and his companion Rosario Murillo who is also a poet (all Nicaraguans are poets) and a representative in the National Assembly. Daniel Ortega does not drink or smoke, runs three miles and works fifteen hours a day. He began to conspire against Somoza when he was thirteen, and of his current thirty-eight years, he has spent seven in prison for robbing a bank to get funds for the revolution. When the Sandinista Front divided into three tendencies, he and his brother Humberto led what was called the 'Third Tendency'. It was an eclectic position between the 'Proletarian' position of Wheelock and Carrión and 'The Prolonged War' group of Tomás Borge and Henry Ruiz. Although the nine comandantes emphatically state that there is complete equality amongst them, Comandante Daniel Ortega has in fact been emerging as the leader, first as the Coordinator of the Government Junta and now as President of the Republic.

I told him that the month I had spent in his country had been schizophrenic, but privileged. Because every day I spoke alternately to Sandinistas and the opposition who, from one hour to the next offer me very dissimilar versions of the same facts. And that I was alarmed at the mutual deafness between the regime and its dissidents. 'We'll gradually get to understand each other,' he assured me. 'We have begun a dialogue with the bishops. And now that the Assembly is beginning to discuss the constitution, we will reopen a dialogue with the parties that abstained in the elections. It'll be slow, but the internal tensions will be resolved. That's not the difficult part. The difficult part is the negotiation with the United States. That's the root of all our problems. President Reagan still wants to crush us, and for that reason, he appears to negotiate but then takes a step back, as in Manzanillo. He doesn't want negotiation. He wants us to surrender. We've said that we are prepared to take out the Cubans, the Russians and the other advisers; suspend any movement through our country of military or other aid to the Salvadoreans, and accept international verification. We have said that all we ask in return is that they do not attack us and that the United States stops arming and financing and then boasting about it to the world, the gangs that come in to kill us, burn our crops and force us to divert enormous human and economic resources that we desperately need for development.'

Since Rosario Murillo then called us to the table, I did not manage to tell him that, in my opinion, the negotiation with the United States seemed to me less difficult than the negotiation with the opposition. Because when the North American government recognizes that the Sandinista regime is not going to be overthrown by the Contras, and that a direct invasion would be catastrophic for the cause of democracy in the rest of Latin America, it will probably negotiate with Nicaragua over what, in the end, is the major concern: to get the USSR and Cuba out of Nicaragua and to cut off aid to the Salvadorean insurrection. That, I have no doubt, Comandante Ortega and his colleagues will grant in exchange for peace.

What they will not concede so readily is what the opposition wants: full democracy. That is, power sharing and placing the outcome of the revolution in the hands of certain variables such as free elections, no press censorship, a division of powers and representative institutions. This is not the democracy for which they went up into the mountains, the legality that they believe in. In line with an old tradition which, unfortunately, is more Latin American than Marxist and which a number of their adversaries share, they think, although they do not admit it, that real legitimacy is bestowed by the arms with which the power has been won, and that once you take power, then there is no reason to share it.

This is why it is so difficult for the regime to reach an understanding with an opposition which also tends to back itself into an 'all or nothing' corner. And yet the survival of the Nicaraguan revolution depends on negotiation, agreement or, at the very least, an accommodation between the two factions. Perhaps it is not the solution for those who defend, against all odds, democratic 'forms' but at least it would help support social justice within a minimally genuine system of pluralism and freedom, so as to avoid becoming prey to the claustrophobia, despair and new forms of injustice endemic to Marxist dictatorships.

Don Emilio, the old conservative ophthalmologist and political guru, told me one night: 'Our *criollo* culture is all powerful, as you can see. It swallows up everything you give it. It assimilates everything and ends up putting its own stamp on it.' I remember that this is exactly what Rubén Darío did, that obscure Nicaraguan who began by imitating the

French symbolists and ended up revolutionizing the poetry of the Spanish language. Is creole culture swallowing the Marxism of these impatient young men and will it turn it into something better? The circumstances are auspicious for this to happen.

April 1985

# My Son the Rastafarian

Until I was invited to take part in that jury at the Berlin Festival, I was convinced that the best thing that could happen to anyone in life was to be a member of a film jury. I had been one in Cannes, in San Sebastián and in Barcelona, for The Week of Cinema in Colour, and on all these occasions I knew for certain that happiness was not a dream, but rather a tangible reality. I love cinema and seeing four or five films a day, even if they are bad, is something that I can manage perfectly well. (It is not the same for everyone. At Cannes, in 1975, one of my fellow jurors, the Lebanese poet Georges Schehadé, confessed to us that all the over-indulgence in films gave him nightmares because, until then, he had been used to seeing, at most, one or two films a year.) The best hotels, the best seats, invitations to all the press conferences, exhibitions, parties and the opportunity, between films, to contemplate the celluloid stars, sometimes in monokinis or *au naturel*: what more could one ask for?

But at the Berlin Festival, I discovered that being a jury member could also be an exhausting task, with unsuspected ethical dimensions. Our president was Liv Ullmann who, in flesh and blood, turned out to be as beautiful and intelligent as in the films of Ingmar Bergman. But she was also possessed by an almost monstrous sense of responsibility, a president who had decided that the jury in her charge would deliver in their verdict nothing less than absolute justice. And she was convinced that this was possible if we would only bring to our task an almost superhuman dedication to analysis, comparison and evaluation, virtually memorizing all the films in competition (24 features and 14 shorts).

In San Sebastián, we discussed gastronomy above all else (the Basque Country has the best cuisine in Spain), and only late in the day, in the course of our tour around the restaurants and bars of the city and the region, would we rather distractedly agree on the merits and weaknesses of the films. In Cannes, the president of the jury was Tennessee Williams. At the outset he made it known to us that the level of violence in the cinema was intolerable (this from a man who had crammed the theatre with brutalities, imaginative perversions and even cannibalism) and therefore he would not see any film or attend meetings of the jury over which he was presiding. We rarely saw him, a mythical figure in the distance, surrounded by a varied entourage of secretaries of both sexes, chauffeurs and a maid to carry the *caniches*. A couple of meetings were enough for his underlings to decide, in friendly after-dinner conversations, the distribution of the prizes.

But from our first moment in Berlin, we knew that our incorruptible president would not be satisfied with an 'I vote for this film for the Grand Prize, for so and so as best director etc.' Each film, director, actor, cameraman, cinematographer, script writer, composer, editor, mixer – to say nothing of each soundman, make-up artist, dresser, extra – would have to pass through the filter of our critical intelligence, be scrutinized, weighed up, compared and balanced against the tally and marks of our colleagues, in sessions that consumed all the free time between the films, reduced our meals to a sandwich and caused us to slump exhausted into our cinema seats.

So as not to be struck dumb or stammer when faced by Liv Ullmann's questions, I had no alternative but to go to the screenings laden with file cards and fill them with notes, recording my impressions of each film. The result was, naturally, that the films were no longer a source of pleasure and became a problem, a struggle against time, the darkness, and my own aesthetic emotions, which had become confused by these autopsies. Since I had to spend so much time worrying about rating each film, my scale of values went into shock and I very soon discovered that I could not easily make out what I liked and disliked and why.

I was in this delicate psychological state when my younger son came to spend a week with me in Berlin: Gonzalo Gabriel, the nepheloid.

2

He was almost sixteen. He was at boarding school in England and I hadn't seen him for a term. The Berlin Festival coincided with a few days' school holiday and I invited him to spend it with me. The organizers had a bed for him in my room and gave me passes so that he could attend the functions and activities of the Festival the days he was in Berlin.

Unlike his brother and sister who talk all the time and are temperamental and obsessive, Gonzalo Gabriel was always extremely reserved and a dreamer. When he was six, he fired a difficult question at me one day. 'Daddy, does God exist?' I tried to get out of that one by explaining to him that for many people, God existed and that for others, He did not, and that there were some of us who could not say whether He existed or not. He listened attentively and went off to bed. But a few days later, early one morning, he woke me up, kicking open the bedroom door and bellowing at me from the shadows, 'God exists and I love him!' It was the only time that I heard him raise his voice. His mother and I always thought that he had his head in the clouds (that's why we called him the nepheloid) and it was always very difficult for us to judge if he was happy, sad, bored, or enjoying himself, and what he thought, felt or wanted. My children spent their childhood changing countries, languages, houses and schools. This nomadic, gypsy life did not much affect the oldest and the youngest, but it did affect Gonzalo Gabriel. We realized this in Barcelona, when we noticed that he was carrying on his back, without ever being separated from it, either to eat or sleep, a small bag full of knick-knacks – matchboxes, stones and butterflies – which he had collected in the garden of the house in London where he had spent his first years. In the dizzying whirl of cities that made up his childhood – London, Washington, San Juan in Puerto Rico, Lima, Paris, Barcelona – that bag must have been the only stable and permanent thing in his life, a sort of amulet against the devil of moving house. He slept clutching the bag, and if we tried to take it away from him, he sobbed his eyes out.

He and his elder brother were very happy at school the year I was a visiting professor at the University of Cambridge. So much so that when Patricia and I went back to Peru, they asked to stay in England as boarders. That is what happened. They were there for five years. They spent their holidays in Lima and we tried to spend at least a term near them.

In these reunions, I was generally surprised at the way they had changed. The one who went through the most abrupt changes was the eldest, Alvaro. In the year before that Festival in Berlin, for example, he informed us at termly intervals that: 1. He was having mystical experiences and that he was thinking of devoting himself to theology; 2. He had left the Catholic Church for the Anglican faith and that he had been confirmed in the Church of England; and 3. Religion was the opium of the people and that he had become an atheist. The changes in Gonzalo Gabriel tended to be more discreet and often imperceptible, usually involving music (from AC/DC to Kiss) or sport (from ping-pong to athletics). Ever since he had reached the age of reason, I had seen him going into a sort of mystic trance in the theatre, and spend a great deal of time in the world of the imaginary, so I thought that he might have the stuff of an actor in him. But Gonzalo Gabriel never showed any sign of being the slightest bit bothered about his future. Except the previous holiday when he had brought a school friend back to Lima. Both dressed like models and told us one day that when they grew up, they would probably become fashion designers like Pierre Cardin or Yves St Laurent.

Perhaps because of this background I was not prepared for what was in store for me that morning when I slid out between two jury meetings and went to Berlin airport in a limousine put at my disposal by the Festival, accompanied by a pleasant, maternal Berliner, to pick up the nepheloid.

'Is *that* your son?', my companion asked me. Yes it was, although it was difficult to recognize him as a hominid. He had appeared at the end of the queue of passengers from London and waved at me through the glass partition. The police won't let him in, I thought. They will expel him as an undesirable. But they did let him in. In three months, he seemed to have grown four inches and lost ten pounds. He looked tall and seemed to have become a kind of fakir – all skin and bones – and what was also new about his face was his fixed, penetrating gaze, of a man-boy who knows the deep truth of things.

An enormous head of hair fell in disorder over his face and swept his shoulders. But what was more shocking than its length was its tangle, a jungle never explored by a comb. The long strands ended in knots and little curls. He was wearing a strange bag, with holes for his arms and legs, made of some undetectable material like patchwork, with clashing colours, in which red, black and gold predominated. With its amorphous shape, its grotesque bagginess and its buttons like sunflowers, it vaguely resembled the garments that adorn clowns or scarecrows. But in those disguises, there is always a note of humour. The mess that Gonzalo Gabriel was swamped in was completely joyless. There was something solemn and disturbing about it, like religious habits or military uniforms. (I later found out that it was a combination of both these elements.) His shoes did not seem to be made of leather or of cloth but of oilskin or cartilage and they were all colours of the rainbow. They went from toe to calf and had no sole, no heel, or any structure, so that they looked like a badly packed prosthesis. He was carrying a bag of the same viscose material that covered his feet. In it, his only luggage, was a Bible.

He greeted me in his usual laconic way, saying hello and giving me a kiss. (His elder brother, on reaching fifteen, decided that such familiarities were excessive and replaced the kiss with the manly Iberian clap on the back.) In the limousine on the way to the Hotel Kempinsky – where I was sure that they would not let him register – I gave him all the family news and then ventured to ask him about his studies. 'The truth is that lately I haven't had time to study.' What had been keeping him so busy?

Fighting against animal vivisection, mainly. Demonstrating in front of those 'murderers' stores', Harrods, Austin Reed, Aquascutum etc., which traded in corpses; brandishing protest placards outside fur shops and shoe shops which displayed their crimes with total impunity in their windows. Furthermore, a lot of 'their' time had been taken up finding out which hunts were being planned and organizing the necessary campaigns which, he explained, consisted of getting between the guns of the hunters and the skins of the foxes and the feathers of the pheasants or the pigeons at which the bullets were being fired. The letters to the Spanish Ambassador had also been time consuming for 'them'. To the Spanish Ambassador in London? Yes, they had written him a letter every day for three months. I asked him the reason for this copious correspondence.

'Genocide,' he replied impatiently. He wasn't referring just to bull-fighting; 'they' had a very full catalogue of all the acts of sadism that were perpetrated in the different regions of Spain, in local fiestas, against horses, dogs, pigs, geese, donkeys etc. I imagined the face of the Ambassador, whom I knew, as he received every morning a letter from my son, admonishing him for every drop of animal blood being spilled by human hands in the Motherland.

In the Hotel Kempinsky, despite my fears, they did not object to him checking in and a bell-boy offered to carry the multi-coloured bag to our room (he didn't let him). Patricia had packed him a suitcase with suits, shirts and ties and had enclosed a list of instructions so that he would attend all the Festival events, 'very well groomed, very elegant and very handsome'. I had carried this suitcase and these exhortations across continents and oceans and now, in our elegant Kempinsky room, feeling totally ridiculous, I gave them to him.

He glanced with quiet disdain at the suits, ties and suggestions and told me that I could have saved myself the trouble since he would never again wear 'bourgeois clothes'. His principles did not allow it. Since I was not up to engaging in a philosophical discussion at that moment, I could only manage a pragmatic objection. 'If you go dressed like that, they might not let you in to see the films.'

His smile told me that, at this stage of his life, there was no sacrifice that he would not be prepared to make in the name of the religion to which he was a new convert. What religion exactly? I didn't dare ask. My obligations as a jury member were calling me away. I told him that there was the official opening of the Festival that night, with the screening of James L. Brooks' *Terms of Endearment* and that it would be a pity if, for a few clothes here or there, he might miss the show . . . and I fled. Liv Ullmann opened the jury meeting with a detailed report on the way the animal sequences had been shot in a Japanese film – *Antarctica* by Koreyoshi Kurahara – which we had seen the previous evening and now had to dissect. Anticipating our predictable anxieties that the dogs, wolves, seals and walruses in the line-up of *Antarctica* might have suffered rough handling or abuse in the course of the filming (a thought that horrified her as much as it horrified us), Liv had made the relevant enquiries (perhaps by not sleeping the two or three hours that we had free for that superfluous activity?) and was equipped with the information that the director Kurahara had filmed *Antarctica* under the supervision of two vets and an observer from the Japanese Society for the Prevention of Cruelty to Animals, whose task it was to verify that the animals did not suffer, even when they were anaesthetized. Along with my colleagues on the jury, I gave the necessary sighs of relief that showed us to be worthy of the delicate sensibility that our President attributed to us, thinking that perhaps after all Gonzalo Gabriel had not gone off the rails and that his ideas were not as strange as I had thought.

When I got back to the hotel, I found the room full of smoke and a terrible smell. The nepheloid assured me that burning incense created an atmosphere for meditation and relieved tensions. Other healthy effects were that it purified the lungs and assured a better flow of blood to the brain.

Hadn't he had problems at school dressing that way? Not at all: he had given his reasons and the teachers respected them. He told me that he would always wear clothes like that because — and he said this as if he was reassuring me about something — they had all been made with skins of animals which had died a natural death. He assured me emphatically that he did not have on his body a single thread that was the result of sadism to cows, sheep, lambs and other animals. As for his stocking shoes, they were from Ethiopia. They could, therefore, be worn with a clear conscience because, despite the very difficult conditions in which they lived, the Ethiopian people had a religious respect for animals. They used for their clothes only the hair and skins of quadrupeds which had died of old age, sickness or in an accident. Looking him straight in the eyes, I asked him if he believed what he was telling me, or if he took me for an idiot. He returned my gaze with the tranquil meekness of one who possessed the truth: he believed it all. Changing tactics, I asked him if he might consider the hypothesis that the shop owner in London or Cambridge where he had purchased these articles might have deceived him, passing off as untainted clothes rags and leathers whose origins were as bloody as the ones I was wearing. His ghost of a smile cut me dead before I had finished. 'Of course not. He is one of us. One of the Twelve Tribes of Israel. A Rastaman!'

It was the first time that I had heard that strange word. So as not to appear too ignorant in front of him, I didn't ask what it meant. Instead I thought that next time I was in England, I would go to see this inspired merchant straight away.

I assumed that, with these ideas, he was now a vegetarian. 'Of course. If you're against the crime, you have to take it all the way.' But a shadow crossed his face. 'Though the truth is that I do have some doubts about food. Perhaps you can advise me.'

Was there a way of bringing him back, through gastronomy, to the world of the sadists? Some hope!

'Many people think that it is not right to eat vegetables either,' he explained, and, for a few seconds his face, or what could be seen of it through the dense undergrowth, was not that of a fanatic, but rather of a bewildered adolescent. Aren't green beans, lettuces, tomatoes, peas born, and don't they grow? Aren't they also living beings?

Dazed, I asked him what these scrupulous perfectionists ate.

'Fruit,' he told me. 'Fruit matures and falls on its own. No one kills it. And the seeds reproduce and continue the strain. So it is not cruel or unnatural to eat fruit. Some people only eat fruit. Just a few. They are considered the purest. They feed themselves without harming anyone, without destroying nature. What do you think of that?'

The call that it was time to leave for the opening of the Festival found me arguing, with all the scientific references that I could muster (which were few), in favour of vegetarianism, denying that rice, gherkins and peas had a 'soul' or could feel pain. Gonzalo Gabriel listened to me with the aloof condescension that pagans inspire in the believer. His face filled with distrust when he heard me say, pointing out how thin he was, that charity began at home. If it so troubled him to inflict harm on other living beings, then he should also show a bit of compassion for his own body. At the rate he was going, he would soon be so weak that a simple cold would carry him to his grave. He replied, of course, that a man should be prepared to die for his ideas.

3

The ushers at the Festival Theatre did not stop him going into the opening function and there he was, dressed like a marionette, with his sorcerer's locks, in the VIP row alongside Jack Nicholson, Jules Dassin, Liv Ullmann, Debra Winger and other stars who did not seem disturbed by their grotesque neighbour. And they did not deny him entry to the party laid on by the Mayor of Berlin, where most of the invitees were in evening dress. When it came to the official presentation, the mayor of the city committed the friendly faux pas of asking him if he was an actor. He replied, with laconic brutality: 'No.' But he refused to eat a mouthful, afraid that the buffet might contain corpses and that the canapés and food might have been the result of some illtreatment to the infinite variety of beings that populated the air, the land and the waters of the world.

In the week that he spent in Berlin, feeding him became a much greater source of mortification than the psycho-aesthetic-analytic sessions that Liv Ullmann inflicted on us. Almost everything placed before him inspired either mistrust or horror, because another ingredient of the phobia that he had contracted had to do with salt. It was difficult for me to recognize the timid and silent Gonzalo Gabriel of three months ago in this young man who caused consternation among the waiters in the restaurants or those in charge of the reception buffets by demanding to be told if the plates of salad that he deigned to accept had been sprinkled with salt (by asking 'do you swear that you haven't put cyanide on it?'). And if, in the first mouthful, he detected any trace of seasoning, he pushed away the plate with the grimace of someone who is afraid of being poisoned. He asked for 'herb tea', a formula that was untranslatable into German because they invariably produced a classic cup of tea. With regard to some foods like milk and eggs, he had devastating doubts. 'They', it seemed, had not formed a clear opinion on them and he had not found a precise guide in his Bible (which, at least in theory, he told me that he consulted for everything, and adhered to strictly in matters of dress and diet). In the dinners or lunches he attended with me, he pulled a face of such disapproval every time, for example, we were brought plates of meat, that I was astonished that our table companions put up with his impertinence with such patience.

Every conversation that we had at night in the dark, before going to sleep after exhausting days of screenings and meetings, increased my dismay, excited my curiosity and, in general, made my hair stand on end. He informed me that he had decided not to go to university. Once he'd finished school, he would go off and work as a volunteer for organizations who looked after children in Ethiopia – like Oxfam, for example. He'd really like to learn Amharic, the official language of the Ethiopians. I hinted that with an academic training he would perhaps be better equipped to give more consistent help to the disinherited of Africa and that if he was interested in African languages, then England was full of universities with humanities departments specializing in all languages, living, dead, and even imaginary. He replied that universities crushed the spirit and created intellectual robots at the service of imperialism, colonialism and Babylon. He paused before adding what I had been fearing: 'Like public schools in England, of course.' I deduced that his flight from school was imminent, if he had not left already.

From these weighty matters he moved on to domestic trivialities, like telling me that we had to convince his mother never to use insecticides or fumigate the house. One had to be consistent. If 'we' thought it was wrong to murder dogs, cows or horses then why kill flies, mosquitoes, rats and cockroaches? Did the dignity of life depend on the size of the living? In that case, why not exterminate dwarfs? Nature should not be destroyed but learned from, since it was all-wisdom. Was that the reason why he did not cut his finger or toe nails, which now seemed like the claws of a beast? Yes. And for that same reason he would never again set foot in a hairdresser's or run a comb through his hair. Not only was he following the commandments of Nature, but also those of the Bible. And he recited to me in English, swearing that it was a verse from the Old Testament: 'Thou shalt not cut thy beard, nor shave thy head.'

One should not alter the course of life. Everything that was 'natural' was good; everything artificial, on the other hand, was dangerous, destructive ('Babylon') and had to be resolutely opposed. Astrology, for example, was as harmful as pork crackling and *ceviche*. His Holiness the Pope was, horror of horrors, the Antichrist. In the midst of the dilemmas and anxiety into which his statements had plunged me, one night I heard him cursing alcohol and spirits, poisons that, like meat, salt and shellfish, exacerbated the worst instincts, causing wars, exploitation, colonialism, crimes, jealousy, robbery and other human calamities. But these moments of relief were transitory because that same night I discovered that the record he listened to most frequently on his portable cassette recorder, with his eyes closed as if in prayer, reciting the words, was called 'Burning and Looting' and prophesied 'burning and looting tonight'.

Wasn't there a certain incoherence between his belligerent pacifism and that apologia for devastation? He replied that Nesta had already illuminated the blind in a *Rolling Stone* interview: it was about burning and looting Babylon symbolically, and that no just man of flesh and blood would be touched.

Trembling, I enquired how drugs were classified in that nomenclature of 'natural' or benign things (children of Jah) and 'artificial' or evil things about which 'they', with the help of the Bible and Nesta, seemed to have such detailed and emphatic knowledge.

'We are against them,' he said without the slightest hesitation. 'LSD, heroin, cocaine are contaminated by chemicals. Or rather, profaned. Chemistry is the most artificial thing in the world. Don't you understand? It would be the same as profaning the body by eating processed food. Our body is a temple, man.'

I confessed that, in the midst of the anguish that his thinness and principles were causing me, it was a consolation – a small ray of light in the shadows – to know that drugs inspired in him the same feelings as chops. And I asked him to forgive me because among the pestilential odours permeating our desecrated room in the Hotel Kempinsky, I thought that I had detected, mixed with the incense, the aroma of marijuana.

'Dad, Dad! Marijuana isn't a drug. It's ganja, it's kaya. A plant, a bush, a marvellous creation of Nature. It sprouts and grows by itself. Like trees. It doesn't need to be pruned, watered or cultivated. What could be more natural than that?'

And with a passion uncommon in him, he lectured me for a long time, without my being able to rebut him – I was petrified. In marijuana, Nesta had found inspiration to compose his songs, like Peter Tosh and the rest of the Wailers, and to sing them in that divine way. Marijuana was the gateway to meditation and knowledge. It made men peaceful, love their neighbour and all living things, sensible and sensitive. If humanity had consumed more marijuana and fewer corpses, there would never have been wars of conquest or colonies or slavery, nor would so much cruelty have been committed. The world would not be this keg of atomic weapons, over which we were perched.

And, ending his peroration, he began to snore beatifically, in the deep sleep of the young and the just, leaving me in a state of complete demoralization. Only that night did I finally understand that Nesta was Bob Marley and that Bob Marley, whom I had stupidly taken for a simple reggae singer – and, even more stupidly I had taken reggae to be simply music – was, for Gonzalo Gabriel, for 'them', a prophet, a messiah, the incarnation of a metaphysical and political truth, and reggae was something like the Gospels in musical form.

This conversation must have occurred halfway through the week. Up to then, in the brief moments when I had time to think between the films and the jury meetings, I had decided that Gonzalo Gabriel's transformation was related exclusively to ecology, the anti-vivisectionist movement and the Animal Defence League which had gained in importance in England over recent years. During that sleepless night I realized that this was merely a further adornment added by my son and his schoolfriends to what was really important. In my ignorance of the subject matter, customs and personalities involved, I had not correctly identified the religion to which Gonzalo Gabriel had converted.

Marijuana raised to sacramental status was, however, an unmistakable clue. Like the desire to learn Amharic, to go off and live in the deserts of Africa and his unbridled love for Ethiopia. A photograph of the by now deposed and dead emperor, Haile Selassie I, in a very formal uniform, plastered with medals, with a cape and flanked by lions, had appeared from the first day on Gonzalo Gabriel's bedside table in our room at the Hotel Kempinsky. Without knowing that I was committing a terrible sacrilege, I asked, 'What's that odd-looking creature doing here?' My eyes were not opened by his scornful reply, full of indecipherable names. 'He's not an odd-looking creature. He's the Lion of Judah, he's Jah, he's the Redeemer.' Nor were my eyes opened by the green, gold and red colours that were repeated with obsessive frequency in the paraphernalia of the ex-nepheloid, in particular on a black beret adorned with these colours which he sometimes wore to hide his profuse locks. 'They seem like the colours of a flag,' I remarked on one occasion. 'They are,' he replied enigmatically, 'the colours of Ethiopia and also of Jamaica.' These three colours were repeated in the mysterious tassels that hung from each of Gonzalo's fingers and when I asked him what they were — were they amulets, adornments, provocations? — he always replied evasively.

The key words, Rasta, Rastafari, had appeared on his lips from the first day in Berlin and I had ignored them, thinking that they were perhaps the title of a song or a new slang word of young people in England. When I realized that these words condensed the new faith of Gonzalo Gabriel, there were only two days left before his return to London. In all the remaining minutes that we could spend alone together, I tried to get him to instruct me in his beliefs, like a catechist. I did not get too many things clear, but what I did understand plunged me into new depths of panic and shock to such an extent that, in order to get through the remaining films and sessions of the Festival, I had to resort to two agents of Babylon, Librium and Valium. I was prepared to accept the extravagances of religious fiction (for which I have always felt curiosity and sympathy). But that God — Jah — had been incarnated in Haile Selassie I (called before his coronation Ras-Tafari-Makonnen) seemed to me a joke in bad taste. It was a fundamental axiom in the Rasta theology. The Negus was the 'redeemer' announced by the prophet Marcus Garvey, a black Jamaican leader who in the 1920s had proclaimed that 'the day of liberation was at hand' because in Africa 'a black king would be crowned'. The king of kings, marijuana, Bob Marley, reggae and the Bible represented good. 'Evil', the devil, discrimination, exploitation, all the forms of human wickedness were summed up in the formula 'Babylon'. Born in the shanty towns of Kingston, the Rastafari religion had achieved international scope and status through Bob Marley. The poor immigrants of the Caribbean had taken the Rastafari customs, trappings and slang to the ghettos of London, Liverpool, Manchester etc.

But how had it spread from there into Albion's public schools? However much I tried to shake it out of him, Gonzalo Gabriel kept silent on this matter. All that he consented to reveal to me was that in his school, the 'Rasta Brothers' numbered more than ten. I told him that he and his friends were being very frivolous, from their comfortable position as privileged young people, in playing at joining a cult that could only be understood as a savage flowering of spirituality among oppressed people of a primary cultural formation. I added that outside the ghettos where it had been born and, above all in the public schools of England, Rastafarianism became a grotesque sham, like 'dressing up as a pauper or a savage'. He replied in a way that caused me to beat a retreat. With biblical tenderness he said that we could discuss the authenticity of his beliefs better in the future, not here, in capitalist Berlin, but in Trench Town or St Ann in Jamaica, or in the villages of Abyssinia; that is, if I deigned to visit him in those places to see for myself whether or not his life lived up to his faith.

I changed tactics and asked him if he had problems, as a white man, in joining a religion whose followers and leaders, all black, were against racial integration and against any white cultural influence that might pervert the 'roots' and whose leitmotif and only discernible political preoccupation seemed to be the return to Africa of the blacks of the two Americas. Despite his best efforts, a tiny cloud crossed his face for a second and I realized that I had got in a low blow.

He spoke at great length, at first in a rather confused way, reminding me Bob Marley was not a pure black but a mulatto since his father had been an Englishman resident in Jamaica. He threw in my face that, from childhood, he had always heard me say that all Peruvians, even those of us who *seemed* white, had traces of Indian or black blood. Did I believe it or not? Yes, I believed it. Well then, he might be, although it didn't show much, a mulatto like Nesta. Beside, wasn't all this stuff about race relative? In the years he had spent studying in England, he had known many English people who were convinced that the 'darkies' began on the other side of the channel and that, for example, Spaniards or Italians (not to mention Peruvians) were as black as Zulus and Jamaicans.

But by the way he spoke, I realized that the arguments he was using to try to convince me did not convince him. He ended up admitting, in a voice racked with grief, that among the brothers there were some racists and intolerant people and that, for example, he'd been thrown out of a few clubs in Notting Hill Gate or Brixton 'for being white'. Full of sympathy for these racists and ever more astonished by his frankness, I asked him how, as a boarder in a school in a country legendary for the severity of its educational discipline (the country of the cane), he managed to spend his life in the street protesting against furriers and shoe shops or trying to get into Rastafarian parties in the ghettos. He reminded me that I had written a novel, *The Time of the Hero,* in which I described how boarders in a military school in Lima flouted the vigilance of their teachers by going to parties and brothels. The English were no less daring or skilful than the Peruvians when it came to escaping from school when they wanted.

The day he left, half in jest and half seriously – anything to get him out of what he'd got himself into – I flashed before his eyes, exaggerating their merits, the rich diversity of superstition, witchcraft, fetishism and barbarism that adorned the religious panorama of his own country. Why complicate his life by becoming a Rastafarian, a sect into which he would never be completely accepted, when he could, for example, join the recently founded Church of the Israelites of the New Universal Pact, which was all the rage in the central Andes of Peru, or any one of the Amazonian cults where he would find all the primitivism that he wanted including, if he looked around a bit, delicacies like cannibalism and head shrinking. He was not amused. (Another result of the Rasta faith seemed to be the extinction of his sense of humour.) He simply replied that he was not interested in the exotic or the picturesque in religion, but only in the truth. And he had found it.

I could not take him to the airport because I had a jury meeting. We said goodbye at the door of the Hotel Kempinsky. In a last ditch attempt at emotional blackmail, I told him that his mother would die of grief when I got back to Lima and told her the state he was in and about his conversion. It was the only time in the week that I had seen him really laugh. 'Die of grief,' he scoffed. 'She'll have a fit, you mean. And she'll want to kill me. *Irie,* Dad! *Jah live*! Ciao!

4

The last jury session, at which we awarded the prizes (*Love Streams* by John Cassavetes won the Golden Bear), lasted for fourteen hours.

Weakened by excesses, both cinematic and analytic, strong emotions and the long Berlin winter, I had gone down with a bad cold and I spent the day sneezing and feverish. My calamitous physical and psychological state did not soften one iota Liv Ullmann's rigorous quest for justice. The third time – it must have been about hour nine – that I warned her that if she didn't put an end to the discussions and let us vote she would have a Peruvian corpse on her hands that she would have to account for to history and to *Jah,* Liv (who was as serious as Gonzalo Gabriel would have been in her place) went out of the meeting room and returned with a saucer of vitamins and decongestants which she placed under my nose. But she did not let us off one second of the session or call for a vote until (leaving us hoarse and half cataleptic with tiredness) she had wrung from all ten jurors the last drop of cinematographic discernment left in us. Jules Dassin was a gratifying and restorative presence, a balm in the claustrophobic nightmare of the jury. In all the previous sessions, the director of *Rififi* and *Never on a Sunday* had displayed his exuberant friendliness and warmth, his good humour and the elegant modesty with which he bore the obligations of fame ('the fame of Melina Mercouri, my wife,' he would say). In this final session Jules Dassin revealed himself to be not only a genial American who had successfully assimilated the rationalist subtleties of his first country of adoption (France) but also a man whose second country of adoption (Greece) had turned into a consummate master of the Machiavellian arts of manipulation and haggling. Calling on one or other of the arms of his tricontinental panoply, prolonging the discussion with innocent questions when the feeling in the room did not coincide with his preferences, winning over doubters to his cause with a snake charmer's wiles or destroying the arguments of his opponents with lethal erudition, Jules Dassin managed to get prizes for almost all his nominees. His devilish enchantment over us was such that he even asked us, with a disarming smile, if, before the real vote, we could have a straw poll so that he could plan his own votes in accordance with ours. We liked him so much that we gave in to him.

I spent the final twenty-four hours in Berlin in bed, befuddled by my cold, the antihistamines and the shocks of paternity. I had the only surrealist dream of my life in which Bob Marley, Haile Selassie I and Gonzalo Gabriel discussed cinema interminably and boringly to the accompaniment of reggae drums and guitars while Liv Ullmann – her blonde hair transformed into the seething locks of the Gorgon – stalked around them, whipping them with a cane every time they fell silent.

From Berlin I had to travel to Central America to write an article on the electoral campaign in El Salvador for *Time* magazine. The journey was timed to the minute and it was difficult for me to cancel or alter it so that I could not do what I was really tempted to do: visit Gonzalo Gabriel's teachers and find out what they thought of his metamorphosis. So I had to settle for a phone call to them from Paris. My conversation with his housemaster was an animated dialogue of the deaf. In an attempt to respect the parabolical system of English conversations, I asked him if 'all was well'. He said that it had rained at the weekend and that there had been very strong winds; apart from that, the winter was 'quite all right'. Being more specific, I said to him that I had been alarmed to find my son so much thinner. Really, he hadn't noticed. He offered a few observations about the stage of development when adolescents grow and lose weight. He promised to take steps to make sure that Gonzalo Gabriel was given extra portions of meat and milk. 'But he has become a vegetarian,' I said. 'Didn't you know?' He coughed and thought it over. 'Frankly, no,' he replied. And, after another pause, 'it's supposed to be healthy.' I asked him if he hadn't noticed recently anything worrying about his way of thinking, acting or dressing. No, he hadn't noticed anything inappropriate. And what about his studies? Good, good. In the last few months, the young man even seemed to have become interested in reading the Bible.

Was the housemaster a moron or was he an accomplice? Had the plague been transmitted to the students from the academic staff?

In the few hours of my stopover in Paris, I went round the bookstalls buying up everything that I could find on the Rastafarian cult and on Bob Marley (I even bought his records and cassettes). This reading was my spiritual sustenance for the ten days I spent in El Salvador, interviewing politicians and travelling the country which was devastated by the revolutionary war.

So that ten days later, when I returned to Lima at the end of my El Salvador mission, I was a specialist on the subject. I'm not exaggerating. One of the advantages of Rastafarianism – doubtless its only advantage – is that the whole corpus of its doctrine fills half a page since it consists of four or five simple ideas buried in extravagant rhetoric. The knowledge of the theology and the liturgy of the Rastas increased my unease to a dizzying degree. Why, out of all the cults on the earth, had Gonzalo Gabriel opted for the one which combined, in abundant measure, bodily filth, historical nonsense, ethical misunderstandings and theological gibberish?

In Lima, my immediate problem was to break the bad news to Patricia. I decided not to spare her any of the details in the hope that, by sharing it with her, my own trauma would be lessened. I told her that Gonzalo Gabriel had lost a few pounds and that he no longer wanted to be an *arbitrum elegantorium* as in his previous holidays. That he had become a vegetarian (and might become a fruitarian), a defender of animal and vegetable life and a militant in favour of the return of all blacks in the Americas to Africa. That he was a novice in the Rastafarian cult which, in terms of dress, meant putting on rags and berets illuminated with the colours of the Ethiopian flag, having the word 'Jah' tattooed on his arm and having tassels hanging from his fingers. That among the precepts of this faith was the conviction that the Pope personified Babylon (the Antichrist) and that to smoke marijuana was to receive a sacrament that made men good and peaceful. That Gonzalo Gabriel had decided not to go to university but to emigrate to Africa to help the needy and to learn Amharic, although there was still the possibility that he would end his days in some ghetto in Jamaica, playing the drums.

My wife went straight to the essentials. 'How long is his hair?' Shoulder length, I said, but what would surprise her most was not its length but rather its tangle and its texture. Because among the decrees of the new religion there figured, alongside the belief that the deceased emperor Haile Selassie (whom 'they' believed was still alive) was God, the biblical abomination of the comb, the brush and the razor. I told her, with a precision taken to sadistic lengths, of the kinds of ablutions that I had seen Gonzalo Gabriel perpetrate on his hair so that it could erupt into those plaits called dreadlocks which had adorned the head of Bob Marley when he was alive: soaping the locks daily and then letting the soap dry on them without rinsing. To illustrate my description, I threw on the bed all the photos and posters of Bob Marley and his brothers reproduced in my Rastafarian books.

Predictably, Patricia transferred her feelings, in the first instance, on to England in the abstract. She spoke of the decadence and degeneration of the ex-imperial powers whose schools had gone from forming gentlemen to producing Rastafarians. And of the idiots who had become Anglophiles in this day and age and had sent their children to be educated in a country in decline which was returning to paganism. Then she blamed me for everything that had happened – I'd been irresponsible and, instead of giving the necessary advice and clips round the ear which would have sorted out his ideas, I must have spent my days in Germany wallowing in the corruptions of Berlin and flirting with Ms Liv Ullmann. And since the inept teachers at Gonzalo Gabriel's school seemed incapable of dealing with what was happening, she announced to me that she would travel to London at once to cut those dreadlocks personally and to cram the young Rasta with all the steaks necessary to save him from tuberculosis. With that, she began to pack her suitcase.

## 5

But it wasn't that easy. The episode went on for a year. In the course of which, every time Gonzalo Gabriel came to spend his holidays in Lima, our house filled up with Ethiopian flags, Caribbean music and live animals (including two rabbits, a hamster, a cockerel and two canaries that we are still not free of).

One day we received a very friendly letter from the headmaster informing us that the school was sorry to have to let Gonzalo Gabriel and some of his friends go, because of an unpleasant matter of *Cannabis sativa* (the technical name with which the naturalist Linnaeus baptized marijuana in 1753).

My curiosity led me to reconstruct, bit by bit, the story of how the Rasta heresy had contaminated the Anglican bastion of the college. Not through a handful of boys from the West Indies who were studying in its halls, but through the unexpected hand of a young Italian, the son of a wealthy industrialist from Milan who had sent his son to that English boarding school hoping to save him from the bad example of his elder brother, a restless youth who, after various musical and drug-related experiences in Europe, had become a Rastafarian and had gone to live in the slums of Jamaica. Not content with subverting the spiritual foundations of the school by disseminating Rasta philosophy, the young Milanese had boldly planted marijuana alongside the well-kept cricket pitches of the institution so that the students converted by his persuasive arts would have a guaranteed supply of the sacramental smoke that would keep them pure and saintly. The young Milanese, an intimate friend of my son, was a true mafioso and irresistibly charming. The last time that we saw him, he came to the house with a bunch of flowers for my wife and shed compassionate tears at the fate of Gonzalo Gabriel and the other boys expelled from school. Because, despite being the high priest of the small Rasta sect, he had avoided expulsion. He was a magnificent actor and had the leading part in an Elizabethan play that was being put on at the end of the year. The headmaster, adopting the doctrine of utilitarianism, was not prepared to lose that histrionic performance.

In his new school, where he was no longer a boarder (with all that had happened, being a 'boarder' seemed a totally superfluous activity), Gonzalo Gabriel preserved his hieroglyphic locks and his colourful rags but we managed to make him promise not to take communion again according to the precepts of his religion. He lived in a small rented room which became a zoo for orphaned, wounded or abandoned animals that he found in the streets and looked after with a sense of responsibility that no other person, activity or thing had ever inspired in him before.

Two years have passed. His life since then has gone through at least two further changes similar to his encounter with the Rastafarian cult, though perhaps less spectacular from the point of view of attire and theology. Nowadays he cuts his hair in a way that his mother finds too old-fashioned and eats all kinds of corpses with great voracity and without the slightest remorse. He still listens to the subversive records of Bob Marley (which, although we would never admit it in front of him, Patricia and I have grown to like) but, thank God, this dangerous influence seems to have been neutralized by other singers less messianic than the prophetic Jamaican since they now merely celebrate, like Prince, incest (*Sister*), premature ejaculation (Motley Crew, *Ten Seconds to Love*), fellatio (Judas Priest, *Eat Me Alive*) or preach the love of animals in the style of W.A.S.P.: *Fuck Like a Beast*.

He has become a student at the University of London and his political ideas show signs of having changed as much as his spiritual inclinations. I now hear him mention, with the same devotion previously reserved for Emperor Haile Selassie, Friedrich A. Hayek, Ludwig von Mises and Milton Friedman and he spends his holidays working as an interviewer in the shanty towns of Lima for the Institute for

Freedom and Democracy which promotes private enterprise and liberal economic theories in Peru. He'll soon be eighteen.

I observe him with curiosity, with envy. And I wonder what surprises are in store for him (for us) in the next chapter.

Lima, 26 December 1985

# The Trumpet of Deyá

On that Sunday in 1984, I had just settled at my desk to write an article when the telephone rang. I did something that I never did at that time: I picked up the receiver. 'Julio Cortázar has died,' proclaimed the journalist's voice on the phone. 'Give me your comments.'

I thought of a verse by Vallejo, 'A Spaniard, to the marrow', and, stammering, obeyed him. But instead of writing the article, I spent that Sunday leafing through and rereading some of Cortázar's stories and certain pages of his novels that were still very much alive in my memory. I hadn't heard of him for a long time. I had no inkling of his long illness and agonizing pain. But I was happy to know that Aurora had been at his side in those last months and that, thanks to her, he had had a sober burial without the predictable antics of the revolutionary crows who had taken such advantage of him in recent years.

I had got to know them both a quarter of a century ago, at the house of a mutual friend in Paris and from that moment until the last time that I saw them together, in Greece in 1967 — we were all three working as translators at an international cotton conference — I was always amazed at the spectacle of hearing and seeing Aurora and Julio maintaining conversations in tandem. The rest of us seemed superfluous. Everything they said was intelligent, cultured, amusing, vital. I often thought: they cannot always be like this. They must rehearse these conversations at home, in order to dazzle their listeners with their unusual anecdotes, brilliant quotations and jokes which, just at the right moment, would deflate all the intellectualism.

They tossed the topics from one to another like consummate jugglers and one never got bored with them. The perfect complicity, the secret intelligence that seemed to unite them was something that I admired and envied in the couple, along with their friendliness, their commitment to literature — which seemed exclusive and total — and their generosity towards everyone and, in particular, towards novices like me.

It was difficult to tell who had read the most and the most productively and which of them said the most incisive and unusual things about books and authors. The fact that Julio wrote and Aurora *only* translated (in her case that *only* meant the complete opposite of what it seemed), I took to be temporary, a transitory sacrifice by Aurora so that at the time there would be only one writer in the family. Now that I'm with her again after so many years, I bite my tongue on the two or three occasions that I'm about to ask her if she's written much, if she's finally going to publish something. She has grey hair, but otherwise she is just the same: small, slight, with those great blue eyes brimming with intelligence and that overwhelming vitality. She climbs up and down those Majorcan hills of Deyá with an agility that always leaves me behind, panting for breath. In her own way she shares that Cortázarian virtue *par excellence*: of being a Dorian Gray.

That evening at the end of 1958, I'd been sat next to a very tall, thin boy, with extremely short hair, a smooth face and big hands that he gestured with when he spoke. He had already published a little book of stories and was about to publish a second selection in a small series directed by Juan José Arreola in Mexico. I was also about to bring out a book of short stories and we swapped experiences and plans like two young people on a literary vigil of arms. Only when we parted did I find out, to my astonishment, that he was the author of *Bestiario* (Bestiary) and of so many texts that I had read in *Sur,* the magazine of Victoria Ocampo and Borges, and the splendid translator of the complete works of Poe that I had devoured in two bulky tomes published by the University of Puerto Rico. He seemed to be my contemporary and, in fact, he was twenty-two years older than me.

During the 1960s and in particular throughout the seven years that I lived in Paris, he was one of my best friends and also something of a model and a mentor. I gave him my first novel to read in manuscript and I waited for his verdict with the apprehension of a catachumen. And when I received his generous letter of approval and advice, I felt happy. I think that for a long time I became accustomed to writing, taking for granted his care, his encouragement or his critical gaze over my shoulder. I admired his life, his rites, his manias and his habits as much as the ease and purity of his prose and that everyday, domestic, cheerful way that the fantastic themes in his stories were presented. Every time that he and Aurora called to invite me to eat — first in the small apartment by the rue de Sèvres and then in the small house in the rue du Général Bouret, it was always fun and party time. I was fascinated by that board full of cuttings of strange news items and the improbable objects that he collected or made and that mysterious place which, according to legend, *existed* in the house, where Julio would lock himself away to play the trumpet and have fun like a child: the toy room. He knew a magic and secret Paris that did not appear in any guide book and from every meeting with him, I came away laden with treasures: films to see, exhibitions to visit, areas to walk around, poets to discover and even a congress of witches in the Mutualité, which bored me enormously, but which he would later evoke, marvellously, as a humorous apocalypse.

It was possible to be the friend of this Julio Cortázar, but impossible to become very close. The distance that he imposed, through a system of courtesies and rules that one had to obey to keep his friendship, was one of the charming aspects of his character: it shrouded him in a certain mystery, gave his life a secret dimension which seemed to be the source of that restless, irrational and violent side that appeared at times in his texts, even the most humorous and cheerful. He was an eminently private man, with an inner world constructed and preserved like a work of art, to which probably only Aurora had access and in which nothing, outside literature, seemed to be important, or perhaps even exist.

This did not mean that he was bookish, erudite, intellectual in the style of Borges, who could write, accurately, 'Few things have happened to me and I have read a great many.' With Julio, literature seemed to dissolve into everyday existence, saturating all of life, enlivening and enriching it with a particular splendour, but without depriving it of sap, instinct and spontaneity. Probably no other writer has bestowed on the game the literary dignity that Cortázar gave it, or made the game such a flexible and profitable instrument of artistic creation and exploration. I am distorting the truth: because Julio never played *in order to* write literature. For him, to write was to play, to become himself, to organize life – words, ideas – with the arbitrariness, the freedom, the fantasy and the irresponsibility of children or madmen. But by playing in this way, Cortázar's work opened new doors, came to reveal unknown depths of the human condition and touched on the transcendental, something that he surely never intended. It is not accidental – or rather it is accidental, but in the sense of the order of the casual that he described in *62 A Model Kit* – that his most ambitious novel should have as its title a children's game: *Hopscotch*.

Like the novel, like theatre, the game is a form of fiction, an artificial order imposed on the world, a somewhat illusory representation that replaces life. It allows man to relax, to forget real life and himself and to live, while that situation lasts, a life apart, governed by strict rules created by himself. Distraction, entertainment, imagination, the game is also a magic way of exorcizing man's atavistic fear of the secret anarchy of the world, of the enigma of his origins, circumstances and destiny. Johan Huizinga, in his celebrated *Homo Ludens*, maintained that the game is the backbone of civilization and that society evolved towards modernity playfully, constructing its institutions, systems, practices and beliefs out of those formal elements of ceremony and rite found in children's games.

In the world of Cortázar, the game recovers this lost potentiality, becoming a serious activity for adults who play to escape insecurity, their panic in the face of an incomprehensible, absurd, and dangerous world. It is true that his characters amuse themselves when they play, but often these are dangerous games which lead them not just to forget temporarily their present condition, but rather to some terrible knowledge, to alienation or to death.

In other instances the Cortázar game is a refuge for sensibility and imagination, the way in which delicate, naïve beings protect themselves against social levelling or, as he wrote in his most mischievous of books, *Cronopios and Famas*: 'to fight against pragmatism and the horrible tendency to achieve useful goals'. His games are opposed to preformed ideas, frozen by use and abuse, prejudices and, above all, solemnity, Cortázar's *bête noire* when he criticized the culture and the nature of his country.

The effect of *Hopscotch* when it appeared in 1963 in the Spanish-speaking world, was explosive. It shook to the foundations the convictions or prejudices that writers and readers had about the means and the ends of the art of narration and extended the frontiers of the genre to previously unthinkable limits. Thanks to *Hopscotch* we learned that to write was a wonderful way of having fun, that it was possible to explore the secrets of the world and of language by having a good time, and that, by playing, we could explore the mysterious layers of life denied to rational consciousness and logical intelligence, those chasms of experience which no one can peer into without grave risk of death or madness. In *Hopscotch*, reason and lack of reason, dream and waking, objectivity and subjectivity, history and fantasy lost their exclusivity, boundaries became porous, stopped being dividing lines and became confused into a single reality, through which certain privileged individuals like La Maga and Oliveira and the celebrated madmen of his future books could roam at will. (Like many couples who read *Hopscotch* in the 1960s, Patricia and I began to speak *gíglico*, to invent our private slang and to translate our tender secrets into its esoteric vocabulary.)

Along with the idea of the game, the concept of freedom is essential to any discussion of *Hopscotch* and of all Cortázar's fiction. Freedom to violate the established norms of writing and narrative structure, to replace the conventional order of the tale with a subterranean order which appears disordered, to revolutionize the point of view of the narrator, narrative time, the psychology of the characters, the spatial organization of the story and the relationships within it. To unwrite the novel, to destroy literature, to break the habits of the 'female reader', to disorder words, to write badly etc, which Morelli insists on in *Hopscotch* all these are metaphors for something simple: literature is being choked by too much conventionalism and seriousness. One must purge it of rhetoric and clichés, restore to it a sense of newness, grace, insolence and freedom. Cortázar's style has all these things, especially when he gets away from the pompous epic prose with which his alter ego, Morelli, pontificates about literature; that is, in his stories which are generally clearer and more creative than his novels, even if they do not display the same colourful fireworks. The novels are revolutionary manifestos, but the real revolution of Cortázar can be found in his stories. It is more discreet but also a deeper and more permanent revolution because it touches the very nature of fiction, that perfect moulding of form and content, means and end, art and technique which the best creators achieve. In his stories, Cortázar did not experiment: he found, he discovered, he created, something imperishable.

Just as the tag *experimental* writer does not do him justice, it would also not be sufficient to call him a *fantasy* writer, although if one has to play with definitions, he would rather have been called the latter than the former. Julio loved fantasy literature and knew it inside out and wrote some marvellous stories in that mode, in which extraordinary events occur, like the impossible transformation of a man into an aquatic creature, in that small masterpiece 'Axolotl', or the moment when, in a rush of enthusiasm, a dismal concert is turned into an enormous massacre and the fevered audience jump on to the stage to devour the conductor and the musicians ('The Maenades'). But he also wrote distinguished stories in a more orthodox realist mode. Like the marvellous 'Tonto', the story of the decline of a boxer recounted by himself which is, in effect, the story of his way of speaking, a linguistic feast of harmony, musicality and humour, the invention of a neighbourhood style and the particularity and mythology of ordinary people. Or 'The Pursuer', which is narrated from a subtle past perfect tense, which dissolves into the present of the reading, evoking subliminally, in this way, the gradual breakdown of Johnny, the genius jazz player, whose crazed search for the absolute, through his trumpet playing, is told to us through the 'realist' (rational and pragmatic) account made by the critic and biographer of Johnny, the narrator Bruno.

In fact, Cortázar was both a realist and a fantastic writer at the same time. The world that he invented was precisely that strange symbiosis that Roger Caillois considered to be the only real definition of the fantastic. In his prologue to *Anthology of Fantastic Literature*, which he also selected, Caillois argued that fantastic art does not come from any deliberate authorial intention but rather by chance or through more mysterious forces. Thus, according to him, the fantastic is not a technique, a literary device, but rather an imponderable reality which, without premeditation, suddenly *occurs* in a literary text. I remember a long and passionate conversation with Cortázar on this thesis of Caillois in a bistro in Montparnasse, Julio's enthusiasm for it and his surprise when I assured him that this theory could be applied exactly to his own fiction.

In Cortázar's world, banal reality begins imperceptibly to crack and give way to recondite pressures which edge it towards the marvellous, but without forcing it completely into that realm, keeping it in a sort of intermediary, tense and disconcerting space in which the real and the fantastic overlap but do not combine. This is the world of 'Blow up', 'Letters from Mamá', 'The Secret Weapons', 'The Condemned Door' and so many other stories with ambiguous endings, which can be interpreted as realist or as fantastic since what is extraordinary in them is perhaps the fantasy of the characters or perhaps a miracle.

This is the famous ambiguity which characterizes certain classic texts of fantastic literature like 'The Turn of the Screw' by Henry James, a delicate story which the master of doubt recounts in such a way that it is not possible to know if what occurs really does occur or is the hallucination of one of the characters. What differentiates Cortázar from a Henry James, a Poe, a Borges or a Kafka, however, is not his ambiguity or his intellectualism, for these are features found in all these writers, but rather the fact that in his fiction, the most elaborate and cultured stories never become disembodied or abstract, but remain rooted in the everyday and the concrete and have the vitality of a football game or a barbecue. The surrealists invented the expression 'the everyday-marvellous', for that poetic, mysterious reality, freed from contingency and scientific laws, that the poet can perceive beneath appearances, through dream or delirium, and which is evoked in books like Aragon's *Le Paysan de Paris* or Breton's *Nadja*. But I think that the expression defines no writer of our times better than it does Cortázar, a seer who detected the strange in the ordinary, the absurd in the logical, the exception in the rule and the marvellous in the banal. No one has dignified in such a literary way the predictable, the conventional and the pedestrian in human life, which, through the magic wand of his pen, can express a hidden tenderness or reveal an excessively sublime or horrible face. To such an extent that, in his hands, instructions to wind a watch or go up a staircase can become, at once, anxious prose poems and sidesplitting paraphysical texts.

The change in Cortázar, the most extraordinary that I have ever witnessed in anyone, a mutation that I often thought to compare with that experienced by the narrator of 'Axolotl', occurred, according to the official version – which he himself endorsed – in May 1968 in France. He could be seen in those tumultuous days, among the barricades of Paris, distributing leaflets that he had written himself and mingling with the students who wanted to bring 'imagination to power'. He was fifty-four years old. In the sixteen remaining years of his life, right up to his death, he would be a writer committed to socialism, a defender of Cuba and Nicaragua, a signer of manifestos and an *habitué* at revolutionary congresses.

In his case, unlike so many of our colleagues who opted for a similar militancy, though out of snobbery or opportunism – a *modus vivendi* and a way of climbing the ladder of the intellectual establishment which was, and to a certain extent remains, the monopoly of the left in the Spanish-speaking world – this change was genuine, dictated more by ethics than by ideology (to which he remained allergic) and totally coherent. His life was organized around this commitment and became public, almost promiscuous, and much of his work was dispersed, scattered among everyday concerns until it appeared to be written by another person, very different from the man who before had always treated politics with ironic disdain, as something remote. (I remember the time that I tried to introduce him to Juan Goytisolo. 'I abstain,' he joked, 'he is too political for me.') As in the first stage of his life, although in a different way, in this second stage he gave more than he received and although I believe that he was often wrong – as when he stated that all the crimes of Stalinism were a mere 'accident de parcours' of communism – even in these errors there was so much manifest innocence and openness that it was difficult to lose respect for him. I never lost this respect or the affection and friendship that – albeit at a distance – survived all our political disagreements.

But the change in Julio was deeper and more all embracing than political action alone. I am sure that it began a year before 1968, when he separated from Aurora. In 1967, as I have said, the three of us were in Greece, working together as translators. We spent the mornings and the afternoons sitting at the same table in the conference room of the Hilton, and the evenings in the restaurants of Plaka, at the foot of the Acropolis, where we always went to have dinner. And we went together on excursions to the museums, the Orthodox churches, the temples and, on one weekend, to the small island of Hydra. When I got back to London, I said to Patricia: 'The perfect couple does exist. Aurora and Julio have managed to achieve this miracle: a happy marriage.' A few days later I received a letter from Julio announcing their separation. I think that I've never felt so confused.

The next time I saw him, in London with his new lady, he was another person. He had let his hair grow and had an imposing red beard like a biblical prophet. He made me take him to buy erotic magazines and he talked about marijuana, women and revolution as once he had talked about jazz and ghosts. He was still warm and affectionate, unpretentious and totally lacking in that self-importance that almost invariably makes successful writers over the age of fifty insufferable. One could even say that he was fresher and younger than ever, but it was difficult for me to connect this person with the one I had known before. Every time that I saw him subsequently – in Barcelona, in Cuba, in London or in Paris, at congresses or round table discussions, in social or conspiratorial gatherings – I became even more perplexed. Was it him? Was it Julio Cortázar? Of course it was, but like a caterpillar which becomes a butterfly or the fakir of the story who, after dreaming of maharajahs, opened his eyes to find himself sitting on a throne, surrounded by courtiers paying tribute to him.

This other Julio Cortázar, I feel, was less personal and creative as a writer than the first. But I suspect that, as compensation, he had a more intense and perhaps happier life than the one before in which, as he once wrote, existence for him came down to a book. At least, every time that I saw him, he seemed young, elated, bright.

If someone knows, it must be Aurora, of course. I have not been impertinent enough to ask her. We do not even talk much about Julio in those hot, summer days at Deyá, although he is always at the back of the conversations, offering the opposing view with the same skill as before. The small house, half hidden among the olives, the cypresses, the bougainvilleas, the lemon trees and the hydrangeas, reflects the order and mental clarity of Aurora, of course, and it is an enormous pleasure to feel the night breeze on the small terrace alongside the gorge at dusk and to see the arc of the moon appearing above the mountain. From time to time I hear a trumpet playing out of tune. There is nobody around. The sound is coming then from the poster at the end of the room, where a young, gangling, fresh-faced boy, with close-cropped hair and a short-sleeved shirt – the Julio Cortázar I knew – is playing his favourite game.

November 1992

# Botero: A Sumptuous Abundance

In one story of *The Arabian Nights* it is told that the most desirable creature in the harem of Harún-al-Rashid was a young woman with such ample hips that she always had to lie down because, if she stood, she lost balance and fell (or perhaps, one should say, she overflowed). The identification of beauty with being slim is Western and modern, probably an Anglo-Saxon and certainly a Protestant prejudice. In ancient societies, in primitive cultures, in rural societies in the Catholic world, thinness provokes disgust and fear since it is associated with hunger and disease. The Greco-Latin tradition established a canon of beauty based on the harmony of the human form, which did not exclude robust figures; rather, in most historical periods, the robust form predominated. Even today, in rural Spain, the word *hermoso* (beautiful) when applied to a person, means fat.

When Fernando Botero was a boy, the tradition which equated beauty with abundance was very much alive in Latin America. It was fuelled by a whole erotic mythology found in magazine drawings, in obscene bar jokes, in fashion, songs, popular literature and, above all in the films that Mexican cinema sent to all parts of the continent. The exuberant forms of those artists with their bouffant hairstyles, who sang boleros, danced *huarachas* and wore tight clothes which emphasized their breasts and buttocks with knowing vulgarity – these were the delights of our generation and stimulated our first desires – must have remained embedded in the subconscious of the boy from Medellín. Later they would become fused, in a strange alliance, with the Virgins and Madonnas of Quattrocento Italy, at whose feet Botero achieved his artistic maturity, to become the primary sources from which the enormous figures of his paintings emerged. Everything in Botero's art comes from this process of alchemy: the aesthetic tradition of the West that he studied with devotion in Italy recast with his experience of the provincial, exuberant and vital Latin America of his childhood.

According to an anecdote recounted by Germán Arciniegas, the figures in his world began to grow fat on a specific day, at a precise place, more or less by accident. It was 1956, in a park in Mexico City. A young 24-year-old Colombian had a pencil and a sketch pad in his hand. In a moment of distraction, in an almost unconscious way, he began to sketch the outline of a mandolin. Without planning it, through the will, one might say, of the fingers that held the pencil, this pencil altered the proportions of the object, shrinking the central hole, with the result that the rest of the instrument seemed to grow, devour the surface of the surroundings and rise up like a giant. Botero would immediately have recognized, when he examined the drawing that had just emerged from his hands, that something essential had happened to him, and would have realized that, from this moment, his work would be different. Did it really happen like that? Like all stories, it must contain some elements of truth. In any event, the first time that figures with inflated bodies appear on his canvases in a systematic way is in the Pan American Union exhibition in Washington, 17 April–15 May 1957, where he exhibited thirty-one pictures painted in the year that he spent in Mexico, including the landmark painting *Still Life With a Mandolin,* the first of the series that would establish his thematics and his style in a definitive way. Many years later, Botero declared that to enlarge that mandolin was, for him, 'like going through a door and entering another room'. (Interview in the Catalogue of the Retrospective of Botero at the Hirshhorn Museum and Sculpture Garden, Washington DC, 1979.) A room which, in years to come, he would enrich until it took on the dimensions of a world: sumptuous, unusual, cheerful, tender, innocent, sensual, in which knowledge and reason, spurred on by nostalgia, are continually delving into memory to rectify life by appearing to reproduce it.

The most salient characteristic of this world is inflation, which affects men, animals and objects, but also the air, the colours and the spirit. When a critic asked him why he painted 'fat figures', Botero replied, 'They are not fat. They seem slender to me.' And he added: 'The problem is to determine the source of the pleasure when one looks at a picture. For me, the pleasure comes from the exaltation of life which expresses the sensuality of forms. For this reason, my formal problem is to create sensuality through forms . . . I make the characters fat to give them sensuality. I am not interested in fat for fat's sake.'(Catalogue of the Botero Exhibition at the Marlborough Gallery, New York, 1972.) There is fatness and fatness. The fatness of Rabelais, of Rubens, of Gauguin, the fatness of the little pot-bellied craft figures, the fatness which comes from abandoning oneself to desires like Bacchus, or which is born of religious faith – Buddha – or ritual sport (the sumo wrestlers in Japan). In each of these cases, and in many others in art, literature, folklore or other aspects of existence, fatness expresses something different, has its own particular features. In Botero, obesity is, as he says, a vehicle for sensuality, but we need to understand this in an artistic rather than a realist sense. Fatness for him is a point of view and a method rather than a concrete reality. His fat people bear witness to a love of form, of volume, of colour. They are a feast to the eye rather than a glorification of desire, a song of praise to appetite or a defence of instincts. Fatness in his work is a way of transforming life, rather than life itself, a way of impressing on the reality recreated in his paintings, prints and sculptures certain personal and irreplaceable characteristics that transcend obesity.

Sensuality is not, of necessity, a synonym of sexuality; it can, in certain cases – one of these cases is the artistic world of Botero – be an antonym. His elephantine women with their immense thighs and oxen necks are fleshy but not carnal. They all – and there are no exceptions to this rule – have an almost invisibly small sex, a tiny mat of hair lost, as if ashamed, in the torrential mass of their legs. This is not by chance. Unlike, for example, the odalisques of Ingres or Courbet's bathers – I'm thinking of the formidable hindquarters of one of *The Bathers* of 1853, which caused the blushing Empress Eugénie to enquire if the bather also came, like the Percheron mares, from the region of Le Perche – where the rolls of flesh and the undulating arrangement of the bodies exude sexuality and hint at the explosion of physical love. In Botero's fat ladies there is no lasciviousness and the sexual component is minuscule, if not non-existent. These are placid, innocent and maternal fat women. Even when they are naked, drinking, dancing up close or lying on the beds of those poor brothels which always bear the name of their owners – the house of Ana Molina, the house of the Arias twins, the house of Raquel Vega – they give the impression of being sexless and inhibited. They look at the world or, better still, they look at us, since the eyes of Botero's characters are usually fixed on the eyes of the viewer in a sort of passive defiance – atonic and bovine, as if petrified by ontological apathy. Their fatness is not only physical, it is also mental, in the precise sense that Cyril Connolly wrote in *Palinurus*: 'Fatness is a mental illness.' In this essentially matriarchal world, the men look to the women for company and protection rather than pleasure. Alongside the women, they seem small and defenceless. Botero's women, with their perms, their scarlet nails and their boneless, luxuriant forms, are not only a stylized fantasy of the 'ideal woman' in the Latin American world of the 1940s and 1950s. Their thick figures embody, above all, the mother/woman, the supreme taboo, which gives life, suckles the species and is the backbone of the home. Rather than a whore, a nun, or a saint, Botero's fat woman is — has been, or will be — a mother (or, as in the oil painting of 1959, *The Sisters,* a woman hoping to be a mother, or frustrated at not having been one). It is this function that prevails above all others and which, in an explicit or implicit way, determines the attitude, both chaste and timid, that men adopt towards her.

By being inflated, Botero's characters and objects become light and serene, achieving a primordial and innocuous state. At the same time, they become still. Immobility descends on them like Lot's wife, when she succumbed to curiosity and looked back. The gigantism that surrounds them and brings them close to the point beyond which they might explode or rise weightless into the air also seems to empty them of all content: desires, emotions, illusions, feelings. They are only bodies, beings uncontaminated by psychology, pure density, surfaces without a soul. However, it would be unjust to call them caricatures since this word has pejorative connotations. They are not degraded versions of flesh and blood beings in the real world: they are plastic beings, citizens of a world of colours and forms imbued with their own sovereignty. Replying to Dr Wibke von Bonin, who used the term 'caricature' to refer to his fat figures, Botero remarked: 'Deformation would be the exact word. In art, if one thinks and has ideas, one is obliged to deform nature. Art is deformation. There is no truly realist work of art.' (Marlborough Exhibition Catalogue.) Indeed, nothing could be further from Botero's paintings than any desire to ridicule or to wound. The fact that among his characters there sometimes appear little dictators, agents of repression or clearly negative examples of war or abuse should not deceive us: like his whores or his saints, those generals and policemen have changed character and achieved the status of benign meekness that fatness bestows on them. They have been stripped of everything except that rich sensory personality which is displayed to our eyes and to our imagination. If we must compare them with something, then rather than using humanity as our point of reference, we should look to something that is much closer to them: toys, that fictional world whose frontiers a child confuses with reality. His innocuous, beautiful, innocent, fixed world is similar to the world of lead soldiers and dolls through its colour, grace and power of enchantment and also because it is removed from time, that curse which intensifies life even as it consumes it. Unlike human life, the world of Botero is frozen, time that has become space.

## The heritage of Latin America

His themes are unequivocally Latin American. But Latin America is a multiple reality which can be represented in the most diverse ways: the *indigenismo* of Diego Rivera and the African totems of Lam, the virgins and archangels of colonial paintings from Cuzco or Quito and the Puerto Rican 'saints', the dwellings of Szyszlo with their pre-Hispanic traces and the luminous 'Caribbean' lanscapes of Obregón, the Haitian primitives, the skulls of Posada, the monsters of Cuevas, Matta's nightmares and Berni's figures made out of urban detritus. The very diverse works of these artists and others like them express some aspect of the kaleidoscope that makes up the Latin American experience. This experience is drawn from a lived history and geography and also from other histories and geographies dreamed by the creators and imposed on reality in the form of artistic works.

The Latin America reinvented by Botero has its roots in the Andean heights of the Antioquian region of Colombia where he was born, into a middle-class family in Medellín, in 1932. Colombia is the country where the Conservatives defeated the Liberals in the classic war which drained the whole continent in the nineteenth century and where the Spanish language and Catholic religion have remained very traditional and impervious to modernization. The same can be said of its customs, morality, rites and institutions. Botero's father was an itinerant salesman and the child would see him setting off on horseback across the mountains which are very green and fertile in that region. From the age of six to eleven he attended primary school at the Antioquia Ateneo and then went to secondary school at the Jesuit Bolívar College. It seems that he was expelled for an article on 'Picasso and nonconformity in art' (which appeared in *El Colombiano,* Medellín, 17 July 1949) that the fathers deemed subversive. He finished his schooling at the San José College in nearby Marinilla, which was considered to be the most conservative city in the country. Although it only lasted for a few months, his immersion into an even deeper stratum of provincial life left an indelible impression on him, as he confessed to Cynthia Jaffe McCabe and Sareen R. Gerson in the Washington interview quoted above. In Marinilla, he told them, 'the atmosphere was very Colombian, the roofs and houses were just as they appear in my pictures. My themes come from that small town, the petty bourgeois towns of that era.' When Botero left Medellín to go and live in Bogotá in January 1951, after a short stay at the Liceo of the University of Antioquia, he was nineteen years old.

He had painted since childhood and while he was still at school he had worked as a designer and illustrator for the literary supplement of *El Colombiano* and had exhibited two water colours in an exhibition of Antioquian painters. He also had a brief experience as a set designer when the Spanish Lope de Vega Company came to Medellín for a season. But it was not the artistic activities of these years – in which, according to his friends, he dreamed of becoming a bullfighter – that would have the greatest resonance in his future work, but rather the impact made on him by the people that he knew, the landscapes that he saw and the things that he did in that isolated, picturesque, ritualistic, traditional world where he lived until the beginning of his adult years. He thought that he would abandon it for ever when he travelled to the capital and to the rest of the world: he was probably, like any ambitious and nonconformist young man, disgusted by its smallness and sanctimoniousness, by its stifling atmosphere and archaic culture and was longing for a cosmopolitan, avant-garde environment. But in fact he had this provincial world branded on his memory and with it he was able to develop his artistic personality. Those images would allow him to create a world of his own and avoid the risk – of which so many Latin American artists fell foul when they discovered the European 'isms' – of becoming lost in imitation and formalism, of being a mere amanuensis.

The world of Botero is American, Andean, provincial, because his themes invent a mythology out of the images lodged in his memory since childhood, that period in which the important experiences of every artist are formed. In his canvases, travellers on horseback ride in the country, as his father had done, and many stable, very Catholic families don their Sunday best and pose stiffly in front of the painter's memory. High buildings do not yet exist and cars are useless because the streets are too narrow and the distances are so short that one goes to the office on foot. A mother's greatest pride is to have a son who is a priest and if he becomes a cardinal, what joy! If another son becomes a military man, it is greeted with general approval. People live in small colonial houses with twin sloping roofs and orange-coloured tiles which nestle peacefully at the foot of the church whose bell tower still dominates the place. Along the narrow flagstone streets the neighbours spy on each other and whisper and from every corner one can see the multi-coloured countryside. The houses have patios and gardens with luxuriant vegetation and abundant fruit: watermelons, oranges, bananas, custard apples, mangos and pears. Kitchens and pantries exhibit their produce with pride among the humming flies and wasps; here to eat well is looked on favourably, it is a sign of health and prosperity, one of the few pleasures admitted by the dominant moral order. It is a world of tidy people with strict routines, of gentlemen with spectacles – lawyers no doubt – who trim their small moustaches to the millimetre, wear waistcoats, never take their tie off and put cream on their hair. The girls love the operatic uniforms of the military and the old women love the iridescent habits of the priests and nuns. There are few pastimes: hunting, walking in the countryside, a picnic in the open air, a party and making love. A repressed, male-dominated world, where instincts are restrained by religion and what people might say, finds its release in that damned and desirable institution, as solid as the family, its alter ego, which people visit by night and by stealth: the brothel. There the punctilious, pettifogging lawyer and the reliable civil servant, the pious landlord and the rule-bound military man can bring out into the open the demons that they keep hidden from their families by day, play the guitar, tell dirty stories, drink themselves silly and fornicate like rabbits. They can even, if the mood takes them, dress up as women and pose as odalisques alongside a black cat on a pseudo-French chair.

One does not need to have visited the Colombian towns in Antioquia in the 1940s to recognize the social reality that serves as a backdrop to Botero's imagination. Just as I inevitably relive in this world the Peru of my childhood – Arequipa in the south, Piura in the north – so any Latin American will recognize in this merry-go-round of images certain ways of feeling, dreaming and behaving typical of the towns in the interior of any country of the continent. Thanks to the paintings' power of evocation, a whole world is revived, true or false, real or fictitious, transformed into art.

Botero has left his own personal seal on this world, radically changing it in the process. Above all, as we have seen, he has inflated it, emptied it of psychology and paralysed it. Not only has he removed it from time, but also from the violence, the misery and the struggles which, in the real world, are the counterweight to idyllic village life. Botero's world gives the impression of peace and stability; no excess seems conceivable in this sleepy atmosphere. It is a compact, non-fragmented, asceptic, self-confident world which, in contrast to the chaotic, disturbed and irrational worlds of contemporary artists, proposes serenity and logic, an everyday order, love and confidence in life, and a sense of elegance and decoration which are classical. Ugliness, vulgarity and horror take on a different meaning; they are appeased and adorned until they are transformed into their opposites. In the work created by Botero there is no room for death, decadence, violence and cruelty.

Is Botero a *naif*? He is if one wants to call the work of Fra Angelico or Miró *naif*, but not in the way the term is applied to Douanier Rousseau, the Pole Wribel or the Haitian *naifs*. The world of Botero is 'ingenuous' in the attitude of his characters, the decorative and affirmative view of existence, his defence of story telling, the picturesque and folklore as means of artistic expression, his lively and contrasting colours, his strong, healthy, optimistic tone and a whole arsenal of motifs that from the outside seem to be akin to popular art: those little vipers curled up in the branches of trees which hang over couples engaged in Virgilian siestas, or which have slithered lustfully into the rooms of the fat ladies; those small worms tunnelling into the body of the fruit; the cats and lap dogs which put on airs and the invasive flies which leave marks on the walls in every room and soil the meat in all the larders; the cigarette butts thrown on the floor and the hills in the landscape which always have the shape of a woman's breast; the little flags flying in the windows and the fox furs of the grand ladies that seem to have escaped from a children's story. What is *naif* is the love of ceremonial and of the trappings of this world. Here clothes do make the man: bishops, nuns, virgins, generals and saints are here not ways of being but ways of appearing and dressing (when they are dressed). Their appearance is all that they are, so that the dichotomy between being and appearing has no meaning for them. Their appearance is their essence.

Although the content and the themes of Botero's paintings border on the *naif*, his pure technique and intellectual approach make his work closer to the Academy than to the street. Perhaps we should put it another way. If Botero's themes root his painting in Latin America, because his sources are there — the provinces, the mythology and the models of the 1940s and 1950s, which give an underpinning in reality to his fantasy — then his techniques, ambitions and resources place him within the Western tradition. Ever since he first discovered this tradition, he has never stopped studying or defending it against those who claim to deny it.

## A Latin American among the classics

Is Latin America culturally a part of the West or a denial of the West? It's an old argument which will never be resolved theoretically because it is a vicious circle and the arguments for and against can be turned inside out, like a glove. But in the work of its great creators — poets, artists, musicians, prose writers — we discover each day that culturally Latin America is and is not Europe and that it cannot be anything other than hermaphrodite. It is not Europe since America is also made up of pre-Hispanic and African elements which have become fused with, or exist alongside, what has reached us from Europe, and has led to different cultural mixtures. But it is also Europe because from Europe came the languages that have integrated Latin America into the rest of the world, the religions and beliefs that structured life and death, the institutions that — good or bad, well or badly applied — regulate these societies and set the coordinates within which Latin Americans think, act, enjoy themselves or suffer. From Europe also came the ideas and value systems which form the cultural context out of which they must affirm their identity — their difference — when they invent, meditate, write or paint. The radical denial of European influences has always produced in Latin America shoddy pieces of work, without a creative spark; at the same time, servile imitation has led to affected works with no life of their own, as can be seen in much of the painting and literature from the Romantic period. By contrast, everything of lasting value that Latin America has produced in the artistic sphere stands in a curious relationship of both attraction and rejection with respect to Europe: such works make use of the European tradition for other ends or else introduce into that system certain forms, motifs or ideas that question or interrogate it without actually denying it.

In few contemporary artists can one see so clearly this Latin American ambiguity – to be and not to be Western – as in Fernando Botero. The profoundly Latin American nature of his art is due to the reworking of his own experiences, but also to his deep, deliberate and lucid immersion in an artistic tradition that the painter has made his own, without any sense of guilt, but rather with the quiet conviction that he has a right to do so. And Europe has helped Botero enormously to be Botero, to express, through his painting, that nuance of the West that is Latin America.

In a famous essay against the whims of nationalists in the cultural sphere, 'The Argentine Writer and Tradition', Jorge Luis Borges has written: 'I believe that our tradition is the whole of Western culture, and I also believe we have a right to this tradition, greater than that which the inhabitants of any Western nation might have . . . I believe that we South Americans can deal with all European themes without superstition, with an irreverence which can have, and already does have, fortunate consequences.' The work of Botero is one of these fortunate consequences. His painting is an exceptional proof of how a Latin American artist can find himself – and express his world – by establishing a creative dialogue with Europe, drawing from its sources, studying its techniques and emulating its artistic standards. The way forward is not to make mistakes in the choice of models, to know how to tap into the genuine wellspring of one's art, not to be sidetracked by ostentation or give up frivolously one's own deep motivations or experiences in order to follow fashion. In this respect, the case of Botero is exemplary.

After earning money from an exhibition at the Leo Matiz Gallery in Bogotá in May 1952, he travelled to Europe, where he stayed for three years. This period in which, instead of painting original works, he dedicated to copying the classics, looking and thinking, transformed this restless young painter, who was already displaying great talent and an extraordinary vocation, into an artist conscious of the complexity of the artistic process and convinced that methodical training, continuous effort and knowledge had to be combined with intuition and inspiration in order to produce authentic originality.

Botero stayed some days in Barcelona, then a few months in Madrid, where he took a course in the Academia de San Fernando, though he spent most of his time copying the Goyas and the Velásquezes in the Prado. He moved to Paris for several months, where he felt a visceral antipathy for contemporary painting exhibited in the galleries, and then took up residence in Florence. There, by learning the techniques of fresco painting in the Academia di San Marco, listening to the university lectures of the critic Roberto Longhi and, above all, copying the Renaissance artists and in particular the masters of the Quattrocento – Masaccio, Mantegna, Andrea del Castagno, Paolo Uccello, Piero della Francesca – he completed his formation. In a double sense: he learned or refined certain techniques and decided what type of painter he wanted to be.

This latter decision was of fundamental importance to his art. It was a very clear one: in favour of the classics and against the avant garde; in favour of tradition and against the 'isms'. This apparently conservative attitude was, in fact, nonconformist. It meant turning his back on frantic experimentalism, the conformism of the moment, the conventional wisdom enshrined by critics and the public, in order to find in the work of the masters who had founded modern sensibility the formal and technical resources which would enable him to produce, in this day and age, a work that would have the solidity, the ambition, the newness and the permanence that these masters achieved in their work.

### Art as pleasure

Perhaps the most Renaissance, the least contemporary, aspect of Botero's work is his concept of pleasure. Enjoyment, happiness, love of life are attitudes that modern art mistrusts and condemns as unreal or immoral. Modern artists assign themselves the function of expressing the great traumas and instability, the suffering, the fury, the desperation and the anguish of modern man. In this way, contemporary aesthetics has established the beauty of ugliness, reclaiming for art everything in human experience that artistic representation had previously rejected. In Botero's world – as in the world of his classical models – life is worth living since happiness is possible. Botero's aesthetic rejects the cult of ugliness, that great achievement of modern art. He is one of the few contemporary artists to adhere to the old belief that the mission of art is not to become involved with the sad, repugnant or abject manifestations of human behaviour and express them in an appropriate way, but rather that it should use its resources to embellish these manifestations and, in an act of artistic magic, through the delicacy and elegance of form, place this sombre reality on to a new plane, where it can only be appreciated and judged as an object of pleasure. He has said so clearly: 'The problem is to determine where the pleasure comes from when one looks at a work of art.'

When we look at his paintings, we also know where the pleasure that they give us comes from: from the pleasure with which they have been painted. Happiness is not to be found in the themes of his paintings. His characters do not seem to be enjoying themselves, they are not smiling but, rather, they are serious, bewildered, even when they are engaged in the most pleasant activities – dancing, drinking, making love. The pleasure is to be found in the luminous, sensual and enjoyable way in which the ample curves are outlined, the miniaturist delicacy with which the brush has puckered the little mouths, thinned the eyebrows, accentuated the moles, the delicacy with which the characters have been adorned and dressed and the lavish generosity of the colours which makes the modest houses in which they live shine like palaces and their ridiculous and old-fashioned suits bedazzle us like royal finery. There is something cheerful and happy in this detailed and splendid form: the hand – the man – that has drawn it has enjoyed doing so and this enjoyment which surrounds his characters and objects like an aura is conveyed in part to us. Many modern painters paint as if they were screaming with pain, committing suicide out of desperation or spewing out insults; for them, creation is self-immolation. Botero paints as if he were making love or eating a delicacy. Everything that he draws, paints or sculpts, through the fact of being drawn, painted or sculpted, arouses his support and affection and is ennobled. The famous statement of Saint-John Perse, 'Je parle dans l'estime', could be his motto. 'I paint in the esteem', that is, with enthusiasm and passion for the beings and things of the world.

Do the innumerable movements of modern art have a common denominator? Yes, in so far as they have established that a moral attitude or an ideological principle can confer aesthetic status. These attitudes and principles vary, they are sometimes at loggerheads, but none of these different movements has adopted the definition which characterized the art of the past, whereby artistic beauty, based on the comparison between the work and nature, was derived exclusively from certain formal norms and standards: composition, perspective, volume, line, colour. Not even at times of the most intense religious belief, such as the Middle Ages, was art judged first and foremost as an act of faith or as a doctrinaire position. The moralizing or catechizing function of art began, for the medieval artist, after the work of art had been recognized as such, that is, when it had achieved a certain aesthetic standard which could be judged according to a system of values which were universally accepted. Originality, an individual phenomenon, threw into relief the shadow of the artist against a homogeneous background, a way of seeing and evaluating shared by his contemporaries. Today, for it to be artistic, a picture or a sculpture should express an idea, propose a certain conception of society, of man or of artistic endeavour, exemplify an ethical position. The confusion that currently reigns in contemporary art is due to the fact that there is no *one* system of values that unites the works which are produced: these works are the result of different points of view, theoretical models or positions which share no common denominator. This proliferation of aesthetics – or rather of attitudes that purport to embody an aesthetic – has become so extreme that it is no exaggeration to state that each artist or artistic work hopes to be understood or judged according to their own terms. The result is uncertainty and anarchy.

Perhaps, apart from his enormous talent as a painter, one of the reasons for Botero's success is that his work reminds us of the order that structured artistic life before the current confusion and proves to us that he can today continue to structure this life since he is not opposed to innovation or invention. His painting is familiar to us: it is a contemporary expression of a way of understanding and producing art which was the same for our grandfathers and fathers and, for this reason, we can judge it according to standards developed throughout the history of the West. His paintings are intelligible and they are, above all else, paintings; their forms and colours are not justified according to any moral standard or list of principles. His references are, simultaneously, the visible world and the artistic tradition from which he derives his techniques and his themes. In a world where artistic values are in crisis – all values have been, are being or will be questioned and replaced by others and these, in turn, will be replaced in a never-ending spin – the work of Botero, with its constant references to the art of the past, its rational balance, its exquisite craft, its benevolent, unified and optimistic vision, devoid of tension or anguish, its sensuality and flashes of humour and above all its artistic hedonism, its passionate defence of the art of painting as an activity that is justified by the pleasure that it produces and displays, restores our confidence and persuades us that the hunger for beauty is still a legitimate appetite.

Lima, August 1984

# Szyszlo in the Labyrinth

From time to time an anguished question is asked: does Latin America exist? Are we different from the rest? And, if we are, how does one define Latin American identity in cultural terms? No one asks if French, Italian or Spanish cultures exist. They seem self-evident and sovereign, unquestionable realities which every painting, novel and ideas system that they produce merely serve to consolidate. Our culture, what is our own, however, seems much less irrefutable. It is as if Latin America might suddenly dissolve and that the multitude of traditions, mentalities and languages which together form it – the pre-Hispanic, the European, the African, the different *mestizo* cultures – might never coalesce into a coherent whole.

Depending on the time and the prevalent fashion, Latin American artists have considered themselves to be white, Indian or *mestizo*. And each of these definitions – Hispanicism, Indigenism, *Criollismo* – has been a form of mutilation since it excludes from our cultural make-up certain characteristics that belong to us just as much as the ones chosen.

But despite the innumerable tracts, articles, debates and symposia on this inexhaustible theme of our identity, what is certain is that every time we are lucky enough to be faced with a genuine work of creation from our milieu, our doubts are immediately dissolved. Latin America exists and is there, in what we see and enjoy, in what disturbs, excites and also identifies us. This is what happens to us with the stories of Borges, the poems of Vallejo or Octavio Paz, the paintings of Tamayo or Matta. And it also happens with the paintings of Szyszlo: this is Latin America in its highest expression, the best of what we are and what we possess.

To trace the tracks of our identity in these disturbing paintings is somewhat dizzying since they map out a vast geography, a labyrinth so complicated and diverse, that even the most skilful explorer can become lost. The son of a Polish scientist and a mother from the coast of Peru, Szyszlo's artistic sources are similarly split: pre-Colombian art, the European vanguard, certain North American and Latin American painters. But perhaps the landscape that has surrounded him for most of his life – the grey sky of the city, Lima, the coastal deserts full of history and death and that sea which figure with such force in his paintings of recent years – have been as influential in his work as the legacy of the pre-Colombian artisans, whose masks, feathered capes, little clay figures, and other symbols and colours frequently appear in quintessential form in his canvases. There is also the refined, bold rejection and attraction of modern Western art – Cubism, neo-figuration, surrealism – without which the painting of Szyszlo would not be what it is.

The roots of an artist are always deep and inextricable, like those of great trees. It is useful to study and investigate them because they bring us close to that central mystery where beauty is born and that indefinable force that certain objects created by man are capable of releasing, which disarms and captivates us. But to know this is also to know the limits of such an enquiry, since the sources cannot explain the totality of a work of art. Quite the reverse: they usually show how an artist goes beyond what formed his sensibility and perfected his technique.

The personal – that obscure area made up of dreams and desires, presentiments, memories and unconscious impulses – is surely as important to Szyszlo as the movements in painting to which his work can be affiliated or which he has consciously admired and emulated. And it is most likely that in this secret redoubt of his personality can be found that inaccessible key to the mystery which, along with his elegance and skill, is the major protagonist of his pictures. Something is always happening in them, something that is more than form and colour: a spectacle that is difficult to describe, although not to feel; a ceremony that seems at times to be a funeral pyre or a sacrifice celebrated on a primitive altar; a barbarous and violent rite in which someone bleeds, disintegrates, surrenders and also perhaps enjoys something which, in any event, is not intelligible, which we must apprehend through the tortuous route of obsession, nightmare and vision. My memory often suddenly conjures up that strange totem, visceral debris or monument covered with disturbing offerings – ligatures, spurs, suns, splits, incisions, shafts – which has long been a recurring character in Szyszlo's canvases. And I have asked myself the same question on countless occasions: Where does it come from? Who, what is it?

I know that there are no answers to these questions. But the fact that he is capable of provoking these questions and keeping them alive in the memory of those who come into contact with his world is the best way of demonstrating the authenticity of the art of Fernando de Szyszlo. An art which, like Latin America, is buried in the night of obliterated civilizations and which rubs shoulders with the newest civilizations from all corners of the globe. It emerges at the place where all these roads intersect, eager, curious, thirsty, free of prejudice, open to all influences. But it is also angrily loyal to its secret heart, that warm and buried intimacy where experiences and teachings are transformed and where reason is put at the service of unreason, so that the personality and genius of an artist can flower.

New York, 1991

# Degenerate Art

A commission of specialists appointed by Hitler's Reichsminister für Volksaufklärung und Propaganda, Joseph Goebbels, went round dozens of museums and art collections throughout Germany in 1937 and confiscated some 16,000 modern paintings, drawings, sculptures and prints. From that vast haul, 650 works were selected which seemed the most obscene, sacrilegious, anti-patriotic, pro-Jewish and pro-Bolshevik. With these, an exhibition entitled Entartete Kunst – Degenerate Art – was organized, which opened in Munich that same year, drawing large crowds. Over the next four years, the exhibition travelled around thirteen Austrian and German cities and was visited by some 13 million people including the Führer himself who, it seems, first had the idea for the exhibition which would reveal the depths of decadence and putrefaction of 'modernism'.

The Los Angeles Art Museum decided to recreate the exhibition and managed to bring together some two hundred surviving works, for when the exhibition was over the Nazis only destroyed some of the paintings. The rest were sold to a Swiss gallery to raise funds. Now the show has reached the Alten Museum in Berlin.

You have to queue for a long time to get in, but it's worth it, for the same reasons as it is worth spending a few days engrossed in the thick volumes that Don Marcelino Menéndez y Pelayo has dedicated to the heretics, the apostates and the ungodly in Medieval and Renaissance Spain: because in these 'heterodox' figures can be found the most creative imaginations of the age. The amanuenses of Goebbels made their selections with almost infallible judgement. Nobody important escaped them, from Picasso, Modigliani, Matisse, Kandinsky, Klee, Kokoshka, Braque and Chagall to the German expressionists and avant-garde artists like Emil Nolde, Kirchner, Beckmann, Dix and Käthe Kollwitz. The same was true of the books, the films and the music that the Third Reich burned or banned. The exhibition also has some rooms dedicated to this work: Thomas Mann, Hemingway, Dos Passos, jazz, Anton Webern, Arnold Schönberg.

The exhibition of Entartete Kunst was perfect for me because of my liking for 'degenerate' German art of the beginning of the century and post World War I and because for some time now I've been taking notes for a short essay on George Grosz, the most original and strident figure of the fertile 1920s in Berlin. He was clearly the star of that exhibition and one of the artists whose work most infuriated the regime. In the famous inquisitorial ceremony of 10 May 1932, in front of the University of Humboldt, more than forty of his books, or books illustrated by him, were burned and Max Pechstein in his *Memoirs* calculates that 285 pictures, drawings and prints by Grosz disappeared under Nazi rule. In 1938 they stripped him of German nationality and, because he had nothing of his own that they could take, they confiscated his wife's possessions.

But at least Grosz saved his life. In 1932, a commando group of black shirts came to his studio with very clear intentions. His histrionic skills served him in good stead; the thugs thought that he was the servant of the caricaturist. He left for the United States just a few weeks before the Reichstag fire and would only return to Berlin in 1959 to die – alcoholic, frustrated and tamed as an artist. His friend of the same generation, the great Otto Dix, stayed in Germany through the Nazi period and the war, banned from painting and exhibiting. When he began to do so again, there was not the slightest trace in his canvases of his former virulence and imagination. Instead of the spectacular horrors that once adorned his canvases, the new work seemed like miniatures: gentle families under the protection of the good Lord Jesus. Many artists who were not driven to concentration camps, to exile, to silence and to suicide by the Nazis became, like Grosz and Dix, mere shadows of their former selves.

The young Germans now visiting the Alten Museum can see and learn all this in a very vivid way. They can listen to the Führer giving a speech at the opening of the German Museum of Art and see the helmeted Aryan nudes and the blonde, virtuous, child-bearing Valkyries of the 'healthy' art which the Third Reich promoted in opposition to the decadence of the West. And they can see the astonishing similarity between this monumentalist, chauvinist and banal aesthetic and the socialist realism which filled the squares and museums of the now defunct German Democratic Republic. They are indistinguishable save for the proliferation of swastikas in the one and hammers and sickles in the other. This is a persuasive lesson that totalitarian systems are alike and that when the state regulates, directs or decides on intellectual or artistic creation, the results are humbug and rubbish.

This is also true for democracies, of course, and there are many contemporary examples of this, albeit more subtle and less crude and controlled than those offered by communism or fascism. I spent two splendid hours at the Entartete Kunst exhibition, but then I began to feel uneasy and upset when I realized that one effect of it could be to increase the visitors' self-righteousness and misguided feelings of having a clear conscience. The worst reaction to the experience would be to say: 'All that was pure barbarism, of course. Things are much better now for art. Today, what democratic government would dare to ridicule or persecute the experimentation and daring of its artists?'

That is true, no Western government would dare call any picture, sculpture, film or book 'degenerate' so as not to be compared with the Hitlerian or Stalinist barbarians and this respect for the freedom of creation is very laudable. It is not so laudable when such prudence goes hand in hand with a complete inability to distinguish between what is good, bad and deplorable in art, and an irresponsible frivolity.

In order to get from the Wissenchaftskolleg to the place where I have my German lessons, I have to walk twice daily along the lively and prosperous avenue full of Berlin's boutiques and restaurants: the Kürfurstendam. As soon as I come out of Grünewald, I run up against a block of grey cement embedded with two cars, located in the Rathenplatz, which I cannot avoid seeing. When once I ventured the opinion that it was a pity that such an attractive city should be strewn with hideous sculptures on its streets and gave the buried car statue as an example, someone remonstrated with me, explaining that it was a 'statement against consumerism'. What statement is the tubular monstrosity that jumps out at me a few blocks later making? Is it against sausages? Bad digestion? The leads that Berliners use to walk their dogs? Its greyish innards rise up, curve and disappear, attached to the ground by a metal rope. I pass several other sculptures on my daily walk and almost all of them are as unattractive and as lacking in ideas, creativity and craft as the two already mentioned.

They are there because they won prizes and were endorsed by commissions and juries which contained, no doubt, very respectable critics who supported them with such iridescent arguments as seeing them as an attack on consumer society or a deconstruction of bourgeois metaphysics. In fact they are there because in our open, advanced societies, the tolerance towards everything that seems new or daring in art has led to a relativism and confusion worthy of Babel itself, in which nobody understands each other, nobody knows what is true creation and what is fake or, if he does know, would not make his views public for fear of being considered a 'philistine' or a 'reactionary'. That is an ideal state of affairs for the wool to be pulled over everyone's eyes. It has been happening for a long time, not just in Berlin, but in cities like Paris, where one might think that the solid tradition of public consensus about aesthetic values and artistic criteria would make them better prepared to avoid such a risk. If not, how can one explain the calm resignation of the French in the face of the coloured columns that turned the patio of the Palais Royal into a chess board and the glass pyramid that spoiled the symmetry of the Louvre?

Unlike the Nazis and the Communists who were convinced that art and literature were 'dangerous' and should thus be controlled and directed by political power, democratic, liberal society has managed to turn art into something totally innocuous, if not fraudulent or laughable, a job divorced from life and its problems, from human needs, a soulless trick, a commodity with which *marchands* can speculate and politicians can promote themselves and assume the mantle of being tolerant and progressive patrons of the arts. That is also another, very baroque, way of 'degenerating' cultural life.

Freedom, which is a secure value in every sphere, resolves fundamental problems but creates others, which demand daring solutions and great imagination. In the case of art, the open society guarantees the artist both tolerance and limitless possibilities which, paradoxically, have often sapped him of force and originality. It is as if when artists feel that they no longer scare or upset anyone, then they lose their resolve, their will to create and an ethical attitude towards their vocation and what we find instead are mannerisms, cynicism and other forms of irresponsibility.

For that reason, although I am very pleased that the East German people have freed themselves from totalitarianism, I am not so glad that they are demolishing so many statues of Marx, Engels and company in the ex-German Democratic Republic, among them that enormous stone Lenin that cost a fortune to take down. Its portentous presence had the involuntary humour of a kitsch construction. Among the different possible forms of ugliness, it will always be preferable to have ugliness that does not need to guarantee its acceptability by employing intellectual sophisms, like the heroic fight against consumerism.

In my daily journey to face up to the confusions and declensions of the German language, the sculpture that I am always pleased to see is a sort of aluminium snake that stretches over the street like an arch. There is something pleasing in its heavy, obvious form that blends in well with the busy pedestrians, the high buildings and the surrounding traffic. Every now and then, it is daubed with Gothic slogans or splashes of colour. Perhaps it is not a sculpture at all, but instead the giant pipework of a building that has had to be moved while the foundations for a planned skyscraper are being laid? That is indeed the case. It is a transitory and casual structure, a 'ready made', which embodies the creative potential of industry, a fiercely sarcastic monument of the collective Berlin subconscious – like those immortalized by Grosz in the 1920s, in this same city – in the face of the complacent degeneration of art in the last gasps of the millennium.

Berlin, March 1992

# A Fleeting Impression of Václav Havel

He's small rather than tall, with very blond hair, a blond moustache and blue, gentle eyes which glance timidly around. He seems rather lost in that immense, very elegant palace, among the people guarding and escorting him, uncomfortable in the obligatory attire of collar and tie and blue suit.

We barely have time to exchange formal greetings before Patrick Poivre d'Arvor of French television, who has organized the meeting, places us under the lights and in front of the cameras and begins the conversation. He first questions Václav Havel. About the dramatic changes he has experienced in his life, those great strides he has taken from prison to President of the Republic, from banned playwright to a public figure revered everywhere. And about the challenges and obligations of the power that he now holds at this crucial moment in the history of his country.

He listens attentively, thinks for a moment and then answers very rapidly, in long, direct sentences, without the slightest hesitation. All his timidity and even his modesty evaporate when he speaks. And in the assurance and firmness of his replies there are flashes of the young Havel who, in 1956, made a shocking speech at Dobris to a group of official writers, which marked the beginning of his long career of opposition to the regime. Or the no less resolute intervention in 1965, at the Union of Czechoslovakian Writers, when he defended the magazine *Tvar* and accused the Union of intolerance and of obsequiousness towards power.

Poivre d'Arvor then asked me if it was true that the events in Czechoslovakia in the spring of 1968 had a great impact on my political ideas. Yes, they did. But they changed my behaviour rather than my beliefs. Because at that time – when I got to know the USSR, when I had begun to take account of the truth that lay behind the mirages of Cuba – I did not have many illusions about socialism. But, like many others, I did not dare make my doubts and criticisms public. Thanks to the armed intervention of the Warsaw Pact countries, I found the courage to do so.

This is the fourth or fifth time that I've been to Prague, but it is my first real visit. All the other times, in the mid 1960s, were stopovers, en route to or from Cuba, because, due to the blockade, the shortest route for a Latin American to Havana was via Prague. They stamped a loose piece of paper, not our passports, and we had to spend a night in a dreadful hotel on the outskirts of the city – the International, which has now been refurbished – and eat in a lugubrious dining room, where an old man, out of another era, dressed in tails, played the violin.

On one of these rapid visits, in the spring of 1968, my Czech translator took me to visit the many houses that the peripatetic Kafka family lived in – they moved continually, but always within the same block – and the Jewish cemetery, which seemed to be out of a Gothic nightmare. But what really impressed me were the streets, the spectacle of hopeful and enthusiastic people, united in a great fraternal and idealistic upheaval. A spectacle that was very similar to the one I had witnessed in Havana during the missile crisis of November 1962 when, with the same naïvety, I thought that I also had clasped that same fatuous beacon: socialism in freedom. For that reason, when the Soviet tanks entered Prague and Fidel made his shameful speech supporting the aggression, I wrote an article, 'Socialism and the Tanks' (see p. 79), which had two long-term effects on my life: I became the enemy of Latin American 'progressives' and I began to think and speak independently once again, a position that I have never since abandoned.

Václav Havel is not surprised that the communist utopia still has so many followers in Latin America. 'No one who has not lived and suffered it in the flesh can know what it is like.' Much less naïve than I was, he was never remotely convinced by the beautiful spectacle in the streets of Prague in the days of Alexander Dubček, because he had never been a Marxist and, from an early age, he had come to an uncomfortable conclusion: that the only socialism compatible with freedom is the one that is socialist in name alone (for example, that euphemism called social democracy). He was not therefore surprised by the arrival of the tanks or the return to obscurantism after the brutal suppression of this movement for democracy.

But this man who did not succumb to the political illusions of '68 and kept his feet firmly on the ground turned out, in the end, to be less prone to depression and better prepared to take on an apparently invulnerable regime than those who had committed themselves wholly to the reform of socialism 'from within', and found their dreams brutally shattered.

Like Milan Kundera. The polemic between these two great writers, the novelist and the playwright, is one of the most instructive of our times. Kundera, one of the intellectual heroes of the reform movement of Czech socialism, came to certain conclusions after the failure of the experiment. The conclusions were gloomy, but they seemed the most lucid of all. Small countries do not count in that great whirlwind that is History, with a capital 'h'. Their fate is decided by the great powers and they are the instruments, and eventually the victims, of these powers. The intellectual must dare to face up to this horrible truth and not delude himself, or others, by indulging in useless actions – like signing manifestos or letters of protest – which often just serve as self-publicity or, at best, as a form of self-gratification at having a good political conscience. When Kundera went into exile in France in 1975, to dedicate himself completely to literature, he had lost all hope that his country would one day emerge from despotism and servitude. I understand him very well. My reaction would probably have been similar to his.

But the one who was right was Václav Havel. Because, in fact, one can always do something. However small, a manifesto, a letter signed with a handful of people, can be the drops of water that wear through the stone. And in any case, these gestures, ventures, symbolic threats allow one to go on living with a certain dignity and perhaps might spread to others the will and confidence that are necessary for collective action. There are no indestructible regimes or powers that cannot be changed. If history is absurd, then anything can happen – oppression and crime, of course, but also freedom.

This modest man, who finds the very mention of the word heroism repugnant, enjoys an immense moral authority in his country. In the market square of Prague I saw an old woman carrying his photo in a handbag, as if it were the photo of a father or a son. He achieved this in those bleak years through his conviction, which was obstinate rather than strident, that even in the most difficult circumstances one can always act to improve the destiny of a country. Thus the Charter of January 1977 was born, signed initially by 240 residents of the 'interior', that would become a landmark in the democratic counter-offensive which twelve years later restored sovereignty to Czechoslovakia.

I don't ask Havel about the six years or more, over three spells, that he spent in prison, because I have read his essays and I know his sober observations on this topic. Instead, I say to him that one of the most mortifying experiences that I had, in my time in politics, was to discover that almost inevitably politics degrades the language in which it is expressed, that its discourse sooner or later falls into stereotypes or clichés, that it is rarely authentic or personal since what is *politic* to say always takes primacy over what should be said. Had he not felt, on occasion, like a ventriloquist's dummy saying things that seemed to be the words of another person?

Yes, it has happened to him sometimes. And it is something that of course worries him and which he tries to watch out for. For this reason he writes his own speeches. Also, I should realize that literary language is one thing and political discourse another. The former can be everything a writer wants it to be. The latter is forced to be clear, simple, direct, capable of reaching the great variety of listeners that make up a society.

Another disturbing lesson of politics for me, I say to him, is the Machiavellian conflict, sometimes latent and sometimes explicit, but always inevitable, between efficacy and truth. Is effective politics possible without pulling the wool over people's eyes, without deceiving them? I tried this and I think that it was one of the reasons – though not the main reason – for my failure. Always to tell the truth in politics is to hand a devastating weapon to an opponent not constrained by morality. In his year of government had he not had to resign himself sometimes to the famous white lies of politicians?

'I have felt pressure to do so many times,' he says, 'but until now I have resisted this pressure. Of course one must always make a great effort so that these unpopular truths become acceptable. One has to explain them thoroughly, go into detail. There can be exceptional circumstances in which certain things are not said, but I can guarantee that in the pursuit of government, I have never lied.'

I am sure that he is telling the truth now as well. I cannot judge if all his political acts have been correct since he was elected president. In the two days I've been in Prague, for example, I have heard criticism of his rash intervention a few weeks back in a demonstration of Slovak separatists, in Bratislava, where he was insulted and almost hit.

But I have read his speeches and what I have always admired in them (apart from their elegance), is how unpolitical they are in their permanent desire to subordinate action to morality.

When the interview is over, there is scarcely time to talk about serious things. We talk trivialities. The cigarettes that he smokes and that I gave up smoking twenty years ago. That we were born the same year and that we both, in our youth, did two years of military service. And that, like all our generation, we drank the waters of existentialism with mixed results. An old friend of his, Pavel Tigrid, is with him. He is one of his political advisers. 'I don't know why he called on an old man like me to work alongside him,' he says to me. I, on the other hand, do know why. When I was president of PEN International, Pavel Tigrid — an expatriate in Paris and director of a magazine of exiled Czechs, *Svedectvi* ('Witness') — was the president of the PEN Committee of Writers in Exile, and fought tirelessly for those colleagues who, in his country, or in Argentina, the USSR, Chile, Cuba, Poland, or in any other part of the world, were in jail. I know that the presence of Pavel Tigrid in that beautiful palace through whose windows I could see the snow falling on the Mala Strana district — what incredible springs they have in this country — is to remind the president at all times of what he fought for when he was a nobody, of those goals that then seemed so difficult to achieve.

In one of his essays, Havel quotes the terrible observation of Eugene O'Neill: 'We have fought for so long against small things that we've become small ourselves.' I trust now that he no longer has to confront the formidable adversities of before, but rather the small and sordid adversities of the daily art of governing, the president of the Czechs will go on being the discreet and pure man that he is still today.

Prague, April 1991

# Swiss Passion

'They have called from the police and from the Rector's office,' Professor Linder told me. 'It seems that the walls of the university are covered in slogans against you.'

I replied that I was very sorry to be the cause of an assault against a building that I imagined to be tidier than a clinic. But he did not smile (this was my first failed attempt, in this day full of surprises, to communicate my sense of humour to the Swiss people). Rather, Professor Linder asked me if I was comfortable in the Hotel Die Storgchen. I was. And the view, over the old quarter, the Limmar, and the bridges of Zurich, was beautiful. In his car, on the way to the slogans, I asked him if it were true that this handful of blocks that we were travelling through held more money than all the countries of the Third World put together. He replied that I should not be worried since the police and the Rector's office had taken all the necessary steps so that nothing would happen to me.

I assured him that I was not worried in the slightest. Rather, I was astonished to be so popular in a city which, for me, was both exotic and hermetic. Although, probably, the slogans were the work of Peruvian revolutionary refugees in this fortress of capitalism, didn't he think so? He emitted a grunt which could have been yes, no, or perhaps.

To cheer him up, I told him how some years ago, in the University of Stockholm, other Peruvian revolutionaries had burst into the auditorium where I was about to give a lecture, given out leaflets and disappeared at the very moment that I was entering the building. And that these cautious compatriots had proceeded with such manic precision so as not to break the law, for if they had acted in this way with me in the hall, they ran the risk of losing their status as political exiles, which guaranteed them, thanks to the Swedish taxpayer, lodging, language classes and an allowance equivalent to several hundred dollars a month. And I told him that I had teased the bureaucrat who had sought me out to give me a vague explanation of what had happened, by informing him that my revenge would be to proclaim through the streets and squares of my country the hospitality that Sweden lavished on political victims of that tyranny which was Peru and then sit back and watch the frantic stampede of ten million Peruvian revolutionaries towards the Nordic snows. (The Swedish bureaucrat did not laugh, nor did my Swiss companion.)

I was now at the University. The austere nineteenth-century façade of the building was indeed daubed with inscriptions in German, in black and red paint, accusing me of being an agent of the International Monetary Fund (an accusation which contained some remote glimmers of truth), and proclaiming that the Swiss people repudiated me and supported 'the war of the people in Peru' (declarations which left me somewhat sceptical).

It was very early and there was no one to be seen, friend or foe. Professor Linder, who had doubtless heard of the proverbial unpunctuality of South Americans, made me arrive at all my engagements an hour early. So that there I was, in an exquisite small room in the Rector's office, greeting the guests to the reception in my honour.

Waiting for them to arrive, I thought once more about the *sertão* in Bahía and my friend Adelhice. It's a memory that haunts me, fatefully, every time I come to Switzerland. For it was there, in that lost village in the north-east of Brazil called Esplanada, and thanks to her, that, for the first time, I seriously considered that strange creation of chance, geography and religion which is the Swiss Confederation, now 700 years old.

I was travelling across the *sertão* in the tracks of a terrible preacher, the Counsellor, researching the war that he had unleashed. I was accompanied on this journey by the husband of Adelhice, the fabulous Renato Ferraz who, after having been an anthropologist and a museologist in Salvador, gave it all up to raise cattle in the middle of the *sertão*. Renato knew the names of all the trees, the plants, the animals and the vermin of the region and knew – above all – how to break through the mistrust of the inhabitants of the *sertão* and make them talk like canaries. Our centre of operations was his house in Esplanada which we left and returned to on each expedition.

But there, in Esplanada, the topic of conversation was always Switzerland and the Swiss. Adelhice felt a mystical admiration for them, a respect and an enthusiasm that I had never witnessed in anyone for any country. As a young woman she had read in a Brazilian paper an advertisement asking for assistants to work in the canton of Zurich.

She sent in her application and was accepted. She worked for three years in a cakeshop in a small village with an unpronounceable name. She was totally happy there. In her case, there was one of those 'encounters with destiny' that Borges's stories speak of. She discovered in that place ways of living, rites, a certain way of thinking and behaving that must have given form to something which obscurely, from a long time back, the young Adelhice must have foreseen and longed for.

In the beautiful evenings in Esplanada, when the suffocating heat of the day abated and the sky was filled with the gold and the blood of sunset, I listened to her with fascination as she evoked the frozen Alps and talked with emotion and nostalgia of the cleanliness and order of the Swiss, the security and punctuality of their lives, their diligence in work, their respect for the law and their mania for doing everything well. Adelhice had learnt to cook there and she prepared some delicious dishes to show me that Swiss cooking went further than fondue, rösti and muesli, and indeed it was all very varied and delicious.

Many countries have embodied for many human beings their idea of civilization, of a model society. But had anyone, apart from the very pleasant Adelhice, seen in the twenty-four cantons of the Swiss Confederation what so many see in France, the United States, Cuba or Beijing? I am sure these people must exist, but I have never met anyone except her. What would Adelhice now think of her revered country if she could see this noble site of the University of Zurich so ignominiously humiliated by graffiti, like any university in her country or in mine?

And what would Adelhice have thought if she had seen what I had witnessed that very morning when, wandering through the centre of Zurich in search of a Modigliani exhibition, I came across that leafy park which the inhabitants of Zurich have now baptized as 'Needle Park'? It is behind the station on the banks of the river Limmat and it has become a sort of stronghold for drug addicts. Its inhabitants are injecting themselves in full view of the public, with needles that the authorities have been obliged to distribute to them to check the threat of Aids, which is spreading in that group. Many live right there in small shelters made up of rags and wood among trees. Would the sight have depressed her as much as it did me?

But the summoned guests had arrived and it was time to return to the present and to Switzerland. Throughout the reception I tried two or three times to make jokes about the slogans, but everyone, starting with the Rector, avoided the topic, so I made a vow (which I didn't keep) never again to try to make a joke in Switzerland. On the way to the Great Hall the Rector whispered cryptically in my ear, 'Everything is going well.'

The Great Hall was on the top floor which was reached by a marble staircase. On the wall was a plaque commemorating the fact that Churchill had given his famous speech on Europe there. The Rector pointed it out to me, to raise my spirits. It was still not necessary to do so, because the audience filling the hall seemed most courteous. I saw that, after I had entered, they closed the doors in a very ostentatious way, with locks and bolts, which made me feel claustrophobic. 'They won't be able to get in now,' Professor Linder murmured. I had to bite back the observation that if someone really wanted to interrupt the lecture, he would probably already be sitting there, as mild as could be, in the audience.

But Swiss revolutionaries do not go in for such dirty tricks. They arrived after me and when they found the doors closed, they did not try to enter. They limited themselves to shouting and making other noises that could easily be heard through the walls of the Great Hall and served as background music to my lecture. While I was reading, I saw in amazement out of the corner of my eye that the public remained completely impassive to what was happening. Not a single expression of bewilderment, alarm or curiosity. Couldn't they hear, like me, the commotion outside, or were they all deaf? I remembered that Zurich had been the birthplace of Dadaism and I felt quite ridiculous reading my lecture as if nothing was happening. I interrupted the lecture – silly me – to make a joke. I asked the audience if they thought that the racket outside had anything to do with me and with what I was saying. Eight hundred heads nodded in agreement and no one smiled.

After half an hour, whatever was happening outside calmed down. But when the lecture was over, Professor Linder and the Rector kept me in the Great Hall until everyone had left and the danger was over. What danger? What had happened outside? They explained it all to me without emotion, with icy objectivity. Soon after the lecture had begun, the revolutionaries – 'between fifteen and twenty of them, no more' – had entered the building, armed with eggs and tomatoes. The two officers sent by the police to maintain order were pelted with these projectiles and had to call up reinforcements. Ten more police arrived, five uniformed and five in plain clothes, and there had been a confused skirmish. But the situation was brought under control and the revolutionaries had retired. In any event, to avoid further surprises, we set off for the restaurant — there was a final dinner — through a secret exit from the university.

Surrounded by half a dozen policemen, like some presidential candidate from the underdeveloped world, I abandoned the Great Hall. A gentleman in plain clothes preceded me. He seemed to be the head of the squad and not only were his shoulders and lapels stained with egg and tomato, but he also had an entire egg hanging grotesquely from his hair on to his neck.

We went down into a labyrinthine and interminable basement which no one seemed to know the way out of. The light kept going out and we were in the darkness, smelling damp things and hearing terrified scufflings. I told the person who was leading us, loud enough for the Rector and Professor Linder to hear, that I would rather face up to revolutionaries than to rats, which inspired complete terror in me and, since nobody seemed to know where we were, I suggested that we should go back to the main entrance and leave the university like peaceful citizens, not skulking away like thieves. And that furthermore these Swiss revolutionaries were not serious, since the egg and tomato throwing incident — luxury items for the people of Peru — marked them down as spoiled brats. And that I was sure that they would all end up as very efficient employees in the banks of the Banhofstrasse. Someone thought that I was making a joke and laughed. But the Rector defended national honour by pointing out that one of the eggs had broken in the eye of an official, who had to be taken for medical treatment.

At last we reached the exit, the street, the cars. But a Peruvian diplomat and his family remained lost in those gloomy catacombs and only appeared in the restaurant where the dinner was being held an hour later, exhausted and smiling. No one mentioned what had happened or, of course, ventured a smile when, as I gave my thanks, I rashly observed that my reception in Zurich had made me feel at home. I did not say, though it was in my mind, that I would like to have found out if those who had adorned the University of Zurich with slogans in favour of 'the people's war in Peru' knew that one of the feats carried out by their Peruvian revolutionary brothers had been to murder four Swiss agricultural experts on a cooperation programme, who had gone out to work with peasant communities in the central highlands of my country.

Back at the Hotel Die Storgchen, alone now, I decided to commit that most typical of capitalist acts: to go and have a whisky. The terrace by the river was closed but they told me that the bar was still open. I went up and sat in that solitary spot. And then – with my eyes like saucers and my heart pounding – I saw Adelhice. Not the phantom of my memory, but a tangible, real Adelhice, of flesh and blood, almost untouched by the twelve years that had passed since I last saw her. There she was, as slim, lively and vivacious as ever, exuberantly good-natured. She seemed as amazed as I was.

When we recovered our voices, I questioned her. She had separated from Renato and had made the journey to Switzerland with her three children, where they had lived since 1988. It had been very tough at first, she'd had to take on the most menial jobs to survive. But thanks to her desire to stay and educate her children here and never go back there – an unshakeable desire, never, ever again – she was beginning to get established. She had rented a couple of rooms where the four of them made the best of it and now the *crianças* were helping her a great deal. Her work here in the bar was not badly paid. They laid on a taxi back to her home and in her free time she was taking a course in pastrymaking and cooking, with the idea of one day running a restaurant. And of course, all the hardships had their compensations here in Switzerland. Her children were going to a magnificent state school in which ... but I did not let her launch into her predictable apologia for her country of adoption – it was clear that her Swiss passion had not diminished one iota – and I led the conversation towards friends in Salvador and the *sertão*.

That night I tossed and turned in bed without being able to sleep – Zurich was as hot as Bahía – thinking how fortunate this country was, at a time when the bored sons of its privileged denizens were trying to ruin the country with pastimes like heroin and solidarity with the terrorists, to have people like Adelhice coming from the other side of the world to save the inheritance of seven centuries of Swiss history.

Zurich, July 1991

# Letter to Salman Rushdie

Who would have imagined that evening when we went to the football game – we got lost and ended up on a terrace full of painted spectators who were singing something like 'La Cucaracha' and knocking policemen's helmets off – that, a short time later, circumstances would make you the most celebrated contemporary victim of that extreme form of violence that is religious fanaticism.

I am sure I told you on that, or some other, occasion the story of a colleague of mine at King's College, whom I sometimes ran into at lunchtime, at a pub in the Strand. He was very well read, a fluent conversationalist and appeared a most civilized man. Until one day I heard him defend, with icy conviction, in the name of tradition and culture – that most dangerous concept known as the 'identity' of the people – the practice of cutting off girls' clitorises to ensure their future abstemiousness.

One of the truths which remains unshakable in these times when the hurricanes of history are sweeping everything away is that civilization is a very thin veneer that can crack on the first impact with the demons of faith, at the first onslaught of social outrage. These demons are wandering loose in the country where they issued the *fatwa* against you, also in my country where another kind of fanatic has decided to construct universal happiness through terror, and are even in Europe where so many, many things have happened recently which could be interpreted as a victory for common sense and rationality over lies and dogma. It has not turned out that way. And you, living from hand to mouth so that the pack of hounds cannot reach you, are there to clarify any illusions and to remind us that the battle has not been – nor will ever be – won.

In Germany, where I now write, which is reunited in democracy thanks to the East German people's extraordinary freedom movement, there are now groups of skinhead savages hunting Turks and chanting the old racist slogans. In the France of the Declaration of Human Rights, respectable politicians from left and right are flirting with the policies of the Front National because it seems that xenophobia and

chauvinism now win votes. In Northern Ireland, in Spain, other 'patri-
ots' blow up innocent citizens to make abstract demonstrations. In
countries where this culture of tolerance, pluralism and freedom seems
most deeply rooted, a culture which, in recent years, so many millions
of people from Eastern Europe have hoped to imitate and attain, we
can see on a daily basis clear examples of that old, narrow spirit which
we thought buried.

The 'return to the tribe', to the particular, the move to wall oneself
up in one's own culture, beliefs and customs, shutting out everything
else, is not an unusual reaction to the rapid process of internationalization that the world, and particularly the West, is living through. It is a
defensive strategy in the face of the unknown and the formidable
challenges offered by a planet on which the development of freedom
has caused frontiers to disappear, making them increasingly artificial
and useless. But if this process is frustrated by the actions of the
retrograde forces opposed to it, forces that the process itself has
thrown up, then humanity will once again have made a pathetic step
backwards, just at the moment that it seemed better equipped than
ever to tame its demons.

We must not allow a complicit silence to shroud the persecution you
are suffering, or allow public opinion to grow accustomed to what is
happening to you. It is our obligation, as writers, for moral but also
practical reasons – because in a world where the threat of a crime
silences those who write, literature could not exist – to keep indignation and protest alive. We must remember that it is an intolerable
injustice and demand that governments and popular opinion should
press for its end, because there are very few cases like yours where the
line – which is so often faded or wavy – between the rational and the
irrational, the just and the unjust, the barbarous and the civilized is so
clearly visible.

Dear Salman, we will go to a football game together again and we'll
learn to sing 'La Cucaracha'.

Berlin, 7 February 1992

# The 'People' and the 'Decent People':
## On Contemporary Peru

The writer Abraham Valdelomar used to say: 'In this barbarous country, they call the delicate dragonfly a "bloodsucker".' The surrealist César Moro penned this aphorism: 'All over the world people make mistakes, but in Peru they only make mistakes.' And the story goes that a crafty old mayor at the beginning of the century calmed the fears of the inhabitants of Lima at the spread of Spanish flu that was wreaking havoc throughout America and advancing on Peru, with these words: 'Here, even flu goes soft in the head.'

One has to beware of the reverse chauvinism or masochistic patriotism that such jokes might disguise, but in fact, in the light of recent events, I have been wondering over the last few days if Peru has not now become what Idi Amin's Uganda or 'Emperor' Jean Bédel Bokassa's Central African Republic once were: one of the world's picturesque eccentricities. When, throughout the entire globe, despotic regimes that seemed quite indestructible are beginning to crumble and where civilian and democratic governments are everywhere replacing dictatorships, in Peru a lawfully elected president is stifling democracy and becoming a dictator, without great difficulty and with the approval of 'all the people and all the decent people of the country', as a distinguished gentleman declared when he rang my house to accuse me of betraying the fatherland for having asked the international community to throttle the *coup d'état* with economic sanctions (a plea that I now reiterate).

The support of 'the people' for the dictatorship is not excusable, of course, but it is understandable: those millions of Peruvians who, for several decades, have been reduced to horrific extremes of poverty by the dreadful populist policies of military and civilian governments and who, besides hunger, cholera, unemployment and filth, have had to cope with terrorism and counter-terrorism and are exposed to the break-up of all forms of legality and security in their poor shanty towns, would find it difficult to have a very clear idea of the medium or long term effects of a *coup d'état,* or the meaning of deeply rooted democratic principles. They put their trust in General Odría in 1948

289

and in General Velasco in 1968 and went out to cheer them, just as they are now cheering the brand new 'hard man', whom, as happened with the others, they will come to detest as soon as they discover that those in power are not their saviours but a bunch of cynical operators (several of whom, furthermore, prospered in the shadow of the previous military regime).

It is more difficult to explain the support for the coup shown by the 'decent people', like those businessmen of CONFIEP, the Confederation of Peruvian Industry, who, after a hypocritical declaration, have become an organic part of the dictatorship, responsible for the Industry portfolio. Those gentlemen are displaying a monumental blindness because, by identifying with a regime which sooner or later will be rejected by the Peruvian people with the same contempt with which they have thrown off *all* dictatorships, they are putting at risk not just their own futures, but something much more important, that has cost enormous effort to introduce and develop in Peru: notions of property, private enterprise, the market economy and liberal capitalism.

We fought and won a formidable battle against the nationalization of the financial system by the previous government with an argument that a significant proportion of Peruvian society came to accept: that political freedom and representative democracy are inseparable from a respect for private property and private enterprise and that to defend the one was also a way of defending the other. These businessmen, who went back on all they said in favour of democracy when they were afraid of being expropriated, have rushed to become the *geishas* of the new dictator and to receive from him the commercial perks by which they have always lived. In so doing, they have provided a magnificent service to supporters of statism and collectivism who had seemed to have lost the argument. They can now go on to the offensive again with renewed energy and raise an accusing finger: 'Isn't it clear that the word capitalist is synonymous with *coups d'état* and militarism in Peru?'

Yes, now it is clear, and it also means having a faulty memory and very few brain cells. Because what these people represented – private enterprise – was threatened in a democracy in 1987 and yet it was possible, by using the institutions and rights guaranteed by this democracy, to mobilize, defend and try to save something that, if it had fallen into the jaws of the state, would have functioned much worse than under their control. On the other hand, when a dictatorship, the dictatorship of General Velasco, decided to expropriate their estates, their newspapers, their fishing companies, their radio stations, their television channels etc., they had to accept the losses meekly, without being able to lift a finger to prevent them.

How, after such an experience, can they still believe that a military dictatorship – because that is what we now have in Peru, although the puppet that presides over it for the time being does not wear the stripes – is a firmer guarantee for private property and enterprise than a State of Law, with freedom of the press, and institutions, however defective, like an elected congress and an independent judiciary which can restrain the abuses and excesses of those in power? In truth, they do not believe it. They do not stop to think about it. They do not stop to think for one moment about the incalculable surprises in store for them and for every Peruvian once the Pandora's box of a regime based on brute force is opened. They are drunk with the illusion that the military can now really 'sort out' the terrorists, killing as many as necessary without having those sinister human rights organizations coming to cause trouble, that their beloved Chichonet will know how to run the unions with a firm hand and that the Minister of the Economy with the curls and cupid face that they have cultivated so assiduously – little Pinochet Boloña – will now begin to protect them, or rather to protect 'national industry', against heartless outside competition. One cannot even hope that when, soon, they discover that the collapse of democracy has increased terrorism, and the disenchantment of the 'people' with the dictatorship which has not given them what they expected, and has increased social violence, then they will learn the lesson. Did they learn it under Velasco?

For me, the most extraordinary aspect of what is happening in Peru is the obsequiousness and the indulgence shown to the dictatorship by certain communications networks that were expropriated by the previous military regime and returned to their owners under democracy (this was the first measure of President Belaúnde Terry when he returned to office in 1980). From the pen of some journalists who are among the most competent in the country and, supposedly, the most committed to freedom, I have read the most lavishly ornate arguments to justify the coup or to whitewash it, presenting it as a 'different coup' which, given the mitigating circumstances surrounding it, should be given a chance. If one were to believe them, then the high popularity of the 'coup' in opinion polls in the first days bears more weight than all those abstract arguments about democracy which, in practice, functioned very badly in Peru. Didn't Parliament sometimes seem like a circus? Weren't the judges corrupt? Didn't the institutions need cleaning up and putting in order? This is what the 'real country' wants, not the 'formal Peru' of political parties, and this is what legitimates the actions of Fujimori and the army. It is regrettable that it had to happen like this. But it has happened and it is too late to turn back, to reopen Congress and re-establish the rule of the constitution. Because that could provoke a 'popular uprising'.

If every dictatorial act approved by 'the people' and 'the decent people' according to opinion polls was irreversible, the director of the newspaper *Expreso* in Lima — which now acts almost as the official mouthpiece of the coup since 5 April — would still be in exile, stripped of Peruvian nationality, and the paper that he edits would still be in the hands of the state that confiscated it, because these outrages, according to the famous intellectual 'mastiffs' of the military regime that committed them, could not have been more popular. But, in fact, this is all a farce, mounted by sections of the media like those who now, instead of defending democracy against those who overthrew it, try to excuse them and find an accommodation with them.

I had (naïvely) considered that people like Manuel d'Ornellas and Patricio Ricketts — to name those who have been most servile to the coup — would be incapable of supporting a dictatorship in return for favours or personal gain. If journalists like these — who seemed to fight so tenaciously for Peru to stop being the barbarous and backward country that dictatorships, above all, had made it, and to embrace once and for all the culture of freedom — approve of what is happening and even try to benefit from it, then what can be expected of those that have neither their background nor their experience? How can the uncultured react lucidly if the cultured deceive themselves and deceive them with false reasons to defend the indefensible?

What makes many people like them in Peru act in this way is a sense of impotence that political democracy sometimes gives rise to in a country where the institutions and the parties are not, as yet, very democratic and where corruption and arbitrary acts often make a mockery of the law. And also the exasperation and moral indignation often felt when those who work within the democratic system seem to use this system in such a way as to prevent it from functioning. Yet history — and above all Peruvian history, which is so new — should have taught them that a dictatorship is a much worse remedy than the ills that it purports to cure. Because the defects – corruption, inefficiency, lack of culture – are not those of democracy but of society and can always find in arbitrary and overbearing regimes a wonderfully fertile ground in which to develop and become worse. It has always been so. And for that reason, after every dictatorship, we have had to start out, further and further behind, on that difficult – but irreplaceable – road of learning about democracy from within democracy itself. Today's setback plunges us back to the bottom of the well from which we emerged, so battered, twelve years ago.

'How can you attack a government that is going to cut down APRA and the communists? Have you already forgotten that they were your enemies?' This is a message I have been sent. Yes, APRA and the communists are my political enemies: I have fought a hard ideological and political battle against them. But as far as I am concerned, this battle can only be fought on equal ground that guarantees freedom and the judge of the contest can only be the people of Peru and not a crooked and thuggish judge who opposes reason with tanks. One of the few hopeful news items coming out of Peru is that the political parties have put aside their differences and disputes and have united in their opposition to the coup, in favour of the re-establishment of democracy – a democracy which is at once both definite and real, which allows coexistence within diversity and is capable, furthermore, of harmonizing within a viable system so many cultures, ethnic groups and different social interests as those which make up the explosive society of Peru. It is good that, from all parts of the political spectrum, the political parties have understood that it is now the first priority for every responsible Peruvian to defend this coexistence within the law, without being terrorized by opinion polls or by the farcical relationship between 'the people' and 'the decent people'.

Berlin, 25 April 1992

# The Death of Che

Nothing illustrates better the extraordinary changes in the political culture of our time than the almost furtive way in which the anniversary of the death of Che has been marked. He was assassinated twenty-five years ago – on 9 October 1967 – by a terrified sergeant obeying orders in a lost village in the east of Bolivia.

The legendary Comandante, with his long hair and blue beret, a machine gun over his shoulder and a cigar smoking between his fingers, whose image travelled round the world and who, in the 1960s, was a symbol of student revolt, the inspiration of a new radicalism and a model for the revolutionary aspirations of young people in five continents is now a half-forgotten figure who inspires and interests no one, whose ideas have become petrified in books without readers and who has been blurred by contemporary history to the point that he is mistaken for those third- or fourth-rank historical mummies lost in some obscure corner of the pantheon.

In these twenty-five years, social and political events have plainly given the lie to everything that Che predicted and have propelled humanity along a path which is diametrically opposed to the one that he wanted. Only the bourgeois democratic version of socialism survives; the socialism that he espoused has been wiped from the face of the earth by the masses which had to suffer its consequences, as in Russia or Central Europe, or has degenerated and changed into a strange hybrid, as in Popular China, where the Communist Party has just triumphantly approved in its last Congress the unstoppable march of the country towards market capitalism under the clear – and unique – direction of Marxist–Leninism. In Latin America and in Africa, the scarce revolutionary groups have died out and their survivors negotiate for peace and form political parties prepared, in word at least, to live with opponents within multi-party systems. It is true that liberal democracy has not spread throughout the world, but it is difficult to deny that it is today the most expansive and dynamic political system, which is gaining the most followers in every continent even if, among the recent converts to the philosophy of freedom, there are many defective, caricaturesque versions. What is now competing with democracy as a political alternative is no longer socialism, for which Che went to fight in Bolivia with a handful of Cuban comrades, but rather Muslim fundamentalist regimes and the reappearance of the furuncules of Fascist groups in the old and the new open societies.

The figure of the guerrilla has lost its former romantic halo. Now, behind the beard and hair blowing in the wind of that prototype, which twenty years ago seemed a generous idealist, we can glimpse the fanatical and cowardly silhouette of the terrorist waiting in the shadows to blow up cars and kill innocent people. To start up 'two, three Vietnams' seemed to many at the time a passionate watchword, the mobilization of the whole of suffering humanity against exploitation and injustice. Now it seems like a really psychotic and apocalyptic raving which could only lead to more hunger and violence than that already suffered by the poor of the world.

His *foco* theory, that flexible and heroic spearhead group whose activities would create the conditions for revolution, did not work anywhere and resulted, in Latin America, in thousands of young people who adopted it and attempted to put it into practice, sacrificing themselves tragically and opening the doors of their countries to cruel military tyrannies. His example and his ideas contributed more than anything to undermine democratic culture and to plant in universities, trade unions and political parties in the Third World a contempt for elections, pluralism, formal liberties, tolerance and human rights as being incompatible with authentic social justice. This delayed by at least two decades the political modernization of Latin America.

The Cuban Revolution that Che helped to establish after an epic campaign in which he was the second great protagonist, is now a pathetic sight, a small, oppressive and retrograde enclave, completely shut off from all forms of change, where the brutal fall in living standards of the people seems to be in direct proportion to the increase in internal purges and repression against the slightest symptoms, not of dissidence, but of the simple anxieties of ordinary people about their future. The society which, in its time, appeared to many as a beacon and as a mirror of a future humanity freed from egotism, profit, discrimination and exploitation, has become an historical anachronism which, in the short or medium term, will collapse dramatically.

Because of all this, and much more, the political and moral balance sheet of what Ernesto Guevara represented – and the mythology that his actions and ideas generated – is tremendously negative and the rapid decline of his image should not surprise us. Yet, that said, there is something in his personality and his life, as there is with Trotsky, which is always attractive and worthy of respect, no matter how hostile we are to his work. Is this because he was defeated, because he died according to his own principles, in a way that was utterly coherent with his political actions? Of course. Because in every field of human endeavour, it is difficult to find people who say what they believe and do what they say, but it is exceptionally rare in political life, where duplicity and cynicism are common currency, indispensable for the success and, at times, the mere survival of the political actors.

But in his case, he was also detached from and even contemptuous of power, when he held it, which is even rarer in political leaders of whatever affiliation. There has been much speculation about the differences that Che had with Fidel over the 'moral' incentives to workers that he favoured as opposed to the 'material' incentives that the Revolution adopted in the years that immediately preceded his leaving Cuba, and about the public criticisms that he made of the Soviet Union during his tour of Africa, which put the Cuban government in a difficult situation with a country that had already, by 1964, begun to subsidize the regime to the tune of a million dollars a day. But even if these disputes might have speeded up Che's departure, it is obvious that the form which this departure took is only conceivable in terms of his very firm commitment to the guerrilla theses that he had upheld. The naïve voluntarism lurking behind these theses was torn apart when, in the east of Bolivia, the peasants helped the army to wipe out the international guerrilla group which had come to save them. But this does not detract from the audacity and importance of his gesture.

Despite the fact that I was in Cuba on two occasions when he still held administrative office – as Minister of Industry and director of the National Bank – I never saw Che Guevara or heard him speak. But in 1964 I had unequivocal confirmation of the few privileges that power bequeathed to the number two in the Cuban revolution. I was then living in Paris, in a very modest apartment with two small rooms (which Carlos Barral, whom I once put up there, further downgraded by calling it *la pissotière*) in the rue du Tournon. And one day I received a message from Havana, from Che's first wife, Hilda Gadea, asking me to have as a guest a woman friend of hers who was returning from Cuba to Argentina and, because of the blockade, had to make the trip through Europe. The lady in question, who did not have the money for a hotel, turned out to be Celia de la Serna, Che's mother. She spent a few weeks in my house, before returning to Buenos Aires (or rather, to prison, and to death soon after). The memory of that episode has always stayed with me: the mother of the all-powerful Comandante Guevara, the number two in a revolution that was already by then spending a great deal of money financing revolutionary parties, groups and grouplets in half the world, did not have the money to pay for a hotel and had to rely on the solidarity of a more or less solvent polygraph.

It is good that the revolutionary illumination and the nihilistic and dogmatic example of Che Guevara has been discredited and that young people are no longer moved by the convictions that Che held, by which justice and progress do not depend on votes and on the laws approved by representative institutions, but on the military effectiveness of an enlightened and heroic vanguard. But it is not so good that the disenchantment with messianism and collective dogma has also brought with it the disappearance of idealism and even of mere interest and curiosity about politics in these new generations, in particular in societies which are now taking their first steps into freedom. For there is nothing that erodes and corrupts a political system as much as lack of popular participation, and that the responsibility for public matters should be confined – at the expense of everyone else – to a minority of professionals. If that happens – and it is happening now, surprisingly, in countries where the struggle against a one-party dictatorship was long and heroic – then all that remains of democracy is the name. It is an empty shell, because in that society, as in a dictatorship, all important matters are plotted and carried out at the whim of the leadership, behind the backs of the majority.

Only when it has disappeared or when it is desired as a beautiful ideal has democracy managed to inspire the sort of extreme commitment and sacrifice which is not so uncommon among the ranks of those who, like Che, fought for a messianic dogma. On the other hand, when the democratic ideal becomes a reality and then becomes routine and problematic, difficult and frustrating, this can breed despair, passive resignation or civic indifference in the majority of citizens. For that reason, paradoxically, the system of legality, rationality and freedom that we call democracy, despite having won so many battles recently, is still precarious and is likely, in the medium and long term, to be faced with new and more dangerous challenges.

Cambridge, Mass., October 1992

# Nations, Fictions

Ever since I first got to know him, many years ago, the Chilean historian Claudio Véliz has been organizing seminars. In the sixties he had his office in Chatham House, alongside Arnold Toynbee's, and he brought to London ideological Latin American economists and anthropologists to verify their inability to deal with the pragmatic English. He invited me to one of these reproductions of the Tower of Babel and I had a very good time.

Like the history to which he devotes his time, Claudio Véliz has become global and now directs La Conversazione, a tricontinental conference that moves intellectuals around between Oxford, Melbourne and Boston to talk about every topic imaginable. The one that has just been held was on nationalism, a theme that has now become topical as, suddenly, old nations have begun to disintegrate and others have begun to reconstruct or reinvent themselves in Europe, Asia and Africa, in a further turn of the screw to this spectacular end of millennium.

The paper that I commented on was by Professor Roger Scruton, a subtle essayist who had marshalled more complex arguments than one normally hears to defend his idea of the nation. The nation, according to Professor Scruton, stems from a communitarian feeling similar to, but much richer than, that of the tribe, that fraternity of the first person plural, the 'we' that incorporates the dead, and those still to be born, into the society of the living, as members with full rights. Language, religion and the land that they share are the basis of nationalist feeling. But writing enriches and 'immortalizes' it when, as in Latin, Hebrew, Arabic or English, with the King James Bible, it takes the form of representative religious texts through which the living speak with their ancestors and descendants. A community cemented in this way frees itself from history and acquires a metaphysical permanence which precedes and is much deeper than the constitution of the State, a modern phenomenon which – in only a few privileged cases, it is true – fits the nation like a glove on the hand.

But in the case of Europe, there is even more mortar to strengthen this structure. Its nations inherited the greatest achievement of the Roman Empire, a system of laws for the resolution of conflicts which are universal and independent of the arbitrary actions of those who govern. This inheritance has been particularly fertile in the case of Britain, where it has created a 'gravitational force of territorial jurisdictions', through which conflicts are resolved, contracts are legalized, institutions are strengthened and one lives in security and freedom thanks to the strong links established between the members of a national 'we' that feels and knows itself to be different from the rest, from 'them'.

I suspect that it would not worry Professor Roger Scruton that his delicate conceptual mechanism for describing what is a nation can only be applied to one nation, Great Britain, and that all the others in the world are exceptions. He is that *rara avis* of our time: an intelligent conservative without an inferiority complex. I always read him with interest, and sometimes with admiration, although his essays – and the provocative journal that he edits, *The Salisbury Review* – often give me confirmation of the difference that Hayek described between a conservative and a liberal.

His thesis seems to me an elegant sophism, an attractive intellectual creation which, as happens in fictions, falls to pieces when set against reality. I have nothing against fictions, I dedicate my life to writing them and I am convinced that existence would be intolerable without them for most mortals. But there are benign and malign fictions, those that enrich human experience and those that impoverish it and are a source of violence. For the blood that it has caused to be spilled throughout history, for the way in which it has contributed to stoke up prejudices, racism, xenophobia, lack of communication between peoples and cultures, for the alibis that it has provided for authoritarianism, totalitarianism, colonialism, religious and ethnic genocide, the nation seems to me to be a pristine example of a malign fantasy.

A nation is a political fiction imposed on a social and geographic reality almost always by force, for the benefit of a political minority and maintained through a system of uniformity which imposes homogeneity, either gently or severely, at the price of the disappearance of a pre-existing heterogeneity and sets up barriers and obstacles which often make the development of religious, cultural or ethnic diversity impossible within its boundaries. Many are now scandalized at the operations of racial and religious cleansing of the Serbs against the Bosnians in the former Yugoslavia, but the reality is that the history of every nation is plagued by savagery of this kind which patriotic history — another fiction — takes charge of hiding. This has happened not only in New Guinea and Peru — two nations that Scruton mentions with scepticism — but also in the oldest and most respected 'imaginary communities', as Benedict Anderson calls them, those which through their longevity and power seem to have been born with the form and spontaneity of a tree or a storm.

No nation has arisen *naturally*. The coherence and fraternity still displayed by some also mask frightening realities beneath the embellishing fictions — be they literary, historical or artistic — in which their identity is formed. In these nations as well we find pitilessly destroyed those 'contradictions and differences' — creeds, races, customs and languages, which are not always minority — which the nation, like Camus's Caligula, needs to destroy in order to feel safe, to guard against the risk of fragmentation. And not even that multitude of African and Latin American nations that have come about as a result of the eccentric demarcations imposed on those continents by the colonial powers have such an arbitrary and artificial lineage as Transjordan, a country invented by Winston Churchill with the stroke of a pen on a Sunday afternoon, according to his famous *boutade*.

The difference is that the old nations seem more serious, necessary and realistic than the new ones because, like religions, they have acquired an abundant literature and also seem to be validated by the oceans of blood that they have spilled. But this is a mirage. Because, contrary to the hypotheses that Roger Scruton lays out in his conclusions, it is extraordinary that, despite the enormous efforts made by the oldest nations to create this common denominator, this protective and isolationist 'we', what are becoming each day more manifest in these nations are the irresistible centrifugal forces that challenge this myth. It is happening in France, in Spain, let alone in Italy and even in Great Britain itself. And, of course, in the United States where the development of multiculturalism frightens conservatives like Allan Bloom as well as progressives like Arthur Schlesinger, who see in this flowering of diverse cultures — African, Hispanic, Native American — a serious threat to the nation (which of course it is). With few exceptions, modern societies display an increasing mixture of 'them' and 'us' in very diverse forms — racial, religious, linguistic, regional, ideological – which weakens and erases the geographical and historic common denominator that Charles Maurras called 'the land of the dead', on which the idea of the nation has been founded since the Enlightenment.

Is Great Britain an exception? Did this truth, this coherent, compact, integrated society formed by the sea, the climate, common law, reformed religion, individualism and freedom, which Roger Scruton evokes so beautifully in his writings, ever exist? Over the past thirty years I have frequently visited and lived for long periods of time in this country – the country I admire the most – and I have observed and studied it with unceasing devotion. But I have never seen what Scruton sees, this metaphysical Albion. And of course much less now than in that winter of 1962 when, as soon as I had crossed the Channel and got on the Dover train, I was presented with a cup of tea and a biscuit, which shook my tenacious incredulity with respect to national psychologies.

Great Britain is today the Austrian Popper, the Latvian Isaiah Berlin and the Islamic fundamentalists who burn *The Satanic Verses* in Brighton and want to kill Salman Rushdie. And it is also the Pakistani Rushdie and the Indian-Trinidadian V.S. Naipaul, the most British of British writers, not only because of the elegance of his English, but above all because none of his colleagues can equal him in those traditional English literary virtues: irony, sardonic wit, gentle scepticism. Can we take seriously a 'we' that includes Roger Scruton, whose political plan for Europe is a revival of the Austro-Hungarian Empire, with the miners' leader Arthur Scargill, who would like to establish the Soviet Socialist Republic of Great Britain and with the drunken and painted hordes that I've had to contend with when I've been to watch Chelsea Football Club? I fear that despite his Celtic and Norman ancestors and my ancestors – an outrageous mixture of Extremadurans with Catalans and Incas – that it would be much more consistent to have a 'we' that would include him and me, the only two writers in the world who admire Margaret Thatcher and detest Fidel Castro.

Nationalism is a form of lack of culture that pervades all cultures and coexists with all ideologies, a chameleon resource at the service of politicians of every persuasion. In the nineteenth century it seemed that socialism would put an end to it, that the theory of class struggle, revolution and the proletarian international would lead to the disappearance of frontiers and the establishment of universal society. The reverse occurred. Mao strengthened the idea of the nation to a chauvinistic degree and now, with the bankruptcy of communism, it is in the name of nationalism that regimes like North Korea, Vietnam and Cuba justify their existence. They allege that their rigid systems of censorship and isolation are there to defend national culture threatened by 'them'.

Beneath these pretexts there lies a truth. All nations – poor or rich, backward or modern – are today less stable than they once were. There is a process of internationalization of life which, in some cases more rapidly, in other cases more slowly, is eroding them, gnawing at those boundaries that had been established and preserved at the price of so much blood. It is not socialism that is perpetrating this outrage in the world. It is capitalism. A practical system – not an ideology – for producing and distributing wealth, which, at a certain moment in its development, found frontiers to be obstacles to the growth of markets, companies and capital. And then, without proclaiming it, without boasting about it, without hiding its intention – to gain profits – behind big words, the capitalist system, through the internationalization of production, trade and property, has imposed on nations other coordinates and demarcations which create links and interests between individuals and societies which in practice increasingly denaturalize the idea of the nation. Creating world markets, transnational companies, disseminating shares and property in societies throughout the globe, this system has been depriving nations, in the economic sphere, of many of the prerogatives on which their sovereignty was based. This has had already an extraordinary effect in the cultural field, and is also beginning to have an effect in the political sphere, where the steps that are beginning to be taken, here and there, towards the formation of vast supranational organizations like the European Community or the Free Trade Treaty in America, would have been inconceivable in any other way.

This process must be welcome. The weakening and dissolution of nations within broad and flexible economic and political communities, under the sign of freedom, will not only contribute to the development and well-being of the planet, lessening the risk of warlike conflicts and opening new opportunities for trade and industry; it will also allow the diversification and development of genuine cultures, which arise and grow out of a need for expression of a homogeneous group, even though they do not serve the will of political power.

Paradoxically, only internationalization can guarantee the right to existence for those minority cultures that the nation has swept away in order to consolidate the myth of its untouchability.

Cambridge, Mass., November 1992

# Saul Bellow and Chinese Whispers

In 1957 the writer Wang Meng published a short story that the Party considered to be suspect of revisionism. Sent for re-education to a forced labour camp and banned from writing, Meng was rehabilitated in 1978. Twenty years of ostracism had not weakened his communist faith or his literary vocation because when he gained his freedom, he continued writing stories, which made him very popular, and he took up political activism once again. In 1986, the Party named him Minister of Culture, a post that he held until 1989. After the events of Tiananmen Square, Meng was part of a great purge against intellectuals who had shown themselves to be lukewarm and did not warmly approve the massacre. He lost his ministry but – part of the indecipherable political hieroglyph of China – he kept his place on the Central Committee. The rumours that pass for information in the land of Mao imply that Wang Meng is part of a 'revisionist' minority in the Party which is quietly waiting for its moment to launch an offensive against the 'ultras' which overthrew it in 1989.

Is this anti-orthodox counter-offensive about to break out? It would appear so. And the signs that point to this, as is often the case in communist countries, can be found in literature. At the beginning of 1989 Wang Meng published a story entitled 'Hard Oats'. In it an enterprising old man decides that his family should become up to date, modernize its customs and that, instead of having a plate of oats when they get up, according to time-honoured local custom, they should breakfast like Westerners. The innovation, however, leads to a number of setbacks for the protagonists who, at the end of the story, go back to the 'hard oats' of the title.

A year and a half after this story appeared, in September of this year, the cultural publication, *Wen Yi Bao,* seemingly controlled by the 'ultra' group, published a violent attack against the story of Wang Meng, accusing it of a major crime: that of criticizing, in course of its gastronomic plot, the policies of Deng Xiaoping. The diviners – the press correspondents – interpreted that an attack of this sort was unthinkable without the approval or the orders of the current Minister of Culture, He Jingzhi, who is considered to be an intransigent 'ultra'. They deduced from all this that a new purge against undomesticated artists and intellectuals was on the way.

But something different occurred. Wang Meng circulated a document defending his story, which he would have sent to all the members of the Central Committee, and, if this were not enough, he decided to instigate a legal claim against *Wen Yi Bao,* demanding reparation and public apologies. Considering that in all the history of Chinese communism, no one had ever dared to put a publication of the Party in the dock, there could only be two explanations. Meng had lost his mind or had solid support in the Party bureaucracy. The latter interpretation has been gaining ground in the last few days because it is said that a tribunal has taken up the dispute, and that various publications in Beijing and in the interior of China have dared to mention it.

This story of 'Hard Oats' and Wang Meng has restored my optimism. I read it in an article by the *New York Times* correspondent in Beijing, Nicholas D. Kristof, after participating with Saul Bellow in a discussion about culture in the modern world which had left me very depressed. Although not all of Bellow's ideas on the subject convinced me, many of them seemed to go to the heart of the matter and describe such a state of disintegration in Western art, thought and literature that it is difficult to know how this can be corrected.

In the United States there are good writers and important intellectuals but, unlike what happens in France or Italy, for example, these two aspects rarely come together in one person. 'Creators' like Melville, Hemingway or Faulkner are often men of action, remote and often disdainful of the university milieu in which 'thinkers' are usually quartered, far from the noise of the world. There are few cases of novelists or poets who have taken on an important, parallel, intellectual function as political ideologues, philosophers, literary critics or cultural historians. Saul Bellow is one of these exceptions.

All his work is a passionate exploration of the ideas which have filled his life, the way that they have filled the life of his characters, the most celebrated of whom, the thwarted humanist Valentin Gersbach in *Herzog,* is a tragicomic exaggerated symbol of the condition of the intellectual. Like Gersbach, Bellow has seen in the work of certain thinkers and artists the development of civilization, the motor force of a long process of the humanization of life, in which man has overcome the state of nature, acquiring a moral conscience and an aesthetic sensibility which protect him against barbarism. And, like the hero of his novel, he has also dedicated part of his life to promoting among the new generations the reading of those great classics in whose pages men and women find reasons and the courage to overcome the prejudices that passed for science, the fanaticism disguised as religion and the stereotypes or superstitions that masqueraded as knowledge. But unlike Valentin Gersbach, who is punished severely by real life for thinking that it can be identified with the life of ideas, one might have thought that contemporary history, instead of giving the lie to Saul Bellow, might rather have confirmed his ideas.

After the disintegration of the USSR and the system that it embodied, is not the type of society represented by the United States the only viable model today? And this is the model of society which, despite raising objections and criticisms to it, some of which have been very severe, Bellow has defended for over thirty years as being the least bad, the most flexible and improvable system, the heir to the best tradition of humanity. To reach these conclusions, Bellow had to break out of many personal religious and cultural strait-jackets. The first of these, his own family, were ultra-orthodox Jews who had emigrated from Russia to Canada and then on to Chicago, were reluctant to become assimilated into North American life and had sent him at the age of four to a rabbinical school to train him as a rabbi. Later came the strait-jacket of what he has called the 'three tyrants' of his youth and early adulthood: Marx, Lenin and Freud.

For many years now, Bellow has given a course on the masterworks of literature at the University of Chicago which has become famous. It has been his way of fighting for the only revolution he believes in: the revolution that is rooted in the spirit and in the imagination and nurtures all other human activities from that impalpable centre. And nothing, according to him, has contributed so greatly to enriching life and attacking the savagery and folly that are also part of the human experience as the great literary creations. Principally, these are the classics which, from Ancient Greece and Rome, the Renaissance and the Middle Ages, have passed all the tests and reach us strengthened by those intervening cultures which inherited them, reinterpreted them and gave them a contemporary meaning. They are the connecting thread of civilization.

Bellow's current pessimism is due to the fact that, in his opinion, this thread has now been broken and that intelligence has a very precarious existence today. The United States might now be without rivals in the military and political spheres but culturally it is a giant with feet of clay. The pseudo-cultural products of mass consumption – which people try to make presentable with the tag of 'popular culture', but which are a base and vulgar form of human invention – have almost completely displaced genuine creativity.

There is a risk of disintegration in the United States, as a result of ethnic exclusivism and the demands of the so-called minorities – racial, religious, sexual and cultural – who, instead of accepting assimilation, want their own life, independent and protected, and in permanent antagonism with the rest. Education which was formally the integrating factor *par excellence* in North American society and the spearhead of its progress, is now instead one of the most active instruments of its decadence and impoverishment.

The university has abdicated its obligation to defend culture against fraud. Of course its technical and scientific departments still train good specialists, efficient professionals, albeit blind to everything outside the confines of their specialist interest. But the humanities have fallen into the hands of falsifiers and sophists of every hue, who pass off ideology as knowledge and intellectual snobbery as modernity and who make young people feel an indifference or a disgust for the life of books. Through the fault of the pharisees without and the philistines within, the great classic tradition of literature and philosophy which made modern liberal society possible is sweetly dying in the campuses of North American academe, with their impeccable gardens and well-stocked libraries.

Saul Bellow wrote a prologue for Allan Bloom's *The Closing of the American Mind* (1987), which is a savage indictment written to show, according to its author, how higher education has betrayed democracy and impoverished the souls of today's students, and although he assures us that he disagrees with Bloom on many issues, the reasons for his pessimism seem to me to be very similar to those outlined in the book. Professor Bloom reproaches North American universities in the same terms as Julien Benda reproached the intellectuals of his day in *La Trahison des clercs:* for having turned their backs on the classic tradition, substituting the cult and the envigorating study of the great thinkers and artists of the past for the fraudulent idols of an alleged modernity. And to have enshrined in the cloisters an aesthetic and ethical relativism in which all ideas are equal, and where there are no hierarchies or values.

If literary works only refer to other works, not to the life of the author, or to history, or to the great moral, social or individual problems, and that there is no point in judging them as good or bad, profound or banal, but only as different manifestations of a protean and almost self-sufficient form which lives and reproduces itself on the margins, without a visceral relationship with humanity, then why read them? To submit onself, through them, to the textual pulverizations, the esoteric sleight of hand, the rhetorical game of mirrors that constitute academic criticism today? How can authentic literature survive among the cretinizing artefacts of the pseudo-cultural industry which corner the market place and the anti-humanist chatter of the universities? Who will believe, in a world like this, that poems help one to live, that novels unveil the hidden truths, that, thanks to great literature, life is not much more violent, sad or boring than it actually is?

How? Who? The one thousand two hundred million Chinese, of course. They know that literature is one of the most important and dangerous things in the world; no sophist will be able to speak for them. If this were not so, would poor Wang Meng have spent twenty years in a labour camp for writing *one story*? Would the story of a few pages, 'Hard Oats', have caused the uproar that I have described if literature were not dynamite in the hands of a good writer? They know that literature is contaminated with life, that it is a good place to go and breathe when the air becomes rarefied and the world asphyxiating, that it is an irrefutable demonstration that the life we lead is insufficient to placate our desires and for that reason it is an irresistible spur to fight for a different life. The Iranians also know it because, if this were not so, why has Salman Rushdie been in hiding now for one thousand and twelve days, to avoid being killed by fanatics? And the Cubans also know it very well, because, if it were not something essential, why would Fidel Castro have ordered his thugs in the 'Rapid Action Brigade' to beat up the poet María Elena Cruz Varela so savagely in her own home a few days ago?

It is true that freedom, the market and economic development, which bring so many benefits to men, often trivialize intellectual life and prostitute not only its teaching, but also the practice of literature itself. For those of us for whom reading poems and fiction is as indispensable as drinking water, this seems terrible. In fact it is not, at least not for the great majority of people. They can carry on quite well without literature and satisfy their thirst for unreality by watching trash on the television or reading romances. Modern democratic society has mechanisms through which important matters can be discussed and criticized without having to go through poetry, theatre and the novel. It is this reality that has contributed to making literature, in these societies, a mere entertainment, or a form of snobbery for a precious few, which has deprived literary endeavour of ambition, depth and vitality.

Fortunately there are a few Deng Xiaopings, Fidel Castros, ayatollahs, Kim Il Sungs and their like still loose in the world. They have tried to bring the heavens to the earth and like all those who have attempted to do so, they have created unliveable societies. In these small and sordid infernos where they reign, literature also reigns, despite – or rather, thanks to – the commissars and the censors, with their tempting mirages and their tender images, who offer answers to problems or the splendid lie of a life that will one day come about.

Berlin, November 1991

# Visual Contact

Class struggle was replaced by racial struggle and this in turn has been replaced by the battle of the sexes as the main issue in North American life. Those who criticized President Clinton for beginning his term of office by opening up a debate with his decision to lift the restrictions on homosexuals serving in the armed forces were wrong to imply that this is a marginal issue. It was up to a few years ago; now it is the most hotly discussed issue in North American public opinion, something which in many different guises appears daily in court cases, administrative disputes, religious campaigns and political actions, and is generating a copious literature, both academic and journalistic.

In the small world of university life which I have been inhabiting for the past few months, first in Harvard and now in Princeton, I see it everywhere: the 'sexual minorities' of gays and lesbians present their demands in official publications and panels, they have offices and assessors provided by the university and, within the academic community, this leads to a hypersensibility laced with fear which ethnic minorities used to cause the last time that I came to teach in this country. Then the worst suspicion that could be levelled at a professor was to be racist; now it is to be sexist.

All this seems to me to be highly civilized, a praiseworthy effort to combat the discrimination suffered in all societies of the world by women and those who do not practice sexual orthodoxy. (The scale of these prejudices could be seen recently in Peru, when President Fujimori threw out on to the street, by a stroke of his pen, one third of the diplomatic service, accusing them of being 'homosexuals', and instead of provoking a storm of criticism, this evil action increased his popularity.) Like economic exploitation or racial discrimination, machismo is the source of innumerable and insidious injustices, legitimated by culture, committed by the strong against the weak – behaviour which Hayek, at the end of his life, argued was the Achilles' heel of democracy: the power of the majority which is detrimental to the minority.

But since, in this case, the origin of the ill is in the warp and weft of culture itself and is part of the nature of that body of ideas, practices, manners, ethical projects, myths and codes that dictates our behaviour, the real remedy for the problem will only come about through profound cultural changes. Administrative provisions and judicial action can lessen its impact, compensate some victims, correct the most flagrant excesses, but it will be difficult to root out. Until there is a deep-rooted reform in the way we understand sex and encourage understanding between the sexes in the world in which we live, prejudice will continue to cause harm and run like quicksilver between those superficial barriers.

And there is also the risk that by striking too often at just one of the enemy's flanks or by seeing enemies where there are none, the fight against sexism is distorted and becomes ridiculous or else causes injustices which are equivalent to those that it seeks to outlaw. This is the theme, an explosive mix of fire and ice, of the most recent play written and directed by David Mamet, *Oleanna,* which opened in Boston a few months ago and has now come to New York.

In a private university, Carol, a student with problems, goes to the office of a professor to discuss her grades. He is just about to buy a house and obtain tenure. John likes to teach and has heterodox ideas which he has expounded in a book in which, for example, he challenges the idolatry of higher education as a universal right and argues that university classes often alienate the minds of the young. He is sure of himself and slightly arrogant. But he seems to be an understanding and responsible teacher because when he sees the insecurity and anguish of the young woman, he offers to help her: he'll forget the grades, allow her to pass the course and he tells her to come to his office to discuss what she does not understand in the classes. He sees her out with an affectionate pat on the back.

This dialogue in the first act, banal in the extreme, then hangs like a magic object which becomes metamorphosed and unimaginably poisoning in the second and third acts when we discover that, deconstructed and reconstructed by Carol (who is now active in a feminist group), everything that John said – all those words that sounded so obvious and insipid – form the basis of an accusation of sexual harassment which will jeopardize the tenure and end up destroying the career of the professor.

The real characters of the play are the words themselves, shifting sands that can swallow up the best intentions at each step, sinister traps which, in an unguarded moment, can ensnare the hunter. For in fact, everything that John said on that occasion could also make him appear abusive and exploitative, someone overreaching his power and taking advantage of his masculine condition. But for this interpretation to become possible, one would have to have listened to, copied down, twisted and adjusted the remarks of John with the sick sensibility of Carol and have imbued his gestures and silences with a significance that only the light of religion or an ideology could have given them.

The ceremony that takes place in the anonymous college of *Oleanna* refers to a contemporary problem and contributes to a lively debate in the United States but, in fact, it reproduces, in modern garb, a very old conflict: between intolerance and its victims, between fanaticism and its devastating effects. It is the old story of the inquisitor delving into the innermost reaches of an inoffensive person to detect heresy and of the commissar who invents dissidents and conspirators to reinforce orthodoxy.

The real tragedy of John, the pernicious consequences of Carol's action, will only begin to be assessed after the curtain has fallen. Because, even if he finds another post, will this purged professor ever trust words again, will he express himself, when he gives his classes, advises his students or writes his books, with the spontaneity and conviction that he had before he discovered, thanks to Carol, how dangerous and destructive words could be? In future he will always have a secret censor crouching at the back of his consciousness, alerting him and restraining him. And although he lives in a society whose laws and rules guarantee freedom, when he comes to think, write and teach, John will never again be a free man.

The benefit to Carol of adopting an ideology is quite clear. What were once inhibitions and complexes with regard to others have become certainties; and the violence within her has been given shape and direction, transforming into a belligerence against men that self-destructive feeling that had previously prevented her from studying, or rather, from learning. But that feminism which she took to sectarian and grotesque extremes is not a mere product of neurosis, an entirely fictional construction. The spectators discover this suddenly, in the final chilling minutes of the drama, when John, beside himself, pounces on the woman, hits and insults her, using the whole range of macho scatology. They discover that, despite all, the dragon in skirts was to some extent right.

This work by David Mamet, like others by him, has a biting vitality because, apart from being constructed with the skill of a consummate craftsman, it is a polemical commentary on a contemporary problem. Does it signal the return of 'committed' theatre, which seemed to have been buried under many layers of happenings, absurd works or terrible musical comedies like *Evita* or *Les Misérables*? In any event, this is real theatre and although it is full of ideas and thought-provoking moments, it is no less imaginative and daring than this other type of theatre I have mentioned, which has a contempt for history and reality and strives for pure fiction, mere spectacle. And the public is responding very well to it, to judge by the interminable queues at the Orpheum Theatre and the prices of the ticket touts.

Some feminists accuse David Mamet of having made Carol a caricature, of having accentuated her defects out of all reality. I think, however, that *Oleanna* gives quite an accurate, and perhaps even understated, description of the excesses in the fight against machismo in certain university campuses in the United States. I have been astonished at the number of cases that I have come to hear about of professors reprimanded, moved or relieved of their posts for supposed misdeeds of this nature. So much so that, exaggerating somewhat but not much, I would venture to say that a spectre is running through the departments of Romance languages in the universities of the United States: sexual harassment. The most nervous are, naturally enough, my Italian colleagues. What most worries them is the so-called 'visual contact', which in some quarters is now accepted as a grave error, something that a student has the right to consider an offence, a sexist attempt at degrading her feminine condition. How to prevent one's expression from taking on unconsciously, at the most unexpected moment, a lustful sheen or sinful glow? By killing libido with doses of bromide, so it seems, or for those enemies of chemicals like me, by always staring at the ceiling, at the wall.

Princeton, NJ, February 1993

# The Penis or Life: The Bobbitt Affair

In a recently published book of essays, *El caimán ante el espejo* ('The Alligator in Front of the Mirror', Ediciones Universal, Miami, Florida, 1993), Uva de Aragón Clavijo advances a polemical thesis: the political violence that has bloodied the history of Latin America, and of Cuba in particular, is an expression and a product of machismo, of 'homocentric culture' that is deeply rooted throughout the continent.

'Militarism and *caudillismo,* the endemic evils of our America,' she argues, 'have their origins, in our opinion, in the cult of virility.' And on another page of her disturbing formulation, she sums up three and a half decades of Castro's revolution with an allegory that the film censors in my youth would have classified as unsuitable for young ladies. 'One man penetrated a female people, which opened its legs to receive him. After the first orgasm of pleasure was over, the genuine thrusts in search of liberation were to no avail. The dead weight of masculine strength still captivates some, kills others and controls the majority.'

On the evening of the book launch at Florida International University, which I attended, Carlos Alberto Montaner, who presented the book with his usual humour and flair, concluded that Uva's formula for peace and tolerance in our people was that the culture of Latin America should be 'gelded'. He told me later that when he said this, a shudder ran through the auditorium and that, to a man, all of us males pressed our knees together. This is an unfounded fear in the case of Uva de Aragón Clavijo, a mild-mannered friend whom I know would be incapable of inflicting such surgery even on a chicken or a rabbit. Her extremism has never moved beyond the intellectual sphere. In politics, she is a moderate within the Cuban exile community, an activist in the Democratic Platform which proposes a dialogue with the regime in order to achieve the island's peaceful transition to democracy. And all the other essays in *El caimán ante el espejo* bristle with exhortations that the hatreds of Cain should disappear and that Cubans outside and inside the regime should at last coexist and collaborate.

But while under the blazing Florida sun in the middle of last year, Uva was elaborating her theoretical accusations against what some feminists have baptized the phallocracy, another 'Hispanic' in the United States (here all Latin Americans are known by this name), Lorena Gallo — a young Ecuadorian woman educated in Venezuela — proceeded, without metaphors of any kind and in the crudest way, to decapitate her husband sexually. This ex-marine infantryman, ex-taxi driver, ex-construction worker and current bouncer was baptized with a name that seems a programme for life: John Wayne Bobbitt.

The story has travelled the world and here, in the past few weeks, no one has talked about anything else — in the newspapers, on the radio, on the television, everywhere, as if a phantom more terrifying than that of the celebrated *Manifesto* was loose in this society: the castration complex. (I am referring, of course, to the phantom of the *Manifesto* of Karl Marx, not to that of Valerie Solanas, the author some three decades ago, as some of you will remember, of a *Manifesto for Cutting up Men,* which the current situation has revived and made fashionable. In the mid sixties, she fired three shots at Andy Warhol, not for the terrible paintings that he was perpetrating, but for the generic crime of being a man.)

I summarize the facts with the objectivity of which I am capable, and which my newspaper sources permit. In the early morning of 23 June last year, at a place in Virginia, John Wayne Bobbitt returned home drunk and forced his wife to make love. Married for four years, the couple got on quite badly, they had had their separations and reconciliations and many witnesses agreed that the husband often illtreated Lorena, a manicurist in a beauty salon. On several occasions her boss and her female workmates saw the marks of conjugal violence on the face and body of the Ecuadorian.

Since there are no witnesses, it is more difficult to prove the 'Hispanic's' accusations that her husband raped her continually and he, of course, denies it, accusing his wife, in turn, of being bad-tempered and a nymphomaniac. In any case, on the fateful night of 23 June, after the sexual act, John Wayne Bobbitt fell asleep. Humiliated and in pain, Lorena stayed awake for a long time and then got up for a glass of water. In the kitchen, she caught sight of a household knife, twelve inches long, with a red handle, which she picked up in a state of almost hypnotic confusion. She went back to the bedroom, lifted up the sheets and, with a skilful butcher's slice, she rid her husband of the emblem of his virility. Then she fled.

While the bar bouncer had an inconsiderate and bloody awakening, Lorena was fleeing through the dark, deserted streets of Manassas, at the wheel of the family car. A mile and a half from her home, she discovered that she still had, in one hand, the weapon and, in the other, the body of the crime. She put on the brakes and threw out of the car window, into some brambles, the kitchen knife and what had been the penis of John Wayne Bobbitt. Both were picked up some hours later by the police and the latter was reinstated on to the body of Lorena's husband in a nine-hour operation which, it seems, has been a major achievement of medical science. According to all accounts, and in particular that of the interested party – I have heard him state this on television – the most photographed and most publicized penis in the history of the United States is beginning to function again, although still weakly and not, I imagine, with the same excesses of old.

But all these are negligible, almost superfluous, details compared with the corollary. The real show came later. Initially, when the story first hit the headlines, it seemed that the hero would be John Wayne Bobbitt, a long-standing resident who had been decapitated and mended and the villain would be Lorena Gallo, the perpetrator of the offence and on top of this, a very recent immigrant and an 'Hispanic'. This seemed to be the case when the court of Manassas acquitted John of the alleged crime of rape on 23 June and he made a successful appearance on the popular Howard Stern programme, whose viewers donated more than $200,000 for his defence costs.

But then came the mobilization and the formidable counter-attack of feminist movements which, in a few weeks, gave the situation a totally different slant and turned Lorena Gallo into a Joan of Arc of the struggle for women's emancipation, the defender of women's rights which, from time immemorial, had been trampled underfoot by the unjust, patriarchal society. They transformed John Wayne Bobbitt into a malign and deservedly punished incarnation of this system, into the embodiment and prototype of that abusive, phallocratic beast which, from the dawn of time, has discriminated against, harassed, depowered and sodomized women, physically, morally, psychologically and culturally, preventing them from fulfilling their potential and taking charge of their lives in as complete a way as possible.

Psychiatry was the leading edge of the attack in the court room where Lorena Bobbitt was on trial. One of the three women doctors called by the defence declared, in the most memorable of all the technical depositions given to the jury, that the accessory that Lorena had cut off was not at all what it appeared to be – that is to say, a cylindrical protuberance made up of flesh and veins and traces of sperm. What was it then? An abstract coefficient, a symbolic structure, an emblematic icon of domestic horror, of servile subjection, of the blows that Lorena received, of the insults that tormented her ears, of the ignominious panting that assailed her in her husband's drunken nights. With an impeccable sense of theatrical effect, she concluded: 'For Lorena Bobbitt the choice was simple: the penis or life. And what is more important? The penis of a man or the life of a woman?'

Alongside this intellectual and scientific offensive, in the streets the activists were growing in strength. Many organizations representing 'Hispanic' communities in the United States had arrived to swell the ranks of the feminist movements in defence of Lorena Bobbitt, which proclaimed that what was really at stake in the Court of Manassas was not an alleged sexual crime, but an ethnic and cultural crime, a typical case of abuse and discrimination against the underprivileged Latin American immigrant by the domineering, racist and exploitative Anglo-Saxon. Would the court legitimate, by its sentencing of the symbolic Lorena, the miserable condition of neglect and ill-treatment suffered by citizens of 'Hispanic' origins in the United States? And in Ecuador a female crowd caught up in the debate threatened to 'castrate one hundred gringos' if Lorena was sentenced to just one day in prison.

In one of his lucid essays, 'Killing an Elephant', Orwell recounts how in his days as a policeman of the British Empire in Burma, he had to shoot a poor pachyderm who had bolted in the streets of the city because the pressure of the crowd that surrounded him did not allow him to act in any other way. This must have been the psychological state of the poor jurors – seven women and five men – of the Court of Manassas, on whose shoulders fell the responsibility of judging the wan Lorena Gallo, whom they naturally let off, declaring that her actions were dictated by irresistible, irrational forces. I am not saying that, judged impartially, they should have found against her. What I am saying is that in these conditions of real national – and even international – hysteria, in which they had to act as judges, it was not possible for them to display impartiality or lucidity or perhaps even a minimum of rationality. The trial was not a trial; it was a political showpiece in which almost all the tremendous contradictions and opposing forces which keep the present North American society in a state of permanent crisis, played their parts. Is this a symptom of health, of constant renewal, or of anarchy and decadence? Until recently, I thought it was the former. Now, along with Saul Bellow, I think that it could perhaps be the latter.

And I think of the depressing sequel to this story which, aside from its picturesque and grotesque aspects, reveals something alarming in what we could call the state of culture in this country. What am I referring to? The fact that both John Wayne Bobbitt and Lorena Gallo seem to have their futures assured thanks to the tragic events in which they were the main protagonists. I read this morning in the *New York Times* that in simultaneous press conferences, the publicity agents of both partners have announced that John has received several film and television offers which, at the moment, he is considering; also contacts for radio and publishing, and that he has already planned a succulent series of appearances on the small screen throughout the year. With regard to Lorena, her agent has registered to date one hundred and five paid audiovisual appearances as well as three offers from Hollywood to sell her story to the cinema. And various publishing houses have sent her tempting contracts to write her autobiography.

I do not want to draw any conclusions because they are all so blindingly, painfully obvious. I will just keep on giving my classes twice a week, in the ice and snow of Washington, looking at the ceiling so that none of my female students can accuse me of 'visual harassment', my loins firmly girded against the cold and, well, just in case.

Washington DC, December 1993

# The Truth of Lies

Ever since I wrote my first story, people have asked me if what I write is 'true'. Although my replies sometimes satisfy the questioners, every time that I answer that particular enquiry, however sincerely, I am left with the uncomfortable feeling of having said something that never gets to the heart of the matter.

The question as to whether novels are true or false matters as much to certain people as whether they are good or bad and many readers judge the latter by the former. The Spanish inquisitors, for example, banned the publication and importation of novels in the Spanish American colonies with the argument that these absurd and nonsensical – that is, lying – works could be bad for the spiritual health of the Indians. For that reason, the Spanish Americans only read contraband fiction for three hundred years and the first novel to be published under that name in Spanish America appeared only after Independence (in Mexico in 1816). By banning not particular works, but a literary genre in the abstract, the Inquisition established something that, in its eyes, was a law without exceptions: that novels always lie, that they all offer a false vision of the world. Years ago, I wrote a study ridiculing these dogmatic men who were capable of making such a generalization. Now I think that the Spanish inquisitors were perhaps the first people to understand – before the critics and the novelists themselves – the nature of fiction and its seditious tendencies.

In effect, novels lie – they can do nothing else – but that is only part of the story. The other part is that, by lying, they express a curious truth that can only be expressed in a furtive and veiled fashion, disguised as something that it is not. Put this way, it seems something of a rigmarole, but, in fact, it is really very simple. Men are not content with their lot and almost all of them – rich and poor, brilliant and ordinary, famous and unknown – would like a life different from the one that they are leading. Novels were born to placate this hunger, albeit in a distorted way. They are written and read so that human beings may have the lives that they are not prepared to do without. Within each novel, there stirs a rebellion, there beats a desire.

Does this mean that the novel is synonymous with unreality? That the introspective buccaneers of Conrad, the languid Proustian aristocrats, the anonymous little men punished by adversity of Franz Kafka and the erudite metaphysicians of Borges's stories excite us or move us because they have nothing to do with us, because it is impossible for us to identify our experiences with theirs? Of course not. One must tread carefully because this road – of truth and lies in the world of fiction – is strewn with traps, and the inviting oases that appear on the horizon are usually mirages.

What does it mean that a novel *always lies*? Not what the officials and cadets thought at the Leoncio Prado Military School, where my first novel, *Time of the Hero*, takes place – supposedly at least – when they burned the book for being slanderous to their institution. Or what my first wife thought when she read another of my novels, *Aunt Julia and the Scriptwriter*. Feeling that she had been wrongly portrayed in it, she published a book seeking to restore the truth altered by the fiction. Of course, in both stories there are more inventions, distortions and exaggerations than memories and, when I wrote them, I never intended to be anecdotally faithful to events and people that preceded or were outside the novel. In both cases, as in everything that I have written, I started out from some experiences that were still vivid in my memory and stimulated my imagination, and I imagined something that reflects these working materials in a very unfaithful way. One does not write novels to recount life, but rather to transform it, by adding something. In the slim novels by the Frenchman Restif de la Bretonne, reality could not be more photographic; they are a catalogue of French eighteenth-century customs. In these laborious costumbrist sketches, in which everything approximates to real life, we find, however, something different, minimal but revolutionary. That in this world, men do not fall in love with women because of the purity of their features, the elegance of their bodies, their spiritual virtues and the like, but *exclusively* because of the beauty of their feet (this has been called, for that reason, *bretonisme*, the fetishism of the shoe). In a less crude and explicit, and also in a less conscious way, all novels remake reality – embellishing or making it worse – just as the extravagant Restif did with such delicious ingenuousness. In these subtle or gross additions to life – in which the novelist gives form to his secret obsessions – lies the originality of a fiction. This originality is more profound the more it expresses a general need and the more readers there are, through time and space, that can identify in this contraband smuggled into life the obscure demons that disturb them. Could I, in the novels that I mentioned, have tried to be scrupulously exact with my memories? Of course. But even if I had achieved the boring feat of only narrating true facts and describing characters whose biographies neatly fit their novels, my novels would not have been, for all this, any less lying and any more true than they are now.

Because it is not the story which in essence decides the truth or lies of a work of fiction, but the fact that this story is written rather than lived, that it is made of words and not concrete experiences. Facts suffer a profound change when they are transformed into words. The real fact – the bloody battle that I took part in, the Gothic silhouette of the young woman that I loved – is one, while the signs that could describe it are innumerable. By choosing some and discounting others, the novelist privileges one and kills off a thousand other possibilities and versions of what he is describing: this, then, is altered: *what is described* becomes *what has been described*. Am I referring only to the case of the realist writer, that sect, school or tradition to which I doubtless belong, whose novels recount events that the readers can recognize as possible through their own lived experience of reality? It would seem in effect that for the writer of fantasy, who describes unrecognizable and blatantly inexistent worlds, that the comparison between reality and fiction does not even arise. It does arise, however, albeit in a different way. The 'irreality' of fantastic literature becomes, for the reader, a symbol or an allegory, that is, a representation of realities, of experiences that can be identified in life. What is important is that it is not the 'realist' or 'fantastic' nature of a story that draws the line between truth and lies in fiction.

Accompanying this first transformation – that words impose upon deeds – there is another which is no less radical: that of time. Real life flows and does not stop, it is incommensurable, a chaos in which each story mingles with all the other stories and thus it never begins or ends. Fictional life is a simulacrum in which that dizzying disorder becomes order: organization, cause and effect, beginning and end. The sovereignty of a novel is not just derived from the language in which it is written. It is also derived from its temporal system, from the way in which existence flows within it: when it stops, when it accelerates and the chronological perspective from which the narrator describes this invented time. If there is distance between words and deeds, then there is always a chasm between real time and the time of fiction. Novelistic time is an artifice fabricated to achieve certain psychological effects. In it, the past can come after the present – the effect precedes the cause – as in that story by Alejo Carpentier, 'Journey to the Source', which begins with the death of an old man and continues up to his gestation in his mother's womb; or it can be just a remote past which never manages to dissolve into the near past from which the narrator is narrating, as occurs in most classic novels; or an eternal present without a past or a future, as in the fictions of Samuel Beckett; or a labyrinth in which past, present and future coexist and cancel each other out, as in *The Sound and the Fury* by Faulkner.

Novels have a beginning and an end and even in the most formless and intermittent of them, life takes on a meaning that we can perceive because they give us a perspective that real life, in which we are immersed, always denies us. This order is an invention, an addition by the novelist, a simulator who seems to recreate life whereas in truth he is amending it. Sometimes subtly, sometimes brutally, fiction betrays life, encapsulating it in a weft of words which reduces its scale and makes it accessible to the reader. This reader can therefore judge it, understand it, and above all live it, with an impunity that real life does not allow.

What is the difference, then, between fiction and a newspaper article or a history book? Are they not all composed of words? Do they not imprison within the artificial time of the tale that boundless torrent that is real time? My answer is that they are opposing systems for approximating to reality. While the novel rebels and transgresses life, those other genres can only be its slave. The notion of truth or lies functions in a different way in each case. For journalism or history, truth depends on the comparison between what is written and the reality that inspires it. The closer the one is to the other, the more truthful it is; the further away, the more deceitful. To say that *The History of the French Revolution* by Michelet or *The Conquest of Peru* by Prescott are 'novelistic' is to scoff at them, to insinuate that they lack seriousness. On the other hand, to document the historical errors in the depiction of the Napoleonic Wars in *War and Peace* would be a waste of time: the truth of a novel does not depend on that. On what, then? On its own capacity for persuasion, on the communicative force of its fantasy, on the skill of its magic. Every good novel tells the truth and every bad novel lies. Because to 'tell the truth' for a novel means making the reader live an illusion and 'to lie' means being incapable of achieving this trick. The novel, then, is an amoral genre, or rather it has its own particular ethics in which truth and lies are exclusively aesthetic terms. Brecht's argument that works of art should strive to achieve 'critical objectivity' misses the mark: without 'illusion' there is no novel.

From what I have said up till now, it would seem that fiction is a gratuitous creation, a casual conjuring trick. Quite the reverse for, however delirious it might seem, its roots draw nutrition from human experience. A recurrent theme in the history of fiction is the risk that is implied in taking novels literally, in believing that life is how novels describe it to be. The romances of chivalry befuddle the brain of Alonso Quijano and propel him along roads where he battles with windmills, and the tragedy of Emma Bovary would not have occurred if Flaubert's character had not tried to be like the heroines of the romantic novels that she reads. Alonso Quijano and Emma suffer terrible damage. Do we condemn them for this? No, their stories move us and we admire them: their impossible attempt to *live the fiction* seems to us to personify an idealist attitude which honours the species. Because the human aspiration *par excellence* is to want to be different from what we are. This desire has been the cause of the best and worst moments in history. It has also led to the birth of fiction.

When we read novels, we are not just ourselves but we are also those conjured-up characters into whose midst the novelist transports us. This transportation is a metamorphosis: the asphyxiating enclosure of our real life opens up and we leave it to become others, to live vicariously experiences that novels make our own. A lucid dream, a fantasy incarnate, fiction completes we mutilated beings that have had imposed on us the terrible dichotomy of having only one life and the desires and fantasies to have one thousand lives. This space between between our real life and the desires and fantasies that demand that it be richer and more diverse is the terrain of fiction.

In the heart of all these fictions, protest is ablaze. The person who imagined them did so because he could not live them and whoever reads them (and creates them through reading) finds in their phantoms the faces and adventures that he needed to add to his life. This is the truth that the lies of fiction express: the lies that we are, the lies that console us and compensate for our nostalgia and frustrations. What confidence, therefore, can we have in what novels say about the society that produced them? Were those men like that? They were, in the sense that they wanted to be like that, that this was the way that they saw themselves loving, suffering and enjoying pleasure. These lies do not document their lives, but the demons that were stirred up, the dreams in which they found pleasure, which made the life they were leading more bearable. An era is not just peopled with beings of flesh and blood; but also by the ghosts into which these beings change in order to break through the barriers that limit and frustrate them.

The lies of novels are never gratuitous: they compensate for the inadequacies of life. For that reason, when life appears full and absolute and, due to a faith that justifies and absorbs everything, men are content with their lot, novels usually have no function. Religious cultures produce poetry and theatre but only rarely great novels. Fiction is an art of societies where faith is experiencing a certain crisis, *where one needs to believe in something,* where the unitary, trusted and absolute vision has been replaced by a fractured vision and a growing uncertainty about the world in which one lives and the afterlife. In the guts of novels we find not just amorality, then, but also a certain scepticism. When religious culture comes into crisis, life seems to slide away from the structures, dogmas and rules that bound them and reverts to chaos; this is the privileged moment for fiction. Its artificial orders give refuge and security and also allow the free display of those appetites and fears that real life provokes but cannot satisfy or exorcize. Fiction is a temporary substitute for life. The return to reality is always a brutal impoverishment: the realization that we are less than what we dream. This means that just as fictions temporarily placate human dissatisfaction, they also fuel it by stirring up desires and imagination.

The Spanish inquisitors understood the danger. To live lives that one does not live is a source of anxiety, a disagreement with existence that can become a rebellion, an insubordinate attitude towards what is established. It is understandable, then, why regimes that aspire to control life totally mistrust novels and subject them to censorship. To go out of oneself, to be another, in however illusory a fashion, is a way of becoming less of a slave and experiencing the risks of freedom.

2

'Things are not how we see them but how we remember them,' wrote Valle Inclán. He was doubtless referring to how things are in literature, an unreality on to which the power of persuasion of a good writer and the credulity of the good reader confer a precarious reality.

For almost every writer, memory is the starting point for fantasy, the springboard that launches the imagination on its unpredictable flight towards fiction. Memories and inventions mix in creative literature in an often inextricable way for the author himself who, although he might pretend the contrary, knows that the recovery of past time to which literature can lead is always a simulacrum, a fiction in which what is remembered dissolves into what is dreamed and vice versa.

For that reason literature is the realm of ambiguity *par excellence*. Its truths are always subjective, half-truths, literary truths which are often flagrant inaccuracies or historical lies. Although the cinematic battle of Waterloo which appears in *Les Misérables* excites us, we know that this was a contest that Victor Hugo fought and won and not one that Napoleon lost. Or, to quote a classic medieval Valencian romance, the conquest of England by the Arabs described in *Tirant lo Blanc* is totally convincing and nobody would dare deny its verisimilitude with the petty argument that in real history an Arab army never crossed the Channel.

The reconstruction of the past in literature is almost always false in terms of historical objectivity. Literary truth is one thing, historical truth another. But although it is full of lies – or rather, because of this fact – literature recounts the history that the history written by the historians would not know how, or be able, to write, because the deceptions, tricks and exaggerations of narrative literature are used to express profound and unsettling truths which can only see the light of day in this oblique way.

When Joanot Martorell tells us in *Tirant lo Blanc* that the French princess was so white that one could see wine going down her throat, he is telling us something technically impossible which, however, under the spell of reading, seems to us an undying truth, because in the false reality of the novel, unlike what happens in our own reality, excess is never the exception, but always the rule. And nothing is excessive if everything is. In *Tirant*, excess is to be found in the apocalyptic battles with their punctilious rituals and in the deeds of the hero who, alone, defeats multitudes and literally devastates half of Christendom and all of Islam. It is to be found in the comic rituals like those of the pious and libidinous character who kisses women in the mouth three times in honour of the Holy Trinity. And love, in its pages, like war, is always excessive and is likely to lead to cataclysmic results. Thus, when Tirant sees for the first time in the darkness of a funeral chamber the insurgent breasts of Princess Carmesina, he falls into an almost cataleptic state and stays stretched out on a bed without eating, sleeping or uttering a word for several days. When he finally recovers, it is as if he is learning to speak once again. His first stammered words are 'I love.'

These lies do not describe what Valencians were like at the end of the fifteenth century, but what they would have liked to have been and done; they do not describe the flesh and blood beings of this terrible time, but their phantoms. Their appetites, their fears, their desires, their resentments are given form. Successful fiction embodies the subjectivity of an epoch and for that reason, although compared to history novels lie, they communicate to us fleeting and evanescent truths which always escape scientific descriptions of reality. Only literature has the techniques and powers to distil this delicate elixir of life: the truth hidden in the heart of human lies. Because in the deceptions of literature, there are no deceptions. At least there should not be any, apart from for those naïve people who think that literature should be as objectively faithful to, and dependent on, reality as history is. And there is no deception because when we open a book of fiction, we adjust ourselves to witnessing a representation in which we know very well that our tears or our yawns depend exclusively on the good or bad spell that the narrator casts to make us live his lies as truths and not on his capacity to reproduce lived experience faithfully.

These well-defined boundaries between literature and history — between literary truths and historic truths — are a prerogative of open societies. In these societies, both coexist, independent and sovereign, although complementing each other in their utopian desire to include all of society. And perhaps the greatest demonstration that a society is open, in the meaning that Karl Popper gave to this term, is that fiction and history coexist, autonomous and different, without invading or usurping each other's domains and functions.

In closed societies, the reverse is true. And, for that reason, perhaps the best way to define a closed society is by saying that in it fiction and history are no longer different things and have started to become confused and to supplant each other, changing identities as in a masked ball.

In a closed society, power not only takes upon itself the privilege of controlling the actions of men — what they do and what they say — but also aspires to govern their fantasy, their dreams and, of course, their memory. In a closed society, the past is, sooner or later, subject to manipulation with a view to justifying the present. Official history, the only one tolerated, is the stage for these magical transformations which the *Soviet Encyclopedia* made famous (before *perestroika*): protagonists who appear or disappear without trace, according to whether they are being resurrected or purged by the powers that be, and the actions of the heroes and villains of the past that, from edition to edition, change their meaning, their valency and their substance as they are accommodated and reaccommodated by the ruling committees of the present. This is a practice that modern totalitarianism has perfected but not invented; its origins are lost in the dawn of civilizations which, until relatively recently, were always vertical and despotic.

To organize collective memory, to change history into an instrument of government for the purpose of legitimating the ruling powers and providing alibis for their misdeeds, is a temptation inherent in all forms of power. Totalitarian states can make this temptation a reality.

In the past, innumerable civilizations behaved in this way. My ancient compatriots, the Incas, for example. They carried out this policy in a powerful and theatrical way. When the emperor died, there died with him not only his wives and concubines, but also his intellectuals, who were called *amautas*, wise men. Their wisdom was fundamentally applied to the trick of turning fiction into history. The new Inca assumed power with a new court of *amautas* whose mission was to reform official memory, correct the past, modernizing it one might say, in such a way that all the achievements, conquests and buildings that were formally attributed to his forebear, were from that moment transferred to the curriculum vitae of the new emperor. His predecessors were gradually swallowed up by forgetfulness. The Incas knew how to make use of the past, transforming it into literature, so that it could help to immobilize the present, the supreme aspiration of every dictatorship. They banned individual truths, which are always contradictory, in favour of an official truth which was coherent and not subject to appeal. (The result is that the Inca empire is a society without history, at least without narrative history, because no one has been able to reconstruct in a reliable way this past that has been so systematically dressed and undressed like a striptease artist.)

In a closed society, history is imbued with fiction, becomes fiction, because it is invented and reinvented in accordance with contemporary religious or political orthodoxy, or more crudely, according to the whims of the controllers of power.

At the same time, a strict system of censorship is usually set up whereby literature must also fantasize within strict limits, so that its subjective truths do not contradict or cast a shadow over official history, but rather serve to disseminate and illustrate it. The difference between historical truth and literary truth disappears and they become fused in a hybrid which bathes history in unreality and empties fiction of mystery, initiative and rebelliousness towards the established order.

To condemn history to lie and literature to propagate the truths manufactured by the powers that be, does not hinder the scientific and technological development of a country or the establishment of certain basic forms of social justice. It has been proved that the Inca system – an extraordinary achievement for its time or for our own – ended hunger and managed to feed all its subjects. And the modern totalitarian states have given a great impetus to education, health, sport and work, putting them within the reach of all, something that open societies, despite their prosperity, have not achieved, because the price of the freedom that they enjoy is often paid for by tremendous inequalities in wealth and – what is worse – in opportunities for its members.

But when a state, in its desire to control and decide everything, wrests from human beings the right to invent and believe whatever lies they please, appropriates this right and exercises it through historians and censors – like the Incas through the *amautas* – a great neuralgic centre of social life is abolished. And men and women suffer a loss that impoverishes their existence, even when their basic needs are satisfied. Because real life, true life, has never been, nor will ever be, sufficient to fulfil human desires. And because, without this vital dissatisfaction that the lies of fiction both incite and assuage, there is never authentic progress.

The fantasy that we are endowed with is a demonic gift. It is continually opening up a gulf between what we are and what we would like to be, between what we have and what we desire.

But the imagination has conceived of a clever and subtle palliative for this inevitable divorce between our limited reality and our boundless desires: fiction. Thanks to fiction we are more and we are others without ceasing to be the same. In it we can lose ourselves and multiply, living many more lives than the ones we have and could live if we were confined to the truth, without escaping from the prison of history.

Men do not live by truth alone; they also need lies: those that they invent freely, not those that are imposed on them; those that appear as they are, not smuggled in beneath the clothes of history. Fiction enriches their existence, completes them and, fleetingly, compensates them for this tragic condition which is our lot: always to desire and dream more than we can actually achieve.

When it freely produces its alternative life, without any other constraint than that of the limitations of its own creator, literature extends human life, adding the dimension that fuels the life deep within us – that impalpable and fleeting, but precious life that we only live through lies.

This is a right that we should defend without shame. Because to play with lies, as the author and reader of fiction do, the lies that they themselves fabricate under the rule of their personal demons, is a way of affirming individual sovereignty and defending it when it is threatened; of preserving one's own free space, a citadel outside the control of power and of the interference of others, where we are truly in charge of our destiny.

Other freedoms are born from this freedom. These private refuges, the subjective truths of literature, bequeath to historical truth, which is complementary to them, a possible existence and a particular function: that of regaining an important part – but only a part – of our memory, that greatness and poverty that we share with others as gregarious beings. This historical truth is indispensable and irreplaceable for us to know what we were and perhaps what we will be as human collectivities. But what we are as individuals and what we wanted to be and could not really be and had therefore to be through fantasy and invention – our secret history – only literature can tell. This is why Balzac wrote that fiction was 'the private history of nations'.

By itself, literature is a terrible indictment against existence under whatever regime or ideology: a blazing testimony of its insufficiencies, its inability to satisfy us. And, for that reason, it is a permanent corroder of all power structures that would like to see men satisfied and contented. The lies of literature, if they germinate in freedom, prove to us that this was never the case. And these lies are also a permanent conspiracy to prevent this happening in the future.

Barcelona, June 1989

# Index

Adán, Martín, 60
Aguilar de Argumedo, Julia, 185, 186, 187, 191–3
Alberti, Rafael, 45, 47
Alegría, Ciro, 132
Algeria
  Camus and, 107, 108, 113
  Sartre and, 138
Alleg, Henri, 135
Alonso, Dámaso, 17
Alvarez Montalbán, Emilio, 209–10, 223
Amazon region of Peru, 13–14, 148–51
Anderson, Benedict, 301
animal rights movement, 229, 230–31, 233, 235
Antonio the Counsellor, 128–9, 282
Antonioni, Michelangelo, 57
Aragon, Louis, 251
Aragón Clavijo, Uva de, 315–16
Arequipa (Peru), 1, 2
Aretino, Pietro, 118
Arguedas, Alcides, 132
Arguedas, José María, 108, 132
Argüello, José, 216
Argumedo, Juan, 185–6, 187, 191, 192, 193, 197
Argumedo, Juana Lidia, 185, 186, 191–3
Argumedo, Rosa de, 185, 186, 187, 191–3
Aron, Raymond, 108, 140
Arreola, Juan José, 246
art
  Botero and abundance in, 254–67
  'degenerate', 271–5
  Latin American heritage and, 258–64, 268–70
  as pleasure, 264–7
  states and governments and, 272–5
Asnières, Dog Cemetery of, 28–31
Asturias, Miguel Ángel, 47, 132
Aucatoma, Venancio, 189
*Aunt Julia and the Scriptwriter* (Vargas Llosa), 12, 321
Ayacucho (Peru), 171, 172, 180–81

Bahía [de San Salvador de Todos los Santos] (Brazil), 127–8
Bakunin, Mikhail, 145
Balzac, Honoré de, 137
Barcelona, World Cup (1982) in, 164–70

Baroja, Pío, 18
Barral, Carlos, 296
Barthes, Roland, 144
Bataille, Georges, 114, 117–26, 147, 157
  *The Blue of Noon*, 123
  *Eroticism*, 119
  *Literature and Evil*, 117, 122
  *The Story of the Eye*, 124
Baudelaire, Charles, 66, 122, 133, 135, 136, 137
Beach, Sylvia, 38
beauty, fatness and, 254–7
Beauvoir, Simone de, 137, 143
  *Les Belles Images*, 56–8
  *The Mandarins*, 55, 99
  *Un mort si douce*, 56
Beckett, Samuel, 55, 323
Beckmann, Max, 271
Belaúnde Terry, Fernando, 182–3, 190, 291
Belinski, V. G., 145
Belli, Carlos Germán, 62, 107
Bello, Andrés, 76
Bellow, Saul, 306, 319
Belmonte, Juan, 8
Ben Schmuel, Uri, 171
Benda, Julien, 308
Berlin, Isaiah, 14, 144–7, 302
Berlin
  Film Festival, 225, 226–39
  modern art in, 273–5
Bernardo (Sacristan of Cuapa), 218–20
Blake, William, 122
Blanco, Hugo, 143
Blest Gana, Alberto, 76
Bloom, Alan, 301, 308
Blume, Ricardo, 18
Bobbitt, John Wayne, 316–19
Bobbitt, Lorena Gallo, 316–19
Bocaccio, Giovanni, 118
Bolivar, Simón, 172
Bolivia, 1
Böll, Heinrich, 200
Bonin, Wibke von, 257
Borge, Tomás, 212, 214, 215–16, 222
Borges, Jorge Luis, 10, 128, 132, 153, 246, 247, 263, 321
Bosco Vivas, Bishop, 217
Botero, Fernando, 254–67